Learning Amazon Web Services (AWS)

The Pearson Addison-Wesley
Learning Series

Visit **informit.com/learningseries** for a complete list of available publications.

The **Pearson Addison-Wesley Learning Series** is a collection of hands-on programming guides that help you quickly learn a new technology or language so you can apply what you've learned right away.

Each title comes with sample code for the application or applications built in the text. This code is fully annotated and can be reused in your own projects with no strings attached. Many chapters end with a series of exercises to encourage you to reexamine what you have just learned, and to tweak or adjust the code as a way of learning.

Titles in this series take a simple approach: they get you going right away and leave you with the ability to walk off and build your own application and apply the language or technology to whatever you are working on.

Make sure to connect with us!
informit.com/socialconnect

Learning Amazon Web Services (AWS)

A Hands-On Guide to the Fundamentals of AWS Cloud

Mark Wilkins

✦✦ Addison-Wesley

Learning Amazon Web Services (AWS)

Copyright © 2020 by Pearson Education, Inc.

Trademarks

All terms mentioned in this book that are known to be trademarks or service marks have been appropriately capitalized. Pearson cannot attest to the accuracy of this information. Use of a term in this book should not be regarded as affecting the validity of any trademark or service mark.

AWS screenshots © Amazon Web Services, Inc.

Cover photo: Sdecoret/Shutterstock

Microsoft and/or its respective suppliers make no representations about the suitability of the information contained in the documents and related graphics published as part of the services for any purpose. All such documents and related graphics are provided "as is" without warranty of any kind. Microsoft and/or its respective suppliers hereby disclaim all warranties and conditions with regard to this information, including all warranties and conditions of merchantability, whether express, implied or statutory, fitness for a particular purpose, title and non-infringement. In no event shall Microsoft and/or its respective suppliers be liable for any special, indirect or consequential damages or any damages whatsoever resulting from loss of use, data or profits, whether in an action of contract, negligence or other tortious action, arising out of or in connection with the use or performance of information available from the services. The documents and related graphics contained herein could include technical inaccuracies or typographical errors. Changes are periodically added to the information herein. Microsoft and/or its respective suppliers may make improvements and/or changes in the product(s) and/or the program(s) described herein at any time. Partial screenshots may be viewed in full within the software version specified.

Microsoft® Windows®, Microsoft Office®, and Microsoft Azure® are registered trademarks of the Microsoft Corporation in the U.S.A. and other countries. Screenshots reprinted with permission from the Microsoft Corporation. This book is not sponsored or endorsed by or affiliated with the Microsoft Corporation.

For information regarding permissions, request forms and the appropriate contacts within the Pearson Education Global Rights & Permissions Department, please visit www.pearsoned.com/permissions/.

Warning and Disclaimer

Special Sales

For information about buying this title in bulk quantities, or for special sales opportunities (which may include electronic versions; custom cover designs; and content particular to your business, training goals, marketing focus, or branding interests), please contact our corporate sales department at corpsales@pearsoned.com or (800) 382-3419.

For government sales inquiries, please contact governmentsales@pearsoned.com.

For questions about sales outside the U.S., please contact intlcs@pearson.com.

Visit us on the Web: informit.com/aw

ISBN-13: 978-0-13-529834-3

ISBN-10: 0-13-529834-2

Library of Congress Control Number: 2019937606

1 2019

Acquisition Editor
Paul Carlstroem

Managing Editor
Sandra Schroeder

Development Editor
Kiran Panigrahi

Project Editor
Lori Lyons

Production Manager
Aswini Kumar

Copy Editor
Kitty Wilson

Indexer
Cheryl Lenser

Proofreader
Abigail Manheim

Designer
Chuti Prasertsith

Compositor
codeMantra

Accessing the Web Edition

Your purchase of this book in any format includes access to the corresponding Web Edition. Your Web Edition contains the following:

- The complete text of the book
- Hours of instructional video keyed to the text

The Web Edition can be viewed on all types of computers and mobile devices with any modern web browser that supports HTML5.

To get access to the *Learning Amazon Web Services (AWS)* Web Edition, all you need to do is register this book:

1. Go to www.informit.com/register.
2. Sign in or create a new account.
3. Enter the ISBN: **9780135298343**.
4. Answer the questions as proof of purchase.
5. The Web Edition will appear under the Digital Purchases tab on your Account page. Click the Launch link to access the product.

Contents at a Glance

Table of Contents

Companion Videos List

In addition to this book, several hours of companion online training videos are available. Throughout the chapters, you'll be invited to watch a video that relates to the topic being covered in that section.

To access the videos, register this book at www.informit.com/register.

Chapter 1: Learning AWS
Signing up for Amazon Free Tier
Terra Firma

Chapter 2: Designing with AWS Global Services
Availability Zones
Choosing a Region
Planning Compliance
Trusted Advisor
Using the Simple Monthly Calculator

Chapter 3: AWS Networking Services
Create a Custom VPC
Creating CIDR Blocks
Public and Private Subnets
Exploring Route Tables
Creating Security Groups
Network ACLs
VPC Flow Logs
Understanding Endpoints
Adding an Internet Gateway
Creating VPN Connections

Chapter 4: Compute Services: AWS EC2 Instances
Creating a Custom AMI
Creating Reserved Instances
Spot Instances
Creating Instances

Chapter 5: Planning for Scale and Resiliency
Installing the CloudWatch Agent
CloudWatch in Operation
Creating a CloudWatch Alarm

Preface

Although the Amazon cloud is well-documented, the Internet includes all types of information. This means you can spend a great deal of time reading AWS technical documentation, only to find that what seems interesting might be five years old or more. There's too much documentation to expect to spend just a couple of evenings researching and getting right up to speed.

My opportunity to create this technical book for understanding AWS began in April 2018 after Mark Taber, an acquisitions editor for Pearson Education, pinged me on LinkedIn. I had written technical books before, and Mark asked if I was interested in writing one on the topic of Amazon Web Services. I asked, "Do people actually buy paper books?" and he replied quickly, "They sure do."

So, I thought about it and realized that most of the customers I had consulted with over the past few years regarding the AWS cloud were smart technical people, but they had been thrown into a bit of a panic because they had to get ready for moving to the cloud—specifically, the Amazon cloud. And they were looking for a starting point to ramp up their technical cloud knowledge and become technically proficient in what was happening in AWS cloud technologies.

I had spent a few years quite involved with AWS cloud services with various clients—including a major Canadian bank, a major American bank, and several small-to-midsize companies working in AWS—because their developers had developed applications they were using quite successfully. The only problem was, they weren't in the AWS cloud.

I thought about all my customers and realized that what was missing was a foundational book on AWS that explained how the core AWS services of compute, storage, networking, scale, security, and automation fit together. I decided to combine a book with a number of videos that would walk through how to set up each service. This approach would allow my customers, and hopefully many others, to visualize how AWS could work for their company or their project.

Writing a technical book is ultimately an abundance of research and rounds of testing, breaking, and fixing until the project comes together. To create a detailed technical overview of Amazon Web Services and how its cloud services fit together, I decided to review all the relevant AWS documentation of the compute, storage, networking, and managed services by following the pattern of reading and testing; then even more reading and testing. I then added some tips and tricks, and finally summarized this last year's work into the technical content found in the chapters of this book. I learned a lot about AWS that I didn't know—that's the great thing about researching and writing a book!

Companion Training Videos

Learning Amazon Web Services (AWS) also has a useful learning companion—several hours of training videos are bundled with the book that will show you how easy it is to set up the core services at AWS and grasp the concepts of what the AWS cloud can offer.

Throughout the chapters, you'll be invited to watch the companion video that relates to the topic that is being covered in a particular section.

Watching the videos will help you get in technical shape to start deploying your company's applications and resources at AWS. The videos take the place of page after page of step-by-step instructions. This reason for no detailed steps is that in the AWS cloud, the steps to perform any task are constantly changing, so up-to date videos as a means of teaching makes more sense. Videos can also be updated easily as changes occur.

The videos can be accessed by registering your copy of this book at www.informit.com/register. The videos can be watched on most any device as they are formatted in a standard MP4 video format. And, don't forget popcorn!

About the Author

Mark Wilkins is an Electronic Engineering Technologist with a wealth of experience in designing, deploying, and supporting software and hardware technology in the corporate and small business world. Since 2013, Mark has focused on supporting and designing cloud service solutions with Amazon Web Services, Microsoft Azure, and the IBM Cloud. He is certified in Amazon Web Services (Architecture and Sys-Ops). Mark is also a Microsoft Certified Trainer (MCT) and holds certifications in MCTS, MCSA, Server Virtualization with Windows Server Hyper-V, and Azure Cloud Services.

Mark worked as a technical evangelist for IBM SoftLayer from 2013 through 2016 and taught both SoftLayer Fundamentals and SoftLayer Design classes to many Fortune 500 companies in Canada, the United States, Europe, and Australia. As course director for Global Knowledge, Mark developed and taught many technical seminars, including Configuring Active Directory Services, Configuring Group Policy, and Cloud and Virtualization Essentials. Mark also developed courseware for the Microsoft Official Curriculum 2008 stream, Managing and Maintaining Windows Server 2008 Network Services, and Active Directory Services.

Mark's published books include *Windows 2003 Registry for Dummies*, *Administering SMS 3.0*, and *Administering Active Directory*.

Acknowledgments

A book is not written by a single person; many help along the way. I'd like to thank Ashley Neace for giving me the opportunity to develop courseware for Global Knowledge way back in 2010 about the AWS cloud, and Rick Morrow, Mark Sluga, and Ryan Dymek for providing their expertise and knowledge over the years working together at Global Knowledge and as valuable technical resources. Thanks also to my editors Paul Carlstroem, Kiran Panigrahi, and Mark Taber for providing support and guidance for this project.

Learning AWS

About This Book

This paper book and companion video library are focused on the Amazon Web Services (AWS) cloud—and specifically what is called infrastructure as a service (IaaS)—to help you learn about the cloud services Amazon offers. Services that AWS offers can be broken down into the foundational services of compute, storage, networking, and security—and a big helping of automation. A handy way to think of AWS is as a massive toolbox with a wide variety of specialized tools that can carry out an assortment of infrastructure tasks. If you're a system administrator, developer, or project manager or you've heard about the AWS cloud and want to know more about it, this book is designed for you as a technical baseline of AWS services, what they can do, the major concepts, one of the major components, and how to set up the service to function. I estimate that I reviewed more than 35,000 pages of AWS documentation and summarized all that technical detail into somewhere between 300–400 pages of AWS information. That doesn't mean you won't read AWS documentation because you most definitely will; but hopefully this book and the companion video library will catapult your indoctrination into the AWS jungle.

You may also want to get certified; however, this is not a book that is directly focused on AWS certification. This book is instead focused on the so-called foundational services. All AWS certification tests are focused on problem-solving based on a particular scenario. Your job is to figure out the best one or two answers; therefore, knowing the foundational services is key. If you want to get certified on AWS cloud services, particularly on AWS architecture, you must know the foundational AWS services inside and out. And you'll have to spend a few hours doing hands-on work with AWS services. If you want to develop applications that will be hosted at AWS, you will need to know the foundational services in even more detail. And forget about learning everything about AWS in a single book; it's just not possible, and the reality is that AWS is constantly changing. That's a notion you will learn to embrace.

Each chapter in this book attempts to deal with a specific concept or AWS service and provide a strong detailed technical summary of the AWS service in question. However, there are not pages and pages of step-by-step solutions because the steps change every couple of months. During the writing of this book, AWS changed the design of its icons used in its technical documentation three times. They also added 600 features and made numerous other changes, from cosmetic to substantial.

To get around the issue of immediate obsolescence, there is a companion video library associated with this book that shows you how to set up and install and configure many AWS cloud services. You can access these videos by registering your book at informit.com/register.

Throughout the remainder of the chapters, you'll be invited to watch the companion video that relates to the topic that we are covering. The companion step-by-step videos can be changed and updated or added to as AWS changes. The beauty of a video is that you can pause or rewind it as you learn. Let's begin the journey and see where we end up. This initial chapter includes the following topics:

- Defining the public cloud
- Where AWS fits with IaaS and platform as a service (PaaS)
- Characteristics of cloud computing according to NIST
- Considerations for migrating applications to AWS
- Operational benefits for operating in the cloud
- The cloud service-level agreement (SLA)
- Data, application, and network security at AWS
- Compliance at AWS
- AWS Well-Architected Framework

Trying to Define the Cloud

The roots of public cloud computing are not new; the public cloud providers Amazon Web Services and Microsoft Azure have been established for well over a decade with strong IaaS and PaaS offerings around the world. The Google Cloud Platform (GCP) and the IBM or Oracle Cloud are other viable alternatives. Gartner's Magic Quadrant (www.gartner.com/en/research/methodologies/magic-quadrants-research) in Figure 1-1 shows four types of technology provider a company can align their goals and strategies with. In 2018, IaaS market penetration dominated two of those categories. Under the Leaders quadrant, Amazon Web Services led in that area, followed by Microsoft and then Google. Google also aligned closely to the Visionaries Quadrant. Alibaba Cloud, Oracle, and IBM fell in the Niche Players quadrant.

When I started my career as a computer technician back in the 90s, most corporations that I supported used several computer-based services that were not located on premise. Accounting services were accessed through a fast (at the time) 1200 baud modem that was connected using one of those green-screened digital terminals. The serial cable threaded through the drop ceiling to connect the terminal was strong enough to pull a car.

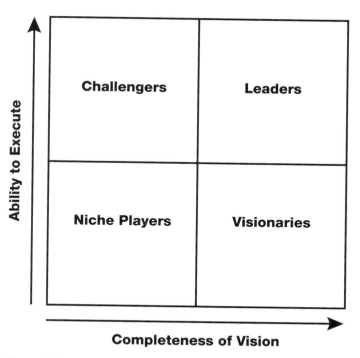

Figure 1-1   Top public cloud providers. Gartner, Magic Quadrant for Cloud Infrastructure as a Service, Worldwide, Dennis Smith et al., 23 May 2018. (Gartner Methodologies, Magic Quadrant, www.gartner.com/en/research/methodologies/magic-quadrants-research)[1]

A customer of mine at the time was utilizing a mainframe computer for accounting hosted locally in town. However, he couldn't access his accounting services any time he liked; he had his allotted slice of processing time every Tuesday, and that was that. Payroll services were provided by another remote service called Automatic Data Processing, or ADP for short. Both service companies and their services are still around today. IBM is continuing to release versions of its z series mainframe, and ADP payroll services was one of the first software as a service (SaaS) companies but remains popular today.

In 2015, IBM bought a cloud provider based in Texas called SoftLayer and merged it into its public cloud offering, today called the IBM Cloud. The z mainframe has ended up being hosted in the IBM cloud providing hosted mainframe services; in April 2018, IBM announced it was launching what it called a "skinny mainframe" for cloud computing built around the IBM z 14 mainframe.

---

[1]Gartner does not endorse any vendor, product or service depicted in its research publications, and does not advise technology users to select only those vendors with the highest ratings or other designation. Gartner research publications consist of the opinions of Gartner's research organization and should not be construed as statements of fact. Gartner disclaims all warranties, expressed or implied, with respect to this research, including any warranties of merchantability or fitness for a particular purpose.

If you work for a bank or financial institution, IBM mainframes probably provide 50% of all your computing services. This could be great news for companies that don't want to have a local mainframe environment to maintain.

Fifty years since the launch of the IBM mainframe, many companies' mainframes are continuing to be relevant and are now part of the public cloud landscape.

The reality is that more than 90 of the world's largest 100 banks, the top 10 insurance companies, a majority of the 25 largest retailers, and most of the world's larger airlines still rely on mainframe computers from IBM.

If you didn't use mainframes, you probably lived through the deployment cycle of Novell NetWare and Windows and Active Directory, and virtualization using VMware or Hyper-V. You likely have a private cloud in your own data centers. You may be wondering why your company is moving to the public cloud.

The reality these days is that it is expensive to build and maintain data centers. Certainly, building a data center is going to cost millions or billions of dollars. Maintaining an existing data center over the long term is expensive as well. Because of virtualization and the rise of the Internet as a useful communication medium, cloud services have replaced many local data centers and will continue to do so. Figuring out the capital costs of hosting your applications in the public cloud instead of running them in your own data center is sometimes categorized as renting instead of buying, as defined in Figure 1-2.

Operational expenses (OpEX) are all you pay for using cloud services. The capital expenditure (CapEX) of building a data center does not have to be borne by a single business. Now let's be clear: operational expenses are still expensive. You might say to your boss, "I don't need $800 million for data center construction, but I will need $2 million a year forever."

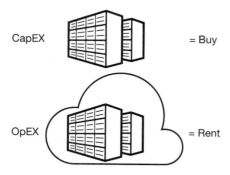

Figure 1-2   No long-term capital expenses

The reality is that the cost of running and hosting your applications in the cloud is cheaper once you add in every expense; however, operating in the cloud is only cheaper if your services being hosted in the cloud are properly designed. Services and applications don't run 24/7; they are turned off or reduced in size when they're not needed. A concept that you may not yet be familiar with is automation. Public cloud providers use automated procedures to build, manage, monitor, and scale every cloud service. By the end of this book, you will understand how automation is the secret sauce for successful cloud deployments. Automated procedures will save you money and allow you to sleep at night.

Let's start by defining the public cloud. The cloud is just a collection of data centers. There is no ownership from the customer's point of view; the cloud provider owns the services, and you rent each service as required. You may be thinking that the cloud is all virtual resources, yet the AWS cloud *can* provide you bare-metal servers. If you want, Amazon will happily host your applications and databases on bare-metal servers hosted in its data centers. Of course, more commonly, AWS will offer you many virtual servers in well over 150 different sizes and designs. Amazon is also quite happy to allow you to continue to operate your on-premise data centers and coexist with cloud resources and services operating at AWS. Microsoft Azure will offer to sell you a copy of its complete Azure cloud operating system to install on your servers in your data centers. As you can see, it's hard to define the public cloud these days other than as a massive collection of compute and storage resources hosted on a network stored in the collection of data centers accessible across the Internet, or by using private connections.

Anything that you host in the public cloud is using compute and storage resources to execute your software application. And anything that used to be a hardware device, such as a router, switch, or storage array, can be replaced by a third-party software appliance or an AWS-managed software service composed of virtual computers, storage, and networking components. This doesn't mean that many companies aren't still using hardware devices. Hardware devices such as routers and switches have incredible speed and can operate much faster in most cases than a software router and switch. But what happens if you can run hundreds or thousands of virtual machines in parallel performing the function of a hardware switch or hardware router device? Perhaps we don't need any hardware devices at all. Most of the AWS-managed cloud services are hosted on virtual machines (defined as EC2 instances, or Elastic Cloud Compute instances), with massive CPU and RAM resources running in massive server farms with custom-designed applications, providing the storage arrays, networking services, load-balancing, and auto-scaling services that we depend on at AWS.

Moving to AWS

Once the decision has been made to move to the AWS cloud, countless moving parts begin to churn. People need to be trained, infrastructure changes must take place, developers potentially need to code in a different way, and IT professionals must get up to speed on the cloud provider that has been chosen; there's no time to waste. Larger companies will usually attempt to convey the message of what moving to the cloud means for them. It's quite common for executives within the company to have strong opinions about what moving to the cloud will do. Sadly, these opinions are not usually based on technical knowledge or real hands-on experience with the cloud provider that has been chosen. Generally, companies utilizing cloud services fall into several mind-sets:

- **The corporate mentality**—You currently have data centers, infrastructure, and virtualized applications. Ever-increasing infrastructure and maintenance costs are driving you to look at what options are available in the public cloud.

- **Born-in-the-cloud mentality**—You're a developer with a great idea, but you don't want to maintain a local data center. In fact, you don't have a local data center, and you want to get going as soon as possible.

- **The startup mentality**—You've just lost your job due to a merger or buyout and are determined to strike out on your own. Your brand-new company has no data center but plenty of ideas combined with a distinct lack of cash.

- **The government client**—You've been told that, to save costs, your government department is moving to the AWS cloud within a defined timeframe.

Each of these starting mind-sets will have differing points of view as to how it should start to migrate or design its cloud infrastructure and hosted applications. Coming from a corporate environment or government department, you will probably expect the cloud provider to have a detailed service-level agreement (SLA) that you can change to match your needs. You will also probably have expectations about how much detail you expect to be provided about the cloud provider's infrastructure and services. In short, you expect to be in control.

If you have started with a public cloud services provider as an individual developer, or you're working with a startup, you will probably have no comparison with current on-premise costs; therefore, the overall costs that you pay for using a cloud provider will be accepted for the short term but, over time, as your experience grows, your overall cloud costs will be analyzed and managed to be as optimized and as cheap as possible.

> **Note**
>
> AWS has options for developers who want to craft and deploy applications hosted at AWS. The site https://aws.amazon.com/startups/ is where you can get further information about how you might be able to qualify for what is called AWS Promotional Credit. There's a possibility of getting up to $15,000 in credits over 2 years, including AWS support and training.

The reality is that moving to the cloud means you will be giving up an element of control. After all, it's not your data center. At AWS, you're not getting deeper into the infrastructure stack than the subnets that host your applications. Remember, the cloud is a data center; it's just not *your* data center. Let's start by looking at the available public cloud computing models of IaaS and PaaS and where AWS fits within these definitions.

Infrastructure as a Service

Most of the services AWS offers fall into the infrastructure as a service (IaaS) definition, as shown in Figure 1-3. This is certainly the most mature cloud model offering; virtualized servers and virtualized storage arrays are hosted on a software defined network with each customer's infrastructure completely isolated as a private resource. Creating resources at AWS typically starts with the creation of what is called a virtual private cloud (VPC). Virtual servers, virtual hard drive volumes, and indeed complete managed services and products can be hosted on your isolated private network. You have the flexibility to create whatever architectural stack you desire at AWS using a vast number of services and utilities contained in the IaaS toolbox. Companies moving to the AWS public cloud will typically first start with IaaS because the compute and storage services closely mirror their current on-premise virtual environment.

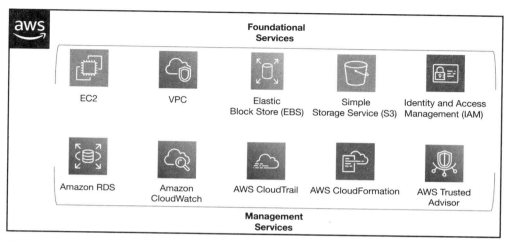

Figure 1-3   Infrastructure as a service at AWS

IaaS cloud services at AWS are bundled with managed services. A managed service is built on the trio of compute, storage, and networking services and customized software providing something you want Amazon to manage and maintain rather than your having to do all the work. For example, AWS offers a managed service called relational database service (RDS). It will build, host, maintain, back up, fail over, synchronize, and monitor a pair of master/standby database servers for you, leaving you the single task of managing your data records. Many other managed services are available at AWS; in fact, many managed services have no additional charges to begin using. For example, an automation service called CloudFormation allows you to automate the procedure of building infrastructure stacks complete with the required compute, storage, networks, and load balancers required for your application stack. In fact, practically anything to do with building, updating, or deleting your infrastructure stacks at AWS can be automated with CloudFormation. Another handy service called CloudTrail is provided free of charge. It tracks and records all application programming interface (API) calls that are carried out in each of your AWS accounts for 90 days. And yes, you can configure CloudTrail to store your API calls forever in S3 storage.

Your internal applications that are running in your on-premise data centers are probably a vast soup of proprietary operating systems (HP, AIX, Linux) and of course Windows. Talk to most departments in a small to midsize corporate environment, and the end users typically express unhappiness with some of the current applications that they use daily. They have learned to live with the ongoing issues of each application. Talk to the IT administrators and developers in the corporate data centers; there very well could be a great deal of unhappiness with the inflexibility of the existing infrastructure that they have to use and manage.

On top of these issues, perhaps each department has its own IT infrastructure. My company once provided compute services for a midsized hospital with 25 separate networks. Typically, in a larger corporation, compute services can be heavily siloed between departments, or each line of business gets to make its own decisions.

Most companies with more than 100 employees have some semblance of virtual infrastructure for their servers typically using VMware. Virtualization was supposed to be the answer to controlling a company's infrastructure costs. However, the cost for virtualization services has become extremely expensive to host, run, and maintain. Companies now know that capital and licensing costs are some of the biggest expenses they incur when running an ever-expanding on-premise private cloud. Replacing VMware with AWS-hosted virtualized servers and services removes a company's need for hypervisor administration expertise. And the landscape of applications used by corporations is now widely available in the public cloud as hosted applications defined as software as a service (SaaS) applications. As a result, there is ever-growing interest at the department level or overall company level in using the public cloud to host applications. And the reality is, you may not have a choice. If you're a Microsoft shop, the odds are quite strong that some of your everyday software applications such as Exchange and Microsoft Office are hosted by Microsoft Azure and Office 365, allowing you to completely replace some of your in-house software deployments. For more details on the compute platform at AWS, check out Chapter 4, "Compute Services: AWS EC2 Instances."

If your company has no experience working with external cloud providers and you are a medium- to large-sized corporation, it's a certainty your company will fit the private cloud model. Most of your company's infrastructure will be hosted within several private data centers. For example, your primary data center may be in Philadelphia, and your second data center could be in Nashville. (If you're a large enough company, your data centers may be spread across multiple continents.) The applications used will number in the hundreds or thousands. You may be lucky enough to have centralized IT standards, but these standards have become an issue due to the applications that multiple departments have installed or created over the years. Maybe if you're unlucky, one of the central applications used by your company was developed by a summer student and plunked into production without a second thought.

At AWS, infrastructure resources are spread across the world in 20 different regions. If you are in a large population center, the odds are that Amazon is close by. If Amazon is not close by, you still may be able to connect into it through one of the edge locations. More details on regions, availability zones, and edge locations can be found in Chapter 2, "Designing with AWS Global Services."

Platform as a Service

Platform as a service (PaaS) cloud providers enable your developers to create custom applications on a variety of popular development platforms such as Java, PHP, and Python. The developers don't have to manually build the infrastructure components required for each application per se; the required infrastructure resources are defined at the beginning of the development cycle and are created and managed by the PaaS cloud provider. After applications have been developed and tested and are ready for prime time, the application is made available to end users using public URLs. The PaaS cloud provider will host and scale the hosted application based on demand. As more users use the application, the infrastructure resources will scale out or in as required. PaaS environments are installed on the IaaS resources of the PaaS cloud provider, as shown in Figure 1-4. In fact, IaaS is always behind all "as a service" monikers. Examples of PaaS providers include Cloud Foundry and Heroku.

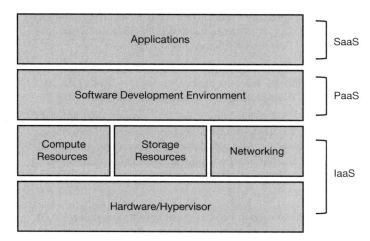

Figure 1-4   IaaS hosts the PaaS layer

Expanding upon Cloud Foundry, this PaaS solution is the foundation of development at IBM Cloud, where the underlying infrastructure is hosted on the IBM public cloud and running a customized version of the Cloud Foundry platform components. Developers can sign up and focus on writing applications. All requests will be handled by the PaaS layer interfacing with the IaaS layer, where the compute, storage, load-balancing, and scaling services operate.

Another popular solution for developing applications in the cloud is Heroku, mentioned in passing earlier. Heroku allows you to create and run hosted applications using a variety of development platforms. Just like the IBM cloud, once the application has been written, Heroku hosts, balances, and auto scales the application as required and sends you a bill for hosting at the end of the month.

If you're dealing with a PaaS provider, remember that programming languages change from time to time; therefore, APIs change as well, and usually without warning. If your developers don't keep up to date, there can be issues when using a PaaS cloud development platform.

Digging into the details on the Heroku website, under "Security," the site states that, "Heroku's physical infrastructure is hosted and managed within Amazon's secure data centers and utilize the Amazon Web services technology." Heroku is owned by another cloud heavyweight, Salesforce. Salesforce indicated in 2018 that future expansion was going to be by utilizing Amazon data center resources. Oh, what a tangled web we weave.

An additional reality is that one cloud provider's PaaS system is not necessarily compatible with another cloud provider's service. Both AWS and Microsoft Azure offer similar cloud services, but internally each cloud provider operates in a completely different fashion with a completely different set of APIs. There is no single standard for defining just what PaaS must be. Compatibility issues begin to reveal themselves at the lower levels of each vendor's proposed solution. RESTful interfaces, manifest file formats, framework configurations, external APIs, and component integration are not necessarily compatible across cloud vendors. AWS deals with platform services using Lambda, the API Gateway, and several code deployment tools.

The applications that your company may have been developing and using internally will be a variety of two- and three-tier architectures with many local dependencies such as network storage, local storage, local users, and databases. The overall architecture design may have been adequate at the beginning but now is straining to function due to the age of the hardware, the sizing of the hardware, and the lack of any flexibility to change.

The distinct difference with on-premise design when compared to hosting applications at AWS is that provisioning hardware and waiting for it to be set up and configured is a thing of the past. In fact, there are many possibilities to consider when designing applications at AWS.

Your choice of language and development framework will determine the PaaS vendor you select. Do you do a lot of development in Python? Are you a Java developer? Amazon has a PaaS solution called Elastic Beanstalk that automates the deployment of applications developed in Java, Python, Ruby, and other development platforms on the required infrastructure components for each application including E2 instances or Docker containers, with load-balancing, auto scaling, and monitoring services.

Amazon has several development solutions, shown in Figure 1-5, including CodeBuild, CodeCommit, Elastic Beanstalk, CodeDeploy. These can be key components in your application deployment at AWS. Chapter 8, "Automating AWS Infrastructure," covers these interesting managed services and additional details on automating your infrastructure.

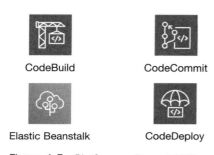

Figure 1-5   Platform options at AWS

Essential Characteristics of AWS Cloud Computing

If you haven't heard of National Institute of Standards and Technology (NIST), a branch of the U.S. government, you're not alone. Around 2010, NIST began documenting the public cloud. After talking to all the major vendors, it released an initial report in June 2011 defining many cloud components that were common across all the public cloud vendors. The report's genius was in defining what the emerging public cloud actually was (the command components). Over the years, NIST's cloud definitions have moved from definitions to becoming standards for how many companies view working in the public cloud. According to NIST, five key definitions of the public cloud have really morphed into a definitive standard methodology of operating in the public cloud:

On-demand self-service—We not only *expect* cloud service to be delivered quickly; we *demand* it. All cloud providers offer a self-serve portal as AWS does, as shown in Figure 1-6. You request a cloud service, and in seconds it's available in your AWS account ready to configure. Gone are the days of requesting a virtual server via email and waiting several days until it's built. At AWS, a virtual server can be started and operational in seconds. Procuring a software-defined network at AWS (called a virtual private cloud) is available and operational in seconds. AWS has an expansive self-serve management console that allows you to order and configure many cloud-hosted services in seconds in any AWS region. Any cloud service that you order from AWS is automatically delivered to you through heavily automated procedures. There are no public cloud providers that survive without a self-service portal driven by heavy-duty automation in the background. This NIST definition is now a standard.

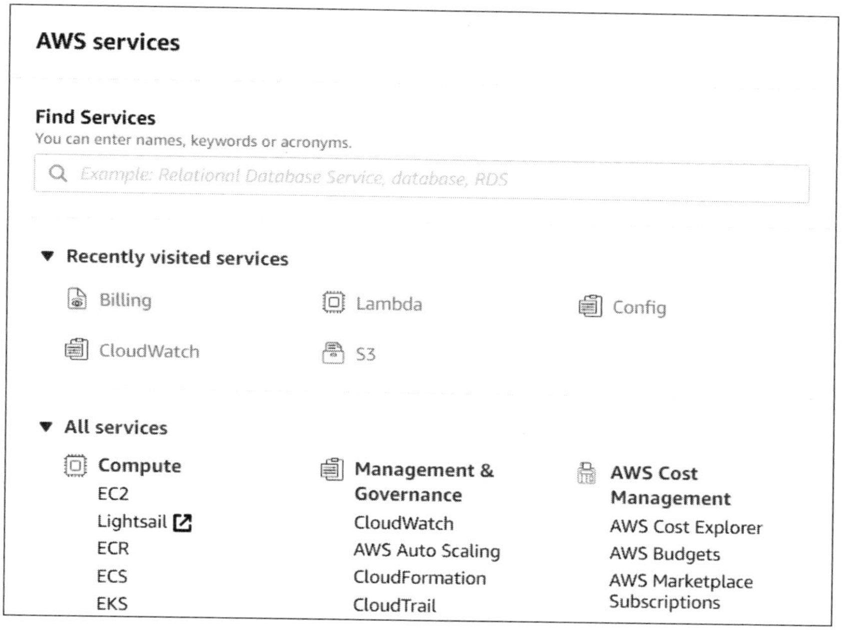

Figure 1-6   The AWS management portal

Broad network access—Cloud services can be accessed from almost anywhere across the globe using the Internet. If you host applications at AWS, perhaps they are public-facing SaaS apps. AWS also provides HTTPS endpoints to access every cloud service hosted at AWS. However, you may not want broad network access, which is defined as public network access to your cloud services. In fact, many companies that are moving to the AWS cloud have no interest in a publicly accessible software solution. They want their hosted cloud services to remain private, accessible only by their employees using private connections. Each cloud customer ultimately defines the real meaning of broad network access. At AWS, applications can be publicly available, or, you can stay completely private. VPN connections from your place of work to AWS are commonplace; in fact, you can order Direct Connect and establish a private fiber connection to AWS running at speeds up to 10 Gbps. Depending on the type of applications you're using in the cloud, high-speed network access is essential. We can even use, access, and administer AWS service from our phone using AWS apps. Certainly, accessing AWS from any device is possible. For more details on networking, check out Chapter 3, "AWS Networking Services."

Resource Pooling—Infrastructure resources for public cloud providers are pooled together in many data centers across the different regions of the world and are dynamically assigned on demand. A company running an on-premise private cloud would pool its virtual machines, memory, processing, and networking capabilities into one or two data centers, and from its own pool offer limited compute resources. All public cloud providers have a massive pool of resources to serve our various needs. AWS has clusters of data centers (known as AZs or availability zones), and each AZ could have over 80,000 bare-metal servers available and online allowing customers to host their application services with a high level of resiliency and failover. Having many available online resources also enables AWS to keep the price down. Without a massive pool of resources, AWS would not be able to offer its cloud services on demand that are able to scale up and down based on customer demand. Having a massive resource pool is a necessary standard for all public cloud providers; customers do not expect to run out of resources. Take, for example, AWS S3 storage, which is unlimited with no defined maximum limit. For more details on regions and AZs, check out Chapter 2.

Rapid Elasticity—Elasticity in the public cloud, or scaling, is *the* key feature required by all hosted cloud applications. Elasticity at AWS is utilized for both compute and storage. Because most services and applications are built on compute and storage, applications in the AWS cloud have the capability to automatically scale, as shown in Figure 1-7. And elasticity, or scaling, is only useful if it's automated based on demand. Turning off a virtual server, adding RAM, and turning it back on is not the elasticity that we are interested in; we want horizontal scale—that is, more application servers—not just a bigger server. Real-time monitoring of a hosted cloud application at AWS allows us to react almost instantaneously before the application's performance is close to degrading. With EC2 Auto Scaling in the background, additional computer resources are automatically ordered and delivered to the application server's cluster, maintaining the application's performance. Rapid elasticity based on demand is only possible with real-time monitoring driving automated scale. This is why the public cloud is so popular; with a massive pool of available cloud resources and the ability to automatically scale applications out and in based on demand, at AWS anybody can easily scale application stacks up and down. For more details on deploying scale and elasticity with EC2 Auto Scale, check out Chapter 5, "Planning for Scale and Resiliency."

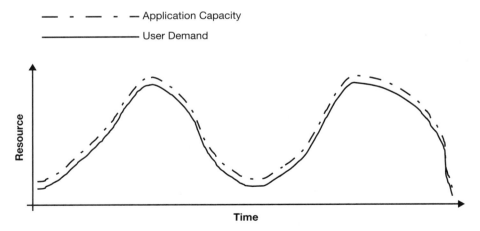

Figure 1-7 Applications can scale based on demand in the public cloud

Measured Service—In the cloud, you are only billed for what you use; that's defined as a measured service. Cloud providers make their money by charging for everything that you use in their data centers, including data transfer costs. Packet flow inbound to the public cloud is usually free; outbound packet flow, or traffic between subnets hosted in different data centers, is usually charged an outbound data transfer fee. Charges are per second, or per minute in the case of computer services like AWS EC2 compute instances, or they are per gigabyte per month in the case of storage services like S3 or virtual hard drives, which at AWS are called elastic block storage (EBS). AWS charges can be broken down into compute, storage, and data transfer charges. If an AWS service is on, the meter is running. Cost management is one of your most important jobs when operating in the cloud. AWS has many useful tools to help you control your costs, including the AWS Simple Pricing Calculator, AWS Budgets, and the Cost Explorer, as shown in Figure 1-8. You can find details on these features in Chapter 2. Being billed for consuming cloud services is a reality that we are all used to. What you also may have to get used to is exactly how you are being billed. Again, you must understand and carefully monitor compute, storage, and data transfer costs. For example, you can order a load balancer at AWS for $30 per month. However, there is an additional charge to be aware of: all the data packets transferred through the load balancer are charged, and that by itself can be a hefty price.

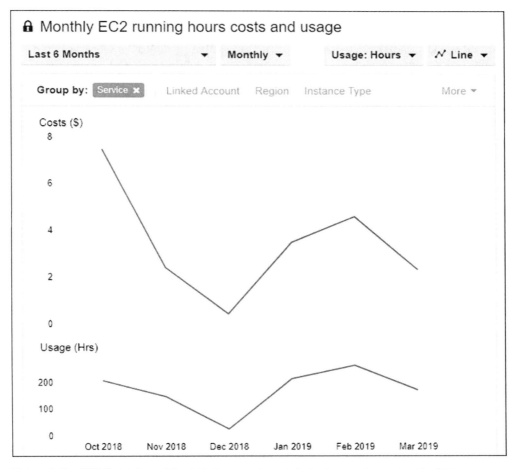

Figure 1-8   AWS Budgets and Cost Explorer track and alert when costs are over budget

Operational Benefits of AWS

Operating in the public cloud has certain benefits. Unlimited access to servers and storage and many management services may make it easier than you expected to operate in the cloud. Table 1-1 summarizes the managed services at AWS that may be able to replace or complement your existing on-premise services and procedures.

Servers—Underutilized servers in your data center are expensive to run and maintain. Moving applications to the public cloud will reduce the size of your on-premise data center. Because you no longer host as many physical servers, your total hosting costs (heating, cooling, and so on) will be lower as well. You also won't have to pay for as many software licenses at the processer level because you're not responsible for running hypervisor services; that's Amazon's job. You may think that moving to the AWS cloud means virtualized resources and only virtualization. However, at AWS, you can get a variety of compute options with virtualization of any size and scale, from a single-core CPU with 512MB of RAM to hundreds of CPU cores and terabytes of RAM. You can also order a bare-metal server and do whatever you want with it. You can find further details on compute options in Chapter 4.

Storage—Using cloud storage has huge benefits due to the unlimited amount of storage promised by cloud providers. Amazon has many options for storage that are similar, but not exactly the same as your on-premise solutions. For storage area network solutions, Amazon has shareable file solutions: the elastic file system (EFS) for Linux workloads, and FSx, a shared file service specifically for Windows File Server workloads. Virtual hard disks are available using EBS. Unlimited storage, and longer-term archive storage, is provided by S3 and S3 Glacier. Details on all the storage options at AWS can be found in Chapter 6, "Cloud Storage."

Managed services—AWS has a variety of managed services, as shown in Table 1-1, that may be able to replace or complement your existing services and utilities currently used on-premise once you move to the AWS cloud.

Table 1-1 **Managed Services at AWS**

IT Operations	On-Premise	AWS Cloud
Monitoring	Nagios, SolarWinds.	CloudWatch monitoring providing metrics for every AWS service. All monitoring and logging data can be stored in S3. All third-party monitoring solutions can access S3 to perform their own custom analysis of log data.
Data backup	Backup tools such as Commvault and NetBackup.	Any third-party vendor that wants to stay in business will be supporting AWS; both Veritas and Commvault have AWS solutions. AWS Storage Gateway can also be installed to cache required content locally, while backing up local disk volumes to an S3 bucket. Backups can be snapshots of local virtual hard disks, or data files from specific volumes can be targeted.

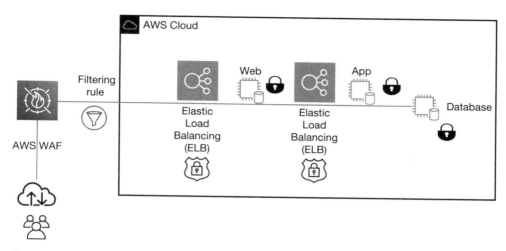

Figure 1-10   Encrypted traffic flow at AWS

Compliance in the AWS Cloud

As a worldwide public cloud provider, AWS operates in many different countries and is subject to a variety of rules and regulations enforced by governments and compliance standards. Depending on the type of business that you operate, there are possibly many different levels of compliance you will have to adhere to when operating in the AWS cloud. Financial, health, and government institutions have strict rules and regulations that must be followed by their clients. In addition, your own company may have specific internal rules and regulations they want to follow.

Many countries in the world are enacting laws, regulations, and mandates in serious attempts to protect the privacy of personal data and the security of corporate information and computer systems. The new data protection laws place the burden of protection and security on the custodian of that data; that is where the data is stored when the data is transferred from source to destination.

The cloud providers have contractual obligations to ensure that when organizations have data records hosted in their cloud, they can adhere to the promises and commitments made in the SLA. Some of the most common compliance regulations that AWS has been successfully audited against include the compliance standards listed in Table 1-3.

Table 1-3   **AWS Supports Many Compliance Standards**

Abbreviation	Scope of Operation	Purpose of Protection	Legal Status
HIPPA	Healthcare	Personal information	Law
GLBA	Financial industry	Personal information	Law
SOX	Publicly traded companies	Shareholder	Law
PCI DSS	Payment card industry	Fraud	Industry regulation
GDPR	EU	Personal information	Law

Health Insurance Portability and Accountability Act—Secures the privacy of individual health information records in the United States.

Gramm-Leachy-Billy Act—Mandates protection of customer information by financial industries.

Sarbanes-Oxley—Ensures the integrity of financial operations of publicly traded companies.

PCI DSS—Ensures the processing integrity of credit card data or authentication data.

GDPR—Protects privacy and personal data for all citizens of the EU. Amazon has a decent compliance page at https://aws.amazon.com/compliance/, which has details about all the AWS certifications and attestations that it has achieved or supports. If you are bound by a specific compliance standard, one of your first steps should be to review the AWS services that are available for each compliance standard, as shown in Figure 1-11.

SOC	^
SERVICES / PROGRAMS	**SOC 1,2,3**
Amazon Athena	✓
Amazon Cloud Directory	✓
Amazon CloudFront	✓
Amazon CloudWatch Logs	✓
Amazon Cognito	✓
Amazon Connect	✓
Amazon DocumentDB (with MongoDB compatibility)	SOC 2 only

Figure 1-11   Check the AWS compliance page to see what services are supported

Playing in the AWS Sandbox

AWS makes it easy to "try before you buy," frequently doling out promotional credits to developers. Even if you are not a developer, every new AWS customer gets limited access to nearly every AWS service for free (Amazon calls this the "free tier") during the first year. This is a great way to experiment with AWS. The only thing you must provide is a credit card that won't be charged unless you choose to use resources that the free tier doesn't cover. After the first year has passed, you'll start accruing charges for every service you use; any AWS resources that you built during the first year remain in your account but start accruing charges.

In addition, AWS has several free hands-on labs. You can sign up for QwikLabs at https://run. qwiklabs.com/home?locale=en and carry out a variety of AWS tasks in the AWS cloud.

Figure 1-12 illustrates some of the learnig and labs that are available from QwikLabs.

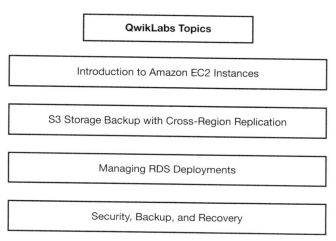

Figure 1-12   QwikLabs has more than 20 completely free labs for AWS services

Running experiments, and performing labs raises additional questions that will help further your AWS cloud knowledge and experience.

MAKE SURE TO WATCH THE COMPANION VIDEO "SIGNING UP FOR AWD FREE TIER."

To access the companion videos, register your book at informit.com/register.

What's the Problem That Needs to Be Solved?

Typical large organizations run hundreds or thousands of applications on thousands of virtual servers. Which applications can be moved to AWS? What should be prioritized?

Start with low value/low risk—It's quite popular to suggest a starting point of high value and low risk when choosing your first application to move to the AWS cloud. Here's a reality check: it's probably going to take you 6 months or longer to move your application to the cloud. Choosing an application with low value provides a valuable timeline to do some additional planning and analysis before finalizing your application in its working form at AWS. I've seen many companies make the pronouncement that applications will be moving to the cloud quickly. It rarely happens successfully because there are so many things to learn and consider. Start with low value. Take your time, and select a working application that has been running successfully for a good time period. Then you can document your lessons learned and what to do differently the next time. The second and third application moved to the cloud generally will be much faster than the first application due to the lessons learned and experience gained.

Create a brand-new application first—The advantage of creating a completely new application at AWS means you are not constrained by anything, such as the type of database that must be used, the type of programming language that must be used, or the type of compute that must be used. Starting anew at AWS allows you to try out some of the new methods to host applications such as serviceless computing, create a mobile application using stateless components, or use DynamoDB instead of SQL. This is where the real learning about what the AWS cloud can do for you will really appear.

Try to solve a single problem—Do you need additional storage? Perhaps that's a great starting point for your adventure in the cloud. Archiving files in S3 Glacier could be as simple as ordering a Snowball device, connecting it up to your network, filling up with files you'd like to archive, and shipping it back to AWS. This is an excellent first project to start working with AWS support, archiving records, and saving your company money.

Define a value proposition—Ideally, the move to AWS is long term and successful. Thousands of companies have been successful moving to AWS; you, too, can be successful. Start off with a defined value proposition that can be validated quickly, in a matter of months rather than years. For developing applications, you could sign up for AWS Cloud9, a cloud-hosted IDE that supports more than 40 programming languages, as shown in Figure 1-13. Armed with a browser, you can try your hand at developing applications at AWS.

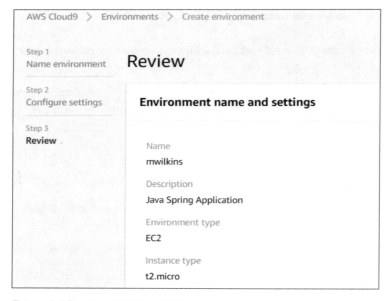

Figure 1-13   Cloud9 IDE at AWS

Access to data records—The number-one problem with larger companies when starting to work with cloud providers is working through the internal politics to allow access to data from the cloud. Data record access, and the steps for successful access, should be considered before you move to the cloud:

- How can we access our on-premise data from the cloud?
- What records have to stay on-premise?
- Are we bound by any compliance rules and regulations?
- Is our data in the right format for what we need?

Migrating Applications

For applications that have been chosen as starting candidates to move to the AWS cloud, several decisions need to be made about the application's journey, or path.

Can the application be moved to AWS and hosted on an EC2 instance with no changes?

Applications that fit into this category could be migrated to AWS as an EC2 instance image. Server migration tools, and database migration tools discussed in Chapter 2, can carry out these migration paths quite effectively. However, applications that are lifted and shifted to the cloud will have other dependencies and issues that will have to be considered:

- The application stores its data in a database. Will the database remain on-premise or be moved to the cloud?
- If the database for the application remains on-premise, are there latency issues that need to be considered when communicating with the database?
- Will a high-speed connection need to be established between the AWS cloud and the database remaining on-premise?
- Are there compliance issues regarding the application data? Does the data have to be encrypted at rest? Does communication with the database need to be encrypted?
- Do users authenticate to the application across the corporate network? If so, are federation services required to be deployed at AWS for single sign-on (SSO)?
- Are local dependencies installed on the application server that will interfere with the application server's operation in the AWS cloud?
- Are there licensing considerations for both the operating system and the application when operating in the cloud?

Is there an existing SaaS application hosted by a public cloud provider that should replace the application because it's a better choice?

This can be a very political issue to resolve. With so many hosted cloud applications available in the public cloud, the odds are close to 100% that there will be an existing application that could replace the current on-premise application.

Should the application remain on-premise and eventually be deprecated?

- The application is hosted on legacy hardware that is near end-of-life.

- The application is not virtualized.

- The application does not have support.

- The application is used by a small number of users.

The Well-Architected Framework

Several years ago, AWS introduced documentation called the Well-Architected Framework to help customers plan properly when moving to the AWS cloud. The goal was to give guidance for cloud architects to build secure, resilient, and decent performing infrastructure to host their applications following recognized best practices that have been developed over time by the experience of many AWS customers. Each best practice still must be evaluated as to whether it meets your criteria. A best practice should not be blindly adopted without understanding why it has achieved a best practice designation.

The documentation for the well-architected framework also has many key questions to ponder that can be found in the well-architected framework blueprint. It is useful to discuss these questions out loud with other technical folks in your company; they will help you make key decisions about your infrastructure and applications hosted at AWS. The framework documentation can be found here: https://d1.awsstatic.com/whitepapers/architecture/AWS_Well-Architected_Framework.pdf. Each application to be deployed at AWS needs to be viewed through the lens of being well architected following these five principles:

Operational excellence—How best to execute, deploy, and monitor applications running at AWS using automated deployment monitoring procedures, continuous improvement, and automated solutions for recovering from failures. Key AWS services to utilize include CloudWatch events and alarms, CloudTrail, EC2 Auto Scaling, AWS Config, and the Trusted Advisor. Check out Chapters 5, 7, and 8. Operational excellence questions to consider include these:

- How are disruptions to applications handled? Manually, or automatically?

- How can you analyze the ongoing health of your applications and infrastructure components hosted at AWS?

Security—How to best design systems that will operate reliably and securely while protecting customer information and data records. Key AWS services to utilize include IAM, AWS Organizations, CloudWatch logs, CloudTrail events, S3 and S3 Glacier, and VPC flow logs. Check out Chapters 3, 6, and 7. Security questions to consider include these:

- How are security credentials and authentication managed at AWS?

- How are automated procedures secured?

Reliability—How can systems and applications hosted at AWS recover from disruption with minimal downtime? How can applications meet your escalating demands? Key AWS services to utilize include ELB, EC2 Auto Scaling, and CloudWatch alarms. Check out Chapter 5. Reliability questions to consider include these:

- How do you monitor resources hosted at AWS?

- How do applications hosted at AWS adapt to changes in demand by end users?

Performance efficiency—How to use compute resources to meet and maintain your application requirements on an ongoing basis. Should your compute solution change from EC2 instances to containers or serviceless? Key services include EC2 Auto Scaling, EBS volumes, and RDS. Check out Chapters 4 and 6. Performance efficiency questions to consider include these:

- Why did you select your database?

- Why did you select your current compute infrastructure?

Cost Optimization—How to design systems that meet your needs at the cheapest price point. Key AWS services include Cost Explorer, Budgets, EC2 Auto Scaling, Trusted Advisor, and the Simple Monthly Calculator. Check out Chapters 2, 5, and 7. Cost optimization questions to consider are as follows:

- How do you oversee usage and cost?

- How do you meet cost targets?

- Are you aware of current data transfer charges based on your AWS designs?

The Well-Architected Tool

In the AWS management console under "Management and Governance" is the AWS Well-Architected Tool, as shown in Figure 1-14. It provides a framework for documenting your work-loads against AWS best practices as defined in the well-architected framework documentation. In each of the five pillars, there are many questions to consider before deploying your application. As you consider each question, you can enter milestones to mark changes in your architecture as it moves through its deployment and build lifecycle. Working with the well-architected tool, you will receive tips and guidance on how to follow the best practices recommended by AWS while carrying out a full architectural review of an actual workload that you are planning to deploy at AWS. It is well worth the time spent.

Before the review begins, you will select the AWS region where your application will be hosted. The first step is to define the workload and choose the industry type and whether the application is in a production or preproduction environment. During the review process, the well-architected tool will identify potential areas of medium and high risk based on the answers to the questions posed during the workload review. The five pillars of design success will also be included in the plan that is presented showing the recommended improvements to your initial design decisions. The plan as shown in Figure 1-15 will also define both high and medium risks, with recom-mended improvements to consider implementing.

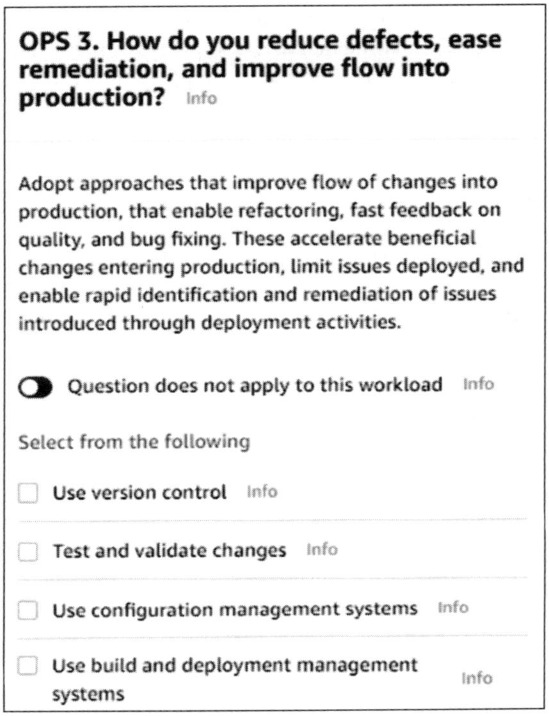

OPS 3. How do you reduce defects, ease remediation, and improve flow into production? Info

Adopt approaches that improve flow of changes into production, that enable refactoring, fast feedback on quality, and bug fixing. These accelerate beneficial changes entering production, limit issues deployed, and enable rapid identification and remediation of issues introduced through deployment activities.

🔘 Question does not apply to this workload   Info

Select from the following

☐ Use version control   Info

☐ Test and validate changes   Info

☐ Use configuration management systems   Info

☐ Use build and deployment management systems   Info

Figure 1-14   Using the well-architected framework tool

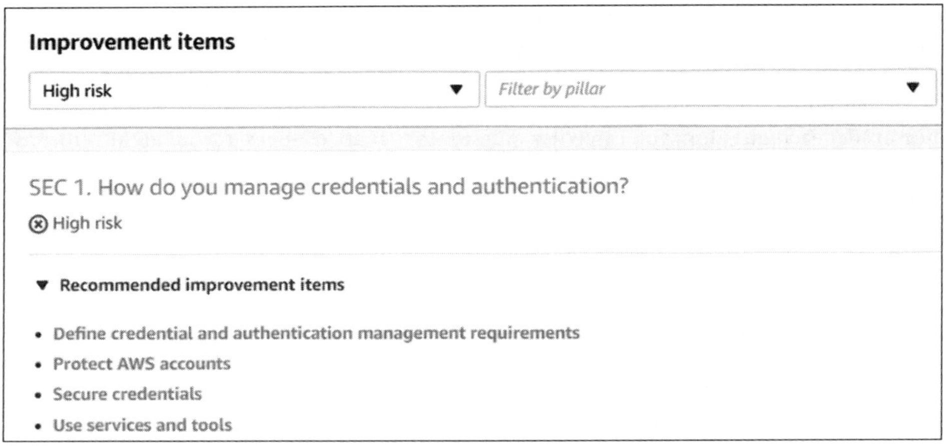

Improvement items

High risk ▼	Filter by pillar ▼

SEC 1. How do you manage credentials and authentication?

⊗ High risk

▼ Recommended improvement items

- Define credential and authentication management requirements
- Protect AWS accounts
- Secure credentials
- Use services and tools

Figure 1-15   Recommended improvements using the well-architected tool review

A failure of an AZ (typically a single physical data center located within the AZ) will not affect and derail the operation of the AWS services that are specifically designed to live outside the AZs. For example, Amazon's S3 storage and Elastic Load Balancing (ELB) services are specifically designed to integrate with the data centers within each AZ; but each of these services functions as a standalone entity that will continue to function even if one or all the data centers located within an AZ have failed.

In addition, services defined as global services are designed to sit outside the regions themselves at the perimeter of AWS, defined as the edge location—specifically, DNS services such as Route 53, and CloudFront, AWS's CDN. You can find more about Route 53 in Chapter 3; for CloudFront, you can find details in Chapter 6.

Even though each AZ is backed by a cluster of multiple data centers, it's important to also grasp that no two AZs share the same single data center. Each AZ is also isolated from the other AZs within the region.

Availability Zone Distribution

The other interesting design criteria to understand is the balancing and distribution of resources hosted in AZs carried out in the background by AWS. If I log into my AWS account, select the US-East (N. Virginia) region, and create a subnet in availability zone A, the physical location of my subnet is probably not the same as another Amazon customer who has also selected the US-East Northern Virginia region and created a subnet in availability zone A. We each have a subnet in "availability zone A," but our subnets are probably not in the same availability zone. We are most likely in different physical locations, as shown in Figure 2-6.

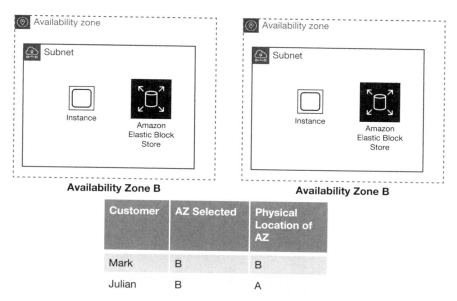

Customer	AZ Selected	Physical Location of AZ
Mark	B	B
Julian	B	A

Figure 2-6   AZ balancing and distribution of resources

Average latency between AZs within a region is around 3 ms. The latency between different instances located in different AZs can be casually tested by running pings between instances located in different AZs. I don't think you'll find that latency between AZs within a region is an issue. Certainly, latency testing can be performed from one instance hosted in one AZ to an instance in another AZ if you're concerned.

Latency from your physical location to AWS can also be tested with the variety of publicly available tools, including Cloud Harmony's speed test for AWS found here: https://cloudharmony. com/speedtest-for-aws.

> **Note**
>
> Each AZ within each region has a name based on the region it is hosted within and a letter code, such as US-West-1A.

Within a single AZ, the data center private network connections are defined as "intra," or local to the AZ. The wiring between the AWS regions is defined as "inter," with international links connecting the regions (see Figure 2-7).

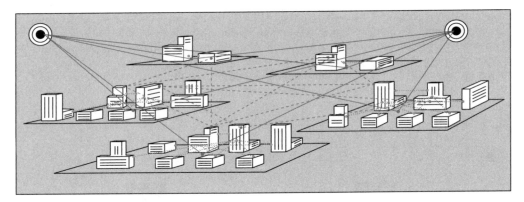

•——• Transit Center connections
•‑‑‑• Inter-AZ connections
•······• Intra-AZ connections

Figure 2-7   Private network wiring for region and AZs

> **Note**
>
> The primary reasons for using AZs in your infrastructure design are for application failover and for database replication.

Multiple Availability Zones

AZs are an important concept to wrap your head around when working with AWS. Key services—specifically the virtual private cloud (VPC), the ELB service, and Elastic Compute Cloud (EC2) Auto Scaling—can function across multiple AZs, providing you, the customer, with the ability to design your applications for scale, resiliency, and high availability. We will revisit availability zones several times throughout this book; specifically, we'll cover them in Chapter 3 and in Chapter 5, "Planning for Scale and Resiliency."

You may remember that a few years ago Amazon had issues in Australia. The media announced that "the Amazon cloud was down!" This was true to a point because an AZ in the Asia Pacific region had issues, but not all the AZs within the region had issues. However, if your application or website was hosted in the unavailable AZ, and you had not designed your application or website for automatic failover to another AZ within the region, as shown in Figure 2-8, then there was a 100% possibility that your applications were not available, in this case for several hours.

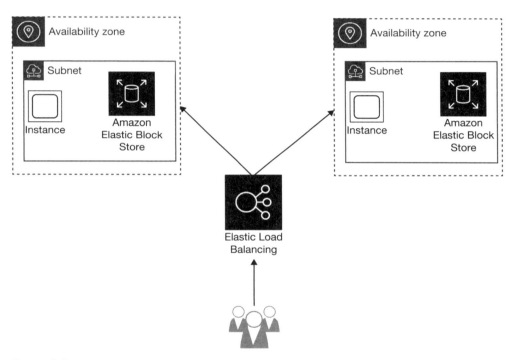

Figure 2-8   Availability zones provide failover possibilities for application stacks

Is this lack of availability of your hosted application Amazon's fault? Nope. It's the customer's fault for not utilizing proper cloud design standards in the hosted applications. In fact, not designing your applications to properly function in multiple AZs negates your service-level agreement (SLA) with AWS. And, if you were down and you had designed your application properly, there was a possibility of getting a credit on your bill for several hours of downtime. But there's a catch; you usually need to prove that your application was down by providing relevant network traces. I say *usually*; I've seen instances in which a credit was automatically given because the outage was so severe it was obvious that it was the cloud provider's problem. More details on the AWS SLA are next.

Remember, your availability zone A is probably not in the same physical location as another customer's availability zone A. Just because it is announced that an AZ is down, there's no real way of knowing what physical data center is down. An AWS customer's solution to this problem is having a properly designed application that can fail over between multiple AZs within each region.

> **Note**
> An AZ is a single point of failure.

MAKE SURE TO WATCH THE COMPANION VIDEO "AVAILABILITY ZONES."

To access the companion videos, register your book at informit.com/register.

What's the AWS Service-Level Agreement?

Cloud SLAs have been described by many technical people over the years as less than adequate. However, this is typically the conclusion made when comparing a cloud SLA with an on-premise SLA. Imagine that you were the cloud provider with multiple data centers and thousands of customers. How would you design your SLA? Would you not tell your customers, "We do the best job we can, but computers do fail, as we know." If you think about the difficulty of what to offer a customer when there are hardware and software failures, you would probably come up with the same solution that all cloud providers have arrived at.

You've probably heard about SLAs. After all, they are a common part of the computer and service industry. Perhaps you have an SLA for on-premise technical support, or you've outsourced your help desk. Each SLA defines the level of support, the hours of support, and the services to be rendered. For example, when hardware breaks down, the response to the breakdown will happen within so many minutes or hours; it will be fixed or replaced within an agreed-upon timeframe. (Perhaps loaner equipment will also be promised.) In every SLA, the guarantee of service availability is the focus of the agreement. Common terms covered in most SLAs also include definitions of quality of service, customer experience, availability, dispute resolution, and, of course, the indemnification clause. Now let's turn our attention to cloud SLAs.

At Amazon, each service may have a separate SLA, but some services don't have a specific SLA at all. Certainly, the building blocks of any application—compute, storage, CDN, and DNS services—have defined SLAs. Before we consider an SLA, the first document you need to consider is the *AWS Customer Agreement,* which lays out the big picture—the terms and conditions that govern your access to the total AWS service. If you've already signed up for AWS and checked that check box indicating that you accepted the AWS terms, you have already accepted the customer agreement. Let's review what you may have already agreed to: the major considerations of the AWS customer agreement.

Changes—The fabled words of *from time to time* in this section indicate that Amazon is free to make changes, additions, or discontinuation of any AWS service. There could also be changes to each AWS service SLA at any time, and this does happen frequently.

Security and data privacy—Each customer specifies the regions where content is stored. Understand that Amazon will normally move your content (data) within the region; for example, a virtual hard disk is created using the EBS service, and Amazon automatically creates a backup copy in a different location. Or an EBS drive fails and needs to be replaced by the backup image. You create an S3 bucket and upload files; these files are replicated to three separate locations within the region that you specify.

Your responsibilities—Accounts, content, security settings, backup, login credentials, logon keys, and the actions of your end users working with AWS services are the customer's responsibility.

Termination of your account—If you cancel your account, your content will be held at AWS for at least 30 days.

Indemnification—You, the customer, will hold Amazon harmless from any losses arising from actions performed by your end users, any violations of the service agreement, and any illegal actions. You will also pay Amazon's legal fees.

Disclaimers—Each AWS service is provided "as is" with no warranty of any kind.

Limitations of Liability—Amazon and its affiliates and licensees are not liable to the customer for anything.

Quality of service—Typically, this term applies to networking performance, or multimedia performance across a network. This term could also mean that the service was slower than expected. Amazon assumes responsibilities for its services; there is a default performance standard for each AWS service that the cloud provider attempts to maintain. Take, for example, the typical complaint of, "This application is so slow it must be the network that's the issue." The customer responsibilities must be taken into consideration:

- Is the operating system kernel up-to-date, or are you using an older version of the operating system that cannot take advantage of faster network speeds?

- Does the chosen instance type have the required network speeds?

- Are elastic network interfaces being used on the latest EC2 instances with the most up-to-date Amazon machine images (AMIs)?

- Are the SSD-backed volumes of your instances optimized with provisioned IOPS (the number of Input/Output Operations per second)?

- Is the instance of Elastic Block Storage (EBS) optimized?

Customer experience—Certainly, the customer experience is based on the "quality" of the service being used. Proper application design using Amazon best practices will result in an excellent customer experience; therefore, the customer experience is the customer's job.

Availability—This is the number-one consideration when using a cloud service: that the service in question remains available. From time to time, certain services will not be available, and you will have to plan for this occurrence. Each separate SLA will detail Amazon's desired availability of the service. We must give Amazon kudos: many times, they exceed the published SLA's specs for months at a time.

> **Note**
> Over at www.cloudharmony.com/status-for-aws, we can review the uptime status of AWS services and locations.

Everything Fails

Here is a concept to get your mind around with every cloud service SLA that AWS provides. Each service is going to fail, and you're not going to have any warning. That's pretty much the only guarantee we have with hosting applications in the public cloud: the underlying cloud services are going to fail unexpectedly. And don't get me wrong; AWS services are stable for months; but failures will still happen unexpectedly.

If you think about it, most of the failures we experience in the cloud are compute failures. An instance fails that is powering an application server, a Web server, a database server, or a caching server. What about the data? Your data in the cloud is replicated, at the very least, within the AZ where your instances are running. (If you're strong, your data records on EBS volumes.) This does not mean you can't lose data in the cloud; if you never back up your data, you will probably lose it. And because customers are solely in charge of their own data, that is certainly job one: 100% data retention.

Recap—Amazon helps us with data retention by having multiple copies of our EBS volume data hosted within the AZ, or in the case of S3 data, replicating the data contents across three physical locations within the region. These and other common cloud services shown in Table 2-2 illustrate how AWS builds redundancy and failover into every service that it offers, except for the single instance. The only SLAs offered by AWS are for these listed services.

Therefore, ordering a single instance to host a website, and not designing your website or with failover to another website instance when issues occur, is simply dumb. Designing your applications stack to fail over between AZs is the bare minimum for being protected by the EC-2 SLA agreement. Customers who don't follow proper AWS design principals and best practices will have no SLA protection.

Table 2-2   **AWS Service Availability and Projected Downtime**

AWS Service	Availability	Projected Downtime per Year	Avoiding Downtime
Instances	99.95%	One hour, 45 minutes	A single instance: none
			Instances that fail over across AZs
Relational database service (RDS)	99.95%	One hour, 45 minutes	Master/slave database design with synchronous replication across AZs
EBS volumes	99.99%	52 minutes	Each volume automatically replicated within its AZ
S3 Storage	99.9%	8.76 hours	Replicated across three physical locations within the region
Route 53	100%	Hopefully none	Anycast design—worldwide replication and updating

Protecting Against Application Failure

It's time to return to the concept of failure. How do we work around service failure at AWS? We must design for failure. Each customer's job is to use the available tools and services at AWS to create an application environment with the goal of 100% availability. When failures occur at AWS, automated processes must be designed and in place to ensure proper failover, with minimum to zero data loss. Computer loss, no matter how painful, we can live with. Data loss is obviously unacceptable and does not have to happen. We will be looking at how to design our application stacks hosted at AWS for automatic failover in Chapter 5.

The other reality to accept is knowing that, for example, although the RDS service as shown in Table 2-2 is designed by AWS to fail a mere 52 minutes per year, that does not mean you can schedule this potential downtime. Just because Route 53, AWS's DNS service, is designed for 100% uptime does not mean that Route 53 will not have issues. The published figures of uptime are not a guarantee; instead, it's what AWS strives for and most of the time achieves.

When a cloud service fails and you're down, you're out of business for that timeframe. Because failures are going to happen, designing your application's hosted AWS for maximum uptime is the goal. You also must consider all the additional external services that allow us to connect to AWS: your telco, your ISP, and all the other moving bits. Considering all services in the equation, it's difficult, if not impossible to avoid some downtime. However, we can greatly minimize our downtime and completely minimize our data loss by following the basic cloud design considerations listed in Table 2-3.

Table 2-3 **Cloud Design Considerations**

AWS Service	Potential Solution
Instance	Load balanced across AZs within a single region
Database	Synchronous replication across AZs within a single region
S3 bucket	Automatic replication to bucket in different region
EBS volumes	Automatic copying of snapshots to different region
100% Application uptime	Geo-load-balancing utilizing Route 53 domain name system (DNS) services across regions

Global Edge Services

Outside of Amazon's regions is the rest of the world where you and other customers are located. Connecting to Amazon resources from your location requires the ability on Amazon's end to successfully direct incoming requests from any location to the desired Amazon resource. This area has a worldwide presence and is defined as the edge location with many points of presence wired to AWS services spread across the globe. More than 155 edge locations are available in 2019 pointing to AWS services from most major cities across the globe.

Each edge location is wired into the local and global telecom provider's mesh of transit networks that are peered and tiered around the world supporting worldwide Internet communications. The cheapest and the slowest way to get to an edge location is across the public Internet You could also use a VPN connection or a private fiber connection, called Direct Connect, from your branch office location, or local data center, to connect to an edge location. There are three data highways connection possibilities found at each edge location:

- Internet connections
- Direct Connect private connections
- AWS private backbone network

Each request to an application hosted at AWS is typically a query for information. Alternatively, my request could be providing an update to existing data records; I have some data I want to move to AWS storage using my application and its associated storage location. It's important to understand that edge locations are for both the fast uploading *and* downloading of information to and from AWS.

Services Located at the Edge

There are several essential services at each edge location; some of these services are provided at no additional charge, and depending on your present and future needs, other services can be ordered and utilized at each edge location as required. The services offered at each edge are as follows:

- **Route 53**—Global load balancing DNS services
- **AWS Shield**—Real-time inline distributed denial of service (DDoS) protection services

- **AWS Web Application Firewall**—Layer 7 protection for Hypertext Transfer Protocol (HTTP) and Hypertext Transfer Protocol Secure (HTTPS)

- **CloudFront**—Content delivery network for the fast delivery of both static and dynamic data

- **AWS Lambda@Edge**—Create lambda functions to control CloudFront delivery

Route 53

As a customer accessing an application hosted at AWS from your phone, tablet, or device, an application query will be carried out. Obviously, you will need an Internet connection or a private network connection for your device to begin communicating with AWS services. What service needs to be working to make the initial query? If you're thinking DNS, you're right. DNS is still the essential service in today's cloud. And because we are now operating in the public cloud, the scope of DNS services has changed from local DNS services per corporation to a worldwide global service that knows about where the Amazon regions are located and each requested AWS service resides.

Amazon's hosted DNS service is called Route 53, named for the standard DNS port number. Route 53 has a public side pointed to the public edge locations that accepts incoming customer requests and then resolves each query to the requested AWS resource located on Route 53's private side, as shown in Figure 2-9.

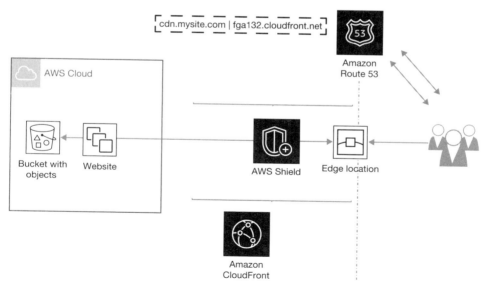

Figure 2-9   Route 53 at an AWS Edge location

For simplicity sake, let's pretend that at the edge location is a single DNS server with full knowledge of all AWS resources. Obviously, it's not a very fault-tolerant design. It would be better to have redundant DNS services wired worldwide that are linked together with full knowledge of all AWS resources. Route 53 is designed using Anycast DNS routing algorithms. In this design, each destination service location is known by all the Anycast DNS servers hosted across the AWS regions. Your physical location will determine the edge location Route 53 directs you to. Once an application request reaches the edge location, the request continues on Amazon's private high-speed network to the preferred AWS service location.

AWS Shield (Standard)

What if a request that enters an AWS edge location is a malicious request like a DDoS attack, or a bot attack? At each edge location is a service running 24/7 called AWS Shield. Its job is to provide multitenant basic DDoS protection with the design requirement that it analyze and block perceived threats within 1 second for known Layer 3 and 4 attacks.

AWS Shield standard protection is for all AWS customers, but AWS is not really protecting each individual customer. It's instead protecting its infrastructure located at the edge for all customers. What if you want or need more individualized DDoS protection? If you don't have the expertise to solve your security issues and would like AWS experts to assist you with real-time custom protection, get out your wallet and connect with the AWS Shield Advanced team.

AWS Shield Advanced

When you can't solve a sophisticated DDoS attack, perhaps it's time to sign up for AWS Shield Advanced by selecting Global threat protection from the AWS Shield console. This option allows you to further protect your two- or three-tier applications running on EC2 instances, sitting behind Elastic Load Balancing and CloudFront services. Choosing AWS Shield Advanced, you'll be working with an expert DDoS response team at AWS with a 15-minute SLA response. After analyzing your situation, solutions to mitigate the more sophisticated DDoS attack are created, applied, and monitored by the team. AWS Shield Advanced customers also get access to a global threat environment dashboard, which reviews the current attack vectors and any DDoS attacks that are currently happening around the world.

An interesting bonus feature is called cost protection, which saves you money if your hosted application that is under attack forces your AWS resources to scale due to the illegitimate demand placed on its services. AWS will refund the additional load balancer, compute, data transfer, and Route 53 query costs borne by you during the DDoS attack. AWS Shield Advanced can run you a few thousand dollars a month, but that may be a drop in the bucket compared to the business losses you may be faced with if your online AWS resources are unavailable due to attacks. You also get the web application firewall (WAF) and the AWS Firewall Manager at no additional cost when you sign up for Shield Advanced.

Web Application Firewall (WAF)

If you want to craft your own protection at the edge, the next service to consider is the WAF for custom filtering of incoming (ingress) public traffic requests at Layer 7 for HTTP and HTTPS requests. The idea behind the WAF is to limit any malicious requests from getting any further into AWS infrastructure to the edge location. Customers can define their own conditions for the WAF to monitor for incoming web requests. WAF rules are created using conditions that are combined into a Web access control list (ACL). Rules either allow, or block, depending on the condition, as shown in Figure 2-10.

The following behaviors are supported by the AWS WAF:

- **Block requests from specific attackers, or attacks**—Block specific IP addresses, countries, and defined conditions.

- **Serve restricted content to specific users**—For example, restrict content to users from a specific IP address range.

- **Monitor incoming requests properties for analysis**—After analysis, conditions and rules can be created for additional protection.

Figure 2-10   Web application firewall rules

WAF rules can be applied to public-facing Application Load Balancers and CloudFront distributions. WAF rules can also be managed across multiple AWS accounts and resources using the AWS Firewall Manager. You can find more details on WAF in Chapter 5.

CloudFront (CF)

CloudFront is AWS's content delivery network service located at the edge with its own points of presence (POPs). Remember that delivery through each edge location goes both ways; content is delivered outbound to customers, and customers deliver content inbound to AWS through each CloudFront point of presence.

Think of CloudFront as the fast doorway into AWS. CloudFront sits in front of the origin of the request, which could be an EC2 instance, an S3 bucket, or a custom origin location such as resources running in your own data center. CloudFront is essentially a caching service, located at each edge location within each region:

- If the requested content is already in the cache, it is delivered quickly.

- If the content is not in the cache, CloudFront requests the content from the origin server or location and then delivers your request. It places the request in local cache at the edge, as shown in Figure 2-11.

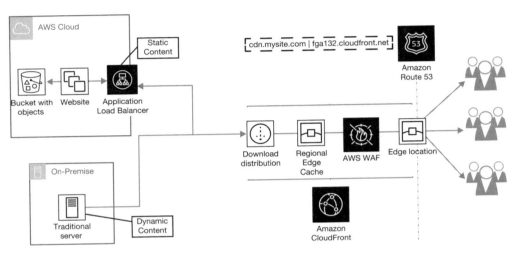

Figure 2-11   CloudFront operation

The delivered data may also be placed in a regional cache, which if available, is a much larger cache location hosted within each AWS region. Think of it as a secondary cache location designed to speed up delivery. If a content request is not in the local edge cache, perhaps it's in the regional cache.

AWS Lambda@Edge

Lambda is a managed AWS service that allows you to craft custom functions to carry out any task written in a variety of programming languages, including Python, Go, C#, Node.js, or Java. Lambda is available as a hosted service at each edge location, which means that you can craft Lambda functions to control CloudFront content requests from end users, and the responses from the origin service. Lambda sits in the middle of the ingress and egress communication and can completely control traffic flow, as shown in Figure 2-12. For example, Lambda could send specific content to users sending requests from a smart phone versus requests from a traditional computer.

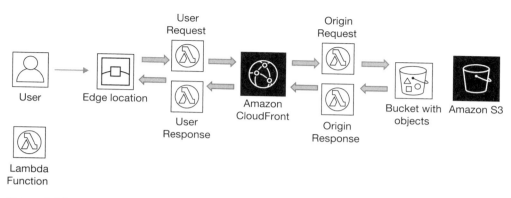

Figure 2-12   Lambda@Edge at CloudFront

Choosing a Region

Reasons to choose a specific AWS region over another usually depend on four interlinked conditions, namely these:

- **Compliance rules**—Where are you allowed to operate?

- **Latency issues**—How far away are you from the desired cloud service?

- **Services offered**—Is the service that you require offered within the region that you've selected?

- **Pricing realities**—Is the pricing reasonable? Pricing is more complicated at AWS than you may first think.

Making a good decision about the best region to operate in takes some quality decision time after evaluating each of these conditions thoroughly. Let's begin by looking at the most important condition: the compliance rules and regulations that you must follow.

> MAKE SURE TO WATCH THE COMPANION VIDEO "CHOOSING A REGION."

Compliance

The rules and regulations that your company follows in its day-to-day business practices should be analyzed for how they're potentially going to change once you start hosting applications in the cloud. There is going to be some loss of control; after all, you are working in AWS's data centers being controlled by their rules.

AWS maintains its data centers, networks, and shared infrastructure adhering to a suite of ISO certifications that mandate a strict level of compliance with security management, information security controls, and best practices while operating in the public cloud. If your company complies by these ISO 27001 standards, perhaps your security standards compared AWS's standards are closer than you may have thought.

> **Note**
>
> AWS holds certification for compliance with the ISO/IEC 27001:2013, 27017:2015, 27018:2014, and 9001:2015 certifications.

AWS is audited on a rigid schedule by third-party ISO auditors to ensure that they maintain and uphold their overall operations to the ISO 2700:2013 security management standard. Other third-party auditors ensure that AWS lives up to the many other compliance standards and assurance programs that it is also aligned with. Once you sign on as an AWS customer, you have access to the compliance reports aligned with the standards, certifications, or attestations that Amazon has currently achieved and maintains. Some compliance reports are available to all AWS customers upon request; others require that you also sign a nondisclosure agreement (NDA) with AWS. The steps to get started with reviewing the available compliance and attestation reports at AWS follow:

1. Sign into your AWS account with the root user account credentials.

2. From the Management console, select Security, Identity and Compliance and select Artifact. The available security and compliance documents are listed.

3. Choose your compliance program and click Get This Artifact.

4. Typically, you are asked to agree to the terms of the AWS Artifact NDA.

5. After acceptance of the security terms, you can download your selected document and review.

Once you gain access to the desired compliance report, you can view the services that were defined as in scope for the review and read the summary information and conclusions.

To begin to understand the compliance rules and regulations that AWS supports, I suggest you follow these steps:

1. Head over to the compliance website at https://aws.amazon.com/compliance/programs/.

2. Review the compliance programs that Amazon currently holds.

3. After selecting a compliance program, review the following details:

    a. What level of certification does AWS hold?

    b. What services are in scope with the selected compliance program?

    c. What does AWS's Attestation of Compliance cover?

AWS and Compliance

AWS supports several compliance programs for a variety of businesses running in regulated industries, including financial, healthcare, and the U.S. government. AWS is an American company, so it stands to reason there are compliance programs supported by AWS that adhere primarily to North American compliance standards. A review of the chart shown in Table 2-5 shows that most of the compliance programs are aligned with U.S. government regulations. Table 2-6 details the global compliance programs AWS is associated with.

Table 2-5   **North American Compliance Frameworks**

Compliance Frameworks	Details
CJIS – Criminal Justice Information Services	Workloads for state and federal law enforcement agencies at AWS
FERPA	Educational agencies and institution's storage of data records at AWS
FFIEC	Rules for federal financial institutions on the use and security of AWS services at AWS
FISMA	Security authorizations for government agencies using systems hosted at AWS. Adhering to NIST 800-37 and DIACAP standards in the AWS GovCloud
GxP	Rules and guidelines for food and medical products data hosted at AWS
HIPAA	Rules for processing, storing, and transmitting protected health information at AWS
ITAR	Compliance with International Traffic in Arms Regulations in the AWS GovCloud
MPPA (Motion Picture Association of America)	Rules for securely storing, processing, and delivering protected media and content
NIST	800–53 Security controls applied to U.S. Federal Information Systems to ensure confidentiality, integrity, and availability (CIA)
VPAT / Section 508	Rules for developing electronic and information technology for people with disabilities

There are also well-known global compliance programs that AWS supports. The SOC 2 audit is a good place to start in reviewing available security controls at AWS.

Note

All current compliance certifications and attestations that AWS is aligned with are audited and assessed using third-party independent auditors.

Table 2-6 **Global Compliance Programs**

Global Compliance Programs	Details
ISO 9001:2015 Compliance	Requirements for a quality management system, including documentation, management responsibilities, and measurement and analysis
ISO/IEC 27001:2013 Compliance	Security management best practices and security controls based on ISO/IEC 27002
ISO/IEC 27017:2015 Compliance	Guidance on the implementation of cloud-specific information security controls
ISO/IEC 27018:2014 Compliance	Protection of personal data in the cloud based on ISO/IEC 27002
PCI DSS level I (Payment Card Industry Data Security Standard)	Security standard applied to the storing, processing, or transmitting of CHD or sensitive authentication data
CSA Security Alliance Controls	Best practices for security controls requirements in the AWS cloud
Statement of Controls SOC 1	Details of AWS security controls and how they should work
Statement of Controls SOC 2	A service auditors report detailing the testing of AWS's security controls as they relate to operations and compliance, availability, security, processing, integrity, confidentiality, and privacy
Statement of Controls SOC 3	A white paper providing details on the AWS services that will be audited by SOC 2

HIPAA

If your business needs to comply with the 1996 Health Insurance Portability and Accountability Act (HIPAA), you must provide protections for what is defined as protected health information (PHI). Each healthcare provider, defined as the "covered entity" using AWS services to architect and host its applications, is solely responsible for complying with HIPAA's rules and regulations. Amazon's role is defined as a business associate.

Since 2013, Amazon has provided a signed contract called a Business Associate Addendum (BAA). In this contract, Amazon promises to properly safeguard the stored healthcare information and lays out the rules and responsibilities that AWS is undertaking, including a listing of the services and tasks that AWS will carry out on the customer's behalf. Each customer who enters a BAA with AWS must use only the defined HIPAA-eligible AWS services defined in the BAA.

Over the past few years, many common services available at AWS are now allowed by HIPAA regulations. However, to be sure, check the current compliance documentation at AWS because certifications and regulations are constantly in flux. For example, the AWS Systems Manager

the service, the longer it might take to get deployed in all regions. And some services can take years to change from preview status to full online status.

For example, the Elastic File System was in preview mode for quite a long time before it was generally available across all AWS regions. Therefore, the services being offered per region might dictate what regions you will choose to operate in. However, core services of compute, networking, and storage are everywhere. It's the newer AWS services that once introduced take time to become generally available in all regions.

Service availability can also be determined by your compliance rules and regulations. For example, if you are bound by FedRAMP rules and regulations, there are a number of services and management tools that are not approved at this time and perhaps never will be.

Calculating Costs

Costs need to be understood when dealing with a cloud provider. The AWS mantra is to pay for what you use; therefore, you pay for everything that you use. Most costs that will concern customers are not bundled in the price of most services. For example, there's no charge to spin up a VPC and add subnets. However, we are going to eventually add instances, and there's certainly costs for hosting, operating, and replicating compute instance traffic across subnets within an availability zone.

> **Note**
>
> There is a price to pay for resiliency and failover; it's a price worth paying. After all, we want our applications to remain available and our data records to be stored in multiple locations.

Costs at AWS depend on the region that you have selected to operate in; you can pay a little or a lot more for the same service compared to other AWS regions However, you may have no choice if compliance dictates where you can operate at AWS.

Choosing the Central region means you are using AWS resources located in Canada, and depending on the currency exchange rate of your country, pricing in Canada may be less. But are you allowed to operate in Canada? What happens if you compare costs with an EU or São Paulo regions? Expect pricing to be a few hundred percent more!

> **Note**
>
> Over at Concurrency Labs (https://www.concurrencylabs.com/blog/choose-your-aws-region-wisely/) are some excellent examples showing the price differential between N. Virginia and São Paulo.

The human resources system at Terra Firma will require an average of 10 t2 medium EC2 compute instances, sitting behind a load balancer. The load balancer balances the user requests spreading the load across the 10 EC2 instances. Although there are many variables when analyzing pricing, when comparing the Northern Virginia regional costs to the São Paulo region for a load balancer sending traffic to 10 t2 medium EC2 instances within the same AZ, you can expect on average up to an 80% difference, as shown in Figure 2-15.

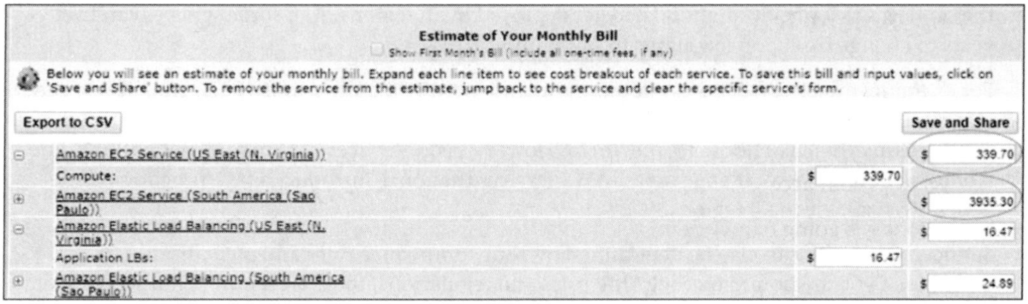

Figure 2-15   Comparing regional prices

The biggest and cheapest AWS region is located in the US-East-1 (N. Virginia) region; it also has the largest number of availability zones and AWS services. Other regions with comparable pricing to Northern Virginia include Ohio, located in US-East-2, and Ireland (EU). Your purchase price can also be greatly reduced in many cases by reserving or prepaying your EC2 compute costs. Reserved costs are explored at various times throughout the book, specifically when we are talking about compute costs in Chapter 4, "Compute Services: AWS EC2 Instances."

Management Service Costs

A management service at AWS can be thought of as a self-contained entity; you sign up for the service, and it performs its various tasks and provides the results. Another concept to consider is how you are charged for using a management service. The cost of a management service at AWS relates to the number of times the service carries out its task (think compute) and the price of storing the results (think storage). How AWS charges for management services used can be broken down by component, as shown in Table 2-7.

Table 2-7   **Management Service Charges at AWS**

	AWS Service	Frequency of Charges	Components	Examples
A	Management tools	Number of times management service is executed per month	Compute, storage, notification, and automation charges	Config, Inspector, GuardDog
B	Compute	Hourly	Compute hours plus data transfer charges from instance	EC2 instance
C	Storage	Monthly per GB stored	Storage, data transfer, and optionally, encryption, or notification and automation charges	EBS, S3, Glacier, snapshots, server logs
D	Data transfer	Per GB transferred	Outbound and inbound packet flow	Across AZs, Outgoing data

Management Tools Pricing: AWS Config

As an example of management pricing, let's look at AWS Config, which gives customers the ability to monitor the configuration of their IaaS resources such as compute, networking, and monitoring against a set of customer-defined rules and capture any changes to the resource's configuration. For AWS Config to operate, it needs compute cycles to execute its review of resources in your account. It then needs to store the results in S3 storage.

AWS Config is going to charge for the number of configuration items being monitored by Config in your account, per region. It is also going to charge you for the number of custom rules you have defined. If you stick with the default set of managed rules provided by AWS, there are no additional compute charges. An example of an AWS-defined Config rule you could deploy is *encrypted-volumes.* (All boot volumes attached to EC2 instances must be encrypted.) The management charges for using AWS Config are as follows:

- When AWS Config compares this rule against all boot volumes in your account, the rule is defined as an "active rule" because the rule was processed by the Config management service. The first 10 AWS Config rules will be charged a flat rate of $2.00 per AWS Config rule, per region per month.

- The next 40 rules will have a slightly lower price per month ($1.50 per processed rule). When you reach 50 rules or more, the price drops further ($1.00 per processed rule).

AWS Config's data-gathering is carried out using Lambda functions. Lambda is an AWS managed service that runs functions that can be created using several programming languages such as GO, Python, C#, Node.js, and Java. There is no additional cost for executing the standard prebuilt AWS Config rules. However, once you create custom AWS Config rules, additional Lambda charges will be applied for the execution of custom rules. Lambda charges are based on the amount of CPU, RAM, and time taken to complete execution of a function. The more custom rules that you create, the longer it takes for Lambda to finish its tasks, and therefore more you are charged.

AWS Config Results

The results gathered by AWS Config are stored in an S3 bucket. Charges for S3 storage depend on the size of the storage results. For example, S3 storage pricing is $0.023 per GB for the first 50 TB per month. AWS Config is also integrated with CloudWatch and sends detailed information about all configuration changes and notifications to CloudWatch events. An event means something happened that you should know about. Events are charged at $1.00 per 1 million events.

One of the main features of AWS Config is that you can be alerted if your defined rules are found to be out of compliance. For example, a developer creates an unencrypted boot volume; AWS Config can alert you using the Amazon simple notification service. As you may expect, SNS notifications are also charged. The good news is that the first 1 million SNS requests per month are free; after that, they are charged at $0.50 per 1 million SNS requests.

Another concept to consider is that an SNS notification could be directed to call Lambda to perform a custom task. Lambda functions can be crafted to perform any task at AWS you want as Lambda functions can invoke any AWS API call. In this example, if unencrypted boot volumes are found, a custom Lambda function could swing into action, perform a snapshot of the unencrypted boot volume, and then delete the offending EC2 instance and unencrypted volume.

Let's say you have 500 configuration items in your AWS account that are checked by AWS Config each month with 30 active AWS management rules in the US-East-1 (N. Virginia) region. Your monthly charges would be as follows:

- AWS Config costs: 500 * $0.003 = $1.50
- AWS Config rules: $2.00 per active rule for the first 10 active config rules = $20
- $1.50 for the next 20 active config rules = $15
- Total AWS Config monthly charges = $36.50

This is just one example of how complicated costs can be to calculate at AWS; there are many moving parts. Hopefully you can see from this one example that pricing is just not composed of just one charge; it *is* complicated. There would also be a very minor S3 storage charge for storing the AWS Config results and possibly additional SNS and CloudFront charges for this example. And if your resource configurations were found not to be in compliance with a defined AWS Config rule, notifications and alerts would be generated by AWS Config, resulting in additional costs.

AWS Compute Costs

Compute (think EC2 instance) costs are defined as pay-as-you-go and depend on the size of the instance and the region location of the instance. And then EC2 instance pricing gets complicated once again. Compute pricing can be greatly reduced by prepaying or reserving your EC2 instances. There are also pricing considerations for shared or single tenancy instances. Perhaps you would like to reserve instances based on a re-occurring schedule. There are several other pricing examples for EC2 instances to also consider. Are you using a public or a private IP address? Do you want your instances to be blue or red in color? (Okay, there are no charges for color and no color choices.) Are you communicating with other instances located within the same AZ on the same subnet, or are you communicating across different availability zones? We will deal fully with compute costs and the many choices in Chapter 4.

> **Note**
>
> An MS SQL RDS EC2 instance db.r4.16xlarge pair located on separate subnets across multi-AZs hosted in the Tokyo region, could cost you in the range of $1.9 million for a 3-year reserved price.

Storage Costs

Storage costs at AWS depend on the storage service being used, whether it's EBS storage volumes, shared file storage using the elastic file system (EFS) or Amazon FSx, S3 object storage, and archival storage using S3 Glacier.

- **S3 Buckets**—An S3 bucket has storage and retrieval and request costs. Optional features such as lifecycle transition costs, storage management, data transfer (outbound directly to the Internet or to CloudFront), transfer acceleration, and cross-region replication to another S3 bucket all have separate and additional costs.

  - **S3 bucket example**—100 GB of standard storage in the US-East-1 (N. Virginia) region would cost you roughly $2.21 per month. This includes 5,000 PUT/COPY/POST/LIST requests and 30,000 GET requests, as shown in Figure 2-16.

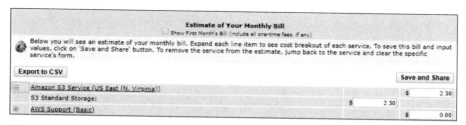

Figure 2-16   S3 storage pricing

- **S3-Glacier**—Glacier storage has storage and retrieval pricing. Retrieval pricing is based on the speed of the data retrieval required. There is also outbound data transfer pricing, which varies based on the destination: outbound directly to the Internet or CloudFront, the CDN network.

  - **S3 Glacier example**—Terra Firma has stored 100 TB of archived records in the US East N. Virginia region with data retrieval of 10 GB per month with an average of 20 requests per month. This would cost roughly $411.92. Switching to other regions does not change the price point.

- **EBS Volumes**—Virtual hard drives can be ordered in several flavors: SSD, SSD drives with provisioned IOPS, throughput-optimized drives, or what is defined as Cold HDD (infrequently accessed hard drive storage). You are also charged for snapshot storage in S3 for your EBS volume snapshots.

  - **EBS example**—A single general-purpose SSD drive sized at 16384 GB hosted in the US-East-1 (N. Virginia) region would cost you roughly $450 per month. Adding 10 GB of snapshot storage space would bump the monthly charge to $5,052. A provisioned, IOPS SSD drive sized at 8000 GB with 16,000 IOPS hosted in the US-East-1 (N. Virginia) region would cost you roughly $4,997 per month, as shown in Figure 2-17.

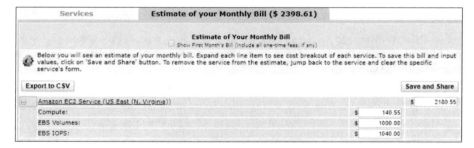

Figure 2-17   EBS price calculations

- **EFS storage**—The EFS is for shared file storage. At a minimum, you pay for the total amount of storage used per month. There is also a GB charge for the amount of data that is copied into EFS per month at $0.01 per GB. You can also optionally pay for faster provisioned throughput in MBs per month.

    - EFS example: Assume the file system hosted in the US-East-1 (N. Virginia) region uses 300 GB of storage for 20 days for a single month. The charges would be as follows:
    - Total usage (GB-Hours) = 300 GB × 20 days × (24 hours / day) = 144,000 GB-hours.
    - Converting GB hours to GB-month = $43.20.

Moving your files to EFS Infrequent Access Storage Class further reduces your storage costs by up to 70%.

Data Transfer Costs

The price for running applications in the AWS cloud is usually thought of in terms of compute and storage charges. However, an additional charge is tacked onto the bill for transferring your packets from source to destination. At AWS, these are called *data transfer costs*, and every customer must spend some time and diligence to understand the actual costs. Your first monthly AWS bill will contain a few data transfer charge surprises. If we looked at every AWS cost, this book would exceed thousands of pages. Data transfer costs are generally higher for data transfer between regions, as compared to inter-region data transfer between AZs.

> **Note**
>
> It's probably a good idea to subscribe to the Amazon simple notification service (SNS) to get alerts when the prices for services change because prices change all the time. See https://docs.aws.amazon.com/awsaccountbilling/latest/aboutv2/price-changes.html.

Typically, a link to a cost calculator is present when you order AWS services, but not all costs will be initially visible. Data transfer costs can be expanded into the following breakdowns:

- Data transfer costs across AZs within a region, which are higher than costs for data transfer within a single AZ

- Data transfer costs between AWS regions

- Data transfer costs by service—egress data sent outbound

- Between AWS services—egress data sent from an S3 bucket through CloudFront

When you transfer data into an AWS region from any service from any other region, it's free. (As a general rule, incoming data transfers are free for all public cloud providers.) Regional data transfer costs are charged based on data transfer within a region or the transfer of data across regions. Within each region, charges depend on whether you are communicating within an AZ or across AZs, as shown in Figure 2-18.

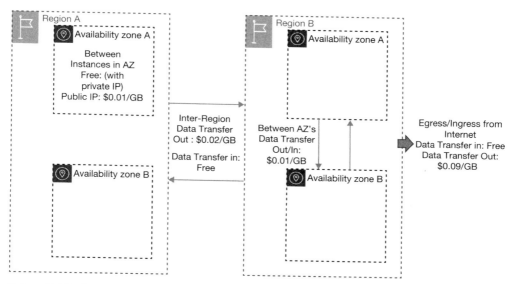

Figure 2-18   Data transfer costs as AWS compared

The design of your hosted applications at AWS will greatly determine your data transfer costs. Here are some design parameters to consider:

- AWS services that are hosted in the same region but that are in separate AZs will be charged for outgoing data transfer at $0.01/GB.

- When data is transferred between AWS services hosted in different AWS regions, the data transfer charge is $0.02/GB to start.

- Data being transferred within the same region and staying within the same AZ is free of charge if you're using a private IP address.

- If you're using an AWS-assigned public IP address or an assigned elastic IP public address, there will be a charge for the data transfer out from the instance. Charges are per gigabyte transfer, and the minimum charge is $0.01/GB.

- The most common replication example is database replication from the master database node to the slave database node. Across AZs, there is a data transfer charge for this replication.

- Always use private IP addresses rather than public IP addresses; public IP addresses cost more to send data.

- Different AWS regions have different data transfer costs.

- Architect your applications and systems for minimal data transfer across AWS regions or AZs.

- Architect your AWS environment so that data transfer is restricted within an AZ, or restricted within a single region.

> **Note**
>
> AWS provides a handy API called the AWS pricelist API that enables you to query for the current prices of AWS products and services. For example: https://pricing.us-east-1.amazonaws.com/offers/v1.0/aws/AmazonS3/current/us-east-1/index.csv

Understand Tiered Costs at AWS

Referring to something as *free* at AWS is complicated. There is a default pricing tier which means you can use a particular AWS service until your data transfer costs exceed the default pre-value, typically 1 GB; then your costs begin to scale based upon a sliding price point. If you then use up to another level, AWS gives you another price break up until another usage or storage point. For example, data transfer out from EC2 instances to the Internet starts at $.09/GB until you reach 10 TB, as shown in Table 2-8. Then additional discounts apply, as shown in Table 2-9. The charge for region-to-region traffic is currently set at $.02/GB, but in the case of US-East-1 and US-East-2, it's a little lower at $.01/GB.

Table 2-8   **Tiered Storage Cost Example**

Data Transfer Out from EC2 Instance to Internet	
Up to	**Price per month**
1 GB	Free
9.999 TB	$0.09 per GB
40 TB	$0.085 per GB
100 TB	$0.07 per GB
Greater than 150 TB	$0.05 per GB
Greater than 500 TB	Call AWS

- **CloudFront**—Outbound CloudFront traffic costs vary based on the geographical location of the cache; pricing starts at $.085/GB in the U.S. regions.

- **EC-2 Instance Traffic**—EC2 traffic between different availability zones hosted within the region costs the same as region-to-region data transfer. ELB-EC2 traffic is free of charge except when the outbound request crosses an availability zone.

- **ELB**—ELB charges are in GB if you are using the Classic Load balancer but switch to LCUs if the Application or Network load balancer is chosen. That's defined as load balancer capacity units. Then the regional location of your load balancer is considered when calculating the price. The LCU is a complicated calculation that measures the dimensions of your traffic. The dimensions are new connections, active connections, the amount of bandwidth, and the number of rules processed by your load balancer. Whichever dimension is highest is the one you are charged.

Optimizing Costs at AWS

Now you know some of the complexity of figuring out costs at AWS. Here's another concept to consider: running resources at a maximum scale at AWS 24/7 will probably bankrupt your budget. The key word in the last sentence is *scale* (as in scale out when additional resources are required to support additional user requests and scale in when resources are not required).

The concept of scale is key to understand and implement at AWS if you want any chance at manageable costs when hosting applications in the AWS cloud. AWS has produced some fine documentation called the Well-Architected Framework, which details best practices for optimizing costs at AWS which we briefly discussed in Chapter 1, "Learning AWS." Let's further summarize the concepts of optimizing costs at AWS. The concepts briefly discussed in this section will be fully fleshed out in later chapters referenced by chapter location.

- **Optimize compute**—Matching the right instance or service to the right workload (Chapter 4)

- **Reserved pricing options**—Reserved pricing for regions and AZs (Chapter 4)

- **Elasticity**—Scaling resources up and down, in effect increasing and decreasing consumption of cloud services based on your needs (Chapter 5)

- **Optimized storage**—Matching storage with the workload (Chapter 6)

Optimizing Compute Costs

Selecting the best EC2 instance for your needs at the lowest possible cost is the overall goal. Let's use our use case for a compute example. Terra Firma started its initial testing in the AWS cloud thinking about matching the EC2 instance size at AWS as closely as possible to the virtual machine size they used on-premise. However, the virtual machine that was utilized on-premise was very large and sized with many CPU cores and gigabytes of RAM.

- Moving to the AWS cloud, Terra Firma knows that its EC2 instance size at AWS will be smaller as multiple EC2 instances will be deployed, on subnets located across multiple AZs, and located behind an ELB load balancer.

- Preliminary testing will evaluate the overall performance of Terra Firma's application stack under a steady-state load. The number of users accessing the application will remain consistent.

- For this initial proof of concept, compute resources will not be scaled up and down; once that application moves from test to production choosing reserved pricing for the compute instances will reduce the price up to 70%.

- During initial testing, the entire development environment could be turned off after hours when it's not being utilized, saving additional compute and data transfer charges.

- If the application load changed to an unpredictable schedule, meaning that the number of users accessing the application changed from a small number of users to a large number of users, adding elasticity into the design of this application stack would automatically add or remove compute instances based on the user demand instead of a steady-state schedule.

In summary; if an AWS service or EC2 compute instance is running in your account at AWS, you're charged for it. Getting used to this fact takes time. After all, you don't turn off your bare-metal servers every night in your own data centers. Why would you? You've already paid for your on-premise resources. However, in the AWS cloud, running all resources 24/7 is not cost-effective. Therefore, each customer needs to decide what remains on 24/7 and what services should be turned off or reduced in operating size when not under high demand, as shown in Table 2-9. This is a major mind shift for customers beginning to work in the AWS cloud.

Table 2-9 **What Services Need to Run 24/7 at AWS?**

AWS Service	On-Premise Operation	At AWS
DNS Servers	24/7	Use Route 53
Dev/test environments	24/7	Turn off when not used
Applications	24/7	Auto Scale based on demand
Databases	24/7	AWS Auto Scale or Serverless
Storage arrays	24/7	24/7 (AWS-managed service)
Websites	24/7	Auto Scale based on demand

Reserved Pricing

If you use instances or specific compute-related AWS services constantly, reserved pricing is a must. Reserved pricing has many variables, per region, per AZ, standard 1-year or 3-year durations, or reservations that can be converted to another reservation type. Reservations are billing discounts that apply to EC2 instances hosted in a specific AZ, or region. The billing discount could be as high as 75% against the standard on-demand hourly rate.

The other concept of reserved pricing that's important to understand is that you are guaranteeing the availability of your EC2 instances in your AZ's when you need them. If you do not reserve EC2 instances in specific AZ's, there is no guarantee that your EC2 instances will be available when you need them. On-demand instance types are not guaranteed to be always available. If you need EC2 instances for scaling up compute capacity, reserving your instances will guarantee their availability when it's time to scale. Most reserved pricing is dealing with EC2 instance capacity. Choices for RI pricing at AWS are shown in Table 2-10.

Table 2-10   **Reserved Pricing Choices at AWS**

Reserved instance pricing options	Details
Amazon RDS	Managed database compute instances
Amazon EMR	Hadoop cluster instances
Amazon ElastiCache	Memcached or Redis support
Amazon RedShift	Data warehouse
Amazon DynamoDB	Database throughput
EC2 instances	Reserved EC2 instances 1, or 3 years

Tools for Analyzing Costs at AWS

For preplanning the costs of using hosted cloud services, AWS has several tools available to help analyze compute and storage utilization.

Trusted Advisor

Trusted Advisor is a built-in management service that executes several essential checks against your AWS account resources, as shown in Figure 2-19. It takes just a few minutes to give you a wealth of information. The information presented by Trusted Advisor depends on your level of support. It is the perfect tool to run against any AWS account to gain a quick analysis on the account's current cost optimization, performance, security, fault tolerance, and service limits. Trusted Advisor can provide you with important cost-optimizing details.

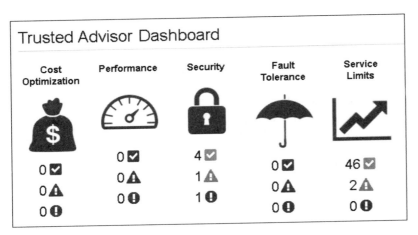

Figure 2-19   Trusted Advisor results

Let's look at the output from Trusted Advisor in the following context. Terra Firma has a two-tier application running at AWS that is hosted in two separate availability zones utilizing EC2 instances and EBS storage volumes. The relational database service (RDS) is part of the database solution. The application stack is hosted behind a load balancer, and EC2 instances are reserved per AZ's for a partial upfront one-year standard term. Running Trusted Advisor would help track and alert you to the following potential issues:

- **Reserved EC2 Instances**—The optimized number of partial upfront reserved instances is calculated based on an analysis of your usage history for the past month.

- **Load balancers**—Checks the load-balancing configuration usage.

- **EBS volume check**—Warns you if any EBS volumes in your account are unattached or have a low access rate.

- **Elastic IP addresses**—Warns you if any elastic IP addresses assigned to your account have not been associated. Charges apply if elastic IP addresses in your account are not used.

- **RDS instances**—Checks for idle database instances.

- **Route 53 records**—Checks for the proper creation of latency record sets that should be designed for replication of user requests to the best region.

- **Reserved reservation expiration check**—Checks and alerts you if your reserved reservation is scheduled to expire within the next month. Reserved reservations do not automatically renew.

The trusted advisor can be run from the management console or from the CLI. The basic account and service checks and recommendations are available for any customer at AWS. Customers with business or enterprise support plans have access to all Trusted Advisor checks, including automatic actions that can be carried out with CloudWatch alerts.

Budgets—Once you start using reserved instances, a budget should be created to track what you expect to spend and what you are currently spending. Each budget defines a start and end date and a budgeted amount to track costs against. Each budget report can include the AWS costs as they relate to the AWS services, the associated tags, purchase options, instance types, region and AZ, and other options. Once your budget forecast hits the defined threshold, which can be defined as a percentage or a dollar figure of a budgeted amount, notifications can send alerts to email accounts and an associated SNS topic.

AWS Simple Monthly Calculator

Be prepared to spend some quality time with the Simple Monthly Calculator, as shown in Figure 2-22. Only by using the calculator will you start to see the integrated costs for infrastructure and the inbound and outbound data transfer charges. On the right side are several sample reports to give you an idea about how you could host a marketing website or create a disaster recovery and backup solution. Of course, these costs will not be your actual costs, but they're certainly enough to get you thinking.

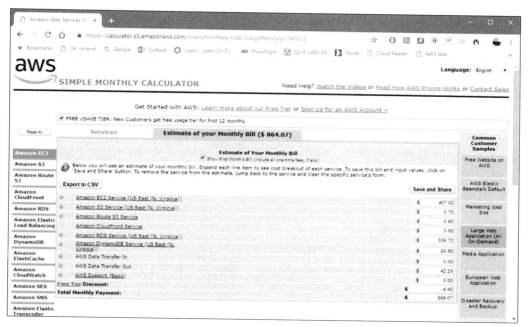

Figure 2-22   The not-so-simple Monthly Calculator

On the left side are the services supported by the Simple Monthly Calculator, which calculates the cost of running a variety of infrastructure as a service (IaaS) components, some developer components, standalone services such as Amazon WorkSpaces and WorkDocs, and the Amazon Elastic

Transcoder Service. Regardless of the service selected, you first must choose a region of operation before you can fill out the details. To really take the most advantage of using this calculator, you must know how your applications are going to be designed and operated at AWS.

Terra Firma's test application is going to use EC2 instances fronted with a public-facing load balancer with EBS storage and a backend SQL database hosted across multiple AZs. Pricing out EC2 instances, after choosing the AWS region for operation, will begin to provide answers to Terra Firma's many questions.

When you look at the number of choices at AWS available for compute instances, database solutions, and load-balancing pricing, it becomes clear that entering the intimate details of how your application is going to be hosted and running at AWS is necessary to get an accurate price. And if you're just starting out, you won't yet know all the answers. But you'll certainly know what you're going to be charged component wise, and that is valuable information to have.

Compute: Amazon EC2 Instances

- The number of instances: 4
- The number of hours used per day: 8
- Type: Linux on m4.xlarge (4 vCPUs, 16 GB memory with EBS storage)
- Billing option: On-demand

Database: RDS

- The number of instances: 2
- The number of hours used per day: 8
- DB engine version and license choice: SQL Server Enterprise Edition 2016 SP2
- Type of database instance: db.m5.xlarge–db.m5.24xlarge
- Number of AZs: 2
- Data transfer: Intra-Region (within the region) or Inter-Region Data Transfer Out

Elastic Load Balancing

- Average number of connections per second: 20
- Average connection duration: 45 seconds
- Average request per second: 20
- Total data processed per hour: 1.1 GB

MAKE SURE TO WATCH THE COMPANION VIDEO "USING THE SIMPLE MONTHLY CALCULATOR."

Total Cost of Ownership (TCO) Calculator

The TCO calculator calculates the cost of your current servers, whether they are physical servers or virtual machines, and their location: on-premise or at a co-location as shown in Figure 2-23. Server types can be defined either as a database or a compute instance. Database choices include running flavors of Oracle, SQL, and MySQL. The non-DB server types can be defined as virtual machines hosted on several hypervisor types: VMware, Hyper-V, or KVM/ZEN. After inputting your server details, you can enter your storage types that you use: storage area network (SAN), network-attached storage (NAS), or object storage. The overall IOPS for each application can also be added for comparison. For networking, you can enter your data center bandwidth, and you can include details on your data center staff's annual salary and the number of VMs assigned to each admin.

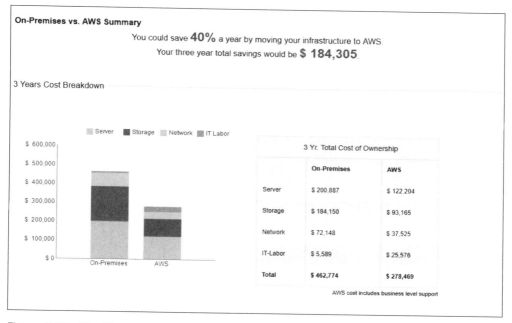

Figure 2-23   The TCO Calculator

The costs that the TCO calculator provide give you a ballpark of your infrastructure cost but do not consider data transfer costs or any other costs, such as load balancing and failover. However, it's a start, and if the total cost of the TCO calculator is more than the totals from the AWS Simple Monthly Calculator, your move to the cloud is probably a financially viable option.

In Conclusion

Whew! We've made it through the gauntlet of regions, availability zones, edge locations, and the criteria for making the best decisions based on location, location, and more location. There's a lot of material in this chapter that you probably must review. There are also several big-picture decisions to be made that you want to take your time with rather than having to make on the fly two years from now when you're under pressure. No one needs or wants that type of pressure. To help alleviate any pressure, political or otherwise, review the top 10 discussion points, bring them into the conference room, and start discussing and arguing, moving toward a consensus. By taking the time to review and discuss this top-10 list, you're performing the proper steps to create your own SLA: what you're willing to accept and to risk, and potentially, what stays on-premise.

Top 10 Big-Picture Discussion Points: Compliance, Governance, Latency, and Failover Considerations

1. What compliance rules and regulations do we have to follow?

2. What AWS compliance reports should we review?

3. What regions are we allowed to use?

4. How many availability zones should we be using?

5. Does our internal auditor need to ramp up quickly on AWS security?

6. Who wants to volunteer costing out our current application stack?

7. What type of reserved instances should we be using?

8. Is AWS Config a useful tool for monitoring our compliance?

9. What does the Trusted Advisor help us with?

10. Should we consider upping our AWS support to the business level for additional Trusted Advisor checks and support discussions with AWS?

3

AWS Networking Services

The odds are 100% that you will be using networking services at AWS. Networking at AWS is called the virtual private cloud, or EC2-VPC. This chapter explores in detail the available networking options for virtual private clouds (VPCs) and how they are set up and configured at AWS. At the end of this chapter, you will have a strong understanding of VPCs, networking services and options available, and understand the necessity of properly planning your networking services.

The reality is that you may need to read this chapter a few times to become comfortable with the networking services at AWS. There are a few changes when setting up and managing networking in the cloud even though the terms might look familiar. In the previous chapter, we looked at the big picture of regions and zones, and edge locations—the bedrock services at AWS that we really can't touch. Networking at AWS, the subnet is the lowest level we can gain access to, and it's all at a virtual level. Yes, there is a physical network at AWS, but we don't get to access it directly. Starting with the lowest point of the stack that we are allowed to control, let's get into networking.

One of the first configuration questions that will be asked of you when ordering an EC2 instance; AWS WorkSpaces, their hosted VDI solution; or RDS, their hosted database solution is this question: what VPC or what subnet do you want to use? The topics for this chapter include the following:

- VPC networking
- Subnets and IP address types
- Route tables
- Security groups and NACLs
- VPN connectivity options
- Route 53—the domain name system (DNS) service

Questions we will ponder and reflect on for this networking chapter focus on our case study Terra Firma and its human resources customer relationship management (CRM) software system. To recap, the company's current CRM system was developed in-house several years ago and is running successfully on VMware server images in the corporate data center. Other details include:

- Management agrees that the current HR system must be migrated to AWS as soon as possible.

- The company's HR system needs to be able to properly scale to handle the increased demand of upper management.

- The human resources system must be available 24 hours a day and needs to be accessed across the Internet and from corporate head and branch offices.

Some of the questions they need to get answered include these:

1. How many VPCs should Terra Firma consider using?

2. How many AZs should Terra Firma use to design for failover?

3. How many subnets should Terra Firma use?

4. Do the Web servers need public or private IP addresses?

5. Can we privately access AWS resources from within a VPC?

6. Are NAT services required?

7. Compliance rules mandate security at the subnet level. Is that possible at AWS?

VPC Networking

The networking layer at AWS is a VPC, and we generally work with networking services using the VPC console, as shown in Figure 3-1. The official name of a VPC is an EC2-VPC, even if we typically just use the VPC moniker. The EC2 (Elastic Cloud Compute) designation indicates that EC2 instances are usually hosted within a VPC. Each VPC is a logically isolated "data center" where your computer instances and various AWS services reside. Software that can run success-fully on a Windows or Linux virtual server can be hosted on EC2 instances hosted in VPCs running as Web/application servers, databases, NAT servers, or any third-party software appli-ance you can think of.

When you order a VPC, AWS's job is securing your VPC as a private isolated software data center linked to your AWS account. AWS's job is to provision, host, and secure the VPC; the rest is up to us. There is also plenty of AWS management going on below the surface of a VPC; your network traffic must be routed and protected based on your network design and needs. In addition, Amazon must ensure the continued separation of your VPC from all other AWS customers. Any failure on Amazon's end in safeguarding and protecting VPC networks just can't happen.

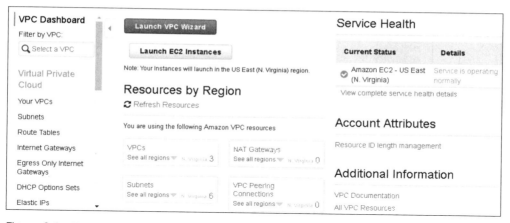

Figure 3-1   The VPC console

There are lots of moving parts and pieces at AWS, which I like to describe as a large toolbox containing a variety of tools and attachments that you can mesh or cobble together any way they suit your needs. Within the VPC "toolbox" are many configurable options, including route tables, public and private subnets, VPN connections, gateways, and private endpoints, to name just a few of the available options. In addition, there are multiple security choices available at every network level allowing you to fully protect your EC2 instances; choices include security groups and network access control lists (ACLs). A VPC also has multiple connectivity options, allowing you to connect your VPC to the Internet, to your own private data center, to other VPCs within your region or outside your region, or to other AWS accounts holders' VPCs.

Partnering with AWS

Hosting your applications in the Amazon public cloud means you have implicitly accepted to work in partnership with AWS in what is typically defined as a shared security model. AWS has responsibilities of building and securing its cloud infrastructure; this is typically defined as *Security of the Cloud*. Your responsibility as an AWS customer is to design acceptable security provisions for your applications and data hosted within the AWS cloud. The level of acceptable security provisions is entirely your choice. The definition for the customer's responsibilities of securing their resources at AWS is called *Security in the Cloud*. Customers can choose to use any of the managed services and utilities provided to accomplish their deployment and security goals. Within each VPC, your compute instances (EC2) are hosted on subnets that you create in selected availability zones (AZs) within the AWS region you chose to operate within. Although the VPC is a managed service, customers make most of the choices and decisions on their own after AWS carries out the initial creation of the VPC.

Because a VPC is defined as a virtual *private* network (VPN), it's easy to forget sometimes that you're still participating within a shared environment when hosting applications in the AWS cloud. AWS customers all share the private network backbone linking shared compute, storage, and services, as shown in Figure 3-2. Of course, the one issue you don't want to experience in the AWS cloud is an unexpected loss of privacy.

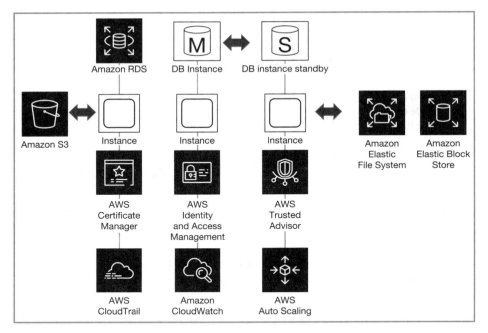

Figure 3-2   AWS networking concepts

Amazon's private global network that hosts all the VPCs has terabytes of networking capacity available. AWS also owns and operates all the fiber connections connecting their data centers, AZs, regions, and edge location equipment together. However, the networking services that are exposed to each customer at AWS are not running on the same network hardware devices that are deployed in your own data centers. Some of the networking service terms we are going to define may also be new to you. And some of the other networking components that are utilized at AWS will hopefully sound familiar—terms like subnets, public and private IP addresses, and route tables. But you will find that your overall design of networking services at AWS will still be different from what you would use on-premise. Hosting hundreds of thousands of customers in a massive shared networking environment means networking can't be the same as your on-premise network due to the size and scope of Amazon's overall operation.

> **Note**
>
> If you're a new customer at AWS, the VPC is the only networking choice currently available for hosting your workloads. There used to be another networking option available at AWS called EC2-Classic. We won't be spending any time on this older style of networking because you don't want and can't access EC2-Classic networking; it hasn't been available for new customers since December 2013. And you wouldn't want to use it instead of a VPC. To begin with, EC2-Classic networking was a flat network design that was shared with all other EC2-Classic AWS customers. The EC2-Classic feature set available is quite minimal compared to the expansive options available with a VPC. However, your company may have EC2-Classic networking if it began working with Amazon before 2013.

To Host or to Associate?

Some services can be hosted within a VPC, and others can be associated to a VPC. There are many additional AWS management and compliance services that you will probably want to use. Some of these services will have relationships with the services and components hosted *inside* a VPC, but the services themselves are not actually *installed in the VPC*. AWS services such as AWS Config (a compliance tool) and ELB (Elastic Load Balancing) aren't installed or hosted within a VPC; instead, they reside on the private or public Amazon network and, once ordered or selected, are then associated or linked to the chosen VPC carrying out their task. Table 3-1 lists several examples of AWS services that are either hosted or associated with a VPC.

Table 3-1   **AWS Services That Host or Link to a VPC**

Hosted VPC Services	Associated Services
EC2 instances	Trusted Advisor
Elastic Beanstalk	AWS Config
Amazon Redshift	VPN connections
ElastiCache	Auto Scaling
Amazon EMR	Elastic load balancing
Amazon RDS	S3
Amazon Workspaces	DynamoDB

The reality is that most of Amazon's offerings are not actually installed inside a VPC. The primary service hosted in a VPC is the EC2 instance.

What's Behind the Networking Curtain?

How is it possible to manage thousands of customers who require hosted private networking services? To complicate this reality, customers change their minds all the time. It's a daunting task. Customers who order a VPC are working within their own private walled garden of virtual networking. The first major concept of networking at AWS is that within each VPC, the networking exposed to each customer is designed and managed at the subnet level—specifically, the Layer 3 subnet address space contained within each availability zone. That's as deep as we're going to get in the network stack at AWS. Full stop.

Your on-premise networking environment is probably composed of virtual local area networks (VLANs), Layer 2 networks, and Multiprotocol Label Switching (MPLS) connections. Why does a customer's exposure to the AWS network then start and end at Layer 3? Because thousands of customers are running on a massively shared network infrastructure, and AWS is running at a scale that far exceeds the scale utilized within your own data centers. As a result, the internal network design offered to each customer needs to be different as well.

AWS is not using VLANs on the internal private network because these technologies cannot scale to the number of customers that Amazon hosts. A VPC also doesn't use MPLS for communications; however, you may be utilizing MPLS connections when connecting to a VPC using an external Direct Connect connection from your on-premise network to AWS. You can find more details on external VPC connections later in this chapter. If you have worked with public cloud providers for several years, you may have experienced ordering networks with an email request and waiting a few days to get set up; or perhaps you waited just a few hours. Waiting a few hours or even days might be acceptable within your own data center. In the hosted public cloud, however, we demand and get cloud resources instantly. Amazon had to figure out a way to combine scale, automation, and instant gratification, and they did. Ordering a VPC takes seconds; if a VLAN had to be set up for each customer network, the process would ultimately take too much time and, as discussed, not be able to scale as required.

Note

If you expect to design a VMware-like network utilizing a stretch layer 2 network design at AWS, it's technically possible between two separate AWS data centers, but it is not recommended. For example, each data center has separate power and cooling, and you don't have access or control of these components at the physical layer; that's Amazon's domain. What happens if a connection goes down between the two stretched data centers? There are multiple redundant connections between the data centers at AWS, but again, the customer does not have access to the physical components or connections between AWS data centers.

Each VPC is a software-defined network built on Amazon's own code and custom network hardware developed by AWS to match its required scale of network operations. There are two networks at AWS: the real physical network that is maintained by AWS, along with physical switches and routers and familiar networking components. The underlying physical network at AWS would be quite recognizable component wise. However, we don't have access to the physical network; that's the folks at AWS's job. It may be obvious, but I'm going to mention it anyway: each VPC runs on top of the physical AWS network infrastructure.

Your instances are running on a hypervisor installed on custom-designed bare-metal servers, as shown in Figure 3-3. The standard hypervisor AWS used was a customized version of XEN for a number of years, but many changes are happening. For several instance types—the C5d (massive computer-optimized instances), the M5d (massive memory-optimized instances), and the new, bare-metal EC2 instances—AWS has moved to what is called the Invocation platform with the Nitro system. Nitro is a customized version of the KVM hypervisor with a published benchmark of less than 1% when comparing virtual EC2 instance performance to bare-metal system performance. Nitro systems are also matched with a customized Nitro security chipset that monitors the firmware and hardware at boot, supports enhanced networking, and has NVMe block storage specifically designed for access to high-speed local storage over a PCI interface with transparent encryption provided on the fly by hardware processes. Scotty, I need more power! Wait a minute. I'm more than okay.

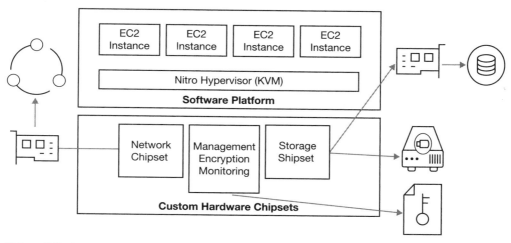

Figure 3-3 Instances hosted by the hypervisor

> **Note**
>
> If your job involves managing VMware and Hyper-V hypervisor, you have no exposure to the hypervisor at AWS. Maintaining and operating the hypervisor is Amazon's job.

Therefore, customized bare-metal servers host multiple AWS customers and their EC2 instances, and all instances are hosted on VPCs. And there are approximately 80,000 bare-metal servers residing in a typical AWS data center. For many years when the hypervisor of choice was XEN at AWS, an emulated software router providing additional security resided just below the hypervisor. However, on the latest and greatest Nitro platform, a hardware router is directly embedded in the physical host. These routers sitting below the hypervisor provide the majority of VPC functionality and at a much greater speed.

It's All About Packet Flow

I find that reducing the concept of the network to the packet level a simple, functional way of thinking about networking at AWS. You have packets that need to be sent from a specific EC2 instance, on a specific subnet, from a specific VPC, to a specific destination or location. At the subnet is where routing decisions are performed for the EC2 instances on each subnet. For example, instances may need access to the Internet, access to the head office, or access to data records stored somewhere on the AWS network.

How's each packet going to get to its preferred destination? The answer is through those specialized routers/routing services hosted on each bare-metal server and some custom external hardware. Before each packet exits the subnet to its destination, AWS stamps the required proprietary data records within each packet, including the VPC encapsulation details as shown in Figure 3-4 containing essential information:

- Which VPC is home base for the packet?
- What subnet does the instance reside on?
- What is the IP address of the instance that sent the packet?
- Where is the destination service the packet needs to be sent to?
- What is the IP on the physical network where your VPC is located?

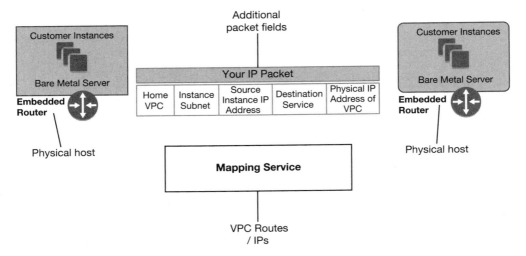

Figure 3-4   VPC encapsulation details

Packet flow is carried out using customized hardware components connecting to each "VPC" called a Blackfoot device, as shown in Figure 3-5. These smart devices sit on the edge of the VPC and perform a conversion for the network traffic based on the final destination each packet is headed toward. Each packet is also encapsulated with its essential personal travel information before beginning its journey. The outermost IP destination will need to identify the target physical host the packet is being sent to. In addition, each packet will have the destination VPC and destination network interface identification.

> **Note**
>
> Blackfoot edge devices translate the traffic residing on the internal VPC encapsulation network to the outside IP network sending each packet to its desired destination.

For example, if the traffic needs to go to the Internet, the VPC encapsulation will be stripped from the packet, and its IP addresses will be changed to a public IP address. If the destination was to an external private connection, the traffic would be directed to the requested VPN service. The Blackfoot device also adds additional protection by performing network address translation as the internal network traffic transitions to an external packet flow. With their current VPC design, AWS has successfully gone past any limitations imposed by using VLANs.

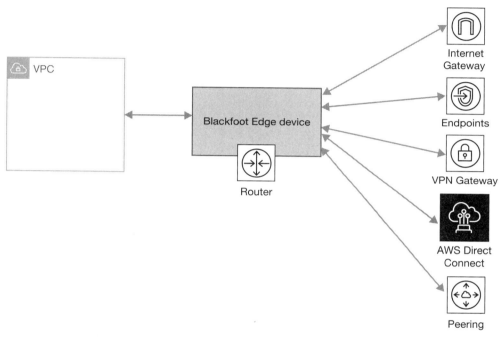

Figure 3-5   Blackfoot edge device forwarding decisions

The Mapping Service

How can all the required networking information be gathered in a timely fashion? AWS uses a process called the mapping service. The mapping service is a fully distributed service in charge of mapping VPCs and their associated network interfaces and the physical locations of each VPC. Mapping decisions are highly optimized using high-speed lookup memory caches. With support for microsecond scale latencies, mappings are cached in the location where they are most used and are proactively validated when routing information is updated. According to AWS, with this design, the overall system latency is reduced to tens of microseconds. The central mapping server knows everything about every IP address, every Media Access Control (MAC) address, and where each component physically lives on the AWS network, as shown in Figure 3-6.

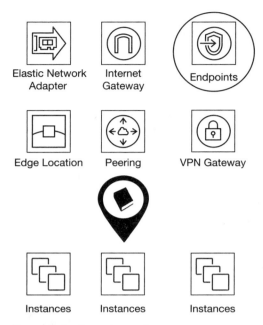

Figure 3-6   Central mapping server

The mapping server replaces the traditional process of broadcasting packets to identify the MAC addresses, and multicasting to distribute information to everybody on the network. You could also think of the VPC as a tagging mechanism, where the tag of each VPC is inserted in the packet information; the packet can therefore be identified using the VPC tag as to where it needs to flow to. Both the source and the destination of each network packet are verified, and any security rules are upheld and maintained by the mapping service.

There are no broadcasts domains at AWS; the need for networkwide broadcasts has been removed. All networking information is instead held and maintained within the distributed mapping tables. On a traditional network, we would first broadcast and find out the destination information and then create the packet and send it off. Not at AWS. Broadcasts from millions of customers would bring down the network; therefore, no broadcasting is allowed outside of each subnet. Hopefully you found the last few pages an interesting summary of some of the cool networking components running inside of Amazon's data centers. Now that we have some background, let's look at creating our first VPC.

Creating Your First VPC

The initial creation of a VPC is either a very simple or a slightly more complex process depending on what tool you choose to use. Two wizards are available: the Launch VPC Wizard and the Create VPC. Each wizard shows up at different levels in the VPC management console, and that adds a bit of confusion because each wizard asks different questions and then carries out different tasks. You can also use the Amazon command-line interface (CLI) and enter a simple command-line string to create a VPC. Each of the choices available for creating a VPC carries out the creation task a little differently.

Example 1: Create the VPC

For our first example, we will click the Your VPCs link from the main VPC Dashboard. You must answer a couple questions when creating a VPC with the Create VPC wizard.

- What is the name tag? That's the name of the VPC being created.

- What is the initial IPv4 CIDR block you want to use for the VPC?

There are two additional menu choices that allow you to add an IPv6 classless inter-domain routing (CIDR) range and make a choice about VPC tenancy. The tenancy option allows you to change from the default mode of running your future instances on shared hardware, called multi-tenancy, or single-tenancy hardware.

Hosting instances at AWS in a VPC on shared hardware resources means that other AWS customers will also be sharing the underlying bare-metal server hardware and hypervisor along with you. You will not know which customers you are sharing AWS resources with. Selecting dedicated tenancy forces you to run your EC2 instances within the VPC designated as dedicated on single-tenant hardware with you being the only tenant, or customer. This may be an important consideration if you're bound by strict governance rules requiring you to operate with dedicated compute instances when operating in the AWS cloud.

Running dedicated EC2 instances at AWS is more expensive than multitenancy operation. A $2 charge per hour will be added when dedicated instances are running. Let's return to the steps for creating a VPC with the Create VPC wizard.

1. Using the Management Console, click Services, and under Networking and Content Delivery, select VPC.

2. From the VPC Dashboard under Virtual Private Cloud, select Your VPCs.

3. Click the blue button Create VPC.

4. In the Name tag dialog box shown in Figure 3-7, enter the name of your VPC.

5. In the IP CIDR Block dialog box, enter the range of IP addresses you want to use in CIDR notation. For example, enter 192.168.0.0/16, which would allow you to create subnets within the VPC that could total approximately 65,530 possible hosts.

6. Optionally change the default tenancy from shared to dedicated.

Create VPC

A VPC is an isolated portion of the AWS cloud populated by AWS objects, such as Amazon EC2 instances. You must specify an IPv4 address range for your VPC. Specify the IPv4 address range as a Classless Inter-Domain Routing (CIDR) block; for example, 10.0.0.0/16. You cannot specify an IPv4 CIDR block larger than /16. You can optionally associate an Amazon-provided IPv6 CIDR block with the VPC.

Name tag	Mobile Development	ⓘ
IPv4 CIDR block*	192.168.0.0/24	ⓘ
IPv6 CIDR block	⦿ No IPv6 CIDR Block ◯ Amazon provided IPv6 CIDR block	ⓘ
Tenancy	Default ▾	ⓘ

* Required   Cancel   **Create**

Figure 3-7   VPC questions using the Create VPC wizard

Example 2: Launch the VPC Wizard

From the main VPC Dashboard for this example, click the Launch VPC Wizard button.

This more powerful wizard option prompts you for answers to additional questions depending on the VPC design that was chosen. In addition to specifying the default CIDR block for the VPC, you also specify the CIDR blocks for the subnets that you want to create.

Other networking information details such as NAT servers and customer gateway configuration settings can also be added. These VPC wizards can be handy to get you started, but they are also limiting; for example, you can't create multiple public and private subnets in multiple availability zones with the wizard. However, the Launch VPC wizard, as shown in Figure 3-8, is useful in visualizing the components required with the available VPC designs. You can use the VPC management console to add additional subnets anytime.

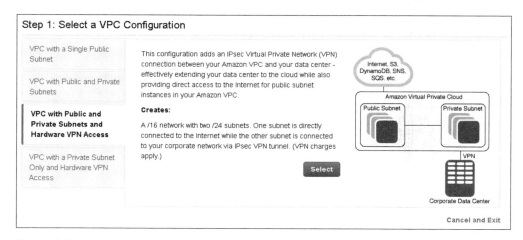

Figure 3-8   Launch VPC starting design choices

The following are VPC design choices we can consider:

1. **VPC with a Single Public Subnet**—This option creates a single public subnet that could be useful for a simple test environment or for a public-facing software as a service(SaaS) application. It might also be useful if you want to design with multiple VPCs for controlling incoming traffic flow through a transit network.

2. **VPC with Public and Private Subnets**—Creating a VPC with public and private subnets allows you to create an environment for a multi-tier application. The public subnets would be utilized for network address translation (NAT) servers or additional public-facing services such as load-balancing services. Multiple private subnets could be created and used for hosting, Web/application servers, and database servers.

3. **VPC with Public and Private Subnets and Hardware VPN Access**—This choice is like the second example above but also allows you to add a private VPN connection.

4. **VPC with a Private Subnet Only and Hardware VPN Access**—This choice is also like the second example, but there are no public subnets created.

After using the Launch VPC Wizard to create your initial VPC infrastructure, you can add additional subnets or connectivity that you require using the other options in the VPC console. The wizards are merely a starting point for most real-world network designs. You can also choose to use the AWS CLI tools to create a VPC, as shown in Figure 3-9.

MAKE SURE TO WATCH THE COMPANION VIDEO "CREATING A CUSTOM VPC."

To access the companion videos, register your book at informit.com/register.

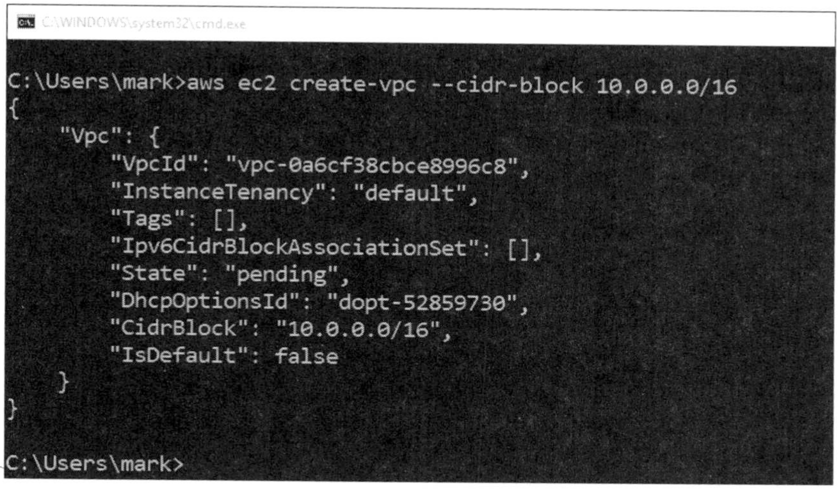

```
C:\Users\mark>aws ec2 create-vpc --cidr-block 10.0.0.0/16
{
    "Vpc": {
        "VpcId": "vpc-0a6cf38cbce8996c8",
        "InstanceTenancy": "default",
        "Tags": [],
        "Ipv6CidrBlockAssociationSet": [],
        "State": "pending",
        "DhcpOptionsId": "dopt-52859730",
        "CidrBlock": "10.0.0.0/16",
        "IsDefault": false
    }
}
C:\Users\mark>
```

Figure 3-9   Creating a VPC using the CLI

If you used one of the VPC wizards or the AWS CLI, congratulations! You have created a VPC. Depending on the wizard or the creation process used, the VPC might be completely empty with just the required IPv4 CIDR block, or you may have fleshed out your design by choosing public, or public and private subnets, and associated network connectivity infrastructure. This is probably a good time to pause and think about how many VPCs you might need. This is a long-term question for your company. You may have many developers with many accounts creating many VPCs without regard for other developers who are also creating VPCs. You might need a single VPC today, but what about tomorrow? How much expansion will you need over the next two years?

> **Note**
>
> Terra Firma's human resources system requires at the very least one VPC, but just how many will they need in the future needs to be discussed? Will their network design require a separate test bed VPC for development? Perhaps an additional VPC to test for quality control, and of course, a VPC for the live application? What if Terra Firma decided to operate in multiple regions? What if multiple developers with multiple accounts worked on the development of the human resources system? You can see how complicated this decision could get.

How Many VPCs?

There are initial limits to the number of VPCs that we can create. The default "soft limit" is five VPCs per AWS account. You can request additional VPCs resources up to the defined hard limit. The current hard limit for VPCs is the current number of VPCs in the region times the number of security groups per VPC. The total figure cannot exceed 1,000. This is but one example of hard and soft limits defined by AWS for each service. Check the AWS documentation for each AWS service that you are planning to deploy to find the current hard and soft limits and plan accordingly.

> **Note**
>
> Hard and soft limits are per AWS account, per region. With 20 regions available at AWS, a single AWS account can create 100 VPCs, 5 per region.

Consider these possible design options for calculating the number of VPCs required:

1. Your company wants to extend, or burst, into the cloud utilizing resources in the corporate data center and at AWS. Your primary need is additional compute resources at certain times of the month. In this scenario, one VPC could be the solution. A single VPC can host many subnets and instances and have private connectivity back to the corporate data center.

2. You are an independent developer creating an application that will be available across the Internet to users around the world. You have no corporate data center. The solution is to start with one VPC. Perhaps you will soon want to have a development workspace, a test workspace, and a production workspace, and you want them all to be separate. Now you have potentially three VPCs within a single region.

3. You're an administrator who has been tasked with utilizing cloud storage at AWS. You need unlimited storage, and you don't know the upper limit of your storage requirements. Your solution doesn't need a VPC. You need storage—perhaps S3 object storage or Glacier archiving. This is an example of the service itself not residing within a VPC. You can find more details on S3 storage in Chapter 6, "Cloud Storage."

4. You work for a large company, with several developers and administrators, and many departments spread across many continents. You may have many AWS accounts and many VPCs to contend with. Don't worry! We can work with multiple VPCs and multiple accounts with VPCs, but it's a great idea to have some long-term plan perhaps 2 to 3 years out if possible. At the end of this chapter, we will look at some discussion points to save you some potential future pain.

5. You work for a large company that is hosted in many different countries with different languages. Your company wants absolute separation; multiple VPCs can be created.

Creating the VPC CIDR Block

A VPC created using either a simple AWS CLI command or the main Create VPC wizard is really a blank slate except for the primary IPv4 CIDR block and the local main routing table. Here are some CIDR details to be aware of:

- Both IPv4 and IPv6 subnets are supported within a VPC; however, it is required that VPCs and subnets have an initial IPv4 CIDR block defined first.

- IPv6 CIDR blocks can be associated with your VPC, but only after an initial IPv4 CIDR block has been created.

- CIDR blocks must not overlap with any existing CIDR blocks associated within a VPC or with another VPC connected with a peering connection. Overlapping CIDR blocks are an issue to be avoided unless it's a deliberate decision to ensure that a VPC cannot connect to another VPC, regardless of the situation.

- The size of an existing CIDR block cannot be increased or decreased; it is locked after creation.

Planning Your Primary VPC CIDR Block

There are many questions, and many possible answers, when plann
VPC. I can't stress it enough that if you are not the prime netw
should talk to your networking team and get advice on what IP
AWS. Two or three years down the road, you may want to conne
to your corporate network, and you might find out that the IP ac
the best choice. Meeting with your network team could save you
save you from a serious meltdown. Your initial IP addressing choi
you without proper planning. We'll explore these issues when we

> **Note**
>
> The primary IPv4 CIDR block that you choose for your VPC will determine the number and size of IPv4 addresses that can be assigned to the subnets created within the VPC. The initial CIDR block that was added when you created the VPC can't be changed; however, you have the option of adding additional secondary CIDR blocks to an existing VPC. We will expand upon using additional secondary CIDR blocks in a few pages.

Let's start with the example of 192.168.0.0, as shown in Figure 3-10. For your VPC starting CIDR address, the network mask you choose will determine the number of possible hosts that can be contained on subnets within your single VPC.

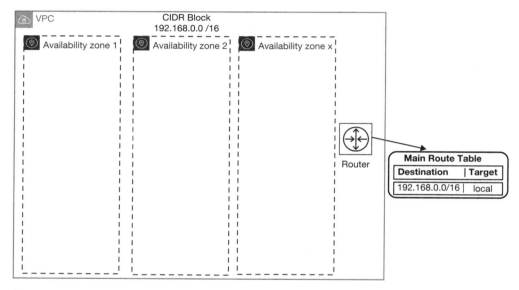

Figure 3-10   The basic VPC components

> **Note**
>
> Amazon supports netmask sizes from /16 to /28.

As discussed, during the creation of a VPC, it's mandatory that an IPv4 CIDR block is assigned to a VPC even if you're planning to use IPv6. However, VPCs can also operate in a dual stack mode communicating over both IPv4 and IPv6 protocols. The subnet CIDR block for IPv6 is fixed at /64. During or after VPC creation, you can choose to associate an IPv6 CIDR block to your VPC d subnets. Reviewing the sample address ranges shown in Table 3-2, you will be able to find an table range of hosts and addresses to match your project. When in doubt, explore increasing et CIDR block size to accommodate more hosts.

Table 3-2   **VPC CIDR Block Examples**

CIDR Block	Addresses Range	Hosts
192.168.0.0/16	192.168.0.4–192.168.255.254	65,529
192.168.0.0/18	192.168.0.4 and 192.168.255.254	16,379
192.168.0.0/19	192.168.0.4 and 192.168.255.254	8,187
192.168.0.0/20	192.1, 68.0.4 and 192.168.255.254	4091
192.168.0.0/21	192.168.0.4 and 192.168.255.254	2043
192.168.0.0/22	192.168.0.4 and 192.168.255.254	1019
192.168.0.0/23	192.168.0.4 and 192.168.255.254	507
192.168.0.0/24	192.168.0.4 and 192.168.255.254	251
192.168.0.0/28	192.168.0.4 and 192.168.255.254	11

Note that the first four IP addresses 0, 1, 2, and 3) and the last IP address (255) in each subnet's CIDR block are reserved for Amazon's use. Using /22 as a standard netmask for all subnets, the maximum number of hosts is 1019, which for a lot of use cases would be fine. However, if you're creating a subnet for hosting thousands of clients utilizing a VDI solution, make sure to pick a larger range for future expansion. On a private subnet for databases, you could go as small as /28. You will not have 11 database hosts on a single subnet.

Adding a Secondary CIDR Block

Up to four secondary IPv4 CIDR blocks can also be associated with an existing VPC. After adding an additional CIDR block, the new route is automatically added to the VPC main route tables, enabling the additional local routing routes throughout the VPC. Keep in mind that the additional secondary CIDR block cannot be larger than the initial primary CIDR block. For example, if you associate a primary CIDR block of 10.0.0.0/24, an additional CIDR block of the same range or larger is not allowed. However, a CIDR block of 10.0.0.0/25 is allowed because it's a smaller range.

The primary advantage of being able to add additional secondary CIDR blocks to an existing VPC is having the ability to add future expansion when necessary. If the initial primary CIDR block caused address space limitations, additional secondary CIDR blocks can be added allowing you to increase the number of IP addresses that can be used within the VPC.

> MAKE SURE TO WATCH THE COMPANION VIDEO "CREATING CIDR BLOCKS."

The Default VPC

You may have come across the default VPC if you have been playing around with AWS and adding an initial instance. The default VPC is available within each AWS region and is created with an IPv4 CIDR block of 172.30.0.0/16, which provides up to 65,531 private IP v4 addresses. In addition, an Internet gateway has been created and attached to the default VPC with a route table entry that sends all IP traffic intended for the Internet to the attached Internet gateway. A default security group and default network ACL are also associated with the default VPC. For each default VPC, subnets have been created for each AZ in the region where it's located. All that's left for you to do is to add instances. Instances placed on the default public subnet within the default VPC receive both a public and a private IPv4 address and public and private DNS host names. Potentially, your Web application is ready to go. Well, hold on just a second.

The idea behind AWS already providing a prebuilt default networking VPC environment is to enable you to start working quickly with AWS, even if you have limited network knowledge. The default VPC can be handy if you want to do a quick demo and don't want to bother setting up subnets and Internet connectivity and think about any CIDR decisions. These networking decisions have been already carried out for the default VPC.

> **Note**
>
> The default VPC's infrastructure is set up for public Internet access. However, the customer still makes the final decision for allowing public Internet access to a VPC by associating a public IP address with an EC2 instance during its creation. Allowing public access to AWS resources is always the customer's choice.

Perhaps having a separate demo AWS account utilizing the default VPC would be useful for demonstrations and more. However, the default VPC can easily cause deployment issues when you are selecting a service that requires network placement. If you're not paying attention, the default VPC will be preselected, as shown in Figure 3-11. And you may not want Internet access, which has been defined for the public subnets of the default VPC. For these reasons, for most deployment options other than a demo account, I would recommend deleting the default VPC from every AWS region in your AWS account. Yes, this means you would have to set up all your networking from scratch. But perhaps long term you'll be happier knowing there's no default VPC with easy Internet access provided to the unsuspecting user. It's a really good idea to understand and control all your networking options when operating in the cloud.

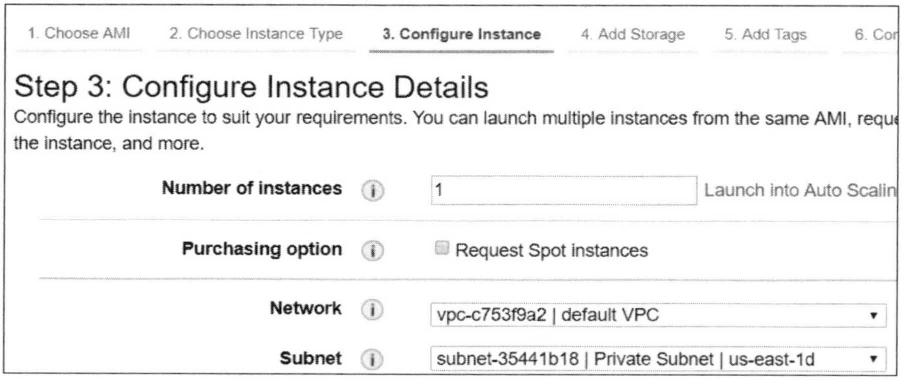

Figure 3-11   The default VPC

> **Note**
>
> The default VPC *can* be deleted. If you want to bring it back, AWS provides a script to re-create it. You also can't assign an existing VPC to become a default VPC.

Revisiting Availability Zones

Availability zones were discussed previously in Chapter 2, "Designing with AWS Global Services." If you are comfortable with the concept of availability zones, you can skip this section. As you may remember, within each VPC, the number of availability zones that are available depend on the region the VPC is created in.

Creating a VPC in the N. Virginia region will give you the option of selecting up to six AZs that can be used within a single VPC to design a resilient network. Choosing the Canadian region, you would have just two AZs to work with. The stated long-term goal is that new AWS regions will have three or more zones. Subnets are created in each AZ. Next, instances are placed on the appropriate subnets. Utilizing AZs allows you to do the following:

- Design for resiliency and failover with multiple AZs in a single VPC.

- Load-balance instances hosted on subnets in different AZs. (See Chapter 5, "Planning for Scale and Resiliency.")

- Auto Scale instances hosted on subnets in different AZs. (See Chapter 5.)

- Deploy RDS primary and slave database servers hosted on subnets in different AZs. (See Chapter 6.)

Creating Subnets

After an initial VPC creation, your next step is to create subnets within the VPC, per AZ(s), depending on your required network design. The AZs that you select for each subnet are already hosted and available within the VPC. It's usually stated that a VPC spans "all of the availability zones within its region" and certainly, there is the potential to include all the AZs within a VPC if your design includes subnets for each AZ. However, AZs don't show up automatically in each VPC; they are added during subnet creation when selecting each subnet's location.

Each subnet that you create resides within its assigned AZ, and although AWS doesn't share the physical details, each subnet is hosted in exactly one data center within the selected AZ, as shown in Figure 3-12. If you choose to design your applications for resiliency and uptime, you'll want to design your solution using at least two AZs. As we know, AZs have been designed with isolation from other AZs; a failure in one availability zone will not affect the other AZs within the VPC and region.

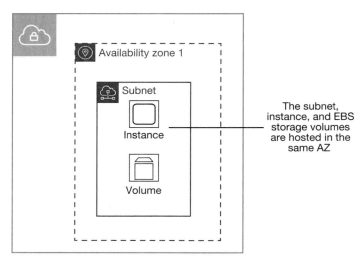

The subnet, instance, and EBS storage volumes are hosted in the same AZ

Figure 3-12   Physical locations for network components

AWS also carries out a balancing of sorts of customers across the listed AZs within a region. If I create a subnet in the N. Virginia region and select availability zone-a, and you also create a subnet in the N. Virginia region, selecting availability zone-a, the odds are high that my subnets are not in the same physical AZ as your subnets. We each have subnets in a selected AZ in N. Virginia. That's as much location detail as were going to get in the AWS cloud.

Every subnet that you create begins life as a private subnet with no connectivity. You may be intent on creating a subnet with Internet access, but you have a few tasks to carry out: you must first add, and then attach, an Internet gateway to the VPC and then manually update the route table associated with the public subnet with a route table entry, pointing to the Internet gateway. Only after every one of these steps is taken will you have an official public subnet.

Note

Subnets are defined by their connectivity options.

- If subnet traffic is routed to the Internet through an Internet gateway, the subnet is defined as a public subnet.

- If a subnet has no gateway or endpoint to direct traffic to, it is a private subnet. Traffic remains on the local subnet and has nowhere else to go. A subnet with no external gateway connectivity is the true definition of a private subnet.

Amazon documentation sometimes defines subnets that are routed to a virtual private gateway as a VPN-only subnet distinguishing that there is another network to connect to—a private gateway location. Therefore, it is not as private as a subnet with no gateway connections. Terra Firma and its human resource application will need the following subnet types:

- Public subnets for load balancers and NAT services
- Private subnets for the database servers
- Private subnets for the Web servers

Subnet Summary

- Subnets are contained within an AZ.

- Subnets host compute instances.

- Public subnets allow you access to the Internet.

- Public subnets are for infrastructure.

- Private subnets are private with no Internet access.

- Private subnets are where instances live privately.

- VPN-only subnets have access to a VPN connection, typically to and from the head office.

> MAKE SURE TO WATCH THE COMPANION VIDEO "PUBLIC AND PRIVATE SUBNETS."

NAT Services

At AWS, a NAT gateway service can be ordered and linked to a public subnet to allow EC2 instances in a private subnet to connect to the Internet and receive required operating system and application updates. The NAT gateway service is always placed in a public subnet and config-ured with an elastic IP address that's a static public IP address, as shown in Figure 3-13. On each created NAT gateway, a network interface is added that is assigned a private IP address from the IP address range of your subnet. The elastic IP address is for public communications, and the private IP address is for the private communications with the private subnets. For additional redundancy, create NAT gateways in each AZ and ensure the route tables, entries in each private subnet point the EC2 instances to the correct gateway location.

Figure 3-13   Ordering a chunk of the NAT gateway service

> **Note**
> The NAT gateway service initially supports up to 5 Gbps of bandwidth throughput and can scale up to 45 Gbps as required.

A NAT EC2 instance could also be built and hosted in a public subnet to allow instances in a private subnet to connect to the Internet through the NAT connection and receive required updates as necessary. However, you must completely configure and manage each NAT instance. If you decide this is the method that you want to utilize to provide NAT services, Amazon recommends that you build your NAT instance using the latest version of the NAT AMI. A NAT security group must also be created and assigned to the NAT instance, and, quite possibly, you will have to create an HA pair of NAT instances for redundancy. When building NAT instances, one configuration change needs to be enabled during installation: source destination checks must be disabled because the NAT EC2 instance is not the final source and destination for the traffic it sends and receives. The only reason I can think of why you would want to build your own instances for NAT services is if your environment needs to support port forwarding. The NAT gateway service that AWS supplies does not support port forwarding.

NAT Gateway Summary

- NAT services are used so EC2 instances residing on private subnets can get required updates.

- The NAT gateway service is a hosted AWS cloud service with no need to install or maintain an EC2 instance.

- A NAT EC2 instance is merely an instance configured for NAT duties.

Working with Route Tables

A subnet route table is a defined collection of rules that dictate where egress subnet network traffic can flow to. As previously mentioned in the subnet discussion in this chapter, each subnet must be associated with a route table; and each VPC has local routing functionality built in implicitly. Multiple subnets can also be associated and controlled with a single route table, and a single route table can be assigned to multiple subnets. You may have multiple private subnets that need routes to the same service, such as a NAT gateway service to get required updates, or to a virtual private gateway for connections to the head office. Here are some common route table considerations:

- Each VPC has a main route table that provides local routing throughout the VPC.

- The main route table can be modified, but don't do this. Instead, leave the main route table with just the local routing routes defined within the VPC. Any custom routes required by a subnet should be allowed with a custom route table. Leaving the main route table in its default state ensures that if you assign the main route table by mistake to a subnet, the worst that can happen is local routing.

- The main route table cannot be deleted. However, it can be ignored and remain unassigned if you do not associate it with any subnets within the VPC.

- Each route table entry defines a destination that is defined by CIDR notation and an external target. For example, a common destination is the corporate network, which can be reached through the virtual private gateway.

- Subnet traffic is matched with the most definitive defined route within the route table that matches the traffic request.

- Existing route tables are not automatically populated with routing rules to any network services that you order within your account. When routing services such as an Internet gateway (for IPv4 public Internet traffic), or Egress only Internet gateway (for IPv6 traffic) are attached to a nondefault VPC, they are not automatically added to a route table. They must be added manually. The exception to this rule is the default VPC, or VPCs created with the Launch VPC Wizard.

Note

After the initial association of the main route table to a newly created VPC, AWS makes no additional routing decisions.

The Main Route Table

As mentioned, the main route table provides local routing services throughout the VPC across all defined AZs, as shown in Figure 3-14. Each route table, whether custom or default, has an entry containing the VPC's initial CIDR designations, and this entry cannot be changed. The main route table also defines the routing for all subnets that are not explicitly associated with any other custom route table after they are created. Only after a subnet is created can the associated route table be changed from the main route table to the desired route table.

Figure 3-14   The main route table

> **Note**
>
> Every subnet, when it's created, is automatically assigned to the main route table of a VPC. This is a protective step as the assumption is made that the main route table will only provide local routing throughout the VPC.

Custom Route Tables

It is considered a best practice to create custom route tables for each tier in your network design. Creation of custom route tables allows you granular control of traffic flow within each subnet. Let's look at an example: Terra Firma is thinking of starting with a two-tier design for its human resource CRM application. It has decided to use two AZs within the VPC to provide for additional availability and failover for the application and database servers.

Public and private subnets will be created within each AZ, with public subnets for hosting the NAT gateway service, which allows instances on the private subnets to get updates as required, and a public-facing load balancer for balancing the user requests across the availability zones. Separate private subnets will also be created for the EC2 instances hosting the application servers, as well as the MySQL database instances, as shown in Figure 3-15. The database servers will utilize synchronous replication from the primary to the secondary server, ensuring the database records remain up to date.

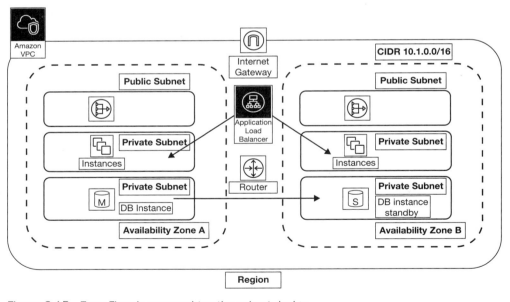

Figure 3-15   Terra Firma's proposed two-tier subnet design

> **Note**
>
> This example is merely a starting design. The actual number of VPCs to be created is still under discussion by Terra Firma. Perhaps the first VPC should be considered for initial design and testing purposes, with other VPCs created for production and quality control. The server and database migration tools provided by AWS also need to be tested and approved.

For our initial design, after the subnets have been created, custom route tables need to be created for the following subnet groupings, as shown in Figure 3-16:

- **Public subnet infrastructure**—ELB, NAT gateway service. A custom route table will be created for the public subnets by adding a route for the Internet gateway enabling public network traffic between network interfaces hosted on the public subnets assigned with public IP addresses and the attached Internet gateway. (Of course, the first task is ordering an Internet gateway; next you must associate the Internet gateway with the VPC.) Internet gateway routes are usually set with a destination route of 0.0.0.0/0 because the destination may be anywhere on the public Internet. For our initial design, perhaps the destination route could be a smaller range of Terra Firma's public IP addresses.

- **Application and database tiers**—The application servers will be hosted on private subnets within each AZ. The master and slave database instances will be either a custom implementation or managed by the relational database service (RDS). To enable EC2 instances hosted on a private subnet to protectively connect to the Internet and receive required updates, the NAT gateway service will be hosted on public subnets within each AZ. Routes pointing to the NAT gateway service must be defined in the route table associated with the private subnets.

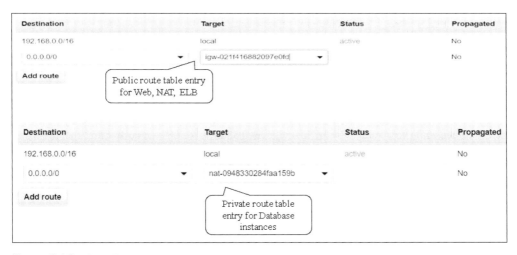

Figure 3-16   Terra Firma's custom route tables

Route Table Summary

- Configure the main route table for local routing.

- Configure custom routes for public subnets.

- Configure custom routes for private subnets.

We now need to talk about TCP/IP address types. IP addresses that are assigned to EC2 instances depend on the subnet types that are selected during the creation of the instance. Let's look at the IP address options available at AWS, starting with private IPv4 addresses.

MAKE SURE TO WATCH THE COMPANION VIDEO "EXPLORING ROUTE TABLES."

Private IPV4 Addresses

When a client launches a new EC2 instance, by default, Amazon assigns a private IP address to the primary virtual network interface card from the range of available IP subnet addresses. (Of course, there could be more network interfaces as well, and they would also have addresses assigned.) Private IP addresses communicate across the private network at AWS. A private DNS host name that points to the associated private IPv4 address is also assigned to each instance. If you choose to manually assign a primary private IP address, the IP address chosen must be available in the subnet's IP address range where the EC2 instance will reside. You can assign any IP address in the assigned subnet range if it is not in use or reserved by AWS.

Note

Once a primary private IP address is assigned, the EC2 instance retains the address for the lifetime of the instance.

Additional, secondary private IP addresses can also be assigned to the network interfaces of an EC2 instance, and these addresses can be unassigned and moved between other EC2 instances that reside on the same subnet at any time. Any network interface other than the primary network interface (eth0) can also be detached and moved to other EC2 instances hosted within the same AZ and within the same VPC.

Note

Let's again discuss the concept of cost at AWS. Communication between EC2 instances residing on the same subnet using their private IP addresses is free of charge. However, EC2 instances using private IP addresses located on subnets in different AZs are charged an outbound data transfer fee for communicating with each other.

The Simple Monthly Calculator is useful to carry out detailed pricing scenarios. http://calculator.s3.amazonaws.com/index.html

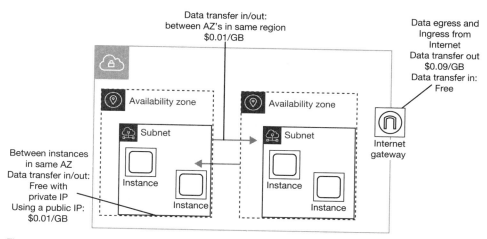

Figure 3-19   Traffic charges at AWS

> **Note**
>
> All inbound communication traffic that an EC2 instance receives is free, regardless of whether it comes from inside AWS or from the public Internet. However, database replication traffic across multiple AZs is charged a data transfer fee.

Bring Your Own IP (BYOIP)

If you have a public IP address range that has been approved for use by your compliance rules, or a specific public IP address has been white-listed as a reputable IP address for a well-known hosted public service, you may want to use these public IP addresses at AWS. The good news is that it's now possible to have control over your own public IP addresses at AWS. BYOIP allows customers to move their existing public IPv4 address space to AWS, as shown in Figure 3-20. Each customer still owns her public IP range; however, Amazon hosts and advertises the public IP address range across the Internet and AWS regions for you. Bringing your own public IPv4 address space to AWS allows you to accomplish the following tasks:

- Maintain your public IP address reputation.

- Avoid any changes to public IP addresses that have been white-listed.

- Avoid changing IP addresses utilizing legacy applications.

- Use a public IP address as a hot standby failover for on-premise resources.

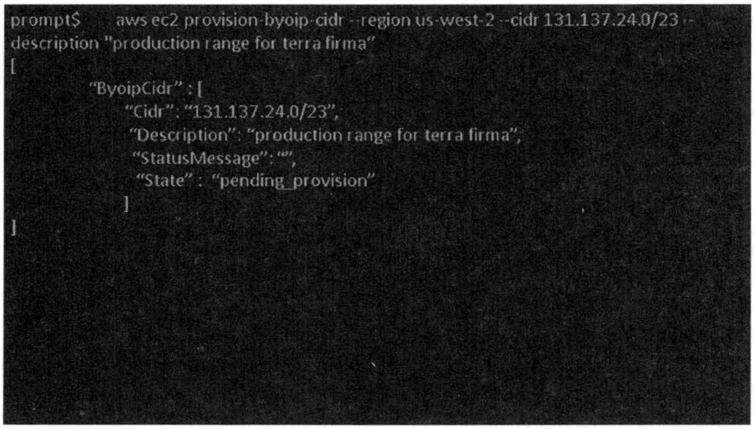

```
prompt$    aws ec2 provision-byoip-cidr --region us-west-2 --cidr 131.137.24.0/23 --
description "production range for terra firma"
[
        "ByoipCidr" : [
            "Cidr": "131.137.24.0/23",
            "Description": "production range for terra firma",
            "StatusMessage": "",
            "State" : "pending_provision"
        ]
]
```

Figure 3-20   BYOIP address architecture at AWS

Reasons for wanting control of your own public address space in the cloud could include the following situations:

- What if you want to keep a recognizable public IP address but have the service assigned to that address hosted on AWS?

- What if you had 10,000 hard-coded lottery machines and you wanted to change the hardware devices to virtual ones at AWS with your public IP addresses?

- What if you had 2,000 hard-coded public IP addresses within your data center and you wanted to change the physical location of your data center to AWS but keep the same public IP addresses?

- What if you had legacy workloads—or older applications relying on specific fixed public IP addresses? These IP addresses can now be moved to AWS.

Note
The specific prefix supported by BYOIP at AWS is /24.

The BYOIP Process

1. Import the public IP address, or the range of public IP addresses, into AWS. AWS creates a pool of these addresses and assigns the address pool to you.

2. Advertise the public address range.

3. Allocate EIP addresses from your AWS hosted pool of public IP addresses.

Step One: Provision Your Public IP Addresses

aws ec2 provision-byoip-cidr --region -cidr <cidr range>

After AWS has analyzed and accepted the range of public IP addresses, the state of the public address range to be hosted at AWS changes to "provisioned" indicating that the IP address request has been accepted. At this point you will be able to use these public IP addresses, but they have not yet been advertised across the Internet or to the peering partners of AWS.

Step Two: Advertise the Newly Created IP Address Pool Using the Advertise Command

aws ec2 advertise-byoip-cidr -- region <cidr range>

After this command has executed, the state of the address space changes from provisioned to advertised, as shown in Figure 3-21. The address range is now advertised across the Internet and to all the peering partners of AWS. Once the advertising process has been accepted and started at AWS, it's time to stop the advertising of the same public IP addresses to avoid any funky duplication routing conflicts.

```
prompt$     aws ec2 advertise-byoip-cidr --region us-west-2 --cidr 131.137.24.0/23
[
        "ByoipCidr" : [
            "Cidr": "131.137.24.0/23",
            "Description": "production range for terra firma",
            "StatusMessage": "",
            "State" : "advertised"
        ]
]
```

Figure 3-21   An advertised BYOIP address range

Step Three: Allocate an EIP from Your Range of IP Addresses

aws ec2 deprovisioning-byoip-cidr--range address range

When using the hosted pool of addresses at AWS to allocate elastic IP addresses, you can select a random IP address from the hosted pool or select a specific IP address.

If, in the future, you decide you don't want AWS to advertise and host your pool of public IP addresses, you can execute a "withdraw" command to change the state of the public IP addresses from advertised back to an unadvertised state. At this point, AWS no longer advertises your public IP addresses. The last step is to run the deprovisioning command to remove the assigned elastic IP addresses.

IPv6 Addresses

Remember that even though IPv6 addresses are fully supported within a VPC, an IPv4 CIDR block must be created first. The allowable format for IPv6 addresses is 128 bits, with a fixed CIDR block size of /56. Amazon is in control of IPv6 addressing; you cannot select your own CIDR range. Note with IPv6 addresses at AWS that there is no distinction between a public and a private IPv6 address.

> **Note**
>
> At AWS, IPv6 addresses are public addresses. Amazon also does not provide support for a DNS hostname for assigned IPv6 addresses.

If your instance is configured to receive an IPv6 address at launch, the address will be associated with the primary network interface. As noted earlier, instances at AWS do not have IPv6 DNS hostname support. Assigned IPv6 addresses are also persistent; you can stop and start your instance, and the IPv6 addresses remain assigned. IPv6 addresses are defined as globally unique because they have a globally unique identifier. Access to the Internet using an IPv6 address is controlled by the subnet route table, or by using security groups or network ACLs.

If you are planning to utilize IPv6 addressing at AWS for Internet access, here is a short summary of the steps to follow:

1. Associate the AWS-provided IPv6 CIDR block with your VPC.

2. Create an Egress only that's outbound only, Internet gateway (EOIG).

   This allows your private subnet to enable outbound communications to the Internet using IPv6; the egress-only Internet gateway prevents inbound communications.

3. Update your route tables to route your IPv6 traffic to the EOIG.

   For instances hosted on IPv6 public subnets, add a route that directs all IPv6 traffic from the subnet to the Internet gateway. Note that that's the regular Internet gateway, and not the EOIG; the EOIG is controlling private outbound traffic from the private subnet.

   For instances on IPv6 private subnets, create a route that directs all Internet-bound IPv6 traffic to the EOIG.

4. Review and update your security group rule, including rules for IPv6 addresses.

Security Groups

Security groups operate at the EC2 instance level. They protect your server's incoming network connections by placing a software firewall around each attached network interface. Each EC2 instance will have a primary network interface (defined as eth0); you may also have EC2 instances with multiple network interfaces, and each interface will be protected with a security group.

Each security group is a collection of inbound and outbound rules that designate the port and protocols allowed into and out of each network interface, as shown in Figure 3-22.

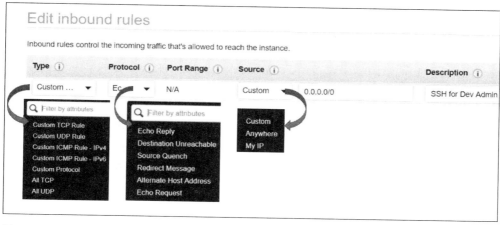

Figure 3-22   Security group details

It may not be obvious, but each network interface is attached to a single EC2 instance, and each security group is assigned to a specific VPC. Here are some details of what we can do with security groups:

- Security groups are associated with a particular VPC.
- Each network interface assigned to an instance hosted within a VPC can be associated with up to five security groups.
- We can allow rules; we cannot specify explicit deny rules with security groups. However, if access is not specifically allowed, you are implicitly denied.
- When you create a new security group, if you don't review and change your outbound rules, all outbound traffic is allowed.
- Outbound rules can be changed to a more specific outbound destination.

Security group rules are defined as *stateful*. Inbound traffic flowing through a security group is therefore tracked to know the state of the traffic; if the traffic is allowed in, the response to the inbound traffic is always allowed outbound. This definition can be flipped; traffic that flows outbound will have its responses allowed back in. Once security groups have been assigned, changes can be made to the security groups assigned to a network interface while the instance is operational. Security group changes will take effect usually within a few seconds.

Security groups show up in several locations in the management console; they appear in both the EC2 and the VPC console. If you were using EC2-Classic networking, the security groups you would have created would have shown up only in the EC2 console.

Think of each security group as a reusable security template stored in your AWS account. Once a security group has been created, it can be assigned multiple times within the VPC where it was created, protecting one or many EC2 instances. Up to five security groups can be applied to a single network adapter, providing an effective set of allow rules mandating what ports and protocols are allowed for both inbound and outbound traffic.

The main characteristics of security group rules are as follows:

- Security groups define allow rules. (You can't create rules that explicitly deny access.)

- Security group rules allow you to direct traffic outbound from one security group and inbound to another security group within the same VPC.

- Security groups don't deny traffic explicitly; instead, they deny traffic implicitly by only stating what is allowed.

- Security groups are defined as stateless; if requests are allowed in, response traffic is allowed out regardless of defined outbound rules.

- For each rule, you define the protocol, the port, or port range, and the source inbound rules or destination outbound rules for the traffic.

- The protocols allowed are TCP, UDP, or ICMP.

- Port Range: for either TCP or UDP, or a custom protocol, this is the range of ports to allow. You can specify a single port such as port 22, or a range of ports if you're dealing with outbound dynamic port mapping. The ports that can be assigned are defined by RFC 5237 and 7045, which define the standard TCP/IP protocols.

One important concept to grasp about security groups is that they don't deny traffic flow. Instead, they allow traffic flow. Another equally important concept is the "direction of traffic flow" allowed by a security group. As we know, the network traffic that is allowed in by a security group rule is also allowed out. However, a defined inbound port request does not use the same port number for the outbound response. For example, if there's a rule defined allowing inbound HTTP traffic across port 80 inbound, the outbound traffic response is allowed out, but the response traffic does not use port 80 outbound. In most cases, outbound traffic uses a dynamically assigned port called an ephemeral port, determined by the operating system of the server making the response. We will explore ephemeral ports when we cover network ACLs later in this chapter.

When a VPC is created, a default security group is also created, as shown in Figure 3-23. Note that all outbound traffic is allowed between the EC2 instances that are assigned the security group; however, any other traffic is implicitly denied. Therefore no one can get into any of the EC2 instances from the outside world because the security group did not allow any external inbound traffic. It's also important to understand that you can't delete a default security group; you also don't have to use the default security groups; you can ignore them and create and assign custom security groups.

If you don't pay attention and don't specify a custom security group when an EC2 instance is created, at launch, the default security group is associated automatically. As we now know, the default security group allows all outbound traffic from the instance associated with the default security group, but accessing the EC2 instance from an external location will not allowed.

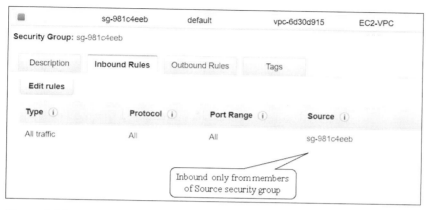

Figure 3-23   Default security group in newly created VPC

Custom Security Groups

What happens when you create a custom security group? First, you must associate the security group with a specific VPC. After it is first created, a custom security group allows no inbound traffic but allows all outbound traffic by default. After the initial creation of the custom security group and selecting the security group properties, from the Inbound Rules tab you create the inbound rules defining the network traffic that's allowed inbound. On the Outbound Rules tab, define the network traffic or security group that is allowed to communicate outbound.

- **Inbound rules**—Define the source of the traffic—that is, where it is coming from, and what the destination port or port range is. The actual source of the traffic could be a single IP address (IPv4 or IPv6), a range of addresses, or another security group.

- **Outbound rules**—Define the destination of the traffic—that is, where it is going to, and the destination port, or port range. The actual destination of the traffic could be a single IP address (IPv4 or IPv6), a range of addresses, or another security group.

  - A prefix list ID for a specific AWS network service, such as an Internet gateway

  - Another security group—This feature allows instances that are associated with one security group to access instances associated with another security group. The security group can reside in the same VPC or can be from a VPC that has been peered together through a VPC peering connection.

> **Note**
>
> Security groups "allow" access; however, security groups are also said to "deny by default." If an incoming port is not allowed, technically access is denied.

The best practice when designing security groups is to restrict what ports need to be opened. If you place a load balancer in front of your EC2 instances, the only ports that need to be allowed by the security group protecting the load balancer are the port or ports your application requires.

For your production applications in your design, it's a good idea to consider picking unique ports based on your production server's tier placement. For example, in a three-tier design, Web servers could be assigned 3020 and application servers 3030, and database instances could have custom ports chosen. That's just an extra level of security to consider. In addition, be prepared to plan for a clean security audit, or for successful troubleshooting by designing and documenting your security group's naming scheme up front. Putting some real thought into all naming conventions pays off when you are under pressure. We have all been in this situation; fill in the blank "what's the blasted name of the --------. Who named it that?" Here are some examples to consider for your security group configurations and initial setup.

App Server Inbound Ports

This security group has rules to allow inbound access of HTTP and HTTPS from any IPv4 address as the traffic is arriving inbound from the public Internet. As shown in Table 3-3, the source IP address of 0.0.0.0/0 indicates the traffic is allowed from any Internet location.

Table 3-3 **Security Group Allowing HTTP Access**

Inbound Rules

Protocol	Number	Port	Source IP	Comment
TCP	6	80 (HTTP)	0.0.0.0/0	Inbound from anywhere (IPv4)

Outbound Rules

Protocol	Number	Port	Destination IP	Comment
ALL	6	80 (HTTP)	0.0.0.0/0	Outbound IPv4 traffic

Database Server Inbound Ports

At AWS, there are a number of managed database server options available with RDS; during configuration, you can choose to use the default port address assigned based on the database product's default port access. You could change this to a custom port number to add an additional element of security. The source IP address could be specified as a single IP address or a range of IP addresses from your subnet of application servers that need to query the database. Default RDS security group database port options are listed in Table 3-4.

Network ACL Rule Processing

Both inbound and outbound rules are evaluated starting with the lowest defined numbered rule. Any protocol that is defined using a standard TCP protocol number can be specified. Once a rule matches the traffic request, it is applied; there is no additional comparison with higher numbered rules that may also match. A misconfigured lower numbered rule that also matches the same traffic request could obviously cause problems. If you designated a higher number rule to deal with specific traffic but instead a lower number rule matched the traffic request, the higher rule would never be used, as shown in Table 3-9.

Table 3-9   **NACL rules out of order**

Rule #	Source IP	Protocol	Port	Allow / Deny	Comments
100	Private IP address range	TCP	22	ALLOW	Inbound SSH to subnet
110	Private IP address range	TCP	3389	ALLOW	Inbound SSH to subnet (Allow rule will be evaluated)
120	Private IP address range	3389	3389	DENY	Inbound SSH to subnet (Deny rule will not be evaluated)
*	0.0.0.0/0	All	All	DENY	Denies inbound traffic not handled by existing rule

Hopefully you can see why the order of your rules is important.

- Inbound rules must list the source of the IP traffic by CIDR range and the destination listening port or range of listening ports.

- Outbound rules must list the destination for the traffic CIDR range and the destination port or range of listening ports.

- Each rule must be defined as either ALLOW or DENY for the specified traffic.

When inbound packets appear at the subnet level, they are evaluated against the incoming, ingress rules of the network ACL. For example, let's say the request is for port 443. Starting with the first rule numbered 100, there is not a match because the first rule has been defined for port 80 HTML traffic. The second rule numbered 110 has been defined for allowing port 443 traffic, as shown in Table 3-10. Therefore, the packet is allowed onto the subnet. If an incoming packet doesn't match any of the inbound allow rules, the packet is denied access.

Outbound or egress responses also must be matched with a defined outbound rule for the traffic to be allowed to exit the subnet. It doesn't hurt to mention once again that NACLs are defined as stateless. The inbound rules are a separate entity from the outbound rules; they pay no attention to each other's defined allow and deny rules. For SSL communication, if the inbound communication is from the Internet, and therefore for the defined SSL rule, the source would be defined as 0.0.0.0/0 because the traffic could come from any location. The outbound rule would use port 443, maintaining the encrypted communication, but the destination would be 0.0.0.0/0 because the destination could be anywhere across the Internet. In this case, both the inbound and the outbound rules for SSL would be set to ALLOW.

For both inbound and outbound traffic requests, we must consider where the traffic originated from. Return traffic from an instance hosted in a VPC, from a destination across the Internet, would be communicating using a dynamic outbound or inbound port called an *ephemeral port*. Let's talk about these ephemeral ports.

Table 3-10   **Custom NACL Setup**

Inbound Network ACL

Rule	Destination IP	Protocol	Port	Allow/Deny	Details
100	0.0.0.0/0	TCP	80	ALLOW	Allows inbound HTTP traffic from any IPv4 address from the Internet
110	0.0.0.0/0	TCP	443	ALLOW	Allows inbound HTTPS traffic from any IPv4 address from the Internet
120	Public IPv4 address for administration	TCP	22	ALLOW	Allows inbound SSH traffic for admins through the Internet gateway
130	Public IPv4 address for administration	TCP	3389	ALLOW	Allows inbound RDP traffic for admins through the Internet gateway
140	0.0.0.0/0	TCP	32768-65535	ALLOW	Allows inbound return traffic from hosts across the Internet that are responding to instance requests in the public subnet
*	0.0.0.0/0	All	All	DENY	Denies all inbound IPv4 traffic not defined by any other rule

Outbound Network ACL

Rule	Destination IP	Protocol	Port	Allow/Deny	Details
100	0.0.0.0/0	TCP	80	ALLOW	Allows outbound HTTP traffic from the public subnet to the Internet
110	0.0.0.0/0	TCP	443	ALLOW	Allows outbound HTTPS traffic from the subnet to the Internet
120	0.0.0.0/0	TCP	32768-65535	ALLOW	Allows outbound responses to clients across the Internet
*	0.0.0.0/0	All	All	DENY	Denies all outbound IPv4 traffic not defined by any other rule

MAKE SURE TO WATCH THE COMPANION VIDEO "NETWORK ACLs."

Understanding Ephemeral Ports

Inbound and outbound rules defined in the network do not always need to be symmetrical. In fact, TCP/IP communications don't utilize the same inbound and outbound ports; symmetric NACL rules do not typically apply. The operating system of the client or the server defines the range of ports that will be dynamically selected for the return communication—that is, the outbound communication. IPv4 connections require two endpoints: a source and a destination. Each source and destination endpoint consists of an IP address and an associated port number.

When a client system connects to a server, several components are employed: the server IP, the server port, the client IP, and the client port. The ephemeral port is a temporary port that is assigned by the computer's TCP/IP stack. The port number is chosen by the TCP/ IP implementation based on the host operating system. In the case of Windows 2008 R2 and above, the ephemeral port range is from 49152 to 65535. If Linux is the operating system, the ephemeral port range is from 32768 to 61000, as shown in Table 3-10. Different operating system versions may use slightly different ephemeral ranges; make sure you check what your operating system uses for ephemeral ports.

When communication is carried out from a source service to its destination, the traffic typically uses the named port for the destination traffic, such as port 22 on a Linux box accepting SSH connections. However, for the return traffic from the server to the client, typically an ephemeral port is used for the return traffic, as shown in Table 3-11. An ephemeral port can be defined as a dynamically assigned port from a range of assumed available port addresses. Outbound packets travel through an outbound port allowed by the security group protecting the network interface. Once the packet is on the subnet, it exits the subnet using an allowed ephemeral port.

If custom NACLs are deployed, ephemeral rules need to appear in both the inbound and the outbound rules to cover the dynamic requirements of communication using ephemeral ports. Outbound communication from an instance hosted on a VPC needs to have an allowed outbound range of ephemeral ports. These ports remain available only during the communication session; each dynamically assigned port is released after the TCP connection terminates. Table 3-11 lists some common inbound port numbers that are typically used. Note that the outbound port is dynamic in most cases, except for port 443; it's returning an answer, returning outbound using a dynamic ephemeral port assigned by the operating system of the client or server that's answering the incoming query.

Table 3-11   **Inbound Port Numbers**

Inbound Ports	Service	Protocol	Description	Outbound Port
20	FTP	TCP/UDP	File Transfer Data	Dynamic
21	FTP	TCP/UDP/	File Transfer Control	Dynamic
22	SSH	TCP/UDP/ SCTP	Secure Shell	Dynamic
25	SMTP	TCP/UDP	Simple Mail Transfer	Dynamic
67	BOOTPS	UDP	Bootstrap (BOOTP/DHCP) Server	Dynamic
68	BOOTPC	UDP	Bootstrap (BOOTP/DHCP) Client	Dynamic

Inbound Ports	Service	Protocol	Description	Outbound Port
69	TFTP	UDP	Trivial File Transfer	Dynamic
80	HTTP	TCP	Hypertext Transfer Protocol	Dynamic
In 88	Kerberos	TCP	Kerberos	Dynamic
123	NTP	UDP	Network Time Protocol	Dynamic
443	HTTPS	TCP	HTTP protocol over TLS / SSL	443
143	Microsoft-ds	IMAP	Internet Message Access Protocol	Dynamic

Network ACL Summary

- Plan your NACLs with names that make sense.

- Discuss your reasons for using NACLs with other technical people.

- Deploy and test on a test VPC before moving to production.

VPC Flow Logs

Network traffic can be captured for analysis or to diagnose communication problems at both the interface, subnet, or VPC. There is no charge for using a flow log, but there can be hefty charges for the data storage. When each flow log is created, it defines the type of traffic that will be captured: accepted or rejected traffic, or all traffic.

Flow logs can be stored in either CloudWatch logs or directly in an S3 bucket for storage, as shown in Figure 3-25. If VPC flow logs are stored as CloudWatch logs, IAM roles must be created that define the permissions allowing the CloudWatch monitoring service to publish the flow log data to the CloudWatch log group. Once the log group has been created, you can publish multiple flow logs to the same log group.

Figure 3-25   Flow log storage location choices

If you create a flow log for a subnet or a VPC, each network interface present in the VPC or subnet is monitored. Launching additional instances into your subnets after a flow log has been created results in new log streams for each new network interface any network traffic flows.

Certain traffic is not logged in a flow log, including AWS DNS server traffic, Windows license activation, instant metadata requests, the Amazon Time Sync Service, reserved IP address traffic, DHCP traffic, and traffic across a PrivateLink interface.

Any AWS service that uses EC2 instances with network interfaces can take advantage of flow logs. Supporting services also include ELB, Amazon RDS, Amazon ElastiCache, Amazon Redshift, EMR, and Amazon Work Spaces. Each of these services is hosted on an instance with network interfaces.

MAKE SURE TO WATCH THE COMPANION VIDEO "VPC FLOW LOGS."

Peering VPCs

Working in the AWS cloud, it is incredibly easy to end up with multiple VPCs. It's quite common to find that a single company has many AWS accounts. This can be a management nightmare, especially if separate accounts and separate VPCs might need to be connected to share resources or common services such as monitoring or authentication, to name but a couple of the options available. Thankfully, we can create networking connections between VPCs through a process called *peering*, enabling you to route traffic between VPCs that have been peered together.

Peering can also be carried out between your own account VPCs or between a VPC assigned to another AWS account. Peered VPCs can also reside in completely different regions. Data traffic between VPCs peered in different regions is encrypted using what's called *AEAD encryption*, the authenticated encryption with associated data protocol. AWS manages the entire encryption process and supplies and rotates the encryption keys.

A peering connection is not the same as a gateway or VPN connection. Instead, peering is set up by first sending an invitation from one VPC to the other VPC; the invitation must be accepted before the peering connection is established. Peering within the same AWS account will use each VPC's ID for identification. Peering VPCs between different AWS accounts requires both the account ID and the VPC ID.

Establishing a Peering Connection

The VPC that starts the peering process is defined as the *requester VPC*, defining the owner of the VPC that would like to establish a peering connection, and the *acceptor VPC*, or the VPC and account owner that needs to accept the request to establish a peer, as shown in Figure 3-26. Here are the basic steps for peering:

1. The owner of the requester VPC first sends a request to the owner of the acceptor VPC.

2. The acceptor VPC owner accepts the VPC peering connection request.

3. The peering connection is activated.

4. Security group rules are updated within each VPC to ensure proper traffic routing to and from the VPCs that have been peered together.

5. Route tables to allow the flow of traffic that needs to be updated to allow communications between two VPCs.

The acceptor VPC might be a VPC that is in your AWS account and therefore one you own, or it could be another AWS account's VPC. This relationship flexibility is important because single companies can have many developers, each with their own VPCs within their AWS account. Another scenario to consider: it could be a third-party service provider that has developed an application that's entirely hosted in a private separate VPC infrastructure, such as a monitoring service or a disaster recovery service.

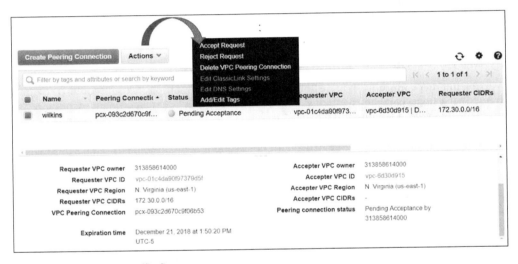

Figure 3-26   Peering traffic flow

Perhaps you would like to subscribe to their hosted service; after you sign up with the service provider, you are invited to create a peering connection with their VPC. This is exactly what Amazon is hoping service providers take advantage of: peered VPCs and PrivateLink connections. PrivateLink endpoints are discussed later in this chapter.

A peering connection will not be able to be established if the CIDR blocks for each VPC to be peered are not distinct—that is, the CIDR ranges overlap or are the same defined range. For example, if each VPC used the Launch VPC wizard and accepted the proposed IP address ranges, there could be future IP address conflicts when peering is attempted. Listed next are some additional considerations for peering VPCs:

- VPC peering connections cannot be created between VPCs that have matching or overlapping IPv4 or IPv6 CIDR blocks.

- More than one VPC peering connection between the same two VPCs is not allowed.

Inter-region VPC peering limitations to be aware of include these:

- Public IPv4 DNS hostnames cannot be resolved from instances on one side of the peered connection to a private IPv4 address on the other side of the peered connection.

- IPv6 communication is not supported.

- The maximum transmission unit (MTU) across the VPC peering connection is 1500 bytes; jumbo frames are not supported.

- Security group rules cannot reference a VPC security group across a peered connection; directing outbound traffic from one side of a peered connection to a security group on the other side of the peered connection is not allowed. A VPN or a Direct Connect connection to a corporate network across a peered connection is not allowed.

- An Internet connection from a private subnet to a NAT device in a public subnet cannot travel across a peered connection to an AWS service such as Dynamo DB or S3. Another example: VPC A is connected to the corporate network using a Direct Connect connection. Users at the head office cannot route through the Direct Connect connection to VPC A and then continue across the peered connection to VPC B. However, they can connect through the Direct Connect connection to VPC A resources.

A VPC peering connection is always a one-to-one relationship between two VPCs. Transitive peering relationships are not supported.

A VPC can have multiple peering relationships with other VPCs, but each peering relationship is always a direct, one-to-one relationship.

Gateway VPC Endpoints

If you're securely operating within a VPC, you probably wouldn't think of accessing Amazon storage such as an S3 bucket or DynamoDB across the Internet as a viable option. However, until a few years ago at AWS, you had to go out across the Internet to access these storage resources. Even though there were secure HTTPS endpoints to access these resources, you still were using the public Internet as the carrier.

We know that EC2 instances hosted within a VPC on private subnets won't have direct Internet access. And typically, updates are performed by communicating with a NAT service hosted on the public subnet, but direct access to other public services is not allowed.

You may be working in an industry that has high compliance and security restrictions that prevent you from accessing public-facing services from the Internet. So how does one get access to S3 storage, DynamoDB tables, or other AWS services while remaining on AWS's private network? The answer is through a private VPC endpoint. VPC endpoints are defined as a gateway, or interface endpoint.

VPC endpoints allow you to connect VPC subnets to an ever-expanding list of AWS services without requiring an Internet gateway, a VPN connection, or a peering connection be set up first. Endpoints are another AWS service designed as a horizontally scaled redundant, highly available service; endpoints scale up when under load from user requests and are designed to be highly available. After all, it's a managed cloud service.

VPC endpoints are controlled by an endpoint policy, which is another name for an IAM resource policy that is attached when you first create the endpoint. IAM stands for identity and access management; IAM policies define the exact permissions allowed or denied. Access to either S3 or Dynamo DB is carried out across a gateway VPC endpoint; the traffic flow is from the private IPv4 address of the instance directly to the selected storage service, as shown in Figure 3-27. Traffic using private VPC endpoints never leaves the AWS private network.

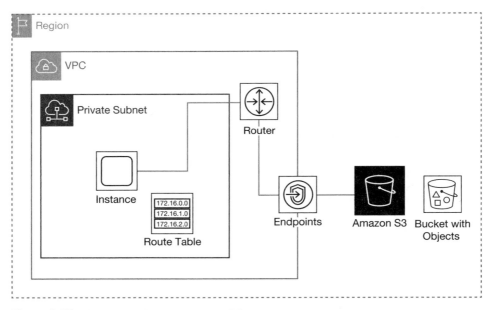

Figure 3-27   Gateway endpoint access to S3

A private VPC gateway endpoint sits in the middle of the source and destination acting as a secure tunnel connection; for example, the S3 gateway connection sits between the instance running a Web application and the S3 data location. S3 and DynamoDB are still accessed utilizing their public IP address location; however, each service is connected directly to the VPC through the private endpoint connection. This may sound confusing. You may be thinking, why don't the gateway services being accessed have a private IP address connection? The path across the endpoint is private, but the destination address doesn't change. However, it's accessed by a private network connection rather than a public connection. Here are steps for creating a gateway endpoint:

1. From the VPC console, select Endpoints, Create Endpoint.

2. Select the desired gateway endpoint (Amazon S3, DynamoDB, or other options if available).

3. Select the VPC and subnets where access is required.

4. Select the route table.

5. Modify the default endpoint policy to match security needs.

6. Update the security groups and network ACLs as necessary.

Endpoint policies are used to define the endpoint access rules and, as mentioned, these policies are IAM resource policies that are established when the endpoint is being created. The default policy allows full access to the service; this is one of those defaults that should be evaluated and changed if necessary.

Note that the defined endpoint policy does not overrule any IAM user policies or S3 bucket policies that are in force. Instead, endpoint policies are controlling access from the VPC through the endpoint to the service from the instance, as shown in Figure 3-28. This resource policy is using a condition defined by the statement **aws:sourcevpc**, which defines the specific VPC that is only allowed access to specific resources.

```
{
  "Version": "2012-10-17",
  "Id": "Policy1415115669152",
  "Statement": [
  {
  "Sid": "Access-from-specific-VPC-only",
  "Principal": "*",
  "Action": "s3:*",
  "Effect": "Deny",
  "Resource": "expenses": {
  "aws:sourceVpc": "vpc-111bbb22"
  }
  }
  }
  ]
}
```

Figure 3-28   Controlling access with an endpoint policy

Interface VPC Endpoints

The newest form of a VPC endpoint supported by AWS is denoted by the term *interface* powered by technology called PrivateLink. The "interface" is a network adapter designated with a private IP address. Not all AWS services are yet supported by interface endpoint connections; however, the long-term goal is to make all AWS services accessible through private interface endpoints.

AWS resources with an interface connection appear to be in your VPC because they are accessed using a private IP address from the linked VPC. If PrivateLink resources are being utilized in a VPC with multiple AZs, multiple private IP addresses will be used, one IP address per availability zone. For customers using Direct Connect to link their on-premise data center with AWS resources, there is also a bonus: AWS-hosted data records and other services can be accessible from your on-premise network.

A Terra Firma developer could sit in his office at work developing applications; the key component, the data records, are being accessed privately during development across the fiber Direct Link connection, as shown in Figure 3-29. Once the application is finished and in production, both the application and data records can continue to be accessed privately through the interface connection from the head office.

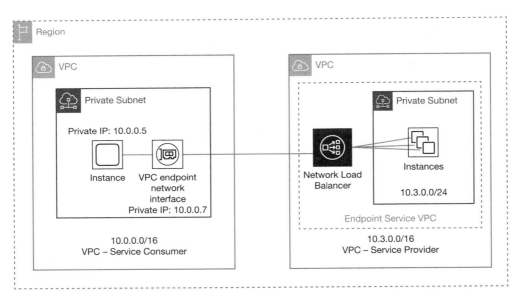

Figure 3-29   Using interface VPC endpoints

There's an elastic IP address, defined as a private static IP address behind every interface connection. Until the PrivateLink service was introduced, an EIP was always defined as a static public IP address. An EIP is now defined as either a static public or a static private IP address, depending on the AWS service.

Most large corporations considering a move to the cloud have massive levels of paranoia when it comes to their data records being stored in the cloud and accessed publicly. In addition, some applications are not going to move to the public cloud anytime soon. For many corporations, the only cloud design that's acceptable is a private hybrid design. PrivateLink endpoint connections combined with high-speed 10 Gbps Direct Connect connections delivers speed, security, and AWS services in a totally private environment. Direct Connect is discussed at the end of this chapter.

> **Note**
>
> Current private endpoints to AWS services includes Kinesis, EC2 Instances, ELB, EC2 Systems Manager, KMS, and Service Catalog, with many more AWS services due to be supported soon.

With no public connectivity, the AWS services that are being accessed using PrivateLink are fully protected from any public attacks, including DDoS attacks because the private interface endpoints are just not reachable from the Internet. When you create an endpoint inside your VPC, the service names are protected because Route 53 DNS services send you to the private endpoint location, ignoring any public routes that also may be advertised. Private endpoints also have regional zonal names designed for keeping traffic within the region, which allows customers to isolate traffic within a specific AZ. Zonal endpoints could also potentially save you additional data transfer charges and latency issues.

The hardware powering interface endpoints is publicly called PrivateLink but internally, AWS calls this new network hardware HyperPlane, which is a massively scalable fault-tolerant distributed system designed for managing VPC network connections. It resides in the fabric of the VPC networking layer, where AWS's software-defined networking is deployed and it's able to make transactional decisions in microseconds. When a VPC interface endpoint is created, it is associated with several virtual hyperplane nodes that intercept network communications at the VPC networking layer and quickly decide what to do with each request. If the request is made to a private endpoint, the transactional decision and the shared state are applied in milliseconds.

MAKE SURE TO WATCH THE COMPANION VIDEO "UNDERSTANDING ENDPOINTS."

Endpoint Services with PrivateLink

Using the PrivateLink technology, AWS hopes to help provide private SaaS services to corporations, as shown in Figure 3-30. The owner of each private SasS service is defined as a *service provider* and the owner of the interface endpoint the *service consumer*; the consumer of the service. Private SaaS services could include monitoring service and disaster recovery services. There really is no limit to the possibilities that are being developed and offered.

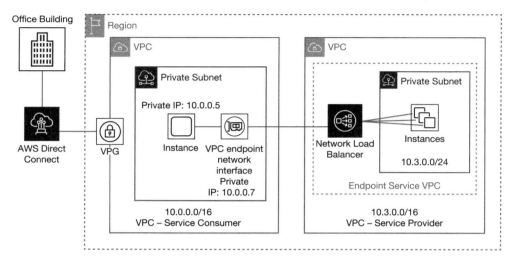

Figure 3-30   PrivateLink endpoints

The customer who wants to access the service makes a request to the vendor; once that request is accepted, a peering connection is established with the customer's VPC. Now the customers can access the service provider's service through the peering connection. To handle access to the subscribed service, behind the "interface" connection is a private Network Load Balancer (NLB) positioned at the entrance hosted service. Third-party micro-service architectures could also be hosted within a private VPC. To the client it's a micro-service, to the service vendor it's a massive fault-tolerant service that scales and fails over as necessary. The service provider VPC can follow the same best practices as recommended by AWS for creating fault-tolerant applications hosted in a VPC. This exact process is how Amazon provides load-balancing services to multiple customers within each region. Applications can be designed with availability targets located in each AZ.

Depending on the tenancy requirements of the customer, for a single-tenant mode of operation, a private NLB could be created for every client customer. Multitenant designs could allow multiple customers to use the same NLB service. There are several additional choices available to separate endpoint traffic from VPCs in a multitenant design:

- Use separate account/password security tokens at the application level.

- Use separate Network Load Balancers (NLB) and different listener ports.

- Utilize the ProxyProtocolV2 preamble, which adds a header to each connection that lists the ID of the destination endpoint.

Note

The costs for PrivateLink are split between the provider and the customer. The provider side pays for the NLB costs. The client side pays for PrivateLink endpoint costs.

The steps for creating an Interface PrivateLink endpoint follow:

1. From the VPC console, select Endpoint Services, Create Endpoint.

2. Select the desired Interface endpoint.

3. Select the VPC and subnets where access is required.

4. Select Enable Private DNS Name if required.

5. Select Security Group.

6. Update route tables, security groups, and network ACLs as necessary.

VPC Connectivity

Connecting a VPC to an external location requires the creation of a public door for direct Internet access, a private door for private access to your corporate data center, or perhaps a private endpoint, which allows connectivity with other VPCs or service providers. We've already talked about peering and endpoints; let's look at public and private connectivity starting with connections to the Internet using the Internet gateway (IGW) service.

Internet Gateway: The Public Door

Before traffic can flow to or from the Internet for Instances hosted on a public subnet within a VPC you must attach an Internet gateway (IGW) to the desired VPC. At AWS, an IGW is hosted by a massive horizontally scaled and highly available server: the standard AWS design criteria farm composed of custom hardware devices AWS calls Blackfoot devices. The IGW service is an example of a hosted micro-service. You may first quibble with this definition, but when you order an IGW, that's exactly what you are ordering: a tiny chunk of the overall IGW service itself. You don't know how the IGW exactly works, and you don't really need to know all the fine details other than it works and continues to work. This mind-set is the same for any service that you order from Amazon, whether you are ordering a gateway service, the ELB services, or auto scaling; we are ordering a service and expect it to function as advertised.

After creation, you need to associate the IGW service with the desired VPC, as shown in Figure 3-31. The IGW still won't be accessible until your route tables have been updated with a route to allow the appropriate subnets to send their public traffic to the IGW. Typically, the default destination route assigned to an Internet gateway is 0.0.00/0, which may be fine for a public-facing application available to the public. However, you can narrow the scope of access to a specific range of public IP addresses from your company, other elastic IP addresses, or specific BYOIP addresses. Public traffic that flows through the IGW also has an additional layer of protection because NAT is performed on all outgoing public traffic from instances with public IP addresses communicating across the Internet.

As we have discussed, if the default VPC is used, the IGW is already enabled and set up with a route table entry for the public subnets. In addition, using either of the first two options to create public subnets with the Launch VPC Wizard from the VPC console creates the public subnets, attaches an IGW, and adds route table entries for the IGW to the main route table.

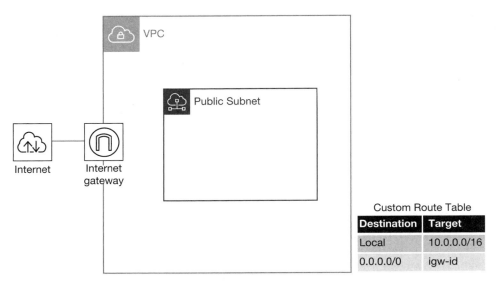

Figure 3-31   Internet gateway routing

> **Note**
>
> Subnets associated with a route table pointing to an Internet gateway are always public subnets.

MAKE SURE TO WATCH THE COMPANION VIDEO "ADDING AN INTERNET GATEWAY."

Egress-Only Internet Gateway

If you require outbound communication over IPv6 from your instances to the Internet using IPv6, you can use an egress-only Internet gateway (EOIG), as shown in Figure 3-32. Internally, the EOIG is a horizontally-scaled, redundant, and highly available service that allows outbound communication over IPv6 but prevents any communication from the Internet from initiating an IPv6 connection with your instances. The design of the EOIG is stateful, meaning that traffic that is forwarded from an instance to the Internet will have its traffic forwarded back to the instance that made the request.

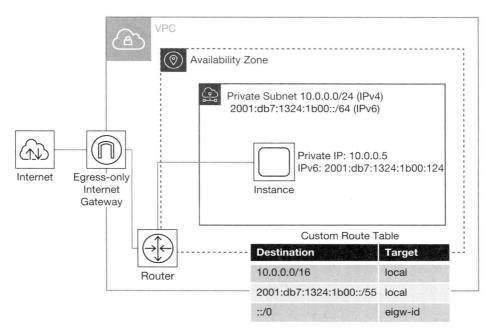

Figure 3-32   EOIG wiring

VPN Connections

It's entirely possible that requiring public access for AWS resources is not part of your network design. Many companies design solutions utilizing a private hybrid design, where their corporate data center is securely connected to the AWS cloud without using the Internet as a public communication medium.

Using a VPN connection to connect to your VPC provides a high level of security using an IPsec VPN connection. A VPN connection is a site-to-site tunnel connection between your VPC and your corporate network. But before your VPN connections can be set up and connected from your corporate data center to a VPC from your remote network, you need to attach a "private door," called a virtual private gateway (VPG), that is directly attached to the VPC where access is desired.

> **Note**
> Both the IGW and the VPG are directly attached to the VPC.

Just the attaching of the VPG does not provide access; you still must manually add access to the VPG through a route table entry before access is allowed. Routing types supported are either static routes or dynamic routes across a VPN tunnel using the border gateway protocol

(BGP). VPN connections with a single static route won't have a failover option, as shown in Figure 3-33.

Dynamically routed VPN connections can reroute traffic as necessary to other available routes. Adhering to Amazon's standards of redundancy, each VPN connection is created with two VPN endpoints on the Amazon side, and each tunnel is assigned with a unique public IP address. IPv4 IPsec VPNs are supported; currently, IPv6 VPN connections are not supported.

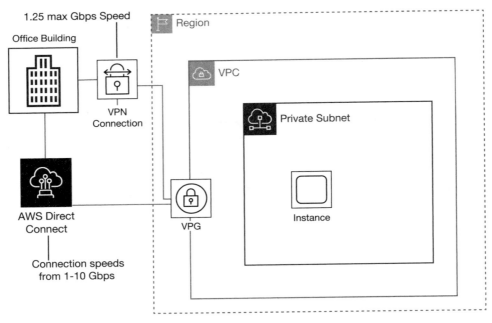

Figure 3-33   VPN connection choices

> **Note**
> There are two choices when connecting your data center to AWS:
> 1. A secure VPN connection
> 2. A fast and secure connection using a Direct Connect high-speed private connection

Virtual Private Gateway

You need to understand several components before you create and complete your VPN connections. The virtual private gateway, the customer gateway, and the VPN connection are shown in Figure 3-34.

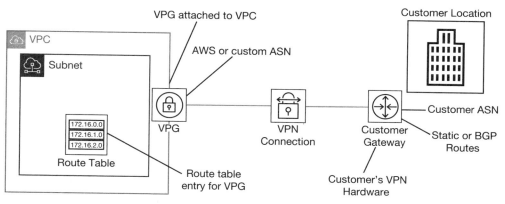

Figure 3-34   VPG connection components

The VPG is the VPN concentrator on the Amazon side of the connection closest to the VPC. During the configuration of a VPG connection, you can accept the default private anonymous system number (ASN) provided by AWS or specify your own custom number. After creation, the VPG needs to be attached to the desired VPC, and appropriate routes need to be added to the route tables to enable communication with the VPG.

Customer Gateway

On the opposite side of the VPN connection, on the customer side, resides the customer gateway. Most customers use a hardware device for their VPN connections, although you could use a software appliance. A key concept: the only hardware in a VPN connection is on the customer side of the connection. Configuration steps for most popular customer hardware are typically provided by AWS; there are many popular supported devices complete with the required configuration information. Examples of devices that AWS supports include Cisco, Checkpoint, Fortinet, Juniper, and Palo Alto. Check the VPC FAQ at AWS for current details on the devices supported as evidence that additional devices are ever changing.

When creating a customer gateway, you need to enter the public IP address location of your hardware device and indicate the type of routing to be used: either static or dynamic. If you choose dynamic, you need to enter your ASN for BGP communications. If your customer gateway is behind a NAT device, you need the public IP address of the NAT device. Once connections are complete on the customer and the AWS side, traffic generated from the customer side of the VPN connection initiates the VPN tunnel, as shown in Figure 3-35. Before creating a VPN connection, the customer gateway needs to be created.

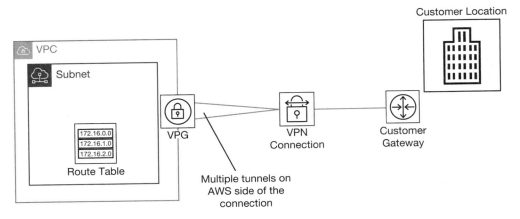

Figure 3-35   VPN tunnel connections

> **Note**
> The maximum IPsec VPN throughput at AWS is 1.25 GB per second.

VPN Connections

When a VPN connection is created, you are prompted to download the configuration file that matches your customer gateway device. Information contained in the document includes device and tunnel configuration. When choosing VPN routing, the best option is to choose dynamic routing using BGP sessions. BGP-capable devices fail over to the second VPN tunnel on the AWS side if the first tunnel goes down.

You can specify the range of inside IP addresses inside the VPN tunnel using the /30 CIDR block from the 169.254.0.0 /16 range. The chosen pre-shared key (PSK) can be between 8 and 64 characters but can't start with a zero (0). If you change your mind about the inside tunnel IP address or the PSK you have selected after you have created your VPN connection, you must delete the VPN connection and create a new one. Modifications are not allowed for existing VPN connections.

A VPN connection at AWS is managed. There are several features to be aware of when creating a VPN connection:

- NAT-T NAT traversal is supported.
- 4-byte ASN numbers are supported.
- Cloud Watch metrics include TunnelState, TunnelDataIn, and TunnelDataOut.
- Encryption options include AES 256-bit, SHA-2 hashes, and DH groups.
- Tunnel options are customized for inside IP addresses and PSK values.
- Custom private ASN numbers are on the Amazon side of a BGP session.

VPN CloudHub

If you have multiple customer locations, you can choose the AWS VPN CloudHub. Multiple remote sites can communicate with the VPC and with each other. CloudHub design follows the traditional hub-and-spoke model. CloudHub is not a new connection feature, and there's no additional speed added because each multiple connection is a separate connection. But it does work and may be an option if your branch offices are small.

On the AWS side, there is still a single virtual private gateway; however, there are multiple customer gateways due to the multiple connection paths shown in Figure 3-36. Each customer gateway needs a unique BGP ASN number to differentiate its location, and each site can have overlapping IP ranges. Remember, the bandwidth of the VPN connection is not that fast. It maxes out at 1.25 Gbps.

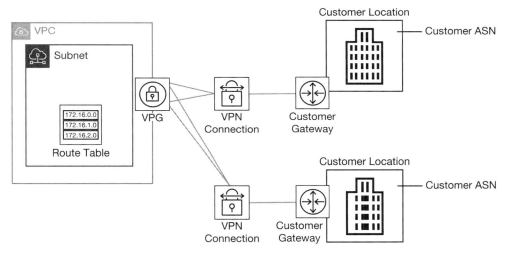

Figure 3-36   VPN CloudHub design

MAKE SURE TO WATCH THE COMPANION VIDEO "CREATING VPN CONNECTIONS."

Understanding Route Propagation

After route table entries have been created allowing EC2 instances to communicate with VPN connections from the customer gateway, you can enable the automatic provisioning of the available routes through a process called route propagation. To enable automatic route propagation, from the properties of the route table, choose the Route Propagation tab, and then select the VPG to assign to the route table.

If static routes are available, when a VPN connection is activated, the static addresses for your customer data center and the CIDR ranges for the connected VPC are automatically added to the route table. Each VPN connection created in AWS will have two tunnels designed for failover on the Amazon side of the connection. Each tunnel will have a unique security association (SA) that identifies each tunnel's inbound and outbound traffic.

Therefore, there are four SAs for the design that uses the default VPN connection of two endpoints on the AWS side with two unique tunnel connections at AWS, and a single connection on the customer side. For this example, any traffic from your network can access any CIDR range on your VPN. To better control your traffic, you can choose to use dynamic routes with tunnels that you define. If dynamic routing is in place, the defined BGP advertisements are automatically added to the route table.

Direct Connect

The purpose of AWS Direct Connect is to connect your internal corporate network to a Direct Connect (DC) location over a private high-speed fiber connection with no Internet connection. This high-speed highway can be ordered with port speeds up to 10 Gbps. There are a range of other slower speeds available from other partners supporting Direct Connect connections.

Each DC connection ordered is a single dedicated connection from your routers to the routers at AWS. If a DC second connection is ordered, it is also provisioned on redundant Amazon routers. If a DC connection fails, traffic fails over to the second DC link automatically. This is an expensive option, but perhaps desired availability makes this an option worth considering.

Direct connections only support 1000BASE-LX or 10GBASE-LR connections over single-mode fiber using the Ethernet transport, using 1310nm connectors.

The connection itself is made using a single fiber pair running from a physical piece of customer equipment that must be in the same facility as the AWS Direct Connect inter-connect.

The hosted connections are connections provided by the AWS Direct Connect Partner from the customer data center to the facility where AWS "Direct Connections" can be made. The available types of connection to the Amazon partner from the customer site is totally up to what is supported by the Amazon partner.

After a DC connection is in place, you can create virtual interfaces to a public AWS service such as S3 buckets or connect privately to a VPC.

To sign up for Direct Connect, from the console, complete the following steps:

1. Request a connection, specifying the port speed and the Direct Connect location where the connection will be terminated. If your port speed is less than 1 Gbps, you must contact an APN partner in your geographical location and order a hosted connection at the bandwidth you desire. Once this connection is completed, the setup of Direct Connect can continue in the console.

2. Once AWS has approved your connection, a letter of authorization and connecting facility assignment (LOA-CFA) can be downloaded and presented to your provider authorizing them to create a network connection to AWS; this is typically called a cross-connect.

3. Create virtual interfaces for connections to either your VPC or to a public service not hosted in the VPC.

4. After virtual interfaces have been created, download the router configuration file, which contains router configuration information to successfully connect to either your private or your public virtual interface.

This is a complicated topic for this book; only the big-picture summary is being provided here. There are many considerations for Direct Connect, including your location, the AWS region you are operating in, the level of redundancy required, and many available options depending on the number of VPCs, public AWS services, or Direct Connect gateways that you may want to connect, as shown in Figure 3-37.

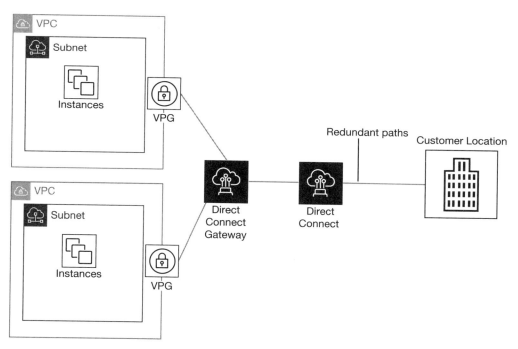

Figure 3-37   Direct Connect options

Route 53

Route 53 is Amazon's DNS service and, of course, it's highly scalable and highly available. Its primary job is to route your end users to hosted applications at AWS. These applications and resources are typically hosted behind AWS services with DNS names that are stored and referenced through Route 53, such as an ELB load balancer, CloudFront, Amazon's CDN, or S3 bucket. Domain names can also be registered with Route 53 directly, or, domain names can be transferred from other registrars. Amazon is also a reseller of the registrar Gandi. Domain names can be transferred to and managed by Route 53.

Route 53 also manages your public DNS records that are connected to public IP addresses; these can be from the short-term public IP address pool provided by AWS, and elastic IP addresses, BYOIP public address ranges, and domain names that are hosted at AWS.

In addition to standard DNS services, Route 53 offers health checking and traffic-steering services for routing selected traffic to a healthy endpoint in multiple AWS regions.

You can also use Route 53 to host a private domain that you've created within a VPC. Each private hosted domain's zone information is assigned to four virtual Route 53 name servers that store the DNS records for your domain.

If you want to migrate from another third-party DNS service provider, exporting your current DNS settings to their own file allows you to import your records into Route 53. Keep in mind that the imported zone file must be empty except for the default NS and SOA records. And DNS is a funny world; if your records are not in a standard BIND format, strictly adhering to RFC 1034 and 1035, there could be migration issues.

> **Note**
>
> By default, each Route 53 account is assigned a soft limit of 500 hosted zones and 10,000 resource record sets per hosted zone; you can increase these values upon request.

Amazon supports a DNS record type called an Alias record. Alias records map resource records within your hosted zone to a variety of AWS services including ELB, CloudFront distributions, and Elastic Beanstalk environments. Alias records also allow you to route traffic from one record within a hosted zone to another record. Alias records as detailed in Table 3-12 work internally like a CNAME record, where DNS domain names are mapped to the desired target resource. However, the interesting difference between an alias record and a CNAME record, as shown in Figure 3-38, is that alias records can contain multiple records associated with a single resource name.

Table 3-12   **Alias Records vs CNAME at AWS**

CNAME Record	**Alias Record**
Not supported for zone apex record	Supported for zone apex record
Route 53 charges for CNAME queries	No charge for alias
Queries are always re-directed	Name and type of alias record must match
Points to any DNS record	Points only to AWS resources
nslookup shows CNAME record	Alias shows as record type (A, AAAA)

Alias records are also used to point your zone apex (your registered root domain name) to a variety of AWS services, including load balancers, static websites hosted by an S3 bucket, and CloudFront distributions. The resources for each of these services can change due to the scaling up or down of the compute resources of each redundant service. With alias records, Route 53 has the changes covered.

For example, the target resource could be a load balancer or a CloudFront distribution. As you know, the load balancer service is designed for failover. As a result, when Route 53 receives a query for a load balancer, an alias record is used to point to the load-balancing resource. Using an alias record allows Route 53 to respond if necessary with more than one IP address for the load-balancing service in times of internal changes to the service. What happens when we query a CloudFront distribution? The alias record provides Route 53 with additional redundancy as multiple records pointing to the multiple IP addresses for the edge servers for accessing your content can be provided, as shown in Figure 3-38.

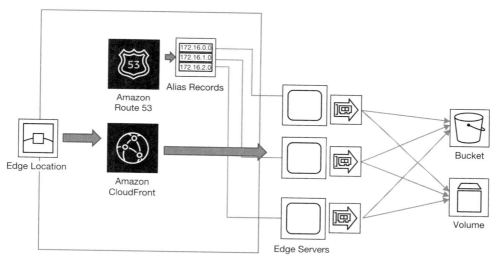

Figure 3-38   Alias records and target AWS services

Using a CNAME instead of an Alias record, only one DNS record could be referenced per service. Route 53 automatically recognizes any changes in the AWS resource when alias records are used to route traffic. Back to our load-balancing example: if your load-balancer fails, Route 53 automatically sends traffic to another load balancer's IP address.

In addition, CNAMEs queries at AWS cost you money; when querying AWS resources using alias records, there's no charge. However, at Amazon an alias record only points to a supported AWS resource or to another DNS record within the hosted zone where the alias record has been created.

Route 53 Routing Options

Route 53 supports a variety of routing protocols, including weighted round robin (WRR), latency-based routing (LBR), and Geo DNS, as shown in Table 3-13.

- WRR allows you to assign weights to resource record sets. Changing the weight of one record in a set of records to a higher number than the other records in the resource record set tells the end user that the resource with the higher number can take more traffic. Assigning values is complicated but is incredibly useful in routing traffic when desired from site A to site B.

- LBR is utilized when you are balancing application performance across multiple regions. Record sets contain multiple AWS endpoints, and Route 53 will do the latency math and determine the best endpoint for the user request.

- Geo DNS gets a little fancier and allows you to balance user requests to specific endpoints based on the geographical location the user request came from. Geo DNS relies on global records with multiple responses defined for all DNS queries. With Geo DNS, it is possible to customize the destination content to regions, and countries within each region. You can also control content based on language preferences, or in the case of compliance, define mandated endpoint locations.

Table 3-13   **Route 53 Routing Options**

Routing Options	Details
Simple	For a single resource; a Web instance
Failover	Active-passive failover; from one resource to another
Geolocation	Route traffic based on user's location
Geo-proximity	Route traffic based on location of resources
Latency	Route traffic to AWS resources with the least latency
Multi-value answer	Answer queries with multiple healthy records
Weighted routing	Route a percentage of traffic to resources; Blue-Green

Each of these routing protocols can be combined in a custom traffic policy design that Amazon calls Traffic Flow. Policies can also pinpoint resource location based on the exact physical location using static IP addresses.

Route 53 Health Checks

What's the point of having DNS records that point to resources that are not functional? That's why there's a need for health checks and failover. Route 53 constantly verifies that your applications are reachable and available through health checks. When health checks fail, requests for resources fail over to the alternate location.

Alias records created with the Evaluate Target Health parameter set to true that point to a load balancer DNS name result in Route 53 managing the health check of the load balancer automatically. Health checks are using DNS names, not IP addresses; for a hosted cloud service, IP addresses are always going to change. But we don't worry about these changes when they occur because we are using DNS names and not IP addresses.

DNS failover can also point to a backup site location such as an S3 bucket or an external location when your VPC becomes unavailable for whatever reason, as shown in Figure 3-39. Internally, Route 53 monitors failed endpoints; once a failed endpoint passes its health check, Route 53 updates its DNS records accordingly. Health checks are supported for HTTPS, HTTP, and TCP.

Health checks can also be carried out using the built-in monitoring service CloudWatch using many defined metrics.

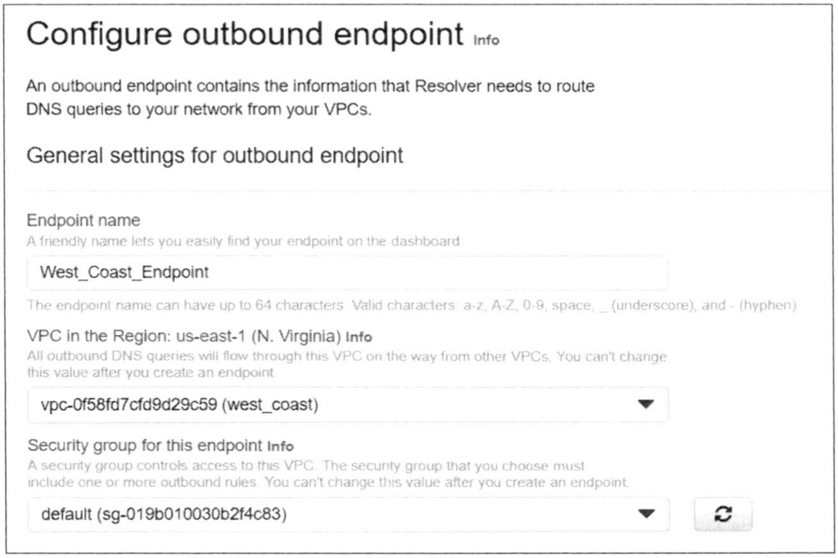

Configure outbound endpoint Info

An outbound endpoint contains the information that Resolver needs to route DNS queries to your network from your VPCs.

General settings for outbound endpoint

Endpoint name
A friendly name lets you easily find your endpoint on the dashboard

West_Coast_Endpoint

The endpoint name can have up to 64 characters. Valid characters: a-z, A-Z, 0-9, space, _ (underscore), and - (hyphen)

VPC in the Region: us-east-1 (N. Virginia) Info
All outbound DNS queries will flow through this VPC on the way from other VPCs. You can't change this value after you create an endpoint.

vpc-0f58fd7cfd9d29c59 (west_coast)   ▼

Security group for this endpoint Info
A security group controls access to this VPC. The security group that you choose must include one or more outbound rules. You can't change this value after you create an endpoint.

default (sg-019b010030b2f4c83)   ▼   ⟳

Figure 3-39   Route 53 failover options

Using DNS with a VPC: Private DNS Zones

Route 53 allows you to have authoritative DNS services hosted within your VPCs with no Internet exposure. After creating a private hosted zone, Route 53 only returns records when queried from within the associated VPCs. Route 53 health checks are also supported for resource record sets within each private DNS hosted zone.

If you want to route traffic for one of your domains and its subdomains that are contained within a VPC, the first task is to create a private hosted zone in Route 53. Within the private zone, you then create Resource record sets that list the resources that Route 53 will direct queries for your domain to. To use a private hosted zone with the VPC, the following settings must be set to true:

> *enableDNSHostnames*

> *enableDnsSupport*

DNS Hostnames

Each custom VPC has attributes for DNS that can be customized. The defaults, or the attributes that will be applied, depend on how the VPC was created. One of the words most overused at AWS is *default*.

If you are using the main VPC Wizard located on the VPC Dashboard, both VPC DNS attributes are set to true.

If you use the AWS CLI or use the VPC link displayed on the Your VPCs landing page Wizard to create the VPC, the attributes are defined differently, as shown in Table 3-14. These attributes determine whether each instance receives a public DNS hostname and if DNS resolution using Route 53 is supported.

Table 3-14 **DNS VPC Attributes**

VPC DNS Attribute	Default VPC	CLI, API, or AWS SDK	Your VPC Wizard	VPC Wizard
Enable DNS hostname (Public)	True	False	False	True
Enable DNS support	True	True	True	True

If both attributes in Table 3-14 are set to true, your instance receives a public DNS hostname, and Route 53 resolves any Amazon-provided private DNS hostnames.

If either or both attributes in Table 3-14 are false, your instance will not receive a public DNS hostname, and Route 53 will not resolve the private DNS hostname provided by Amazon.

If you have private IP addresses provided by AWS, the private DNS hostname resolves to the private IPv4 address of the instance. The private DNS hostname can be used to communicate between instances hosted on the same network.

If you are using the default VPC to deploy instances into, each instance will have a public and private DNS hostname that will correspond to the public and private IPv4 addresses assigned to the instance. Keep in mind that Route 53 is responsible for routing requests to specific domains and applications hosted at AWS. Best practice is that user requests should be routed to a load balancer and not directly to the instance. Therefore, DNS resolution directly to the instance is not required.

In Conclusion

Whew. Okay, this was a long chapter, but I don't really think there's anything we could've cut out for understanding of networking at AWS. Certainly, we could go a lot deeper, but it's important to get the bedrock architecture components understood. Then you can sit back and think about what you are doing with networking in your own data center and how that differentiates between what you're going to have to do at AWS. You can't call up AWS folks and say, "Hey, I'm not doing it your way." That's a short one-sided conversation. Make sure to watch the companion videos to get more details on network deployment at AWS. Then look at the discussion points with your trusted team of tech experts or people at work who are going to be making these types of decisions. And start asking some of these questions out loud and finding out what the answers are from your company's point of view.

Top 10 Discussion Points: Networking Considerations for Security, Failover, and Connectivity

Review this list and then ask the questions out loud. Discuss. Argue. Compromise. Agree or disagree. Only then will you know the real answers.

1. What IP address ranges should I use for my VPC?

2. Why do I need more than one VPC?

3. Why am I using public subnets for my Web servers?

4. Do I have existing Public IP addresses that can be moved to AWS?

5. What AWS networking services can replace existing hardware devices?

6. Are my VPN hardware devices compatible with AWS?

7. Have I finished constructing my security groups required for my two tier or three-tier application?

8. Do I have to use network ACLs to conform with my compliance rules and regulations?

9. Do I have to use elastic IP addresses?

10. Would Direct Connect help my hybrid design connectivity?

4

Compute Services: AWS EC2 Instances

Amazon Elastic Compute Cloud, or the moniker EC2, is a huge topic. The basic EC2 documentation from AWS is currently over a couple of thousand pages because every cloud service AWS offers is powered by some form of compute service, whether it is an instance providing the processing power for your application, a managed service such as the elastic block storage (EBS) storage arrays supporting block storage, or Simple Storage Service (S3) object storage; in the background, there's always some manner of computer power running in the background.

Compute services are also a key component in auto scaling, load balancing services, and networking services. These are all important topics that are important enough to have their own chapters; in this chapter we're going to look at the compute instance and how it is built and hosted, how you launch it, and some of its dependencies. We will also look at pricing, which is a complicated category unto itself, and some of the administrative duties required with creating and maintaining instances.

In this chapter, we will learn about what Amazon provides for virtual machines and virtual hard drives. Because we are working in the Amazon cloud, there will be different names for everything. It doesn't take that long to get used to calling virtual machines *instances* and virtual hard drives *EBS volumes*. There is an amazing amount of choice when it comes to choosing the size of your instances and the type of instance. You can even order an instance that is a bare-metal server now, obliterating the earlier National Institute of Standards and Technology (NIST) definitions of cloud. Let's dig in. The topics for this chapter include the following:

- Virtualization at AWS
- Instances
- Amazon Machine Images
- Instance storage options
- Instance pricing options
- Migration tools

Questions that we will reflect on throughout this chapter regarding the available compute options at AWS are based on our case study Terra Firma:

1. We have a VMware environment on-premise. How can we use our current images at AWS?

2. Can we migrate our database to AWS? If we can, what tools are available?

3. Is there a lot of choice when it comes to virtual machine options?

4. What if we don't want to use virtualization? Are there bare-metal servers available?

5. What's the hypervisor used at AWS?

6. We have some developers who want to spin up resources quickly without having to do a lot of work. Are there any managed services that can speed up the provisioning process?

7. What does AWS mean by the word *backup*?

8. How redundant are EBS volumes?

A Short History of EC2 Virtualization

The purpose of this short history lesson on virtualization is to illustrate the amount of change that has occurred over time with the virtualization process and the hypervisors that AWS currently supports. Amazon builds custom bare-metal hardware for the singular use of hosting EC2 instances; as a result, it tunes its data centers and the hardware and software stack for EC2 instances. This tuning includes the ongoing tweaking and customization of the hypervisors used at AWS: both Xen, which is slowly being deprecated, and KVM, a component of the Nitro hypervisor.

For many years, the standard answer for "what hypervisor does AWS deploy?" was a customized version of the Xen hypervisor. Initial versions offered Xen paravirtualization for the Linux operating system and, over time, the hardware virtual machine (HVM) for support of the Windows operating system. Paravirtualization allows the customization of the Linux operating system kernel, which permits the Linux guest operating system running on EC2 instances to access storage and networking using a *hypercall*, communicating directly to the Xen hypervisor, which in turn called the physical CPU on the bare-metal host carrying out each request.

EC2 instances running Windows were initially hosted differently from Linux using the previously mentioned HVM. HVM virtualization meant that the underlying hardware platform on the host bare-metal server was fully virtualized and accessible by the Windows instance using hardware extensions. Windows clients are completely isolated and unaware of the virtualization process.

Paravirtualization was possible with Linux because it was an open source operating system. On the other hand, Windows remains a closed operating system; therefore, paravirtualization is not possible with Windows EC2 instances. Both of these separate technologies began to be assimilated in 2012.

2012—In 2012, the customized version of Xen used by AWS ran in a hybrid model that installed on Intel processors equipped with hardware virtualization (VT-x). These processors offered faster CPU and memory access. They also used paravirtualized drivers to access the network and storage devices as quickly as possible. These two separate virtualization features were beginning to be combined in a hybrid model called PVHVM (paravirtualization and hardware-assisted virtualization technology combined), as shown in Figure 4-1.

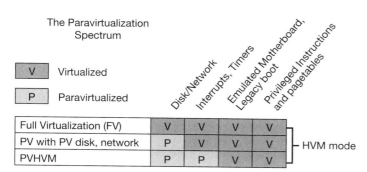

Figure 4-1   PVHVM hybrid model

2013—At the start of 2013, the Xen hypervisor supported a combination of PVHVM drivers and hardware virtualization for the network interfaces called single-route I/O virtualization (SR-IOV). Several EC2 instances also began to offer support for enhanced networking, using SR-IOV, which offered initial speeds of 10 Gbps. Today speeds can reach 25 Gbps, or 100 Gbps with GPU instances. After testing this new network stack, Netflix published test results showing networking processing speeds of close to 2 million packets per second.

2015—AWS introduced the C4 instance, as shown in Figure 4-2, in 2015. Amazon had been working with a startup company called Annapurna Labs, which created custom semiconductor circuits; it is now an AWS company. AWS was interested in Annapurna Labs' application-specific integrated circuit (ASIC) chipsets that provided enhanced networking services and several other custom semiconductor designs, which would greatly increase speeds for storage, networking, and encryption. The C4 instance that used the custom chipsets designed with Annapurna offered such a high level of storage and network performance that EBS-optimized volumes were offered by default at no additional charge; in fact, all new instances AWS offered since the C4 instance was released include EBS-optimized volumes at no additional charge.

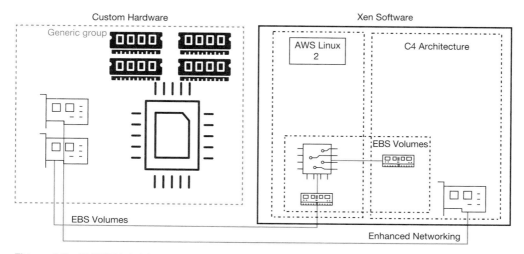

Figure 4-2   PVHVM hybrid model

2016—The X1 instance was released with 128 virtual CPUs (vCPUs) and 2 TB of memory. Custom chipsets allowed access to the high-speed instance storage. An enhanced networking interface that had been specifically designed for EC2 instances was also introduced.

2017—The i3 platform was released in this year. This family of a high-performance instance allowed the offloading of communication, with EBS storage achieving an even higher level of overall performance.

At this point in the redesign cycle, the performance of storage, networking, and management services was vastly improved with the addition of the custom chipsets. Massive increases in speed happened because hardware was replacing software emulation. The next task AWS carried out was replacing the Xen hypervisor with a new lightweight hypervisor called Nitro. I say *lightweight* because several of the emulation tasks and communication jobs that a typical hypervisor would undertake and manage instead were being performed by hardware chipsets.

The C5 instance launched in 2017, as shown in Figure 4-3. It was deployed using the Nitro hypervisor and offloaded the networking, storage, and management tasks such as encryption duties to hardware, greatly reducing the duties of the hypervisor and increasing the speed at which operations were carried out. In this new hypervisor design, there is minimal hardware overload for management of storage, networking, and encryption services; these services are carried out with custom hardware chipsets.

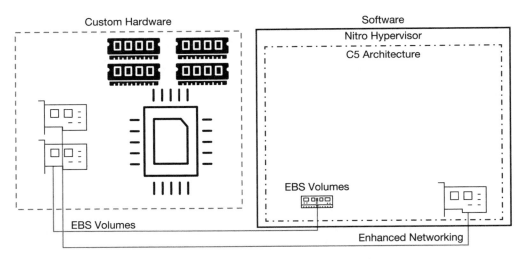

Figure 4-3   C5 instance architecture

The Nitro System

In 2017, the new Nitro hypervisor was launched. As mentioned, the heart of the Nitro hypervisor uses just the KVM core kernel and a streamlined virtual machine manager (VMM). Older KVM emulation components such as QEMU are not used. The term *direct metal access* has been coined by AWS providing the performance equivalent of a bare-metal server. To achieve this goal, AWS designed custom silicon chipsets that use hardware processes for faster access to storage, networking, interrupts, and carrying out security processes such as encryption.

The EC2 instances and the associated hardware storage devices are isolated at the hardware level, providing an additional layer of security. Over time, Nitro will be the only hypervisor used at AWS, except for the AWS i3.metal instances, which don't use a hypervisor but are still called instances. Embedded in the hardware of the new bare-metal instances are the Nitro system components, as shown in Figure 4-4.

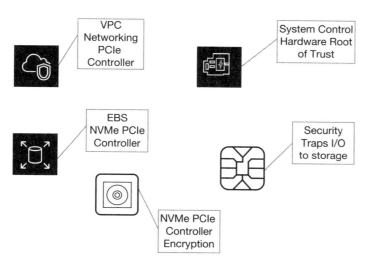

Figure 4-4   Nitro System components

Local NVMe Storage—Custom chipsets provide direct access to high-speed local storage over a Peripheral Component Interconnect (PCI) interface connection, a standard used to connect EC2 instances to the local block storage. All traffic is also transparently encrypted using dedicated local hardware. It's important to realize that the encryption process is now offloaded from the local CPU to local hardware, the Nitro system, greatly speeding up the encryption process at AWS.

Nitro Security Chip—The main component handling security in this design is the Nitro security chip, which, if you're familiar with Intel TXT, is carrying out many of the same security functions: protecting the system's boot process, and monitoring and approving or denying instance request calls for access to the storage resources.

Nitro Networking—Hardware-level networking supports the mapping service for the virtual private cloud (VPC), enhanced networking, and the elastic networking adapter (ENA).

> **Note**
>
> If you are using older versions of Linux, you may still be running virtual machines that require paravirtualization. Although this approach is still possible at AWS, there is only limited support for the older paravirtualization methods, and it is not recommended.
>
> For many years, Linux users were encouraged to use paravirtualization. That is not the case today due to design improvements in both the hypervisor and the hardware platform AWS is currently using. Current generation instances now only support hardware virtual machine (HVM) images. If you still want to use paravirtualization, you will not be able to take advantage of the performance gains of the Nitro system and Nitro hypervisor. You can read more about Amazon machine images (AMIs) later in this chapter.

EC2 Instances

Now that you have some knowledge of how Amazon is designing and retro-fitting its hypervisors, EC2 instances, and bare-metal systems, let's move into a discussion of the instance families at AWS. At AWS, virtual servers are called Elastic Compute Cloud (EC2) instances. At the most basic level, each instance is a virtual server running a version of Windows or Linux. Instances run as a guest operating system hosted by the hypervisor, which in turn is directly installed on a bare-metal server. AWS first launched instances back in August 2006, and there was just one size: the M1.

> **Note**
>
> There are more than 150 instance choices available at AWS.

Each instance is configured at launch with a select amount of memory, vCPU cores, storage, and networking bandwidth. An instance can be sliced and diced in many different patterns and configurations. Regardless of the instance size and type, each configuration has several mandatory parts, as detailed in Figure 4-5.

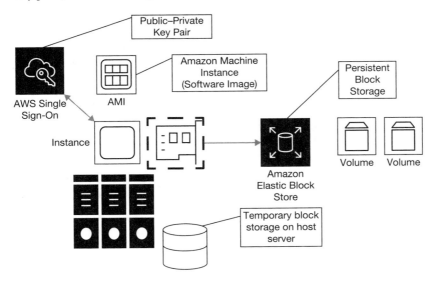

Figure 4-5   Instance architecture and components

The following components are part of each configuration:

- Built by preconfigured images called Amazon machine images
- Authenticated using a unique public/private key pair per instance
- Storage options of persistent block storage and temporary storage volumes
- A mandatory firewall called a Security Group that protects your network interfaces
- Basic or enhanced network adapters
- Shared or dedicated hardware options

Instance Families

Instances are members of several *compute families*, whereby instances are grouped and defined by a name and generation designation. For each instance's name, the first letter that you see is the instance family that it belongs to (see Figure 4-2); this letter describes the resources allocated to the instance and the workloads that the instance is best suited for. The letter also stands for something; for example, the letter *C* stands for compute, *R* for RAM, and *I* for input/output per second (IOPS).

The next number that you see is the generation number. You can think of this number much like a software version number. Therefore, a C5 instance is newer than a C4 instance, and so on. And, interestingly, a newer C5 instance is cheaper than a C4 instance.

Features define the key characteristics of the instance. For example, in c4d; the "d" denotes solid state drives (SSD) for the instance storage. The last component of the instance's name deals with the size of the instance; sometimes this is called a *T-shirt size*. Sizes range from small up to 32 times larger than the smallest size, as shown in Figure 4-6. (The size of an instance is based on the amount of vCPU cores, the amount of RAM, and the amount of allocated network bandwidth.) For example, the C4.8xlarge is eight times larger than the c4.large in areas of vCPU cores, RAM, and network bandwidth.

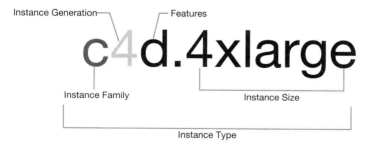

Figure 4-6   Decoding an instance's name

> **Note**
>
> Once an instance has been ordered, the resources (vCPUs, memory, network bandwidth) allocated to an instance are assigned to your account and are never shared with any other AWS customer.

Your on-premise virtual design may overcommit your virtual resources to the available physical resources; therefore, if every virtual machine in your vCenter design was powered on, you possibly wouldn't have enough physical resources to run all your virtual servers at the same time. At AWS, there is no common pool of compute resources constantly being shared among customers; ordered resources are assigned to the customer's AWS account until they are deleted.

The older public cloud concept of the "noisy neighbor" has been redesigned by dedicating the assigned resources to each customer. Running a smaller instance at AWS means you have a smaller portion of the physical server assigned to your instance, whereas running an X32-sized instance means you probably have the entire physical server assigned to you. Regardless of the instance ordered, your allotted memory, CPU cores, storage, and network bandwidth remain isolated for each AWS customer. Because customers are virtually isolated from each other, this isolation also forms a key element of security.

What's a vCPU?

AWS defines the amount of CPU power assigned to each instance as a virtual CPU (vCPU). A vCPU is a part of a physical CPU core. A process called hyperthreading associates two virtual threads to each physical core—an A and a B thread working in a multitasking mode, as shown in Figure 4-7. Think of each physical core as a brain that can be split into two logical brains; each thread is the communication channel linking each instance to a specific amount of processing power. Both Linux and Windows process these virtual threads differently; Linux enumerates the first group of threads (A) before the second group of threads (B); Windows interleaves the threads, selecting first the A and then the B thread. Dividing the vCPU count listed in the EC2 console by 2 will show you the actual physical core count, which might be important if the licensing for your software requires a physical core count, as Oracle databases do.

4 Core CPU / 8 Threads

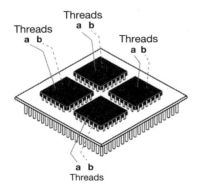

Figure 4-7   Virtual cores

The required core count of your on-premise applications is something to check for before they are migrated to AWS; if hyperthreading is already disabled for your applications running on-premise, you'll probably want to disable this process at AWS. If you're running financial analysis or mechanical design applications, after migrating these types of applications to AWS, you may need to disable hyperthreading on the instance to achieve maximum performance.

> **Note**
>
> To get a listing of the actual core count, visit https://aws.amazon.com/ec2/virtualcores.

Rather than getting overwhelmed by all the choices available in the management console, I suggest you first think of your application and its needs. For initial testing, I'd start with a general-purpose instance that matches your recommended or current specifications for the application. Of course, we must also consider the operating system and its needs. Next, install your application and, if possible, carry out testing on the chosen instance with real user access instead of using a synthetic load-testing tool. Put your instance through its paces as close to a real workload as possible. Remember, you can easily shut off your instance, change its size, and turn it back on and test it again and again until you're happy.

> **Note**
>
> You can run Lstopo on a virtual instance to get a view of the physical topology of the hardware you are running on, the sockets, the level I to level 3 cache, and the physical core mappings.

EC2 Instance Choices

The EC2 console has more than 150 instance types to choose, from general purpose to instances designed for compute, storage, and memory-optimized workloads, as shown in Figure 4-8. There are even bare-metal instances such as an i216xlarge you could consider ordering. After logging into AWS and using the EC2 management console to choose an instance, the initial available choices are defined as "current generation."

Filter by: All instance types ∨   Current generation ∨   Show/Hide Columns

Currently selected: t2.micro (Variable ECUs, 1 vCPUs, 2.5 GHz, Intel Xeon Family, 1 GiB memory, EBS only)

Family	Type	vCPUs	Physical Processor	Clock Speed	Memory (GiB)	Instance Storage (GB)	EBS-Optimized Available	Network Performance
Compute optimized	c5.18xlarge	72	Intel Xeon Platinum 8124M	3 GHz	144	EBS only	Yes	25 Gigabit
Compute optimized	c5d.18xlarge	72	Intel Xeon Platinum 8124M	3 GHz	144	2 x 900 (SSD)	Yes	25 Gigabit
Compute optimized	c5n.18xlarge	72	Intel Xeon Platinum 8124M	3 GHz	192	EBS only	Yes	100 Gigabit
Compute optimized	c5n.2xlarge	8	Intel Xeon Platinum 8124M	3 GHz	21	EBS only	Yes	Up to 25 Gigabit

Figure 4-8   Instance choices at AWS

If you want, you can still order the original m1.small instance that AWS offered in 2006, but it's not recommended to do so. M1 instances should not be used for any workload in production today because there are many more powerful and cost-effective options available. The reality is that AWS rarely deprecates anything; it's easy to pick an older instance choice. Let's *not* start with the cheapest and the smallest instance that you could order.

> **Note**
>
> What also is important is the type of image (AMI) that you use at AWS to build your instance with. The Linux instance types defined as current generation do not support the older paravirtual (PV) images of the past decade. If you still need or still use older PV images, at AWS you are limited to a smaller number of instances that support PV images (c1, c3, hs1, m1, m2, m3, and t1) and a limited number of regions that support PV AMIs, including Tokyo, Singapore, Sydney, Frankfurt, Ireland, São Paulo, North Virginia, Northern California, and Oregon. Windows AMIs support only HVM images.

Micro Instances—There's only one instance type in this class: the t1.micro with an unidentified processor; that means it's probably an Intel processor. The clock speed is not identified, but you have .613 GiB of memory with low networking performance. It supports 32- or 64-bit workloads and only shows up in the management console if you search for the All Generation types of instances. Certainly, a small test instance is not meant for production, right? That's for you to decide. Perhaps you have a micro-service or a logging server that matches up perfectly with the specifications that a micro-service provides.

General-Purpose Instances

General-purpose instances have a deceptively vague name; however, the underlying concept for a general-purpose instance is to provide a baseline of CPU processing, network, and storage.

AWS recommends the general-purpose M5 instance as shown in Table 4-1 as a starting instance to begin testing and learning for Web and application servers, small to medium-sized databases, and other various applications. Keep in mind that there are several versions of the M5 instance type. The overall AWS recommendations for using general-purpose instances are not that exacting. Your definition for the required resources for deploying a small Web server might also vary.

Obviously, launching a massive instance with plenty of memory, CPU cores, and high-speed storage will host many different types of applications effortlessly. But remember, when operating in the cloud, you're paying for everything you use that is running 24/7; the AWS cloud uses different cost variables than what will be used on-premise. Properly sizing the selected instance to match your application needs is of key importance when running production workloads at AWS. But what is also important is the cost of running each instance. Obviously, database instances run 24/7. Application and Web server instances should not be running at a maximum scale all the time—at least not at production scale in the middle of the night. We will look at one of the solutions to this potential problem in Chapter 5, "Planning for Scale and Resiliency."

Table 4-1 **M5 Instance Specs**

Instance Type	Hypervisor	Maximum Size	Storage	AMI
m5	Nitro	96 vCPUs with 384 GB of memory and up to 25 Gbps of enhanced networking	Instance storage offered by M5 instances is fast local NVMe SSD volumes located on the bare-metal server host EBS-optimized storage is provided at no additional cost	64-bit HVM AMIs that include drivers for enhanced networking and NVMe storage
m4	Xen	64 vCPUs, 256 GB of memory, up to 25 Gbps of enhanced networking		

Instances Designed to Burst

Some general-purpose models, such as T2 and T3 instances, are designed with the ability to burst above an initial assigned CPU baseline of performance. Using CPU credits that the instance can earn while it is not running under load, these models can burst above their initial CPU baseline as required. T2 instances have the lowest cost per hour at AWS; t2 nano instances cost you half a cent per hour. The use case for these T instances includes applications where the CPU requirements are not constant and fluctuate up and down over a 24-hour period.

When you launch a T2 or T3 instance, depending on the size, you get a baseline of CPU performance ranging from 5% up to maximum, as shown in Table 4-2. The design of a T instance banks CPU credits for the time that your CPU is idle. Banking your CPU credits allows you to use them when your application needs to burst above the assigned performance baseline. The idea is much like this: the typical server doesn't run flat-out at 100% but instead has peaks and valleys in its performance baseline. Therefore, you can achieve your desired performance when it is necessary using banked CPU credits.

Table 4-2 **T Instance Specs**

Instance Type	Hypervisor	Burst Mode	Features
T3	Nitro	Moderate baseline: unlimited mode allows unlimited CPU bursting	Intel Xeon–scalable processors ranging from 1 to 8 vCPUs and up to 32 GB of memory; network speed is moderate
T2	Xen	CPU credits are half the amount earned compared to T3 instances	EBS-only storage
T3a	Nitro	Unlimited mode by default	10% cost savings over T3 instances

At launch of a T instance, there are enough CPU credits allocated to carry out the initial tasks of booting the operating system and running the application. A single CPU credit has the performance of one full CPU core running at 100% for one minute. After a T2 instance is powered on, it earns CPU credits at a defined steady rate determined by the size of the instance; the larger the instance, the more CPU credits are earned up to a defined maximum value. Earned credits expire after 24 hours. If the CPU credits were not used, the running application didn't need them.

CloudWatch, the built-in monitoring service at AWS, has available metrics allowing you to monitor the credits being used and the current credit balance, as shown in Figure 4-9. The metric CPU credit balance is showing the CPU usage, and the metric CPU credit usage is showing the decrease in CPU credits as the CPU performance increases. When the CPU stops working, over time the credit balance increases once again.

If you run out of CPU credits, your CPU performance is reduced to the assigned CPU baseline based on the type of T instance you are running. Therefore, using a T instance for applications that require maximum CPU performance for unknown lengths of time is not a good design idea. On the other hand, AWS also allows you to choose an unlimited mode of operation for a T2 instance. Therefore, you may be able to use a T2 instance in this mode and pay a flat additional rate based on vCPU usage. AWS documentation details the baseline, breakeven, and maximum CPU utilization details when running T2 instances in unlimited mode. If your T2 instance manages to run under 42% utilization, the unlimited mode will make sense. If you are over this value, it may be more expensive than you think. Pricing *is* complicated!

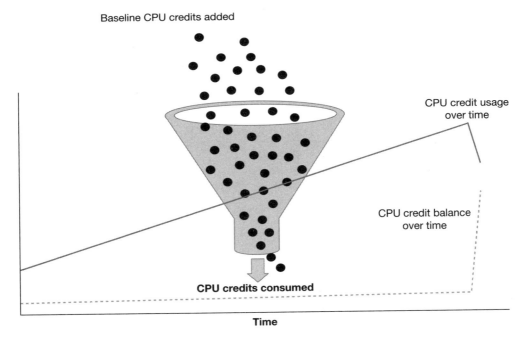

Figure 4-9   T2 credits

Compute-Optimized Instances

Compute-optimized instances are designed for batch processing workloads, media transcoding, and high-performance applications or Web servers. The C5 architecture as shown in Table 4-3 takes advantage of the Nitro system components for enhanced networking. There are no performance constraints on compute-optimized instances.

Table 4-3   **C5 Architecture**

Instance Type	Hypervisor	Maximum Size	Storage	AMI
C5	Nitro	Maximum 72 vCPUs, 144 GB of memory, enhanced networking up to 25 Gbps	EBS-optimized storage with dedicated EBS bandwidth up to 4,000 Mbps	64-bit HVM AMIs that include drivers for enhanced networking and NVMe storage
C4	Nitro	Maximum size of 36 vCPU and 60 GB of memory, enhanced networking up to 10 Gbps	Local instance storage using NVMe solid-state drive (SSD)	

> **Note**
>
> For Linux builds, AWS suggests that you use at a minimum the 3.10 kernel, or newer for NVME instances. What is recommended is Ubuntu 14.04 or later, Centos 7 or later, or Windows Server 2008 R2 or later. Don't expect great performance with an old kernel.

Memory-Optimized Instances

Workloads that need to process vast data sets hosted in memory, such as MySQL and NoSQL databases, or Memcached and Redis in-memory cache stores, should use a memory-optimized instance. Specifications are shown in Table 4-4.

Table 4-4   **x1 Architecture**

Instance Type	Hypervisor	Maximum Size	Storage	AMI
r5	Nitro	96 vCPUs, 769 GB of memory, enhanced networking speeds up to 25 Gbps	EBS-optimized storage with dedicated EBS bandwidth up to 4,000 Mbps	64-bit HVM AMIs that include drivers for enhanced networking and NVMe storage
r4	Nitro	16 vCPUs, 488 GB of memory, enhanced networking speeds up to 25 Gbps	Local instance storage using NVMe SSD	
x1	Nitro	128 vCPUs, 1952 GB of memory, enhanced networking speeds up to 25 Gbps	14,000 Mbps of EBS-optimized storage bandwidth	CPU configuration of both the C-state and the P-state registers is possible on the x8, x16, and x32xlarge models.
x1e	Nitro	128 vCPUs, 3904 GB of memory, enhanced networking speeds up to 10 Gbps		

> **P and C State Control**
>
> C states control the power-saving features of your processor. If you need maximum perfor-
> mance, you can control the idle state on your Linux instances and achieve much higher clock
> frequencies on your CPU. A P state control might be useful for applications that heavily use
> AVX2 on all cores, such as gaming servers. Make sure to select an instance that allows
> access to the C and P states, such as c4.8xlarge.

x1 instances—Can have a massive number of assigned resources, including up to 128 vCPUs,
4 TB of dynamic random-access memory (DRAM), and enhanced network speeds up to
25 Gbps. x1 instances are designed for in-memory databases, big data processing projects,
and high-performance computing (HPC) workloads.

Each physical processor is wired to a local memory footprint, as shown in Table 4-3. Using a
bus called the quick path interconnect (QPI), each physical core can also access all the installed
memory in the physical computer, not just its local assigned memory footprint. The larger
x1e.32xlarge instance has four physical CPUs, each with 32 vCPU cores. Each physical processor is wired to a 1 TB RAM footprint but also has access to the other remote memory footprints
assigned directly to the other physical CPUs.

High-memory instances—Are bare-metal servers featuring up to 224 virtual cores (hyper-
threaded as 448 logical processors), 12 TB of memory, enhanced networking up to 25 Gbps, and
14 Gbps EBS-optimized storage running.

z1d instances—Are hosted on the Nitro hypervisor and are designed with sustained all-core
frequency using Intel Xeon scalable processors with 48 vCPUs, up to 384 GB memory, and 1.8 TB
of instance storage.

Accelerated Computing (GPU)

Accelerated computing instances—Use NVIDIA Tesla GPUs in a variety of designs and are
designed for use within a cluster placement group with enhanced networking speeds of up to
100 Gbps of network bandwidth if the p3dn.24xlarge instance is selected. The p3.16large offers
8 NVIDIA Tesla K 80 GPUs, 64 vCPUs Intel Xeon Broadwell processors, 488 GB of memory, and
128 GB of GPU memory.

For high-performance computing or for machine learning application use cases, you can choose a
P3 GPU instance, which offers a PetaFLOP of compute performance using an NVIDIA V100 Volta-
based GPU chipset.

g3 instances—Are designed for graphic-intensive applications using NVIDIA M 60 graphics
processing units (GPUs). g3 instances also can enable the NVIDIA GRID Workstation feature,
which has support for four 4096 × 2160 high-resolution monitors and enhanced networking
providing up to 25 Gbps of network bandwidth within a cluster placement group. g3 instances
can be useful for VDI solutions, including Citrix XenApp and VMware Horizon.

f1 instances—Are deployed with hardware acceleration image (FPGA Image) combined with a custom AMI allowing your application to operate at incredibly fast processing speeds utilizing field-programmable gate arrays (FPGAs). f1 instances are suitable for financial computing, genomics, accelerated search, and image-processing applications.

Storage-Optimized Instances

Storage-optimized instance are designed for workloads that require local SSD storage for large data sets. Performance requirements as shown in Table 4-5 provide continual high sequential read and write access with high IOPS performance due to the local storage.

Table 4-5   **Storage Optimized Instances Specifications**

Instance Type	Hypervisor	Maximum Size	Processor	Features
h1	Xen	64 vCPUs, 256 GB memory, 4 × 200 GB of instance storage, up to 25 Gbps enhanced networking	Intel Broadwell E5-2686V4	1.15 Gbps read-write with 2 MB block size
d2	Xen	36 vCPUs, 244 GB memory, 24 × 2048 GB of instance storage,10 Gbps enhanced networking	Intel Xeon E5-2670v2	EBS optimized
i3	Nitro	36 vCPUs, 244 GB memory, 8 ×1900 GB of instance storage, up to 25 Gbps enhanced networking	Intel Broadwell E5-2686V4	1.4 million write IOPS

Note

Your selected instance size directly affects your overall throughput. The available EBS performance is directly related to network performance. The larger the instance, the larger the available EBS and network bandwidth. Make sure to match your volume size and type to the desired instance.

Bare-Metal Instances

The bare-metal platform at AWS is used to host the VMware cloud on AWS. i3.metal instances have two physical Intel processors connected with a high-speed QPI interconnect bus having 72 vCPU cores. RAM is 512 GB and eight, 1.9 TB SSDs of instant storage, and 25 Gbps enhanced networking connections. For those developers at Terra Firma who like to host databases on bare-metal servers for the maximum amount of performance, bare-metal server might be an acceptable option to consider. Bare-metal instances were first created for VMware to be able to host their environments at AWS. Figure 4-10 details the bare-metal instance architecture.

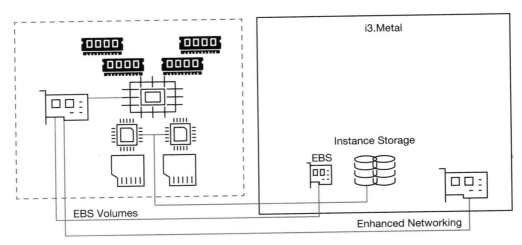

Figure 4-10   Bare-Metal Architecture

Dedicated Hosts

Choosing a dedicated host involves choosing a dedicated physical server with a defined EC2 instance capacity just for you. A dedicated host allows you to control the hardware that your instances are running on; you also get to control the *affinity*, or placement of your instances, on the host that you desire. Dedicated hosts support per-socket, per-core, or per-VM software licenses. There are some AWS limitations and restrictions when ordering and using dedicated hosts:

- The instance size and type of instance placed on a dedicated host must be the same type.

- Red Hat Enterprise Linux and Windows AMIs cannot be used with dedicated hosts; the only type of AMIs that can be launched on a dedicated host are bring your own license (BYOL) Amazon Linux and Amazon Marketplace AMIs.

- Instances hosted on a dedicated host must be launched in a VPC.

- Amazon relational database service (RDS), placement groups, and EC2 auto-scaling groups are not supported.

Billing charges are just the hourly charge for each active dedicated host because you're not billed for instance usage from the dedicated host. Pricing is based on on-demand pricing unless you have set up dedicated host reservation pricing.

> **Note**
> A dedicated host is not the same as ordering an i3 bare-metal server; there is still a hypervisor installed on a dedicated host.

Dedicated Instances

You could also choose to use dedicated instances if your compliance rules and regulations require compute instance isolation. Each dedicated instance runs in a VPC on dedicated hardware resources. Dedicated instances have the same performance and security as instances hosted on a dedicated host but also have some limitations to be aware of:

- You are not allowed to target your instance's placement.

- No access or control of the sockets and physical cores of the physical host is allowed.

- EBS volumes that are attached to a dedicated instance are not running on single-tenant hardware; EBS storage is a shared storage array.

EC2 Network Performance

The type of instance that you select will determine the available network bandwidth. If you've selected an instance from the T or m4 families, the reserved network performance is defined vaguely as low, low to moderate, or high. Proper benchmarking is the only guaranteed method of finding out exactly what bandwidth you have on any instance with a vague network performance tag. However, a nano, or micro instance, is in the baseline range of 100 Mbps, and instances with assigned high-network performance max out in the range of 2 Gbps.

All other instance families have a defined level of network performance that either scales up to a defined speed, such as up to 5 Gbps, or a defined figure, such as 10 Gbps. Network speeds at AWS are also showing the outbound and inbound traffic speed. For example, a 10 Gbps or 25 Gbps network speed is the one-way speed for either inbound or outbound traffic. Over time, all advertised network speeds are gradually increasing at AWS.

Until the launch of the C5 instance, default network communication at AWS was performed by the Xen network driver. Because the Xen hypervisor was involved, there were limitations on the maximum speed of the network connections that could be achieved. Network speeds for older instances were using the elastic network interface (ENI) for network communication.

Enhanced networking uses the elastic network adapter (ENA) to greatly increase an instance's network speed using SR-IOV, where the physical network driver on the bare-metal server is directly exposed to the EC2 instance. The beauty in this design is that the hypervisor does not have to be involved in network communications. Enhanced networking is available on all supported EC2 instance types at no additional cost, but a specialized network driver needs to be installed before enhanced networking can be enabled on the instance.

Note

Enhanced networking may also not be enabled on the instance that you are using, so it's a good idea to check. Use the CLI command **Get-EC2Instance -InstanceId instance-id.Instances. EnaSupport**. If enhanced networking is enabled, the response is true.

Enhanced networking is provided when you select instances that support enhanced networking and use an HVM AMI that includes enhanced networking drivers. Both the AWS Linux AMIs support enhanced networking, as does Ubuntu 14.04 and 16.04, and Windows Server 2008 R2 and above. The ENA supports network speeds of up to 25 Gbps for supported instance types; network speeds up to 10 Gbps are supported by the Intel 82559 virtual function (VF) interface.

> **Note**
>
> You can check out all the details of an instance by using the following CLI command: **aws ec2 describe-image-attribute –image-id ami_id.**

Once you have chosen and enabled enhanced networking, your instance can take advantage of the additional bandwidth for several use cases:

- Connections to S3 storage can send and receive at 25 Gbps.

- Instance-to-instance communication hosted in the same or different availability zones (AZs) within a single region can communicate up to 5 Gbps for point-to-point communication, or 25 Gbps.

- Instance-to-instance communication hosted in a cluster placement group can communicate at 10 Gbps for single-flow traffic, or 25 Gbps for multiflow traffic.

> **Note**
>
> Using a test tool such as iperf can provide your actual network bandwidth speeds at AWS.

Amazon Machine Images (AMIs)

The AMI is *the* important component to understand when deploying EC2 instances because all instances are created using an AMI. Many folks at AWS pronounce the term *AMI* as *amee*, like *maamee*, but with an *a*. The precise definition of an AMI is a template, as shown in Figure 4-11, that contains the desired software configuration; an operating system and a root device boot volume at a minimum; and optionally, an application and perhaps some additional supporting software. After selecting an AMI, you choose the instance type where the AMI will be installed.

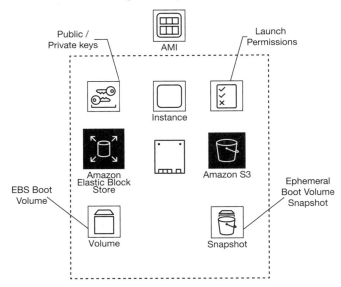

Figure 4-11   AMI details

Each AMI contains the necessary technical information required to launch all instances hosted at AWS. You must use an AMI to launch an AWS instance. There are two types of AMI to consider: an EBS-backed AMI providing a persistent block storage boot volume, and a local instance store-backed AMI, which is installed on a local block storage hard drive that is temporary. Your different needs and requirements dictate which type of AMI to create and use; if you want super-fast block storage and your design works with temporary storage volumes, perhaps a local instance store makes sense. If you are used to using virtual hard disks (VHDs) and snapshots, EBS-backed AMIs are widely available. You can also mix and match with an EBS boot volume and additional local ephemeral volumes. Each AMI includes the following components, which are described by the XML manifest file:

Boot volume—Describes what will be used as the root boot volume for the instance: either an EBS boot volume created from a snapshot or a local instance storage volume copied from an S3 bucket.

Launch permissions—Define the AWS accounts that are permitted to use the AMI to launch instances with. Default launch permissions are set to private, which means that only the owner who created the AMI can use it. Permissions can also define a select list of AWS accounts. Switching permissions from private to public means anyone in the overall AWS community will have access.

Volumes to attach—The volumes to attach to the EC2 instance at launch are contained in a block device mapping document. If the initial root device volume is a local instance store volume, it is listed as ephemeral0 to ephemeral23 depending on the number of instance store volumes to be created. Instance stores can be backed by solid-state drives (SSDs) or NVMe available with some of the newer instance types. For EBS volumes to be created, the ID of the snapshot to be used when creating the block device volume will be specified along with the size of the volume to create.

Default location—AMIs are region specific. When you create your AMI, you will be operating in a specific region; therefore, it is stored in the region where it was initially created. You can use an AMI in any of the AZs contained by the region where it was created. When you launch (think create) an instance, you can only select an AMI that's currently hosted in the current region; however, AMIs can be made available in other regions by copying them to the desired region.

Operating system—The operating system will be a version of Linux or of Windows.

Root device storage—There are two options available: either backed by Amazon EBS or backed by an instance store volume.

- The EBS root volume will be created from an EBS snapshot stored in S3.

- The instance store volume will have its initial root volume created from a template stored in S3.

Choosing an AMI

There are many prebuilt AMIs available in the Amazon Marketplace and in the EC2 management console.

AWS Linux AMIs

Prebuilt AMIs supplied by Amazon include Amazon Linux 2, as shown in Figure 4-12, and Amazon Linux AMI. Amazon Linux 2 is the latest version of Amazon Linux, and it's recommended if you want to start with a Linux AMI. Amazon's Linux distribution is based on Red Hat Enterprise Linux. The Linux 2 AMI supports EC2 instances, including EC2 bare-metal instances and Docker containers. Even more importantly, Amazon Linux 2 can be used on-premise for development and testing purposes because it is available as a virtual machine image for use on many other third-party virtualization environments such as KVM, Oracle VM VirtualBox, Microsoft Hyper-V, and of course VMware ESXi. Amazon Linux 2 can be used on all instance types that support HVM AMIs; it does not support instance types that require paravirtualization functionality.

The Linux 2 AMI also includes a variety of software packages and configurations that seamlessly integrate with many AWS services, such as CloudFront monitoring and the Systems Manager Patch Manager and the MATE GUI desktop environment. Other bundled tools include the AWS CLI, the command-line interface, and cloud-init, which is used for automating user data scripts at boot. Long-term support is provided by AWS until 2023, including updates from a private repository stored within the AWS region where the instance is located.

The older version of Linux that AWS offers is the Amazon Linux AMI. It is supported for use on EC2 instances at AWS but cannot be downloaded for on-premise development and testing. If you are starting out in AWS and want to use a Linux distribution that AWS provides, choose Linux 2.

Figure 4-12   Amazon Linux 2 in the EC2 console

Linux AMI Virtualization Types

Amazon as a cloud provider has been around since 2006. Virtualization has changed a great deal since then; therefore, there are different virtualization choices available at AWS when launching a Linux instance due to backward compatibility. There are two types of virtualization: PV and HVM. There is also an older hybrid combination of technologies with the HVM embedded with paravirtualized drivers for networking and storage.

When you view the available instance types in the AWS management console, by default, the current generation types are initially displayed, as shown in Figure 4-12. The term *current generation* means the latest and greatest virtualized choices available; however, changing the view to All Generations reveals that the older virtualization choices still exist. Amazon recommends that you use what are defined as current generation instance types and HVM AMIs.

Even though the earliest AWS instance types are still available, be warned; choosing paravirtualization or selecting an older instance type means your applications will be running much slower at AWS. However, your on-premise builds may be hosted on older versions of Linux or Windows versions, and perhaps they must stay that way. If that's the case, a variety of instances and regions still support the older paravirtualized builds. Long term, you will be better served by first doing the grunt work of upgrading your on-premise operating system versions to the latest versions. Then you can start with the current generation instance types and HVM AMIs; you'll be happy, and so will your bosses.

- HVM AMIs support enhanced networking and faster GPU processing
- PV AMIs cannot take advantage of enhanced networking and faster GPU processing

Windows AMIs

Amazon has worked with Microsoft to make available a library of AMIs, including SharePoint 2010 and Windows Server versions from 2008 to 2016 (just the base operating system or the base operating system bundled with versions of SQL Server Express to SQL Server 2016 Enterprise). License choices include instances that bundle the licensing fees in their cost (Windows Server and SQL Server licenses) and BYOL, or with a feature called License Mobility. License Mobility is available to customers who are covered with Software Assurance (SA) contracts that allow the movement of eligible Microsoft software to EC2 instances. Windows AMIs that AWS offers by default are patched within five days of Microsoft's patch Tuesday release.

AWS Marketplace

The AWS Marketplace has thousands of AMI options to choose from, as shown in Figure 4-13. Several third-party software appliances are available, such as Cisco, Juniper, F5, and an Open VPN Access server image, to name just a few. After you select a custom AMI from the AWS Marketplace, the typical decisions to be made include licensing, the AWS region, and the size of your instance to deploy the AMI.

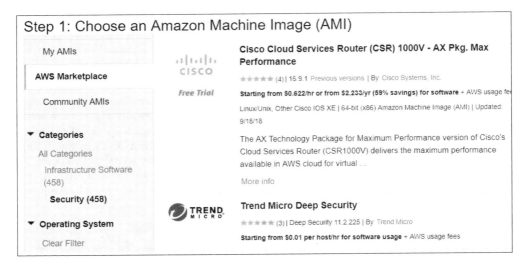

Figure 4-13   AWS Marketplace AMI choices

Creating a Custom AMI

You can create a custom AMI after an instance has booted. Amazon uses the word *custom* in many situations to indicate that you have created something different from the initial default option. Suggested options to consider before creating a custom AMI are installing additional software and applications, defragmenting your hard drives for faster operations, deleting temporary files, and cleaning up existing user accounts and passwords.

Once the EC2 instance is exactly as desired, power the instance off. Then create the image as shown in Figure 4-14. You can add additional volumes as part of this AMI before the creation process is complete. The block device mapping is created, the launch parameters are documented, and the registration of the AMI and creation of the snapshots are carried out automatically. The EC2 service creates snapshots of the instance's root volume and any other EBS volumes that are attached. After the AMI has been created, the instance is rebooted to check the file system integrity of the just-created image. Once a custom AMI has been created, it should be considered a *golden AMI*. This definition means that the image is as perfect as possible; there are no customizations or tweaks that need to be made. If instances stop functioning properly, replace them with their golden AMI instead of trying to troubleshoot the problem.

MAKE SURE TO WATCH THE COMPANION VIDEO "CREATING A CUSTOM AMI."

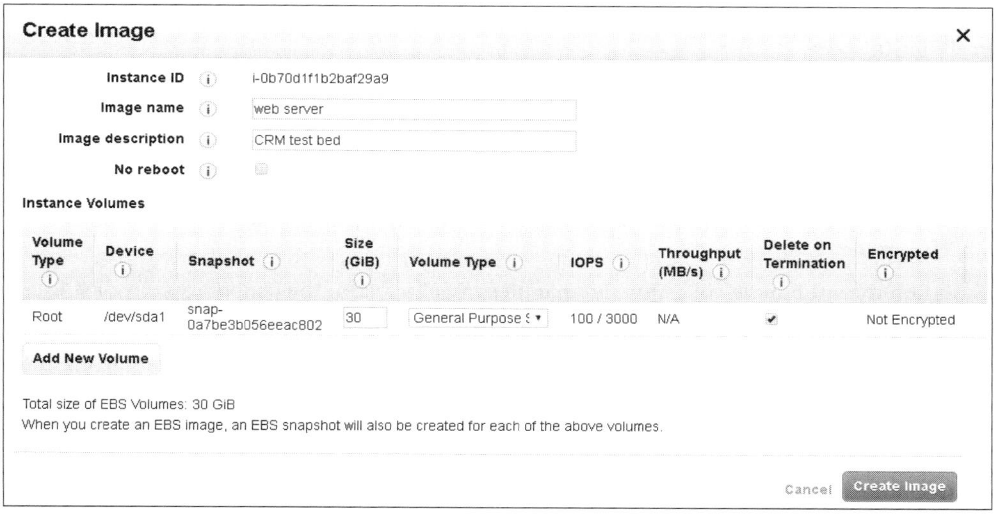

Figure 4-14   AMI creation

To access the companion videos, register your book at informit.com/register.

You can choose Windows or Linux AMIs from the following locations:

- **The EC2 console**—Various Windows or Linux AMIs are available.

- **Amazon Marketplace**—Many custom Windows or Linux builds are available.

- **My AMIs**—This is for AMIs you have created that are stored in your account.

- **Migrated AMI**—Using the Server Migration Service, or the VM Import/Export service, on-premise virtual machines can be migrated to custom AMIs that are stored in your account in S3 storage.

To create an EBS-backed Windows or Linux AMI—First choose a compatible Windows or Linux AMI with an EBS boot volume. After you log on and customize the instance software build, you can create a new AMI from the instance. For EBS-backed instances, creating an image is a simple process using the management console, or the CLI. After you customize the instance-making changes and additions as you see fit, an AMI can be created using the management console by selecting Image from the context menu and then Create Image.

To create an instance store–backed Windows or Linux AMI—Choose a compatible Windows or Linux AMI with an instance store boot volume. After you log on and customize the instance software built, you can create a new AMI from the instance. The process for creating instance store-backed AMIs is a little more complicated because it is not a completely automated process.

To create an AMI from an instance store-backed Amazon Linux instance, you need to carry out the following tasks:

1. Install GRUB.

2. Install the partition management packages.

3. Install the command-line-based AMI tools and the AWS command-line interface (CLI).

4. Create a signing certificate using the command openssl genrsa, and save the output to a .pem file.

5. Run the ec2-bundle-vol command that prepares a *bundle*, or the temporary copy of your instance store boot drive.

6. Run the ec2-uploadbundle command that copies the bundle (the instance boot drive) to an S3 bucket, as shown in Figure 4-15.

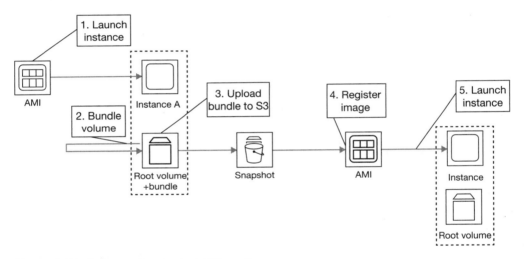

Figure 4-15   Instance store-backed AMI creation

Custom Instance Store AMIs

The differences between instances backed by Amazon, EBS volumes, and an instance store are shown in Table 4-6. Even though the boot time of an instance store instance is slower, perhaps it's an option worth considering. The storage is much faster than EBS storage, and there's one other important point: Web and application instances don't have locally stored data records in the cloud; data is stored in a database. Therefore, instances should be considered as an engine, the engine of your application. Instances that get into trouble operation wise can be discarded and replaced by a golden AMI.

Table 4-6   **Differences in Instance Storage**

	EBS Root Device	Instance Store Root Device
Boot time	Fast; under a minute	Not so fast; approximately five minutes because root drive image must be copied from S3 storage
Root Drive	16 TB maximum	10 GB maximum
Volume type	EBS block storage	Local instance, block storage located on bare-metal server hosting the instance
Data persistence	By default, EBS root volumes are deleted when instance terminates	No persistence when instance store root device turned off or terminated
Changes	EBS storage, AMI, and snapshot storage in S3	AMI storage in S3
State	When instance is turned off, root volume is persistent EBS	Can be either in a running or in a terminated state

> **Note**
>
> AMIs that support the Nitro hypervisor must be HVM in design to be able to support enhanced networking and the ability to boot from EBS storage that uses an NVMe interface. The latest AWS AMIs crafted for Linux and Windows are HVM by design in addition to the latest AMIs of Ubuntu, Debian, Red Hat Enterprise Linux, SUSE Enterprise Linux, CentOS, and FreeBSD.

Proper AMI Design

Just what should you include in an AMI? There's no definitive answer because each use case for each customer will be different. However, when creating any AMI, you must choose Linux or Windows as the operating system. Of course, the operating system is the only absolute component; you may also be ordering an AMI from the AWS Marketplace that has been preconfigured and designed as a software appliance, such as an F5 load balancer or a Cisco router.

As previously mentioned, after you have installed your additional software components and security patches, a finalized AMI should be thought of as a golden AMI. Think of a golden AMI just like a finely tuned engine that you're about to place in a racecar. There are no parts that haven't been tested and approved, and there are no additional parts or changes that are needed. There is no data or configuration stored within the image that can't be re-created. It's a good idea to consider the goals of each golden AMI you create.

- **Base OS-AMI**—Limited to building an exact AMI of a particular operating system version.

- **OS-AMI + Apps + Middleware**—Fully baked, including full configuration and installation of all software components and middleware.

- **AMI-Software Appliance**—From the AWS Marketplace.

- **Base OS-AMI with additional components procured from a management platform such as Chef, Puppet, or Ansible**—A bare-bones configuration of an operating system and software must be updated dynamically at first boot. In this example, the instance could take quite a bit of time before it is ready for operation; however, the AMI is being kept up to date by referencing external components that are up to date.

- **Fully Baked AMI**—At launch, an instance created from a fully baked AMI has all the necessary software components ready to go, as shown in Figure 4-16. Because there are no additional components to install, the instance can boot immediately and be placed in operation. The complexity of an application stack may dictate a fully baked design to ensure a proper build every time.

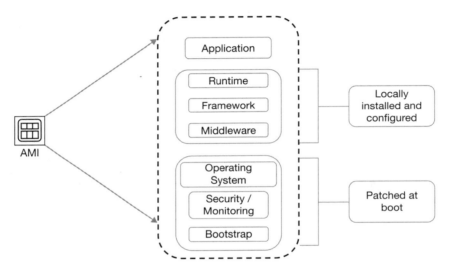

Figure 4-16   Fully baked AMI

- **Hybrid AMI**—In a hybrid design as shown in Figure 4-16, a portion of the core software is installed: the operating system and the application, or just the operating system. Required software components are updated after the first boot using a user data script that runs after the successful first boot of the instance. This approach produces a dynamic build of the instance at launch. If your software builds are constantly changing, this is an approach to consider.

- **Take Me to My Leader AMI**—In this design shown in Figure 4-17, sometimes described as a minimalist approach, just the operating system and the third-party configuration management agent are installed. After the system boots for the first time, the agent calls home to its management platform. Included in the first phone call is a stream of consciousness metadata that informs the management platform of the type of instance, the location of the instance, and any other pertinent information. The instances will be ready to serve after the automation services take over and complete the build. Third-party examples could be Ansible, Chef, or Puppet, or Amazon's own automated solution AWS Systems Manager.

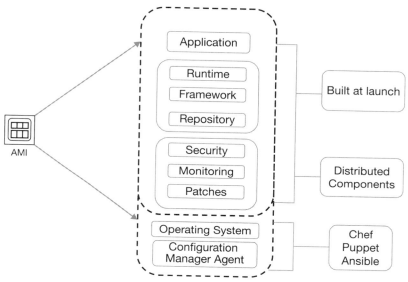

Figure 4-17   Minimalist AMI

AMI Build Considerations

Over time, you will develop a standardized procedure for building and maintaining AMIs. Make no mistake, this is a big job. And it's an ongoing job because operating system fixes and application fixes are also ongoing in the long term.

- Are your instances being placed in an Auto Scaling group? If so, you'll have to properly time how long it takes for the instance to be launched and ready to go. Read more about auto scaling in Chapter 5.

- How static or dynamic are your updates to your workloads?

- Are manual configurations necessary for licensing?

- How often do you plan to update your AMIs? By default, AMIs supplied by AWS have rolling operating system updates applied. This process can be changed, or locked, which ensures that no further updates will be applied after the initial installation of the AMI.

Designing a proper sequence to ensure a workable workflow when creating golden AMIs is a must. You must also consider when you will decommission AMIs that are no longer up to date with the required updates and fixes. The proper process to consider creating is a defined pipeline for creating, validating, approving or rejecting, distributing, and decommissioning AMIs, as shown in Figure 4-18.

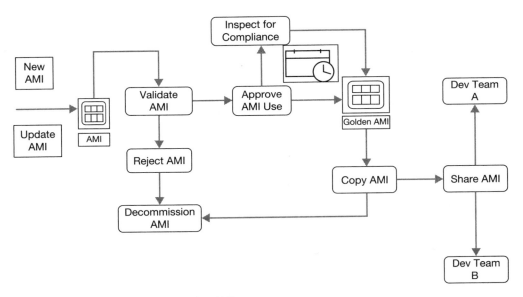

Figure 4-18   Building and maintaining AMIs

> **Note**
>
> Amazon has released a golden AMI pipeline sample configuration that is available at this GitHub location: https://github.com/aws-samples/aws-golden-ami-pipeline-sample. Here, you will find a readme guide with step-by-step instructions, including cloud formation templates to help you set up a golden AMI pipeline for creation and distribution of AMIs.

AMI Best Practices

There are several best practices for starting to build AMIs that I suggest you follow. Many best practices depend on your circumstances, but the following best practices are certainly worth following over the long term.

Adopted best practices are useful if they match up with what you're trying to accomplish and maintain. Any adopted best practices must also match up with what your company and its technical staff can realistically carry out. Understand that adopting a best practice is also accepting that changes will occur in how you and your technical staff will carry out your daily tasks moving forward; and if everybody on your team doesn't change, company-wide, adopting a best practice won't end up being that useful. AWS best practices are probably best defined as lessons learned from hard experience by many AWS customers. A worthwhile best practice is not meant to sell product; instead, best practices are suggestions to help you achieve success operating at AWS. After you have thoughtfully reviewed these suggestions with your entire technical team, if you have complete buy-in—in agreement and in practice—it will be a success.

Create and maintain AMIs for your Web, application, and database servers on a strict update schedule. Consider whether the schedule for updating an AMI can be driven by the application updates; if your instances are hosted on the private network in private subnets as they should be, security updates could be combined at the same time as application updates. Updating based on security updates will be much more frequent and may be unnecessary.

Both the application and the operating system need to be patched at some point in the future, creating a new golden AMI. What sort of patching policy should you adopt? Should you adopt a patching policy of every three months? Every six months? Let's think about this. Should you patch the operating system with service pack releases and ignore any hot fixes (unless the hot fix specifically solves an issue that you're dealing with)? Should you be patching based on your application needs, which may be linked to the operating system fixes that need to be applied?

- Don't embed passwords or security information in the AMI; instead, use IAM roles and AWS Secrets. For more details on security, check out Chapter 7, "Security Services."

- At a minimum, use a standard bootstrapping process with user data scripts. User data scripts allow you to automate processes after the first boot of your instance, including updates and configuration.

- Properly tag your AMIs for identification purposes. Tags are used for monitoring, automation, security, and billing.

Adopting a Best Practice: Tags

AWS feels, and I strongly feel, that you should use tags. A *tag* is a custom piece of metadata that a customer can create as a customer-defined key and value pair that can be attached to most AWS resources. Think of a tag as a custom descriptor of an EC2 instance, such as an Apache web server from a particular department. Up to 50 tags can be assigned to most AWS resources. Departments, organizations, date created, developer names, and more should be tags that every administrator or developer is assigning to every EC2 server instance created. Creating and mandating a tagging strategy also helps you when identifying, scaling, or monitoring your EC2 instances. Tags can also help you separate the costs of resources assigned with the same departmental tag. The possibilities are endless.

I'll bet you're nodding your head, but you might not be so excited if you were picked to deploy a tagging strategy because you might not have the time. Tags are a great best practice, but only if there's companywide buy-in. Let's look at some of the best practices AWS suggests when it comes to using tags:

- **Identification tags**—These are tags such as technical, ownership, product line, and version.

- **Billing**—Billing is departmental; it alerts when costs are higher than expected.

- **Automation**—If on, turn it off, and scale out or in.

- **Security**—Use tags to control access.

Using Launch Templates

Instead of manually entering all the configuration details every time you create an instance, launch templates can be created that contain the configuration details you wish to use for EC2 instances. Launch templates as shown in Figure 4-19 can be used for a variety of instance types, including when requesting spot instances, which are discussed later in this chapter. Launch templates help you maintain standards when deploying AMIs. These are some of the parameters that can be used in a launch template:

- **Image creation**—AMI ID, instance type, key-pair name, the VPC subnet, and security group

- **Networking information**—Create up to two additional network interfaces, subnet locations, public and private IP addresses, and assigned security groups

- **Storage volumes**—Instance store or EBS volumes, size, IOPS, encryption, and tags

- **Advanced options**—Purchasing options, IAM profile, shutdown behavior, termination protection, detailed monitoring, tenancy, and user data

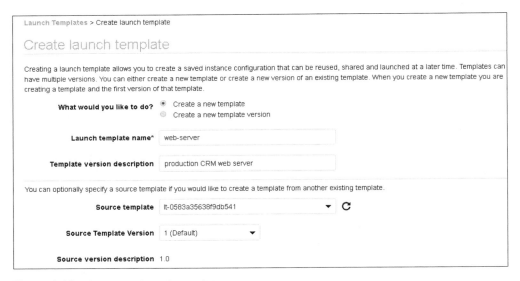

Figure 4-19   Creating a launch template

Changing the Current Instance Type

During initial testing, your needs will change; your initial EC2 instance will be too small, or too large. The size of your EC2 instance can be changed, as shown in Figure 4-20, but there are some compatibility caveats:

- A PV or instance cannot be resized to an HVM instance.

- Resizing a 32-bit instance is limited to an instance type that supports a 32-bit AMI.

- Older instances that are launched in EC2-Classic networking cannot be resized and placed in a VPC.

- ENA drivers must be installed for enhanced networking.

- NVMe drivers must be installed for NVMe storage devices.

- The AMI must support enhanced networking and NVMe block storage devices.

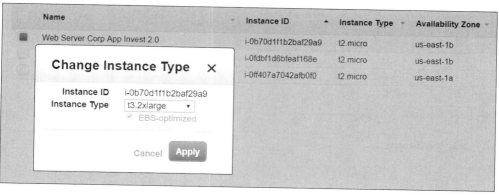

Figure 4-20   Changing current instance type

EC2 Pricing

When you first start with AWS, you won't even think about it. You will use on-demand pricing for your instances. After all, you're working with AWS for the first time. Over time, once you move into production, there are a variety of compute pricing options to consider. On-demand pricing has no long-term contract and requires no upfront payments, but it's the most expensive pricing option. You are billed by the second for Linux instances and by the hour for Windows instances. Each EC2 instance will also have a specific billing cycle during its lifetime of operation.

- An EC2 instance that is turned on and assigned to your account will be billed a compute charge while it is powered on.

- Once an EC2 instance is turned off, the billing cycle finishes. There is no further compute charge.

The only additional charges that will be associated with an EC2 instance are for the attached EBS storage volumes and any snapshots or AMIs that have been created. Storage charges at AWS are per month per GB of EBS or S3 storage. Note: there is no separate charge for EC2 instance storage. The cost for the local block storage is included in the price of the EC2 instance.

Once you've signed up for AWS, you are probably thinking that you can spin up as many EC2 instances as you want; however, you can't because there are limits. There are limits to what you can do in any data center, particularly in AWS data centers. AWS services generally have a defined default soft limit. For example, many instance types have a default soft limit of 20 per account, per region. There are also soft limits on the number of EBS volumes or snapshots that you can create. You can usually increase soft limits with a simple request from the management console, as shown in Figure 4-21.

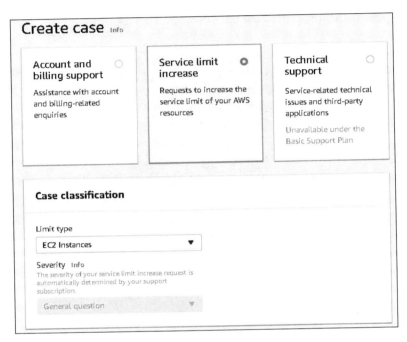

Figure 4-21   Requesting a soft limit change

Because you've probably never talked to AWS support, how are they possibly going to know what you intend to do in the cloud? If you suddenly called up your on-premise data center staff and said, "I need 100 virtual machines right away," the answer might be, "We can't do it right now. You'll have to wait because we don't have the capacity." Amazon is no different; it may not have the capacity of the types of instances that you want in your region, unless you reserve your instances with *reserved pricing*. If you're running production workloads, especially workloads that need to scale up at a moment's notice, you're going to want to guarantee that your EC2 instances are available to scale when required. AWS offers a variety of options to keep the bill as low as possible, including reserved instances, or spot instances. You will definitely be using reserved pricing for production workloads. You also have several other options to consider depending on your use case. Let's explore RIs and some additional details on reserving instance capacity.

Reserved Instances (RI)

You're going to want a reduction in your compute price after your first AWS bill. If you have application or Web servers that are on 24/7, and applications that routinely scale out and in a predictable pattern, RI pricing is essential. An RI is not a special type of EC2 instance; it's merely a billing discount that is supplied to an on-demand instance currently being used or to be used in your account. Let's suppose you have a C5 instance that is exactly what you want to use except for the on-demand price. The RI discount could be as high as 75% when compared to the on-demand instance price, as shown in Figure 4-22. Each RI is defined by the following attributes:

- **Instance type**—The instance family and the size of the instance
- **Scope**—The region or AZ location of the reserved instance
- **Tenancy**—Shared default hardware or single-tenant, dedicated hardware
- **Platform**—Windows or Linux

If you purchase an RI that matches the attributes of a running C5 instance currently in your account, the RI is applied immediately.

RI pricing is also applied when you launch a new instance with the same specifications as your RI price.

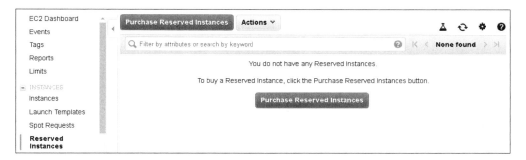

Figure 4-22   Reserved instance pricing

Reserved Instance Limits

The number of regional RIs that you can purchase depends on the current soft limits that have been defined within your AWS account for your on-demand instances. Remember, RIs are simply a discount applied to an on-demand instance in your account.

RIs also have limits based on each region and the number of AZs within the region itself. RIs are defined as regional or zonal—that is, per region or AZ.

For each region, you can purchase RI pricing based on the number of on-demand instances within the selected AWS region and an additional 20 zonal RIs for each AZ within the region. At first, these limits seem more complicated than they really are.

If your soft limit for on-demand instances is 60 instances of a specific instance type, purchasing 60 regional RIs would apply an RI discount to the 60 on-demand instances.

Zonal RIs are an RI discount for a specific AZ within the AWS region. Once you add AZs into your design, the zonal reservation is a capacity reservation for the selected AZ, in addition to the discounted RI price. Therefore, purchasing zonal RIs can increase the number of instances that you can launch in an AZ.

Before you purchase RIs, as previously mentioned, your AWS account also has several predefined soft limits that allow you to only run a certain number of instances within each region. If you're operating in the N. Virginia region, and you wanted to run c5.large instances, your default soft limit is 20, as shown in Figure 4-23.

For xle.xlarge instances, your default limit in the N. Virginia region is 10. If you want to run xle.8xlarge instances, your limit is probably 0. Apparently, there is no xle.xlarge instance available in N. Virginia at the time I'm writing this chapter. In addition to your on-demand soft limits, there is an RI limit that really should be named a "Zonal Reserved instances" limit because it defines the total number of RIs purchased per AZ in a specific region per month.

For the N. Virginia region with six AZs, the initial limit is 120 zonal RIs (20 per region limit × 6 regions = 120), plus whatever the current on-demand soft limit is for each instance type you want to launch.

The big takeaway is that your account's soft limits can be increased, and the RI number you are probably interested in is the zonal number; that is how many RIs can be launched per AZ.

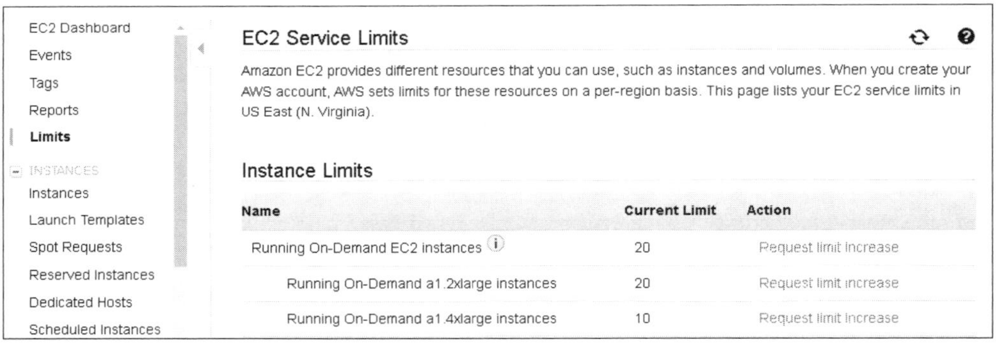

Figure 4-23   Reserved instances soft limits

When you're purchasing reserved EC2 instances, make sure that you are purchasing the type of RI you're looking for: either a regional or a zonal reservation. Zonal provides you with a capacity guarantee per AZ and a discounted price. A regional reservation does not provide you with a capacity reservation; however, it provides flexibility to use the EC2 instances in any AZ, and it allows you to change the EC2 instance size (for example, the C4 family) within the selected instance family sizes as long as you're running Linux instances with default shared tenancy.

The pricing for regional reservations is based on a normalization factor, and you may have to be a math major to figure out exactly how regional reservation pricing will be charged to your account. However, there is a discount and a formula fully documented in the AWS documentation for EC2 instances.

Let's review the steps that you should follow when purchasing instances:

1. What region are you going to be operating in?

2. How many AZs are you going to use?

3. How many EC2 instances do you want to run in each AZ?

4. What size of EC2 instance are you planning to run?

5. How many of these EC2 instances need to be running 24/7?

6. What are my soft limits for each EC2 instance type per AWS region?

7. Do I need to request a limit increase for each EC2 instance type to match my needs?

8. Do I need to request an RI limit increase?

9. Where is my technical calculator?

> **Note**
>
> You can also request reserved EC2 capacity if you need to guarantee that your on-demand instances are always available for use in a specific AZ. It's important to remember that after you've created a capacity reservation, you will be charged for the capacity reservation whether you actually use the instances or not.

Reserved EC2 Instances Types

There are two flavors of RIs: a standard RI and a convertible RI, as shown in Figure 4-24.

Standard Reserved Instance—A standard instance reservation gives you the biggest discount and can be purchased as repeatable one-year terms or a three-year term. After you've purchased a standard instance reservation, you can make some changes within your reservation: you can change the AZ you are using, the instance size, and the networking type. After you've purchased a standard instance reservation, most likely your needs will change. What to do? Register as a seller and sell your standard instance reservation through the Reserved Instance Marketplace, yet another Amazon store.

Convertible Reserved Instance—If your needs are a little different—for example, you may have to change instance types, operating systems, or want to switch from multitenancy to single tenancy compute operation—then you should consider a convertible RI reservation. The convertible reserved discount could be over 50%. and the term can be a one- or a three-year term. Note that a convertible RI reservation can't be sold in the Reserved Instance Marketplace. However, a convertible RI reservation has more flexibility because numerous changes can be made during the length of the reserved term.

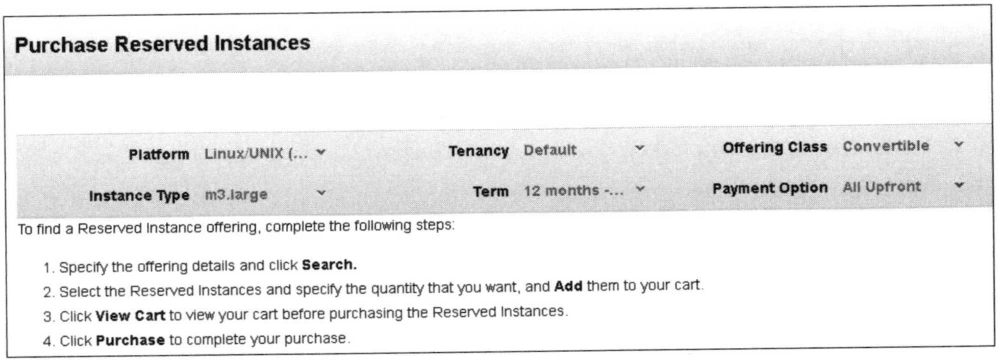

Purchase Reserved Instances

Platform Linux/UNIX (... ⌄		**Tenancy** Default ⌄		**Offering Class** Convertible ⌄	
Instance Type m3.large ⌄		**Term** 12 months -... ⌄		**Payment Option** All Upfront ⌄	

To find a Reserved Instance offering, complete the following steps:

1. Specify the offering details and click **Search.**
2. Select the Reserved Instances and specify the quantity that you want, and **Add** them to your cart.
3. Click **View Cart** to view your cart before purchasing the Reserved Instances.
4. Click **Purchase** to complete your purchase.

Figure 4-24   Reserved instances options

Once you've chosen your RIs option, pay everything up front, make a small payment upfront, or pay nothing upfront. I think you can guess which option gives you the best price. Paying everything up front is the most cost-effective option.

> **Note**
>
> Reserved instances, once expired, do not automatically reapply or renew. Instead, you are charged on-demand prices for continued EC2 usage. Billing alerts can be set up to warn you of any billing changes.

MAKE SURE TO WATCH THE COMPANION VIDEO "CREATING RESERVED INSTANCES."

Scheduled Reserved EC2 Instances

A scheduled RI reservation allows you to buy capacity reservations for a daily, weekly, or monthly term. The specific start time, and length of reservation time that can be requested is for a maximum of one year. Once the instances have been reserved as scheduled, you pay for the reserved compute time, regardless of whether the instances are used. You also can't cancel, modify, or resell your scheduled instance reservation.

> **Note**
>
> Scheduled instances are supported by C3, C4, C5, M4, and R3 instance types.

Spot Instance

A spot instance is spare compute capacity that AWS is not currently using. Potentially, you can save up to 90% of the purchase price; however, when AWS takes your spot instance back, it only gives you a two-minute warning and then, poof; your spot instance is gone. Spot instance pricing is based on supply and demand; the spot instance is available until another AWS account offers a higher spot price for the same type of spot instance in the same region. To counteract this possibility, you can define a maximum spot price that you're willing to pay; therefore, when spot instance prices are volatile, only when the current spot price rises above your maximum spot price that you're willing to pay are your spot instances reclaimed by AWS. Over the past year, the options for terminating spot instances have become much more sophisticated.

- You can now choose to have your spot instance hibernated or stopped when it is interrupted instead of just being terminated. When your spot instances are hibernated, the data held in RAM is stored on the root EBS drive of the hibernated instance, and your private IP address is held. Spot hibernation is not supported for all instance types and AMIs, so make sure to check the current support levels for hibernated spot instances.

- You can now choose a spot instance price based on a guaranteed term of 1 to 6 hours, as shown in Figure 4-25.

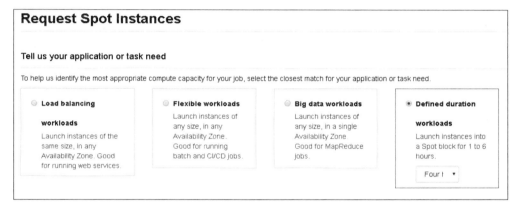

Figure 4-25   Spot instance pricing options

Spot instances have their own language. Let's define the spot terms AWS uses:

- **Spot Instance Pool**—A current number of unused EC2 instances of the same instance type, operating system, and AZ location

- **Spot price**—The current per-hour price of a spot instance

- **Spot instance request**—The maximum price you're willing to pay for a spot instance. When your spot price is higher than Amazon's current price, as long as capacity is available, your spot request continues to be fulfilled. You can request a spot instance as a one-time purchase, as a persistent request, for defining up to a 6-hour duration for the spot instance.

- **Spot fleet**—A number of spot instances are launched based on type and price.

- **Spot instance interruption**—When the spot price exceeds your maximum price or capacity is no longer available, spot instances are terminated, stopped, or hibernated. A spot instance interruption notice, a two-minute warning will be generated before any changes are carried out.

> **Note**
> The number of spot instances that you can request depends on your defined spot limit for the region you are operating in.

MAKE SURE TO WATCH THE COMPANION VIDEO "SPOT INSTANCES."

Spot Fleet

A spot fleet allows you to launch a desired number of instances, called a *fleet* of instances, based on the desired price and number of spot instances types. You can include additional variables, such as the different instance pricing options of on-demand, reserved instances, and spot instances that you want your fleet pricing to use when calculating the type of instance to launch in your fleet. A spot fleet could be helpful if you want to launch a certain number of instances for a distributed application, a long-running batch processing job, or perhaps a Hadoop cluster.

When making a spot fleet request, you first define the desired the total target capacity of your fleet, and how much of your fleet must be on-demand. This is a bit of protection for your workload and ensures that you always have a set amount of capacity available. As shown in Figure 4-26, target capacity is set for 20, on-demand as 14, and the remaining 6 instances will be spot. Each spot fleet request has, by default, a lowest price strategy. Other allocation possibilities include distributing the requested spot instances across all or selected spot capacity pools.

Figure 4-26   Spot fleet allocation request

> **Note**
> The spot fleet API that had been around since 2015 has been replaced by the EC2 Fleet API.

After you request a spot fleet and indicate the amount of compute capacity required, the EC2 fleet attempts first to meet the desired capacity using your spot instances requests.

You can include multiple launch specifications that can separately define a number of variables, including the EC2 instance type, AMI, AZ, and subnet using a launch template. The EC2 fleet then attempts to select a variety of available spot instances to fulfill your overall capacity request based on the launch's template specifications.

Spot Capacity Pools

To design resiliency with spot instances, you also can create spot capacity pools, as shown in Figure 4-27. Each pool is a set of unused EC2 instances that has the same instance type, operating system, AZ, and network platform.

Figure 4-27   Spot capacity pools

To make sure you always have the desired capacity available, even if some of your spot instances are suddenly removed, you can direct Spot Fleet to maintain your desired compute capacity by using on-demand instances if there are not enough spot instances available that match your launch specifications. Spot Fleet attempts to save you money by launching the lowest-priced instance type it can find whether a spot instance or on-demand instance is chosen.

Therefore, your spot capacity pools could have both spot and on-demand instances depending on what spot instances are available at the time of your request.

Once your fleet has been launched, Spot Fleet maintains the desired target compute capacity when there are changes in the spot price or capacity available. The allocation strategy for your defined spot instances is based on the lowest price by default; you can also choose to distribute the available spot instances across the spot instance pools that are being used.

Your fleet of spot instances can be defined for cost optimization or for cost optimization and diversification by designing them to run in multiple pools. If your target capacity was 50 instances, you could request that the spot fleet specifies 5 pools, with 10 spot instances in each capacity pool. For this example, if the spot price changes affecting your spot request, only 20% of the total number of instances would be affected.

Each spot capacity pool can also have a different price point. The built-in automation engine helps you find the most cost-effective capacity across multiple spot capacity pools when you're using a spot fleet. Both Linux and Windows operating system instances are available as spot instances.

Remember that spot fleets operate within the defined soft limits of your AWS account, which include the number of spot fleets per region, the number of launch specifications per fleet, and the target capacity per spot fleet.

Although spot instances can be terminated with a two-minute warning, according to Amazon's analysis, most spot instance interruptions are from customers terminating their spot instances once work is completed.

> **Note**
> A spot fleet can't span regions or different subnets within the same AZ.

EC2 Fleet

Amazon EC2 Fleet is an update to Spot Fleet that also allows you to automate the deployment of your EC2 capacity using a target capacity that can be defined by vCPUs. Your target capacity is defined by weights; think of the weight as the preferred choice. The default mode of operation with EC2 Fleet is still based on the lowest instance price available.

For example, if I needed to create a grid of 3,000 parallel processing nodes to carry out risk analysis, an EC2 Fleet request could be created with m4 and m5 instances that have a vCPU-to-memory ratio of 4 GB of memory to 1 vCPU. Weights are defined based on the number of vCPUs per instance that match up to the desired worker node in the parallel processing grid shown in Table 4-7. Two thousand vCPUs are provided with on-demand instances and 1,000 vCPUs with Spot.

If the on-demand price per vCPU for the m5.24xlarge instance is lower than the on-demand price per vCPU for the m4.16xlarge instance, EC2 Fleet launches the needed number of m5.24xlarge instances to hit the desired target of 2000 spot vCPUs. The remaining capacity is launched with the cheapest on-demand instances available. If RI discounts have been purchased for your AWS account, when instances launch that match up, RI discounts are automatically applied.

Table 4-7   **EC2 Fleet Instances with Assigned Weights**

Instance Size	vCPU-to-Memory Ratio	Weight
m5.24xlarge 96/384 ratio 4:1	4:1	96
m4.16xlarge 64/246 ratio 4:1	4:1	64

Using a single CLI command, I can launch the EC2 Fleet, as shown in Figure 4-28. This command can also be automated as a CloudWatch alert building EC2 Fleets when needed based on monitoring metrics. For more details on CloudWatch, see Chapter 5.

```
$ aws ec2 create-fleet --cli-input-json file fleetrequest.json

"LaunchTemplateConfigs": [
    {
       "LaunchTemplateSpecification": {
          "LaunchTemplateId": "GN-128876933999",
          "Version": "1"
       }
    "Overrides": [
    {
      "InstanceType": "m4.16xlarge",
      "WeightedCapacity": 64,
    },
    {
      "InstanceType": "m5.24xlarge",
      "WeightedCapacity": 96,
    },
   ]
    }
  ],
  "TargetCapacitySpecification": {
    "TotalTargetCapacity": 3000,
    "OnDemandTargetCapacity": 1000,
    "SpotTargetCapacity": 2000,
    "DefaultTargetCapacityType": "Spot"
  }
}
```

Figure 4-28   EC2 Fleet JSON file

EC2 Instance Storage Options

There are three main types of storage that instances can directly utilize: persistent block storage volumes (elastic block storage, or EBS) and temporary block storage, also called instance or ephemeral storage. There are also shared file storage options, such as the elastic file system, Amazon FSx, and S3 block file storage. EFS, S3, and the other available storage options are fully covered in Chapter 6, "Cloud Storage."

Local Instance Storage—SSD or Magnetic Disk

An instance store volume is a temporary block storage SSD hard drive that is physically attached to the bare-metal server; the local drive storage is shared between the multiple virtual machines hosted there. Depending on the instance type, there could be one or several SSD hard drive volumes attached that are exposed as local block storage devices to the instances. Instance storage volumes are numbered from 0 to 23 and are labeled as ephemeral 0 to ephemeral 23, as shown in Figure 4-29.

Block Device Mapping		
Type	Device	Snapshot ID
Ephemeral	/dev/sda	Instance store volume: ephemeral0
Ephemeral	/dev/sdb	Instance store volume: ephemeral1
Ephemeral	/dev/sdc	Instance store volume: ephemeral2

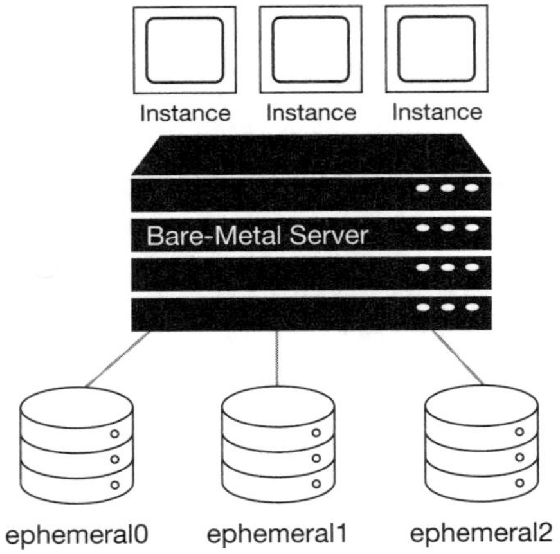

Figure 4-29   Instance storage architecture

Instance storage volumes are a nonpersistent data store; when your EC2 instance is turned off or terminated, the instance storage is discarded; however, it *does* survive a reboot. Instance storage data records do not have durability because they are not automatically replicated to another location, and there is no integrated support with the existing EBS snapshots service.

Testing has shown that instance storage is more than 5 times faster than EBS SSD general drives for uncached reads, and more than 10 times faster for writes. Systems with both EBS volumes *and* ephemeral storage could provide some advantages:

- Boot drives could be EBS volumes providing faster boot times, and the ephemeral storage could be used to store cached data or logs of the hosted Web application.

- Could be considered for workloads, where you do not need the data records to persist as a Web or application server hosted behind a load balancer.

Another example use case for using instance storage would be if you needed a high-performance database storage instance.

- Choosing ephemeral storage, for example, an i2 instance for a large SQL Server database, would provide incredible speed at the local storage level for the database records.

- For redundancy, additional EBS magnetic hard drives designed for a further level of throughput optimization could be added as more volumes provide for full and partial backups and transaction logs.

- A third-party VSS-aware snapshot utility could be installed locally on the SQL server instance performing backups to the throughput-optimized EBS volumes.
- EBS snapshots could then be taken of the EBS volumes for safekeeping.

> **Note**
>
> With proper planning, you could take advantage of instance storage volumes. And ephemeral storage is included in the compute price of each EC2 instance.

EC2 Auto Recovery

On modern instances (C3, C4, C5, M3, M4, R3, R4, T2 and X1 families) that have only EBS volumes attached, you can take advantage of a feature called EC2 auto recovery, as shown in Figure 4-30. Once enabled, in the background the monitoring service CloudWatch has permitted an alarm with an instance metric called StatusCheckFailed_System. If your instance fails, the defined recover instance workflow swings into action. The failed instance is launched on different hardware and retains its instance ID, the instance metadata, private IP and elastic IP addresses, and the EBS volumes that were previously attached.

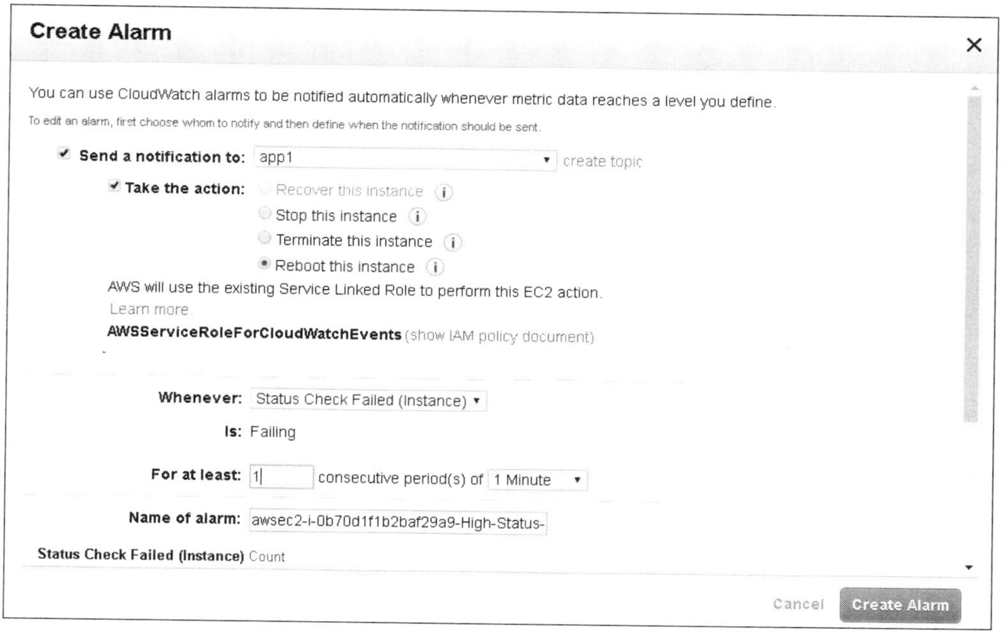

Figure 4-30   Enabling auto recovery

> **Note**
>
> By default, EBS boot volumes that are attached to an EC2 instance are set to be deleted when an instance is selected to be terminated. Data volumes do not follow the same criteria; data volumes by default retain their persistence state.
>
> The key concept with these default EBS boot volume parameters is that you will already have a snapshot of the boot volume because you will have a current AMI of your golden instance. Therefore, when an instance is terminated, you are left with your data volumes. Rebuild an instance with a golden AMI and attach the data volumes, and you're back in business. The flag Delete on Termination can be set to true when you want select EBS volumes to be deleted when the instance it is attached to is terminated.

Ordering an Instance

Now that you know about instance types, AMIs, snapshots, and data storage volume choices, it's time to order an instance and see where these components and pieces fit together.

The first step is to log into the management console with a user account with enough permissions to create an EC2 instance.

From the management console, before you click the blue button Launch Instance, check the top-right corner region listing to make sure that you are in the desired region, as shown in Figure 4-31. Then click the EC2 link.

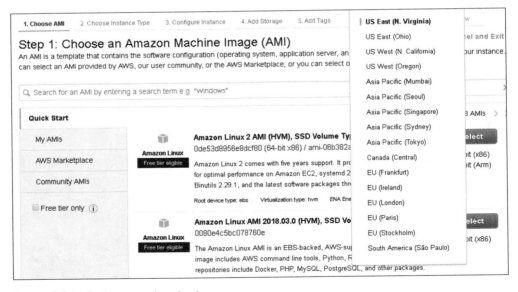

Figure 4-31   Perform a region check

After clicking the blue Launch Instance button, our next choice is to choose an AMI. There are several AMIs that show up by default in the QuickStart section. If you have already created an AMI, select My AMIs and choose your image. Then click Select. You could also choose a prebuilt AMI from the AWS Marketplace or choose an AMI from the AWS Community AMIs. Assuming this is your first time, we will choose the latest Amazon Linux version: Amazon Linux 2 AMI.

Review the Linux 2 AMI for the root device type. Either EBS block storage or instance storage is supported, and the supported virtualization type is HVM, as shown in Figure 4-32.

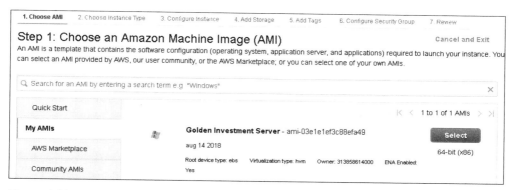

Figure 4-32   Review the AMI details

Our next task is to choose an instance type. Scroll down and select the m5.large instance as shown in Figure 4-33, which provides two virtual cores with 8 GB of RAM, an EBS root boot volume, and a network connection that provides up to 10 GB of network speed.

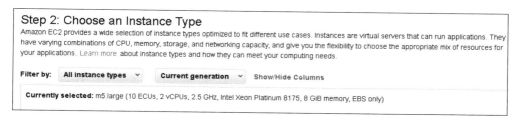

Figure 4-33   m5.large instance details

That was the easy part. Now we must make decisions about the hosting details of our EC2 instance. The configuration window shown in Table 4-8 is full of choices that may be difficult to quickly answer without some thought and discussion.

Table 4-8 **Configuration Choices**

Settings	Comments	Optional
Number of instances	Controlled by AWS account soft limit; depends on instance type selected	Add instance to an auto scaling group
Purchasing option	Can change pricing to spot instance pricing	Request spot instances
Network	Select a specific VPC or the default VPC	Create a new VPC
Subnet	Select desired subnet	Create new subnet
Auto-assign Public IP	Enable auto-assigned public IPv4 address	Can disable auto-assigned public IPv4 address
Auto-assigned IPv6	Enable auto-assigned public IPv6 address	Can disable auto-assigned public IPv6 address
IAM Role	Define security role for instance	Can be added later
Shutdown behavior	Stop or terminate	Can be changed later
Placement group	Choose placement group instal-lation for maximizing bandwidth	Selected instance type must support placement groups
Capacity reservation	Reserve on-demand instance capacity in a specific AZ	Depends on soft limits and availability
T2/T3 Unlimited	Burst beyond baseline as required	Only applicable to T2/T3 instances
Termination protection	Protect against accidental termination	Can be changed later
Monitoring	Select detailed monitoring	Monitor at 1-minute intervals including memory
EBS-optimized instance	Enable dedicated communica-tion channel for EBS storage	Must select the supported instance
Tenancy	Default is shared compute hardware; can select dedicated hardware or dedicated host	Must launch instances into a VPC
Network interface	Add additional network inter-faces and subnet connection	Choose primary and secondary IP addresses
Kernel ID	Linux instances only	Only valid for paravirtual AMIs
RAM disk ID	Linux instances only	Only valid for paravirtual AMIs
Advanced details	Add user data script for initial customization after first boot	Add script or link to existing file

Our next option is to add additional storage. Storage options are detailed in Table 4-9.

Table 4-9   **Storage Options During Instance Creation**

Settings	Comments	Optional
Type	Instance store or EBS volume	Depends on instance chosen
Device	Select volume to attach	Shows available volumes
Snapshot	Snapshot ID	Can select public snapshots
Volume type	Instance or EBS volume	Depends on instance chosen
IOPS	Provisioned EBS volume	Up to 32,000 IOPS
Delete on Termination	Default for root volume	Can be changed
Encrypted	KMS default encryption key	Can use customer-supplied keys

Depending on the instance type chosen, there could be a single EBS volume or one or more ephemeral volumes, as shown in Figure 4-34.

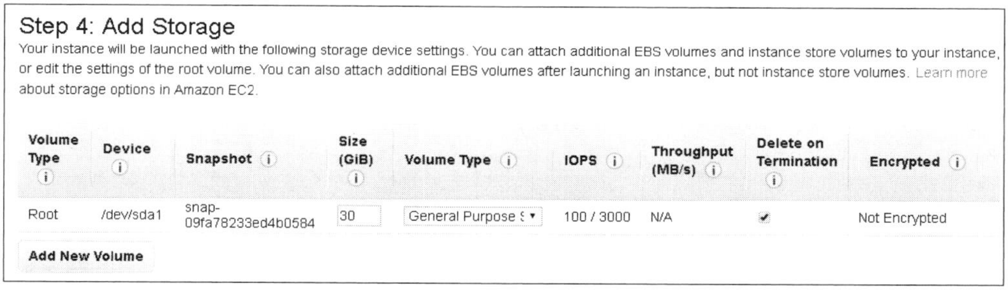

Step 4: Add Storage

Your instance will be launched with the following storage device settings. You can attach additional EBS volumes and instance store volumes to your instance, or edit the settings of the root volume. You can also attach additional EBS volumes after launching an instance, but not instance store volumes. Learn more about storage options in Amazon EC2.

Volume Type ⓘ	Device ⓘ	Snapshot ⓘ	Size (GiB) ⓘ	Volume Type ⓘ	IOPS ⓘ	Throughput (MB/s) ⓘ	Delete on Termination ⓘ	Encrypted ⓘ
Root	/dev/sda1	snap-09fa78233ed4b0584	30	General Purpose S ▾	100 / 3000	N/A	✔	Not Encrypted

Add New Volume

Figure 4-34   Default instance volumes

Note that the EBS volume will be created from the associated snapshot listed under Snapshot, and for the m5.large instance, the ephemeral volumes will be NVMe SSD drives. Adding additional storage requires clicking the button Add New Volume and selecting and configuring your volume choice, as shown in Figure 4-35.

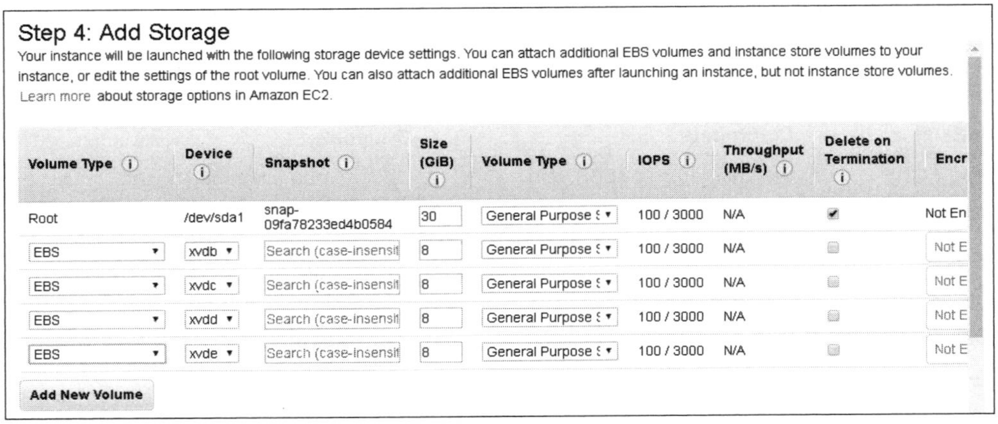

Step 4: Add Storage

Your instance will be launched with the following storage device settings. You can attach additional EBS volumes and instance store volumes to your instance, or edit the settings of the root volume. You can also attach additional EBS volumes after launching an instance, but not instance store volumes. Learn more about storage options in Amazon EC2.

Volume Type (i)	Device (i)	Snapshot (i)	Size (GiB) (i)	Volume Type (i)	IOPS (i)	Throughput (MB/s) (i)	Delete on Termination (i)	Encr
Root	/dev/sda1	snap-09fa78233ed4b0584	30	General Purpose S ▾	100 / 3000	N/A	☑	Not En
EBS ▾	xvdb ▾	Search (case-insensit	8	General Purpose S ▾	100 / 3000	N/A	☐	Not E
EBS ▾	xvdc ▾	Search (case-insensit	8	General Purpose S ▾	100 / 3000	N/A	☐	Not E
EBS ▾	xvdd ▾	Search (case-insensit	8	General Purpose S ▾	100 / 3000	N/A	☐	Not E
EBS ▾	xvde ▾	Search (case-insensit	8	General Purpose S ▾	100 / 3000	N/A	☐	Not E

Add New Volume

Figure 4-35   Additional storage volumes

We're almost ready to launch our instance, but we should add some tags. Tags are an associated, case-sensitive key-value pair. For example, a key value of investment and the value of web server are shown in Figure 4-36. Note that the created tags will be added to the instance and to the EBS volumes associated with the instance.

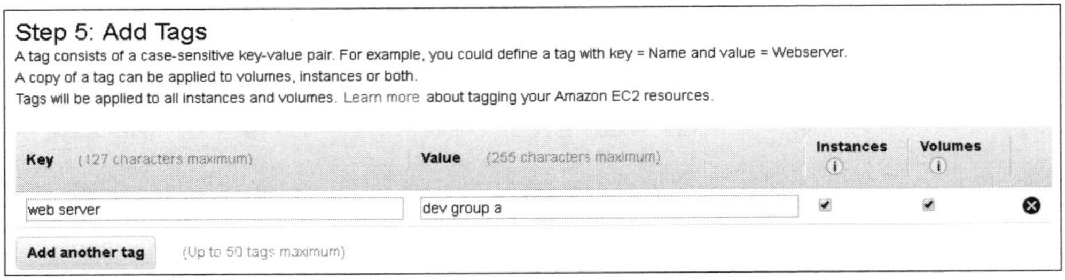

Step 5: Add Tags

A tag consists of a case-sensitive key-value pair. For example, you could define a tag with key = Name and value = Webserver.
A copy of a tag can be applied to volumes, instances or both.
Tags will be applied to all instances and volumes. Learn more about tagging your Amazon EC2 resources.

Key (127 characters maximum)	Value (255 characters maximum)	Instances (i)	Volumes (i)	
web server	dev group a	☑	☑	✖

Add another tag   (Up to 50 tags maximum)

Figure 4-36   Adding custom tags

One of the last tasks that is required is to create a security group, a firewall to protect the network adapter, by clicking Configure Security Group. If we decide to accept the default security group, AWS creates a default security group for us. The default security group initial settings depend on the type of operating system to be installed with the selected AMI. Linux results in a security group allowing us to use Secure Shell (SSH), but a Windows installation results in a security group allowing us to use Remote Desktop Protocol (RDP). The best practice is to create a custom security group. For this example, we will create a security group for administration access, as shown in Figure 4-37.

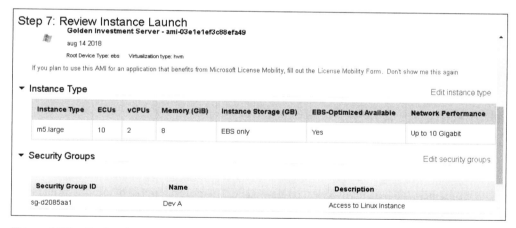

Step 6: Configure Security Group

A security group is a set of firewall rules that control the traffic for your instance. On this page, you can add rules to allow specific traffic to reach your instance. For example, if you want to set up a web server and allow Internet traffic to reach your instance, add rules that allow unrestricted access to the HTTP and HTTPS ports. You can create a new security group or select from an existing one below. Learn more about Amazon EC2 security groups.

Assign a security group: ○ Create a **new** security group
⦿ Select an **existing** security group

Filter VPC security groups ▾

Security Group ID	Name	Description	Actions
☐ sg-dffb0dad	accounting admin	launch-wizard-3 created 2017-10-09T15:30:35.904-04:00	Copy to new
☐ sg-981c4eeb	default	default VPC security group	Copy to new
☑ sg-d2085aa1	Dev A	Access to Linux Instance	Copy to new

Inbound rules for sg-d2085aa1 (Selected security groups: sg-d2085aa1)

Type ⓘ	Protocol ⓘ	Port Range ⓘ	Source ⓘ	Description ⓘ
SSH	TCP	22	0.0.0.0/0	SSH for Dev Admin
SSH	TCP	22	::/0	SSH for Dev Admin

Figure 4-37   Creating a security group for administrative access

On the final splash screen, all may be well; however, there may be some complaints about your instance's level of security depending on your choices made when creating or selecting the security group's open inbound ports, as shown in Figure 4-38. After reviewing the complaints, clicking Launch starts the building and starting up the instance for the first time.

Step 7: Review Instance Launch

Golden Investment Server - ami-03e1e1ef3c88efa49

aug 14 2018

Root Device Type: ebs   Virtualization type: hvm

If you plan to use this AMI for an application that benefits from Microsoft License Mobility, fill out the License Mobility Form. Don't show me this again

▼ Instance Type   Edit instance type

Instance Type	ECUs	vCPUs	Memory (GiB)	Instance Storage (GB)	EBS-Optimized Available	Network Performance
m5.large	10	2	8	EBS only	Yes	Up to 10 Gigabit

▼ Security Groups   Edit security groups

Security Group ID	Name	Description
sg-d2085aa1	Dev A	Access to Linux Instance

Figure 4-38   Final review before launch

There's just one more decision to make: what key pair would you like to associate with this instance? If you have not created a key pair, choose Create a New Key Pair and then download the just-created key pair to your local machine, as shown in Figure 4-39. Select the check box that acknowledges that you have a copy of the associated key pair. If you don't have a copy of the key pair associated with your EC2 instance, your system is safe; no one will ever be able to log in. And perhaps you don't want to log on to the server; there is a choice that allows you to proceed without associating with a key pair. Click Launch Instance. In a few minutes, you can watch your new instance come to life.

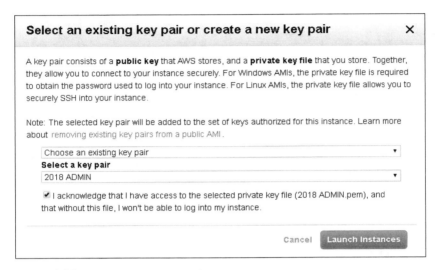

Figure 4-39   Creating a new key pair

Make sure to watch the companion video "Creating Instances."

Migrating to AWS

If you're considering using migration tools to move your application servers and databases to the AWS cloud, there are several AWS and third-party tools available to consider.

- For databases, you could use the AWS Database Migration Service to migrate your on-premise database to AWS with no downtime. There are a number of options available; an AWS is focused on getting your data into one of its hosted databases, such as Aurora or DynamoDB, or into its data warehousing service Amazon Redshift.

- For VMware and Hyper-V servers, you could use the Server Migration Service.

- For migrations of virtual machines and virtual hard drives to AWS from the command prompt, you could use the VM Import/Export Service.

- For performing a premigration discovery of existing servers, you could choose the AWS Application Discovery Service, which is included in the AWS Migration Hub.

- Third-party migration tools integrated with the AWS Migration Hub's GUI console include these:

  - **ATDATA ATAmotion**—Migrate live workloads directly to a VPC from a physical, virtual, or cloud location.

  - **CloudEndure Live Migration**—This provides continuous replication in the background for all workloads, including databases and legacy applications.

  - **River Meadow Server Migration SaaS**—Migrate workloads across virtual private network (VPN) or Direct Connect connections.

The listed third-party migration tools are designed for large enterprise organizations with corresponding large budgets. Perhaps the first tool that you should consider reviewing is the AWS Migration Hub. The Migration Hub is integrated with the AWS migration tools, including the AWS Application Discovery Service, the AWS, Server Migration Service, and the AWS Database Migration Service.

Migration Big-Picture Steps

Before we look at the tools, let's look at the process of migrating a locally hosted blog running on Terra Firma's local virtualized environment migration to AWS. This is an ideal migration test because the blog and the database server are as simple as things get: a two-tier application stack of an Apache Web server and a back-end MySQL database server, each hosted on its own virtual machine.

1. **Create your AWS environment**—At a minimum, you'll create a single VPC test bed with a public subnet for the Web server and a private subnet for the database server. An Internet gateway would be attached to the VPC to provide Internet access, and the AWS NAT gateway service would be ordered and configured for providing NAT services for the database server. Route tables would need to be updated for both the public and the private subnets to enable access to the Internet gateway and the NAT service. Thinking long term, perhaps subnets will be created in multiple AZs for Web server failover, and master-standby database replication.

2. **Replicate and test your database at AWS**—To migrate the MySQL database to AWS, you could use the AWS Database Migration service. The migration service requires a source database, a target database solution, and a replication instance that is created and hosted within your VPC. The replication instance hosts the software that manages the database migration through established connections from the source database to the target database hosted at AWS, transferring data and monitoring the overall migration, as shown in Figure 4-40. Note that the source database can be on-premise, hosted at AWS, or even at another cloud provider. The on-premise MySQL database could also be converted to Aurora, a hosted RDS MySQL-compatible database solution with plenty of power.

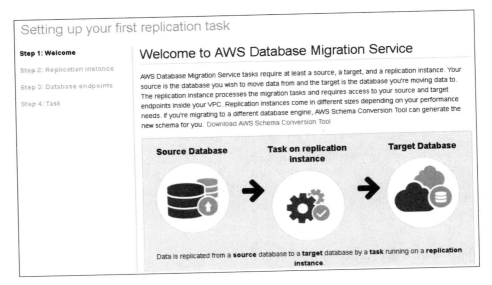

Figure 4-40   Database migration

3. **Configure Server Migration Service (SMS) and AWS Security**—Both your hypervisor and the SMS need credentials to carry out their appropriate tasks. At AWS, an IAM user needs to be created with the ServerMigrationConnector policy. A service account must also be created in the on premise Active Directory Domain Services for the Server Migration Connector, the AWS software appliance that will migrate the on-premise Apache Web server to an EC2 instance AMI.

4. **Download the SMS appliance**—The next task is to download, install, and configure the SMS connector with the IAM user that will be carrying out the migration and the Active Directory service account.

5. **Create a replication job**—The first task is to import your virtual machine catalog from on-premise to the SMS connector. Once that task is completed, select the Web server instance in your local VM catalog to migrate, and create a replication job. The time it takes to replicate depends on your bandwidth and the size of the VM being migrated. You can also choose to migrate your entire catalog of VMs to AWS.

6. **Create and launch your Web server**—Deploy an EC2 instance, choosing the appropriate size, and select the SMS connector that AMI created. After checking out the new Web server, change the configuration files to point to the new Amazon Aurora database server. After testing and confirming that the application stack works, your final task is changing your DNS information via Route 53 and updating your address records for your blog server.

AWS Migration Hub

Opening the AWS Migration Hub console, you can perform a discovery of your existing servers or applications hosted on servers, as shown in Figure 4-41. After the discovery process has completed, you can separate the discovered servers into groups of applications that should be migrated together.

There is also a fun option to just migrate without discovering. Who wants to wait? Ah, that magical pushbutton approach. We certainly would like a pushbutton that would do it all, but sadly, it isn't going to work that easily.

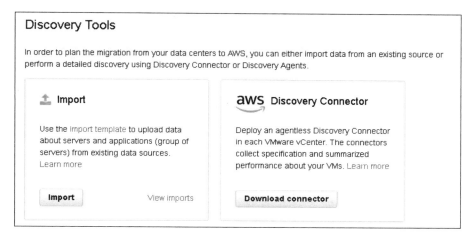

Figure 4-41   Performing discovery using the migration hub

To discover your on-premise application servers, you must make a choice about what discovery tool to use. Your choices include the AWS Discovery Connector or the AWS Discovery Agent.

The Discovery Connector is a prebuilt virtual machine with embedded software that carries out the discovery process hosted in your VMware vCenter. Or, optionally, you could install the Discovery agent on every virtual machine or physical server in your environment. If your virtual environment is Hyper-V, you could also choose to use the Server Migration Service.

At first glance, these migration tools sound fantastic; however, I would caution you that pushbutton migrations to the cloud are not going to be successful if your virtual machines are complicated builds, with many tasks and dependencies. A virtual machine defined with a single task might very well migrate successfully to AWS. I don't mean to suggest these migration services don't do their job; they certainly do. But what you're left with won't be an ideal cloud application server solution in many cases. Let's look at some of the potential issues you may have to overcome before you begin a migration of your application servers:

- Hyper-V environments support Generation 1 VMs (containing 32-bit operating systems), using either VHDS or VHD partitions. Generation 2 VMs must only use VHDX partitions.

- VMware environments must use VMDK disk images.

- Linux VMs must use 64-bit images.

- Linux VMs should use default kernels.

- Linux VMs must have 250 MB of disk space on the root volume for installing additional drivers and software. Windows VMs need a fixed page file size and 6 GB of free disk space on the root volume.

- IP version 6 addresses are not supported. In addition, public IP addresses are not assigned to any VM migrated into a VPC. This can be solved by associating an elastic IP address with the migrated instance.

- Virtual machines that have been created using a P2V conversion tool—that's from physical to virtual—are not supported.

- SMS supports bringing your own license (Linux and Windows) or AWS-applied license (Windows only).

If you can make the appropriate changes to match up with the criteria of the server migration service, technically, your migration job may be a roaring success. However, before you begin, consider the complexity of your existing application stack; are there several or many components that have local dependencies embedded in your design? If so, the migrated image or instance may successfully boot but have an unsuccessful life at AWS for these following reasons:

- The failure of a single local component could result in failure.

- Multiple local components with local dependencies won't be able to horizontally scale.

- Vertical scaling means your instance is offline while changes are applied.

- It will be difficult for a migrated instance to fail over to another AZ without design changes.

AWS Server Migration Services

The SMS is a graphical user interface (GUI) tool that can be accessed from the AWS management console. The VM Import/Export service is accessed at the command line using the AWS CLI, or the EC2 CLI, which can be installed for Linux, Windows, and Mac systems. The AWS SMS allows you to automate the process of importing your VMware or Hyper-V resources to AWS. However, you must use the VM Import/Export service if your images are in Citrix Xen or raw format and if you want to export EC2 instances back to your own environment.

Import/Export Prerequisites

- **Operating systems**—Windows Server (2003 until present), Windows 7 through Windows 10, in 32- or 64-bit flavors. Linux support is for 64-bit versions only and includes the popular variants including RHEL, Ubuntu, SUSE, CentOS, Debian, Oracle Linux, and Fedora Server.

- **Importing images**—OVA Open Virtual Appliance, Stream-optimized ESX\vSphere Virtual Machine Disk (VMDK), fixed or dynamic virtual disks (VHD/VHDX) which are compatible with Microsoft Hyper-V and Citrix Xen, or raw.

- **Instance imports**—Windows supports most instance types; Linux doesn't support as many instance types when importing, so be sure to check the current AWS documentation. Current support includes general purpose, compute, optimized, memory optimized, storage optimized, and accelerated computing instances.

- Initial volume types and file systems:

  - **Windows 32- and 64-bit**—MBR partitioned volumes formatted with NTFS file system.

  - **Linux 64-bit**—MBR partition volumes formatted with ext2, ext3, ext4, Btrfs, JFS, or the XFS file system.

Image and Snapshot Limitations

- Boot partitions must use master boot record (MBR) partitions. Extensible Firmware Interface/Unified EFI (EFI/UEFI) BIOS partitions are not supported.

- GUID partition tables (GPTs) are supported for nonbootable volumes that are less than 16 TB.

- Imported Linux VMs need 250 MB of free disk space on the root volume.

- Windows Server VMs need 6 GB of free space and a fixed page file size of 16 GB. Windows Server 2019 needs an additional 7 GB of memory to ensure the updating process doesn't fail because of a lack of free memory.

- Multiple network adapters are not supported.

- Public IP addresses must be manually added after import.

Server Migration Big Steps

1. **Download and deploy the prepackaged OVF template** and set up the connector (which is a virtual appliance) for the applicable virtual environment you are migrating from. There are some mandatory setup requirements for your virtual environment VMs, including firewall configurations for stateful outbound connections for Dynamic Host Configuration Protocol (DHCP), domain name system (DNS), Hypertext Transfer Protocol Secure (HTTPS), Internet Control Message Protocol (ICMP), and Network Time Protocol (NTP) services.

2. **Import the server catalog and select the server or servers** that you want to replicate from the on-premise location to S3. SMS supports up to 50 concurrent VM migrations.

3. **Choose a license type for the AMIs** that will be created by the replication job.

4. **Schedule a migration job**. Migration jobs can begin immediately, or you can define the date and time for the migration task to start. Each migration job has a maximum amount of time that it can run. The minimum replication frequency cycle is every 12 hours, and the maximum is 24 hours. The entire lifetime of the migration stage is set at 90 days.

5. **Take a snapshot of the selected server**, exporting the VM to an Open Virtualization Format (OVF) template.

6. **AMI is uploaded** to the selected S3 bucket.

Importing and Exporting Virtual Resources

If you don't want to reinvent your entire infrastructure, you can selectively choose what to move using the VM Import/Export service importing your VM into AWS as an image, as shown in Figure 4-42.

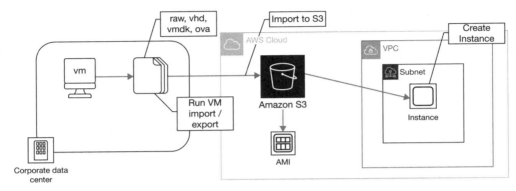

Figure 4-42   Exporting resources using the VM Import/Export service

Retaining your VMs as an AMI allows to maintain your current installed software base and its custom configurations. The VM Import/Export service has some decent migration options to consider:

- **Migrate a local VM to AWS**—Import a VM from your own virtualization environment into AWS as an EC2 instance (Amazon Machine Image). You can then create AMIs from the instance.

- **Import VHDs**—Your existing VHDs can be imported into AWS as an elastic block storage (EBS) snapshot stored in an S3 bucket in your account.

- **Export an existing EC2 instance**—Do this from AWS back to your virtualization environment.

Other Ways to Host Workloads at AWS

Virtualized workloads have been around for quite a while with on-premise applications and have been the prime method for hosting workloads in the cloud. You can continue using instances to directly host your Windows and Linux workloads at AWS. However, there are a couple of other compute choices to be aware of. It all depends on the type of application stack you're trying to build or host. Do you need a full virtual platform that contains multiple services, such as a full LAMP stack? (That's a Linux instance with an Apache Web service, a MySQL database, and a scripting environment such as JavaScript or Python.)

Your first thought may be that an instance is the way to go; after all, it worked just fine on-premise. However, once you start operating in the cloud, there's a good chance that over time you're going to start taking advantage of the hosted services that are present and supplied by AWS. Therefore, in the case of the LAMP application stack, the database could be hosted by AWS using the RDS; the scripting environment would be provided as part of the cloud provider's operating system environment. That leaves you with a single service: the Apache Web service. What if you could deploy the Web servers in a container instead of an instance?

Containers

Another way of running applications at AWS is by using containers. The concept of containers involves changing the underlying virtualization from a complete emulation of a computer system to just the virtualization of the operating system components that are required for communication: the necessary libraries, system tools, and runtime. A container shares the host operating system's kernel and its system libraries using a control plane, or in the case of Docker, the Engine allows the application hosted in the container to have read-only access to the host operating systems file system and network stack, as shown in Figure 4-43. The result is less duplication of operating system components to run applications.

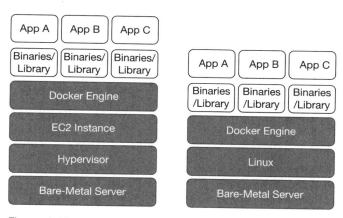

Figure 4-43   Container architecture options

The biggest concept to understand about using containers is that they can run anywhere: in the cloud, at AWS, at Azure, at Google, on Microsoft Azure, on-premise, on a Windows 10 laptop, or on a Windows server.

The operating system that hosts the Docker engine can be a bare-metal server or a virtualized operating system allowing you some flexibility in how to host your containers at AWS. You could choose a bare-metal server or a large instance. Both are hosted within your VPC to install the Docker environment. Comparing the operating concepts of containers versus instances, there are some potentially interesting advantages, as detailed in Table 4-10.

Table 4-10   **VMs Versus Containers**

VMs/Instance	Containers
Full stack	Lightweight
Each app has its own VM	Containers share the host OS
Startup in minutes	Startup in seconds
Gigabytes in size	Megabytes in size
FIPS 140-2 approved	FIPS 140-2 validation
Virtualization technology	Application delivery technology
Application server	Service inside of a container

There are several different types of containers; one of the first was Linux containers sitting on top of the Linux operating system, allowing for multiple isolated containers on a single physical host. There are also Windows containers, and Kubernetes container environments. The most popular container environment at AWS is Docker. The engineer who created the Docker container environment started with Linux containers as the initial model but has created a container ecosystem with many features, including orchestration and integrated container security bundled into the Docker Enterprise container platform. Docker also has a complete development platform for both Windows and Mac environments to allow developers to build containerized applications on their laptops.

Amazon Elastic Container Service (ECS)

Amazon provides a complete container management system supporting Docker containers and Windows Server containers and is certified conformant with Kubernetes, allowing you to use all third-party plug-ins and customizations from the Kubernetes community. ECS allows you to set up a cluster of EC2 instances running Docker in a selected VPC; it then manages the deployment of the containers across the cluster of instances by managing the placement of the containers throughout the cluster, making sure there are enough resources available to run each container. Containers are launched using a task definition, as shown in Figure 4-44, that defines the following criteria:

- The Docker image to be pulled from the private registry for the container

- The CPU and memory requirements

- Links that need to be established between containers

- Data volumes

- Network and port settings

- IAM security settings

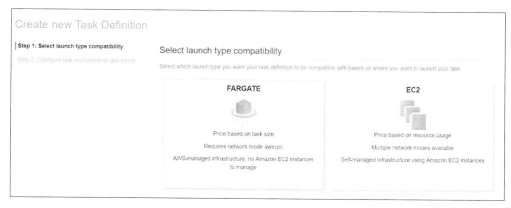

Figure 4-44   Task definition options

The ECS follows what is called a *task placement strategy* using the defined task definition when launching your containers. For example, your strategy might be to spread the containers that are launched across multiple instances and across multiple AZs. Other task placement strategies can include running a task per EC2 instance and your own custom-designed tasks. ECS also monitors all running tasks and can restart tasks if they fail.

ECS is fully integrated with the monitoring services at AWS (CloudTrail), load-balancing services (ALB), role-based security (IAM), and your own private network (VPC). A private Docker image repository called Amazon ECR is available for storing and encrypting your container images at rest.

AWS Fargate

Fargate is a container management service that allows you to run your applications in containers at AWS but not have to manage the underlying instances and clusters. With Fargate, you have the option to specify the container image and memory and CPU requirements using an ECS task definition. Fargate then takes over scheduling the orchestration, management, and placement of the containers throughout the cluster, providing a highly available operation environment. Optionally, you can still launch your container environment using the traditional EC2 launch patterns of the basic ECS service.

AWS ECS for Kubernetes (EKS)

There are other popular container management services in the cloud, including Kubernetes, which Amazon supports with ECS for Kubernetes (EKS). Similar to the concept of AWS Fargate container management, Amazon deploys and hosts the Kubernetes control plane, which controls clusters of worker nodes hosted across multiple AZs.

EKS has been certified Kubernetes conformant, so any third-party plug-ins or tools that you are using or have developed can be migrated to AWS. AWS is also integrated with Elastic Load Balancing (ELB), IAM security services for authentication, VPC hosting for isolation, and AWS CloudTrail.

As a managed service, EKS monitors and replaces any unhealthy control plane nodes and controls the upgrading and patching of your worker nodes. EKS workload clusters can be deployed on any type of EC2 instance. Currently, EKS supports Kubernetes 1.10.11 and 1.11.5 versions.

Amazon LightSail

Want to deploy an application and have AWS do most of the infrastructure work? LightSail allows you to quickly build an application stack from a preconfigured blueprint installed on an instance, as shown in Figure 4-45. Current choices include the following:

- **Applications stack**—Choose an operating system (Linux or Windows), and then choose an application stack blueprint such as WordPress, a LAMP stack, or Nginx. Compute/storage plans are charged by the month and are based on memory, processing, storage, and data transfer.

- **Databases**—Build a MySQL database in a preferred region and choose a database plan of Standard creating your database in a single AZ, or High Availability, which uses two AZs. Plan pricing is based on memory, processing, storage, and data transfer.

- **Networking resources**—Order a static public IP address, create a DNS zone, or add a load balancer to your LightSail design.

- **Storage**—Create EBS block disk volumes in a selected AZ for your LightSail instances. Pricing is always a monthly charge.

- **Snapshots**—Create snapshots of existing LightSail instances.

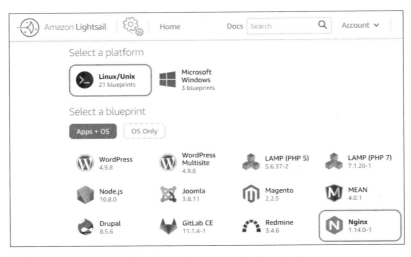

Figure 4-45   Using LightSail to order an application stack

Lambda

Although this is not a development book by any stretch, a discussion about compute options at AWS would not be complete without talking about serviceless computing. Serviceless computing is an inappropriate name because there are servers in the background at AWS; they're just not your servers. Let's explain.

Imagine you have a node.JS Web server, an instance running at AWS. The job of the server is to carry out a specific task or maybe several specific tasks.

- Maybe it runs a batch process several times a day.

- Maybe it converts files uploaded to an S3 bucket into three different formats.

- Maybe it's a fully functional Web server that runs a certain number of tasks based on HTTPS inputs.

For each of these use cases, instead of spinning up your own instance, consider uploading and executing each task as a Lambda function or as Lambda functions to Amazon's hosted instances, as shown in Figure 4-46. Your concern is your custom Lambda function; Amazon's job is hosting and executing your function. That's the basic concept of Lambda; here are the big-picture steps:

1. Upload your function to Lambda as a zip file.

2. Define how long the function will execute.

3. Define how much compute and memory the function requires.

4. Define the trigger that starts the function.

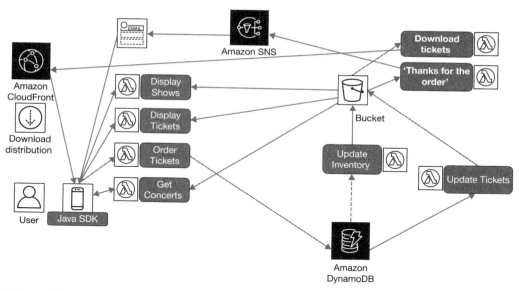

Figure 4-46   Lambda in action

There are many areas in the AWS ecosystem where Lambda is triggered to execute a custom function:

- File uploads to an S3 bucket

- Information being added to a Dynamo DB table

- A CloudWatch alarm or defined event

- Infrastructure components that fall out of AWS Config compliance rules

Each of these actions uses a Lambda server farm hosted at AWS (that is load balanced, auto scaled, and monitored following AWS best design practices) to execute a specific function when required. For public cloud providers, serviceless computing is the future. We'll get into more detail on Lambda and serviceless computing in the final chapter of this book. If Lambda is processing trillions upon trillions of executions per month, perhaps the engine that launched Lambda in 2014 needs a tune-up with AWS Firecracker.

AWS Firecracker

- As Lambda has increased in popularity, the compute engine that executes all the functions has a new engine. Underneath the hood of Lambda is a custom virtualization environment using KVM that launches a micro virtual machine in 125 msec.

- The combination of the fast startup time and the extremely small memory footprint of less than 5 MB for each microVM allows you to store thousands of microVMs on a single hosting Firecracker machine. Virtual machines of this size begin to offer great flexibility for hosting isolated functions. Although Firecracker is not available in the console yet, once it is available, you will be able to use it to host your micro-services in microVMs

- Thinking toward the future, Firecracker VMM is built to run on Intel, AMD, and Arm processors and has been open sourced under Apache version 2.0 to encourage further development.

In Conclusion

There is a lot of detail in this chapter dealing with EC2 instances and their associated bits and pieces, including pricing, images, volumes, snapshots, and migration options. When you look at the available instances, there will be even more choice and more features. Pricing will probably be lower, and change will be constant. That's just the way it is running workloads in the cloud. Keeping on top of changes that affect your designs is a big job but a necessary one; after all, the changes are probably something that you've been looking for. Sit down with your team and start to check off the big-picture discussion points for this chapter. Bring lots of coffee.

Top 10 Big-Picture Discussion Points: Migration and Planning Considerations

1. What database will we first migrate to AWS for testing purposes?

2. What virtual machine will we migrate and test first?

3. What versions of operating systems are we currently using? Are they the latest and greatest versions? If not, why not?

4. Do our virtualized images require paravirtualization support?

5. Do we know what instance size and type to choose for our application servers?

6. Do we know what instance size and type to choose for our database servers?

7. Are there prebuilt AMIs at AWS that we should start with?

8. What tagging strategy should we deploy?

9. What will be our snapshot strategy at AWS?

10. Do we want to use encryption for EBS volumes? If the answer is yes, is using AWS managed encryption keys compatible with our compliance rules and regulations?

5

Planning for
Scale and Resiliency

This chapter looks at the concept of "scaling our applications" that are hosted in the AWS cloud. Scaling is the secret sauce for all public cloud providers: everybody has this feature, and everybody uses this feature. Every application that you like to use on your phone or tablet is controlled by some elements of scale. If your application is slow, perhaps it's because there are too many users currently accessing the application. If your application has decent performance, the odds are that the application is being carefully monitored, and resources are being added or removed based on demand.

Are you watching a movie on Netflix? If you're watching a popular movie, the odds are that other people are also probably watching. Being able to scale or increase the resources that host the movie based on user demand, Netflix has happy customers. When you've shopped at Amazon, can you remember slow page loads and slow response times? Certainly, it has happened, but the odds are that it rarely happens because of AWS's ability to scale its cloud resources based on demand.

In Chapter 1, "Learning AWS," we looked at the definition of what the public cloud seemed to be based on the National Institute of Standards and Technology (NIST) proclaimed definitions of what public cloud providers were currently doing. One of the NIST characteristics of the public cloud was defined as rapid elasticity featuring the statement "capabilities can be elastically provisioned and released in some cases automatically, to scale rapidly outward and inward commensurate with demand."

Let's break down this definition into something more readable: "capabilities can be elastically provisioned and released" describes a situation in which a hosted cloud application can seemingly be changed on demand to provide the desired level of performance by adding performance or taking away the level of performance. Accurately making these types of decisions is completely based on the real-time monitoring of your cloud applications and resources. If you don't know the current state of your application—such as the exact amount of current load being placed on your application servers at this exact moment—then it's impossible to know when you should add or remove additional compute power or storage.

Note

Here's the first rule of running applications in the cloud: you don't know what's going on unless you're monitoring your application resources 24/7.

The next part of this definition, "in some cases automatically," means that you can perform the task of scaling automatically. Most AWS services have a dashboard where you can view the current status of your service and make changes. AWS services can use CloudWatch alarms, or SNS notifications alert you via text or email if there are performance issues. However, the last word of the definition, *automatically*, is the goal. For applications hosted in the cloud that need to be able to handle more users or additional queries at a moment's notice, automated scale is the goal, and it's one that can be accomplished using built-in AWS management services.

The last part of the NIST definition was defining the process of automated scale based on demand—"scale rapidly outward and inward commensurate with demand"—and the ability of your applications to *scale outward* (add resources on demand) and to *scale inward* (remove resources that aren't required any longer). Real-time monitoring is required to automatically scale applications out and in on demand. The ability to automatically add or remove application resources in the cloud is also due to virtualized resources and horizontal scaling. We are not changing the size of our servers to be bigger; vertical scaling of compute resources requires downtime. Scaling in the cloud is horizontal scaling—automatically adding or removing application servers to an existing load-balancing cluster based on demand.

The best example is Amazon and its online store, which of course is powered by Amazon Web Services. On Black Friday or during the holiday season, one could reasonably expect additional Web and application servers to be required to handle the unknown number of customers who will be buying stuff on Amazon. In the initial few years of operation of Amazon.com, the number of servers running was based on expectations—trying to have enough resources available when there were lots of customers. It was a proactive but very expensive design.

Running too many resources costs Amazon a lot of money and will also cost you too much money if hosted resources are on and available but not being fully utilized. Today, Amazon uses monitoring and automation to horizontally scale its Web and application compute resources out (adding more compute power) and in (removing compute power) based on demand. If Amazon can do this, you can as well. Once you're running just the right number of servers based on current demand, and then based on higher or lower levels of demand, dynamically scaling out and in as required, you'll be saving rather than wasting money. And your customers will be happier because your applications will remain sized automatically based on current requirements.

The AWS cloud has many services that take advantage of scale. AWS also calls scale *elasticity*. Look at the naming of the services that make up AWS: Elastic Cloud Compute (EC2), Elastic Load Balancer (ELB), AWS Auto Scale, and EC2 auto scaling. Scale is either implied or part of the name of the AWS service. Typically, when scale is being defined, we are talking about scaling compute resources. However, at AWS, compute (which includes containers) *and* cloud storage such as elastic block storage (EBS) volumes and global DynamoDB tables can also be scaled automatically.

Note

The automatic scaling of compute resources at AWS is dependent on the monitoring of the compute resource that needs to scale using CloudWatch metrics.

Another one of the NIST cloud definitions is *resource pooling*, which is also related to the ability to scale. You can't scale your resources (adding to the number of EC2 instances supporting your application) unless you have the actual resources available to add. Remember: all AWS resources have defined *soft limits* that limit the number of AWS resources that are available to you as an AWS customer. Therefore, scaling in the cloud is only possible if you have the required resources available when you need to add them. And if you're not monitoring your resources, you won't know when to add more or to remove resources when they're no longer required. For more details on soft limits and the type of compute resources available at AWS, make sure to review Chapter 4, "Compute Services: AWS EC2 Instances." In this chapter, we focus first on monitoring, move on to load-balancing, and finish off with auto scaling. These three services work together providing scalable applications at AWS.

The topics for this chapter include the following:

- Monitoring with CloudWatch

- Alarms and alerts

- Elastic Load Balancing

- Application Load Balancing

- Network Load Balancing

- EC2 auto scaling

- AWS auto scaling

Terra Firma is just about finished testing its applications in the cloud, and they seem to work as expected. But now the company needs to look at providing redundancy and failover in scale. Terra Firma also wants to know how the applications are working before problems start occurring. And it wants to control the developers' spending habits. (They also drink too much coffee, but that's manageable.) In a nutshell, the developers need to know the answers to these questions:

- What kind of monitoring service is available at AWS?

- Is it possible to be notified when problems occur with applications?

- Can automated solutions be set in place for applications that are overloaded?

- Can the load balancer perform decryption and authentication?

- Can we track user authentications when problems occur?

- How complicated is it to set up automatic scaling?

The Concept of Monitoring

Back before cloud became mainstream, one of the common reasons for hosting application servers as virtual servers—that is, using VMware—was that most physical servers were found to be percolating along at a 15%–20% load on average. (Obviously, a database server was usually under a much higher operating load.) Companies found that using a large physical server with lots of

RAM and CPU cores running multiple virtual servers was a much better use of the existing hardware. Enter the VMware age.

Experience showed that if multiple VMs were hosted on a physical server, proper monitoring of the hosted virtual machines was essential to ensure that each virtual server's performance was adequate and to make sure that each VM was not running out of RAM, CPU, and storage. And because virtual resources were being utilized from physical resources, additional RAM, CPU cores, and storage could be added and removed as required.

Because of proactive monitoring techniques, we knew when issues and problems arose. If we didn't monitor, we'd run into trouble. When hosting applications in the AWS cloud, monitoring is even more essential; if you don't monitor your AWS resources, you're not going to know when there are issues; therefore, you're going to get in a lot of trouble.

Most AWS services, such as EC2 instances, are integrated with the built-in monitoring service CloudWatch, as shown in Figure 5-1. As you order and configure AWS resources, basic metrics associated with each AWS resource are loaded into CloudWatch, enabling you to monitor your resources.

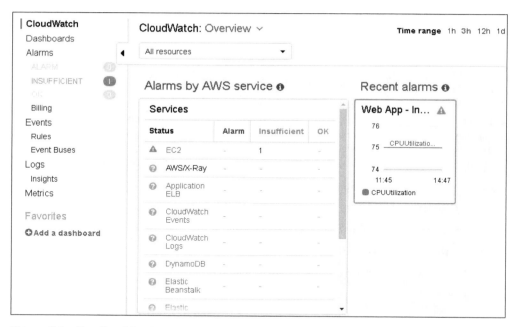

Figure 5-1   The CloudWatch monitoring console

Now, to be clear, you can add your own third-party monitoring solution's monitoring agent to your EC2 instances. You don't *have* to use CloudWatch; you might have specific needs and requirements that CloudWatch can't match. However, if you're using hosted

AWS resources that employ EC2 instances or containers hosting applications—or database servers hosted by RDS—and you don't have another monitoring solution, then you should consider using CloudWatch monitoring because AWS resources are already wired into the CloudWatch monitoring service. Perhaps you already have a monitoring solution that can integrate with CloudWatch datapoints using the CloudWatch application programming interface (API) in conjunction with your third-party monitoring solution such as Loggly or Datadog.

CloudWatch is a frugal, economical monitoring solution that will never be as powerful as a third-party monitoring tool. In fact, Amazon engineers have stated this fact many times. CloudWatch's basic claim to fame is auto scaling EC2 instances hosted behind an ELB load balancer. It manages the auto scaling process quite well. The following are useful features of CloudWatch to consider implementing:

- **Auto scaling with CloudWatch alarms**—Automatically adjust your applications based on need with EC2 auto scaling, ELB, and CloudWatch alarms.

- **Filter logs with metric filters and alerts**—Be notified when specific data patterns occur in your logs, and act accordingly using CloudWatch alerts, metric filters, and simple notification service (SNS) notifications calling Lambda to run custom functions for custom tasks.

- **Billing alarms enabling you to monitor costs**—Control costs by matching billing alerts to actual budget targets using billing alerts and SNS notifications.

- **Logging CloudTrail IAM API calls to CloudWatch logs**—This involves creating CloudTrail trails, storing the trails in CloudWatch, and using metric filters on root account activity.

> **Note**
>
> Any third-party monitoring service you use today, such as Splunk, Datadog, New Relic, and many others, supports integration with AWS CloudWatch data records and S3 buckets.

What Is CloudWatch?

CloudWatch is a monitoring service embedded in the AWS cloud operating system. Many AWS services use CloudWatch to collect metrics that you can use to analyze how your service is currently operating. After ordering specific AWS services, metrics are enabled and available for evaluating the performance and operation of most AWS services, including EC2 instances, EBS volumes, Elastic Load Balancers (ELBs), Auto Scaling groups (ASGs), relational database service (RDS) DB instances, DynamoDB tables, Route 53 health checks, SNS topics and Simple Queue Service (SQS) queues, Storage Gateways, and S3 buckets, as shown in Figure 5-2. Only once an AWS service has been ordered and begins operation is there any data flow, and subsequently, CloudWatch metric data records published to the service's CloudWatch dashboard.

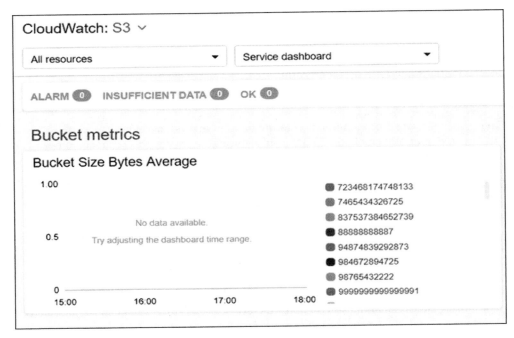

Figure 5-2   Basic metrics for S3 buckets displayed in CloudWatch

Monitoring

Basic monitoring provided by CloudWatch is free of charge and, depending on the AWS service, a select number of metrics are enabled. Metrics report to CloudWatch on a variety of intervals. There is no default among all the services that are supported. For example, for EC2 instances and containers (elastic container service [ECS]), metric data is sent to CloudWatch every 5 minutes. For RDS databases and ELB, a selection of metric data is sent to CloudWatch every 60 seconds. EC2 instances also can enable detailed monitoring, which increases the reporting period to every 60 seconds; however, detailed monitoring is not free.

There's no exact rhyme or reason as to why there are initial differences between the exact number of metrics that are bundled with each AWS service for basic monitoring. Make sure to check what basic monitoring options are available for each service in the AWS documentation; new metrics are being added to CloudWatch all the time, further enhancing its monitoring ability. With every AWS service, there are additional metrics you can choose to also use in monitoring. The CloudWatch metrics shown in Figure 5-3 have been enabled for this particular AWS.

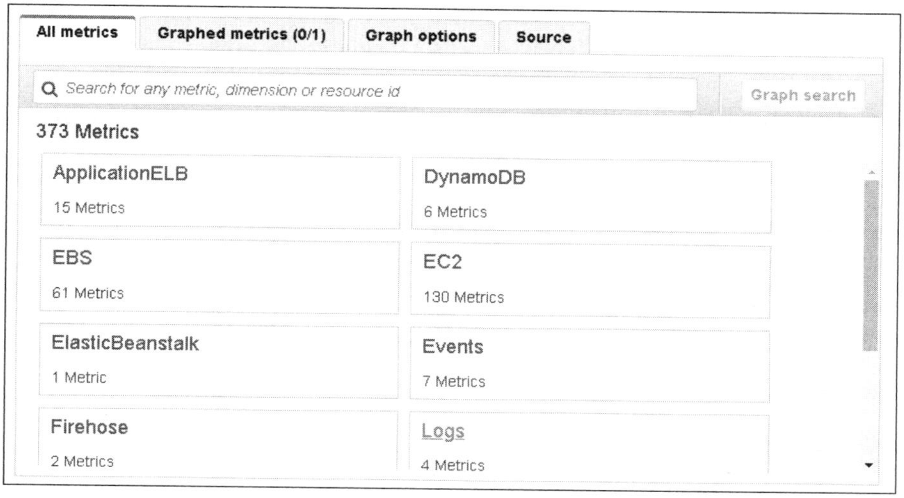

Figure 5-3   CloudWatch metric choices

Logging

CloudWatch also has a logging service that allows you to send your log data from your Linux and Windows instances to CloudWatch log groups. This enables you to further analyze and search your log data for any specific patterns, such as errors or system issues, that you want to analyze further (see Figure 5-4).

The CloudTrail managed service tracks all API calls made to an AWS account for 90 days. The creation of "trails" allows you to send all CloudTrail event information to a CloudWatch log group. CloudWatch log data can also be monitored by creating a metric filter that looks for a specific data pattern or patterns. Once a matching data pattern is found, a CloudWatch alarm can fire off an SNS notification about the issues that have been found (for example, 404 status codes in an Apache access log).

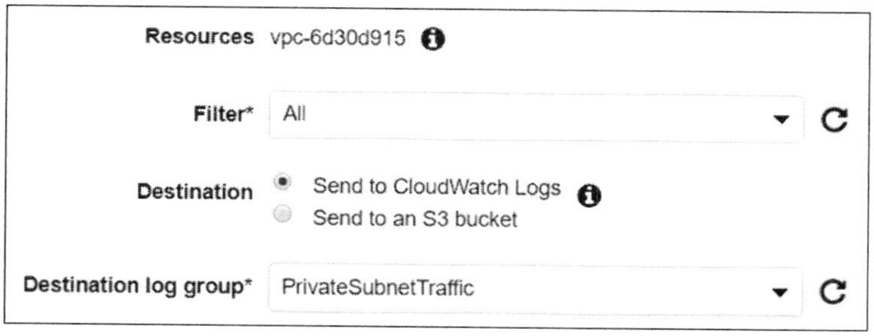

Figure 5-4   VPC flow logs integrate with CloudTrail

Another example of CloudWatch log groups is a virtual private cloud (VPC) network feature called VPC flow logs. Once those logs are enabled, network traffic can be captured from a single network adapter, a single subnet, or all network traffic within a VPC to a CloudWatch log group, providing the ability to analyze your network traffic.

Collected data stored in a CloudWatch log can be analyzed further by selecting one of the following options, as shown in Figure 5-5:

- **Export log data to Amazon S3**—Log information on a defined date range can be exported to a Simple Storage Service (S3) bucket for analysis by any third-party monitoring application.

- **Stream log data to AWS Lambda**—When a log event matches a specific filter, Lambda can swing into action and carry out its defined task. Amazon warns you that streaming log data might cost you; it recommends creating a budget that alerts you when you are close to exceeding your defined budget.

- **Stream to an Amazon ElastiSearch Cluster**—Do this and visualize your data using the open source data virtualization tool Kibana.

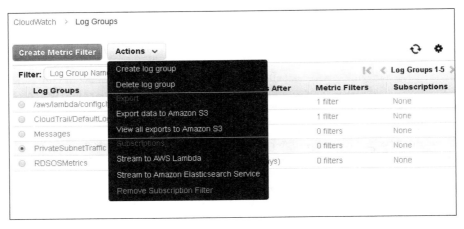

Figure 5-5   CloudWatch log data export options

Terra Firma developers can use the CloudWatch logs to analyze network traffic, and the company's auditors will be able to analyze any API call made to any of its AWS accounts.

> **Note**
>
> The default retention of CloudWatch logs is forever; however, you can decide on a retention timeframe of up to 10 years. Retention of records stored in S3 buckets can be managed with lifecycle rules.

Collecting Data with the CloudWatch Agent

Like any monitoring service, the back-end engine of CloudWatch receives and stores metrics or log data from a CloudWatch agent installed on the EC2 instance, or, optionally on Linux or Windows Server 2016 or later server images that are located on-premise. Supported Linux operating systems include all Amazon Linux versions since 2014, Ubuntu (14.04 and 16.04), CentOS (6.5 and 7.0), RHEL (6.5, 7.0,7.4, and 7.5), Debian 8.0, and SUSE Enterprise Server 12 or later. Amazon machine images (AMIs) of supported operating systems have the CloudWatch agent installed by default.

CloudWatch Agent Install Steps

1. If you migrate your virtual machines to AMIs, you need to install the CloudWatch agent yourself. The agent also requires an identity and access management (IAM) role to transfer data to CloudWatch.

2. If you want to install the CloudWatch agent on servers located on-premise, then an IAM user must be created that will in turn enable the agent to upload data to CloudWatch. You can download the agent from a public S3 link provided by AWS: https://s3.amazonaws.com/amazoncloudwatch-agent/<operating_system>

3. Create the CloudWatch agent configuration file that defines the metrics and logs for which the agent is going to collect proxy settings, IAM role or user credentials, and region information.

4. Run the CloudWatch Configuration Wizard to install the agent.

5. Start the CloudWatch agent with either a fetch-config command line, a PowerShell command, or an AWS Systems Manager run command.

MAKE SURE TO WATCH THE COMPANION VIDEO "INSTALLING THE CLOUDWATCH AGENT."

To access the companion videos, register your book at informit.com/register.

Planning for Monitoring

When deciding what to monitor, the best suggestion is to keep it simple when first starting. If you make it too complicated in the beginning, you'll probably give up. We are monitoring because we want to know when our AWS services are not operating as we expect. Perhaps the service seems slow and we want to understand why. We are ultimately monitoring to be kept abreast of potential problems before they occur and when problems occur. Monitoring allows us to become proactive in solving problems. Monitoring also allows us to proactively react to problems through automation.

Also, it won't be obvious at first, but after you start monitoring and evaluating the results, the light will turn on; your data will indicate what trends are happening, and you will begin to discover why monitoring your applications is essential.

The types of things you can monitor include the following:

- **Performance-based monitoring**—Monitoring your application's compute speed (database, application, or Web server) over time allows you to develop your own initial baseline of operation and what you deem to be an acceptable level of performance. For example, monitoring an application server over a longer time period—for multiple weeks or months—provides valuable data insights as to when the application server gets busy, when there are quiet times, and whether it is busier at the end of the month or at certain times of day. The same criteria can apply to a Web server or a database server. EC2 instances, ECS containers, and RDS instances have CloudWatch metrics; in fact, all AWS services have some integration with CloudWatch.

- **Resources to Monitor**—The initial components to monitor with regard to compute performance are the same ones we have always monitored: CPU, memory, storage, and networking.

- **CPU and RAM utilization**—EC2 instances have the CloudWatch agent installed, which collects many system metrics from EC2 instances. On EC2 instances running Windows Server, all counters in Performance Monitor can be collected by the CloudWatch agent. Linux instances collect system information using metrics for CPU, disk, memory, and networking.

- **Available disk space**—Hard disks with more than 70% disk space used are typically on the edge of causing problems due to lack of available free space. EBS volumes have disk performance and disk read and write operation metrics, and the CloudWatch agent can report on total disk space, used space, percentage of total disk space, and many other metrics. We can also quickly scale our EBS drives at AWS.

- **IOPS**—CloudWatch has metrics for EBS volumes, as shown in Figure 5-6. In addition, the overall read and write performance of EBS volumes can be monitored and increased if necessary by raising input/output per second (IOPS) performance to 64,000 IOPS.

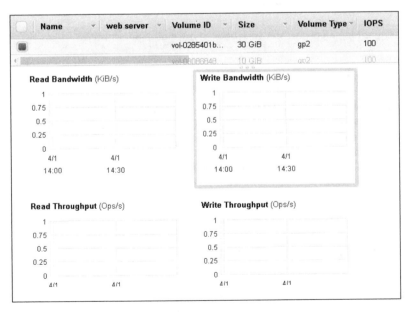

Figure 5-6   EBS CloudWatch metrics

- **Network traffic**—Traffic includes subnet traffic but can also include load-balancing and connections to the cloud, including VPN connections and Direct Connect connections. CloudWatch metrics are available for the ELB service, network address translation (NAT) gateway, transit gateway, and VPN connections. VPC flow logs also capture pertinent network information that is stored at CloudWatch. Additional metrics are available for EC2 instance networking.

Note

At AWS, you can set up notifications for emailing, texting, or sending a notification to an SQS queue, SNS topic, or even better, to Lambda, which could carry out an automated solution using a custom function.

CloudWatch Integration

The following list details some of the AWS services that are embedded with CloudWatch:

- **SNS**—It is used for communication to humans or to other AWS services for sending automated alerts when CloudWatch alarms or events fire.

- **ELB**—Load balancer metrics include active connection count, request count, healthy host count, transport layer security (TLS) connection errors, HTTP responses, and errors.

- **S3 buckets**—Storage metrics detail the number of objects and bucket size; request metrics include all requests, get requests, bytes uploaded and downloaded, 4xx errors, and 5xx errors.

- **EC2 instances**—Once an instance has been launched from the Monitoring tab, 14 metrics are displayed, as shown in Figure 5-7. These include options for CPU utilization and credits, disk read and write operations, network traffic and packet flow, and status checks.

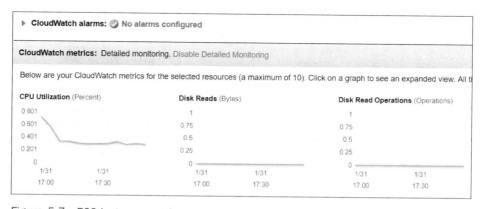

Figure 5-7   EC2 instance metrics

- **EC2 auto scaling**—This allows you to launch or terminate instances controlled by CloudWatch alarms. Metrics include auto-scale group metrics such as the minimum and maximum group size and the in-service, pending, standby, and total instances.

- **CloudTrail**—After a trail has been created, CloudWatch writes the API calls fired in your AWS account to a CloudWatch log file stored in an S3 bucket.

- **AWS Config**—All evaluated rules that fall out of compliance can invoke CloudWatch alarms, which in turn call Lambda.

- **RDS**—Metrics include database connections, disk queue length, free storage space, read and write throughput, solid-state drive (SSD) burst balance, and CPU credit usage.

- **IAM**—All authentication attempts, both successful and unsuccessful, can be monitored by a CloudWatch alarm. When the alarm is fired, SNS notifications can notify humans and automated responses.

- **Trusted Advisor**—metrics include color-codes: green (good), red (there's issues to check), and yellow (there's warnings to consider).

- **VPC**—Metrics include NAT and transit gateways.

CloudWatch Terminology

CloudWatch has its own language to understand with specific terms and definitions.

1. When you create a CloudWatch alarm, choose the metric you want to monitor.

2. Choose the evaluation period that the metric will be monitored for, as shown in Figure 5-8, and what statistical value to measure. Value examples include minimum, maximum, average, and SUM.

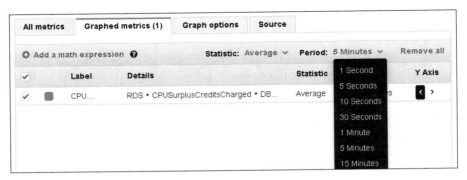

Figure 5-8   Defining the metric evaluation period

3. For each alarm, set a threshold. Choose whether the alarm will trigger when the value is greater than (>), greater than or equal to (>=), less than (<), or less than or equal to (<=) the defined statistic.

- **Namespace**—Each AWS service stores its CloudWatch metrics and associated data in its own container. At this writing, there are more than 74 AWS services that use CloudWatch metrics.

- **Metrics**—Each metric is a variable within an AWS. Each monitored variable produces a data set that is collected over a time period resulting in a graph defined by data points. The data points represent the metric data received from the variable being monitored at an exact point in time based on the range of times selected. For example, with EC2 instances, you can monitor the metric CPU usage, as shown in Figure 5-9. Over the last hour, which is shown on the x-axis, the data points represent the data collected over the last hour in 5-minute increments, defined as the period of time. The y-axis shows the percentage of CPU utilization.

Figure 5-9   Data points summarized every 5 minutes

- **Statistics**—Each metric that you select for analysis collects data based on a defined time period. Graphed data will be categorized statistically using some of the following terms:

  - **Minimum**—The lowest value seen during the specified time period
  - **Maximum**—The highest value seen during the specified time period
  - **Sum**—All values are added together based on a specific time period
  - **SampleCount**—The number of data points over a time period
  - **Average**—Calculated from **Sum** divided by **SampleCount** based on the time period

- **Dimensions**—A dimension describes the metric and what data it stores. Multiple dimensions can be multiple instances assigned to the metric CPU utilization.

- **Units of measurement**—Statistics are defined by bytes, seconds, count, or percentage.

- **Timestamp**—Each metric is stamped with a timestamp that references the exact time when data was received. Each timestamp includes the date, hours, minutes, and seconds based on the current time in UTC format.

- **Time Range (Period)**—The length of time data is collected based on a metric calculated on the defined statistical value. Periods of time can be set from 1 minute up to 15 months. The number of periods define the number of data points that are presented on the graph.

- **Alarms**—An alarm starts an action based on the state of the metric's data over the defined time. Alarms can be notifications using SNS topics, an EC2 action, or an auto scaling action. Each of the CloudWatch metric's data output can also be analyzed against a custom baseline of defined measurement; if the data is below a defined threshold, all is well. However, once the metric's results exceed the baseline or exceed the baseline for a defined time period, CloudWatch alarms can fire, notifying you that there's potentially an issue. Even better, CloudWatch can alert another AWS service that there's a problem, and the problem can be fixed—automatically in some cases. Once enabled, every CloudWatch alarm has three possible states:

  - **OK**—This means that the associated metric is still okay; the data that has been collected and evaluated by CloudWatch still fits within the defined alarm threshold. For example, you may have defined the CPU utilization at 60%. CloudWatch's analysis of the metric's data points over a defined evaluation period indicates that CPU utilization is currently at 52%; therefore, everything's still okay.

  - **ALARM**—Everything's not okay; the metric's data indicates that the established baseline of acceptable CPU utilization has been breached.

  - **INSUFFICIENT DATA**—Everything might still be okay; there's just not enough data yet to make a definitive analysis.

- **Events**—CloudWatch provides near real-time stream of system events for most AWS services based on a defined pattern, such as API calls indicating Root account usage within the AWS account or any IAM API calls. The stream can be stored in a CloudTrail log group and tracked by a metric filter, as shown in Figure 5-10. The target that is notified when the event rule fires can be several AWS services, including an SNS topic, a Lambda function, or an SQS queue. Terra Firma can use events to track any issues with user authentication to AWS.

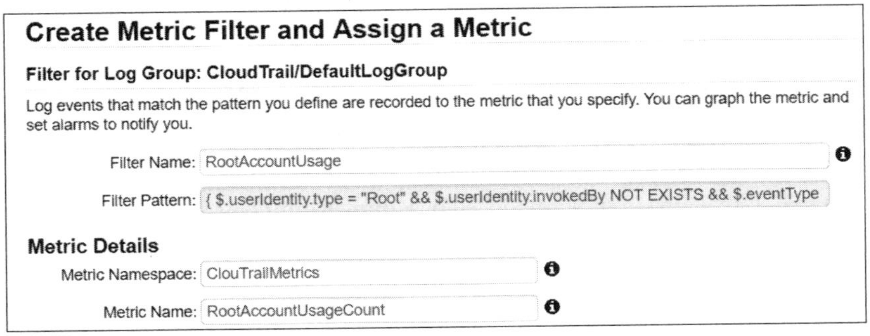

Create Metric Filter and Assign a Metric

Filter for Log Group: CloudTrail/DefaultLogGroup

Log events that match the pattern you define are recorded to the metric that you specify. You can graph the metric and set alarms to notify you.

Filter Name: RootAccountUsage

Filter Pattern: { $.userIdentity.type = "Root" && $.userIdentity.invokedBy NOT EXISTS && $.eventType

Metric Details

Metric Namespace: CloudTrailMetrics

Metric Name: RootAccountUsageCount

Figure 5-10   Defining a CloudWatch event

All metric data is stored with a timestamp referencing a specific point of time; at AWS, these time-stamps are defined as a data point. By default, metrics are defined as standard resolution, which has a resolution of 1 minute. You can change the resolution of the data point from 1 minute to 1 second, resulting in a much more granular distribution of data points. Once you have stored your data in high-resolution format, you can then retrieve it in periods ranging from 1 second up to multiple minutes.

Note

Pricing for CloudWatch is based on the type of metric, the number of dashboards, and the number of alarms that fire. The first 5 GB of CloudWatch log data storage is free; additional storage will be charged. The AWS services that are integrated with CloudWatch send their associated basic metric information to the default CloudWatch dashboard with no additional charges.

One of the best example of AWS service integration and automated problem-solving is the relationship between the gang of three essential AWS services: CloudWatch, Auto Scale, and ELB (load-balancing), which can work together seamlessly. Of course, there is still the need to manually carry out the initial setup of ELB, Auto Scale, and CloudWatch. Once setup is complete, we have an automatic monitoring, alerting, and scaling response. Here's how the gang of three AWS services work together:

1. Instances hosted on subnets in different availability zones (AZs) can be protected by a load balancer. The instances can be monitored by CloudFront on a select metric such as network packets in or CPU utilization, as shown in Figure 5-11.

2. Once the selected metric on the instances has exceeded the defined performance threshold for a defined time period—let's say 75% for five minutes—CloudWatch can promptly fire an alarm that calls the auto-scaling service.

3. Auto Scale starts the build of an additional instance; once ready, the instance is added to the pool of instances targeted by the load balancer. The performance problem is automatically solved without human intervention.

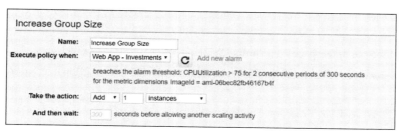

Figure 5-11   CloudWatch and EC2 Auto Scaling in action

MAKE SURE TO WATCH THE COMPANION VIDEO "CLOUDWATCH IN OPERATION."

Using the Dashboard

Opening CloudWatch from the management console displays the default dashboard listing all the current AWS services in your AWS account and the alarm states of your services. If you are currently using fewer than six AWS services, custom dashboards of each service are displayed along with key metrics of each service, as shown in Figure 5-12. Selecting one of the custom dashboards allows you to focus on a specific service.

Figure 5-12   Default CloudWatch dashboard

Creating a CloudWatch Alarm

The first task is to choose the appropriate metric that we want to link with an alarm function. You then need to define the threshold that, when breached, fires the alarm.

1. From the CloudWatch console, choose **Alarms**. Choose **Create Alarm** and then **Select Metric**.

2. From the service namespace (for example EC2), choose your metric or metrics.

3. Select the Graphed metrics tab, as shown in Figure 5-13, and set the following options:

All metrics	Graphed metrics (1)	Graph options	Source				
⊕ Add a math expression ❓				Statistic: Average ⌄	Period: 5 Minutes ⌄		Remove all
✓	Label	Details		Statistic	Period	Y Axis	Actions
✓ ▣	CPUUtilization	EC2 • CPUUtilization • ImageId: ami-06bec82fb4...		Average	5 Minutes	◀ ▸	⌂ ⎘ ✕

Figure 5-13   Define metric behaviors

- **Statistics**—Choose Minimum, Maximum, Sum, or Average.
- **Period**—Choose the time frame that data is sampled, such as 1 minute.

4. Define the alarm with a defined name and the threshold for the alarm to fire, as shown in Figure 5-14.

  - **Whenever**—Define the metric, which in this example is CPUUtilization.
  - **Is**—This can be defined as greater than (>), less than (<), or greater than or equals (>=).
  - **For**—This lists the number of data points and the number of sampling periods (in our case, 3 data points).

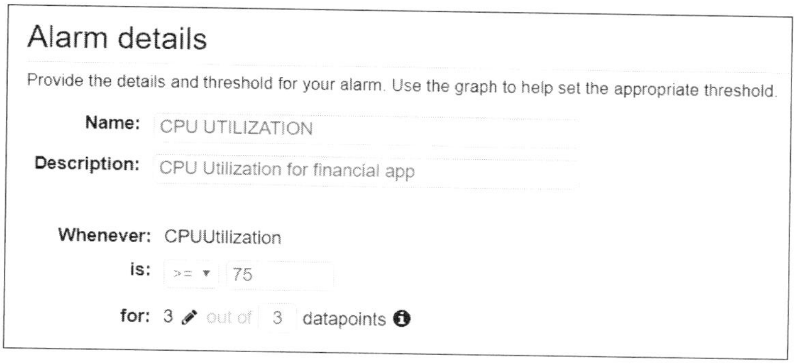

Alarm details

Provide the details and threshold for your alarm. Use the graph to help set the appropriate threshold.

Name: CPU UTILIZATION

Description: CPU Utilization for financial app

Whenever: CPUUtilization

is: >= ▾ | 75

for: 3 ✎ out of 3 datapoints ❶

Figure 5-14   Set CloudWatch alarm details

MAKE SURE TO WATCH THE COMPANION VIDEO "CREATING A CLOUDWATCH ALARM."

Additional Alarm and Action Settings

There are some complicated settings that can define how the stream of metric data is handled when it is stored in CloudWatch:

- Perhaps the instance ran into problems and didn't send data; if that was the case, the default setting of Missing means that the alarm doesn't worry about any missing data points in its evaluation of whether to change state from OK to ALARM. In other words, any missing data isn't considered critical.

- You can also choose to treat the missing data points as being within the defined threshold; in this case, you would choose Not Breaching. Or you could choose to treat the missing data points as reaching the threshold, thereby choosing Breaching.

- In our example, we chose Breaching; the assumption is going to be made that if data points are not being delivered to CloudWatch, there's a problem with the EC2 instance; as a result, the missing data points are critical.

Actions

Actions define what is going to happen when a defined alarm fires; for EC2 instance metrics, we have several choices:

- Send an SNS notification via email or text.

- Choose an auto scaling action that would be appropriate if we were monitoring a cluster of instances. In this case, we would order additional instances to be added to the cluster, thereby reducing the CPU utilization.

- Choose EC2 Action, also called Auto Recovery, which could recover, stop, terminate, or reboot the instance.

Monitoring EC2 Instances

EC2 instances send their basic monitoring metric data to CloudWatch every 5 minutes. You can view the CloudWatch basic metrics from the properties of an EC2 instance and select the Monitoring tab. Detailed monitoring must be enabled on an EC2 instance before you can increase the period to 1 minute. When an EC2 instance is ordered and launched using an AWS-supplied AMI, the CloudWatch agent is installed as a component of the AMI. Instances can use two levels of monitoring: basic, or detailed monitoring.

Basic monitoring includes 12 preselected metrics that report every 5 minutes and 3 status check metrics that report every 1 minute. Detailed monitoring, which is charged, increases the frequency of reporting of each metric to 1-minute intervals.

Automatically Reboot or Recover Instances

CloudWatch alarms can be created to help you automatically reboot or even recover an EC2 instance with no additional CloudWatch charges. The metrics StatusCheckFailed_Instances and StatusCheckFailed_System are provided for this feature, which is called EC2 Auto Recovery.

Reboot—This is for when instances have health check failures. An instance reboot is the same as an operating system reboot. The instance remains on the same physical host. The public DNS name, the private IP address, and data on any instance store volumes are retained. The metric used for rebooting instances as shown in Figure 5-15 is the StatusCheckFailed_Instance.

Recover—This is for system health check failures that can occur when a loss of network connectivity, system power failure, or hardware/software issues occur on the hosting server.

When the system status checks fail, they trigger the StatusCheckFailed_System metric alarm, starting the recovery action for the instance. The failing instance is migrated during the instance reboot to new hardware, and any persistent EBS storage volumes are reattached. Any public IP address is retained; however, any in-memory data contents are lost. Instance types (A1, C3, C4, C5, C5n, M3, M4, M5, M5a, R3, R4, R5, R5a, T2, T3, X1, and X1e) are supported that are hosted on default or dedicated tenancy. Instances must also be hosted in a VPC to use EC2 Auto Recovery.

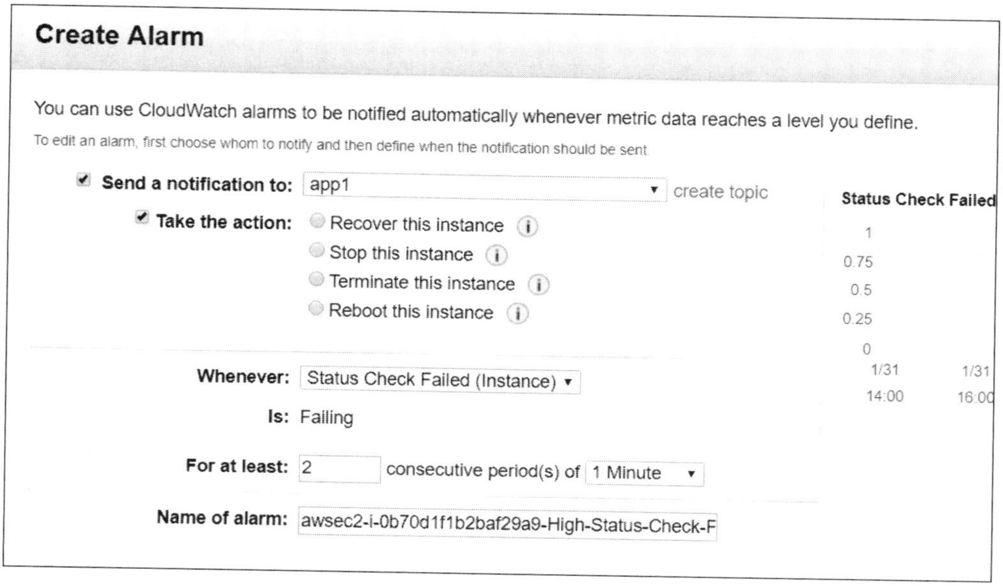

Create Alarm

You can use CloudWatch alarms to be notified automatically whenever metric data reaches a level you define.
To edit an alarm, first choose whom to notify and then define when the notification should be sent.

☑ **Send a notification to:** app1   ▼ create topic

☑ **Take the action:** ○ Recover this instance ⓘ
                        ○ Stop this instance ⓘ
                        ○ Terminate this instance ⓘ
                        ○ Reboot this instance ⓘ

Whenever: Status Check Failed (Instance) ▼
Is: Failing

For at least: 2   consecutive period(s) of 1 Minute ▼

Name of alarm: awsec2-i-0b70d1f1b2baf29a9-High-Status-Check-F

Status Check Failed
1
0.75
0.5
0.25
0
1/31   1/31
14:00   16:00

Figure 5-15   Instance status check monitoring with EC2 Auto Recovery

MAKE SURE TO WATCH THE COMPANION VIDEO "DEPLOYING EC2 AUTO RECOVERY."

Elastic Load Balancing Services

Load balancing is certainly not a new networking service; long before the cloud became popular, load balancing was used in data centers to balance network traffic across two servers. The load balancing could have been static, with defined paths, or it could have been dynamic based on the bandwidth utilization of the available paths.

Load balancing also provides a level of redundancy; if one server in the cluster of servers being load-balanced fails, the application or service is still available.

Operating in the AWS cloud, most AWS services are offered with a standard level of redundancy; in fact, the only service offered by AWS without built-in redundancy is the EC2 instance. Redundancy for your EC2 compute resources at AWS is accomplished by having additional instances or containers and placing these resources behind a load balancer. The load balancer that you choose to use could be from the trio of options provided by the ELB service, as shown in Figure 5-16. Or you could choose from a variety of third-party options, including but not limited to Nginx, Cisco, and Broadcom software appliances. Obviously, because this is a book on AWS, we are focused on AWS services, but many customers use third-party products.

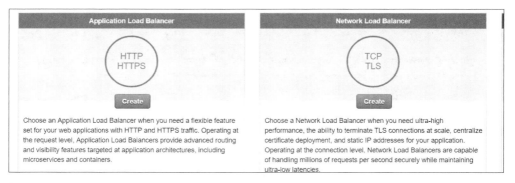

Figure 5-16   AWS load balancer choices

Each load balancer ordered is assigned a traffic profile with a prescribed amount of throughput capacity. The ELB service monitors each online load balancer and scales the capacity required based on the incoming requests.

Each load balancer is charged a monthly fee plus a data transfer charge based on the number of load capacity units (LCUs) used every hour. The LCU is the hourly aggregate total of incoming traffic based on new and active connections, consumed bandwidth, and the number of listener rules that were evaluated. If your workload requires a massive amount of throughput capacity, you can ask Amazon to "prewarm" your load balancer to ensure the load balancer performance is there when required; you need to provide the start and end dates, the expected amount of traffic per second, and the total size of the requests/responses. AWS may tell you that the load balancer that you've ordered will be able to handle your expected traffic levels without prewarming, but it's still a good idea to check if you are going to be hosting applications with massive traffic and scale possibilities at AWS. For most applications, the ELB service can and will scale as required.

The ELB service can distribute the incoming application requests to EC2 instances, containers, and IP addresses hosted in a single AZ or multiple AZs. Sending requests to IP addresses can be redirected to on-premise resources. Target groups define the resources that will be "targeted" by the load balancer listeners. Route 53, AWS's domain name system (DNS) service, resolves the incoming client's request using the DNS name of the load balancer, which is presented as standard address (A) record. However, because the load-balancing service is a redundant AWS service, Route 53 will use Alias records that contain multiple IP addresses' entries, providing for regular and failover resolution to the requested load balancer.

All domains externally hosted outside of AWS need to update their A record to point to the AWS DNS name of the ELB. The load balancer is placed in front of your application servers and hosted in the public subnet, providing the only point of contact for all incoming application requests and protection for your applications; your Web and application servers can reside on private subnets with no direct access from the Internet.

AWS offers three options for load balancing: the Application Load Balancer (ALB), the Network Load Balancer (NLB), and the Classic Load Balancer (CLB). Each ELB option has its features; however, the CLB is only available due to its continued use by existing AWS customers. The ALB and NLB are the only two AWS choices to consider implementing; their feature sets cover the available options of the CLB, as shown in Table 5-1.

Table 5-1 **ELB Choices and Features**

Feature Set	CLB	ALB	NLB
Protocols	TCP, SSL/TLS, HTTP, HTTPS	HTTP, HTTPS	TCP
Networks	Classic, VPC	VPC	VPC
Health Checks	X	X	X
CloudWatch metrics	X	X	X
Logging	X	X	X
Connection draining	X	X	X
Zonal fail-over	X	X	X
Multiple port load balancing on EC2 instances		X	X
WebSockets		X	X
IP address targets		X	X
Lambda as a target		X	
Delete protection		X	X
Path-based routing		X	
Content-based routing			
Host-based routing		X	
HTTP/2		X	
Define idle connection timeout	X	X	
AZ load balancing	X	X	X
SSL offload	X	X	
Sticky sessions	X	X	
Server Name Indication (SNI)			
Back-end server encryption	X		X
Static IP			X
Elastic IP address (EIP)			X
Preserve Source IP			X
User authentication	x		
Web application firewall (WAF) protection	x		

Redundancy by Design

From the customer's point of view, Amazon's ELB service is really a micro-service; behind the scenes it's actually a large redundantly hosted regional service that can scale on demand; as your load balancer handles more requests in the background, the ELB service scales up to meet the demand. We order a "micro-piece" of the ELB service; we don't need to know the inner workings other than that it does its job of load balancing.

ELB can be a key component in your overall application design stack to ensure a highly available and redundant application. If the load-balancing components that ELB assigns to you fail, you are automatically failed over to another load balancer within the massive regional server farm that makes up ELB. Remember: Route 53 alias records are designed to be able to point to multiple ELB resources, ensuring a seamless transition when problems occur.

If you choose to use a third-party load-balancing appliance, you have to design for redundancy and failover by deploying your load balancer in a high availability (HA) pair of load balancers. You also have to monitor for failures and carry out a much higher level of proactive administration when compared to using EBS resources. However, the third-party resource might be a better fit for your organization due to its feature set and your level of experience with the device.

EC2 Health Checks

Certainly, one of the most useful features of all ELB load balancer options is the EC2 instance health check, as shown in Figure 5-17. There's no point in sending user requests to instances that are not available when needed; health checks can be defined to ensure both instances and containers are responding in a timely fashion to the health check requests from the load balancer.

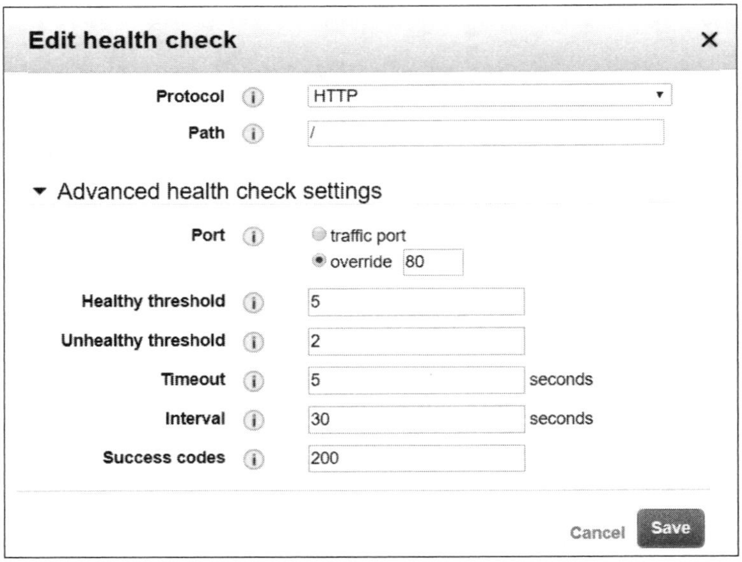

Figure 5-17   Load balancer health check settings

Each load balancer performs health checks at a specific interval to all registered instances. If the instance's response exceeds what's defined as the healthy threshold for consecutive responses, the instance is considered unhealthy and is taken out of service. Note that the load balancer is going to wait for the entire time period defined by the Timeout setting; if this setting is defined at 2 minutes plus 3 retries before the unhealthy threshold is reached, 6 minutes in total will pass before the instance is marked as unhealthy. If the instance responds within the defined response timeout period, the load balancer marks the instance as in-service, and incoming user requests are again routed to the healthy instance.

> **Note**
>
> Route 53, AWS's DNS service, can also perform health checks at the regional level against the load balancer within each AZ. Therefore, ELB health-checks on your Web and application tiers, with both tiers fronted by a load balancer. Route 53 health-checks on the load balancers fronting your Web and application tiers.

Additional ELB Features

Each AWS load balancer has specific features due to its design goals. There are three load-balancing choices. We are going to discuss the two relevant models: the ALB and the NLB. The ALB has more security features than the NLB because it typically routes public traffic coming across the Internet. Additional features of the ELB service to consider are listed next.

SSL/TLS Traffic Decryption—The ALB supports SSL offload, performing SSL/TLS decryption on the incoming connection request, which terminates the SSL traffic on the load balancer before sending the decrypted requests to the application. Certificate management integration is also provided with the AWS Certificate Manager, as shown in Figure 5-18.

The ALB also supports an identification process called server name indication (SNI), which lets the ALB use more than one certificate per ALB. This allows you to use multiple websites with separate domains behind the same ALB. SNI allows the assigning of the correct secure sockets layer/transport layer security (SSL/TLS) certificate to the associated server allowing the ALB to send the website or domain's public key to the end user to establish a secure connection with the load balancer. ALB supports the classic RSA, the industry standard in asymmetric keys, and the newer Elliptic Curve Digital Signature Algorithm (ECDSA), which is defined as elliptic curve cryptography. Both of these certificate options can be currently used for faster authentication purposes. However, most SSL/TLS certificates are still being signed with RSA keys. However, the newer ECDSA standard has a couple of features that make it appealing for mobile communications. First, a 256-bit elliptic curve key provides the same amount of protection as a 3,248-bit symmetric key. Second, a smaller number of keys requires less back-and-forth communication and therefore less bandwidth for mobile applications to securely authenticate using ECDSA keys. Tests have shown that when ECDSA is compared to Rivest–Shamir–Adleman (RSA) in regard to the TLS handshake, ECDSA communication is 9 times faster. ECDSA was popularized due to its use by Bitcoin. It is also used by Apple's iOS and iMessage. ECDSA may be something to consider for mobile applications hosted behind an ALB.

> **Note**
>
> Up to 25 certificates can be attached per ALB.

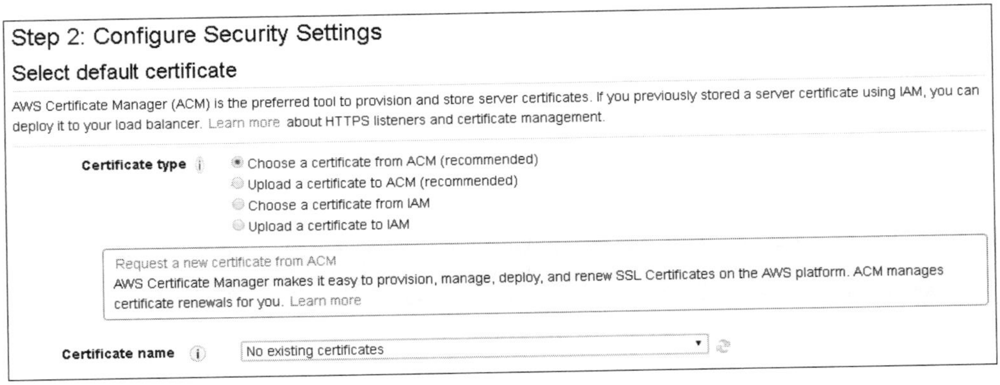

Step 2: Configure Security Settings

Select default certificate

AWS Certificate Manager (ACM) is the preferred tool to provision and store server certificates. If you previously stored a server certificate using IAM, you can deploy it to your load balancer. Learn more about HTTPS listeners and certificate management.

Certificate type ⓘ ◉ Choose a certificate from ACM (recommended)
                    ○ Upload a certificate to ACM (recommended)
                    ○ Choose a certificate from IAM
                    ○ Upload a certificate to IAM

> Request a new certificate from ACM
> AWS Certificate Manager makes it easy to provision, manage, deploy, and renew SSL Certificates on the AWS platform. ACM manages certificate renewals for you. Learn more

Certificate name ⓘ | No existing certificates ▼ | ↻

Figure 5-18   AWS certificate manager can help manage SSL/TLS certificates

IPv4 or v6 support—The IP address type for your Internet-facing load balancer supports both IPv4 and IPv6 addresses; internal load balancers must use IPv4 addresses.

Routing—Using the ALB, content-based, path-based, and host-based routing are supported, allowing connection requests to individual services contained within a domain or container based on the type of the request. Routing to multiple domains hosted in multiple target groups is supported based on the host field or URL path of the HTTP header.

Dynamic port mapping—The ALB supports load balancing containers running the same service on the same EC2 instance where the containers are hosted. When your ECS task definition is launched multiple times on the same EC2 container instance, the containers are running the same service but are individually accessible because the dynamic port mapping process assigns a random port to each container task. Within the target group, the targets for each service will have different dynamically assigned ports. Dynamic port mapping is not supported on the CLB.

> **Note**
>
> ELB load-balancing options integrate with EC2 instances, EC2 auto scaling, Certificate Manager, CloudWatch, Route 53, and, if you're using the ALB, you can also add a web application firewall (WAF) ACL for additional protection.

Connection draining—Once an EC2 instance that is registered with a load balancer is tagged as unhealthy by failing its health checks, the connections to the instance are closed through a process called connection draining. Connection draining from the point of view of the load balancer keeps existing connections open until the client closes them but prevents new requests from being sent to the instances that are tagged as unhealthy.

Connection draining is also a handy administrative option to remove instances from a load balancer target group when maintenance is required; for example, it's time to update a healthy instance with a new version of itself. Performing the deregistration process on an instance as shown in Figure 5-19 starts the connection draining process keeping the existing connections open, providing enough time to complete all ongoing requests. An instance that is in the process of deregistering will not accept new connection requests.

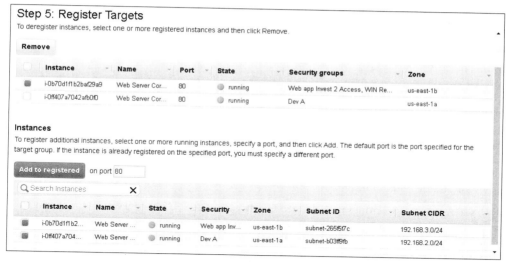

Figure 5-19   Connection draining deregisters instances from target groups

MAKE SURE TO WATCH THE COMPANION VIDEO "CONNECTION DRAINING."

Cross AZ support—Load balancers distribute the incoming traffic requests evenly across the associated AZs. If one AZ has six instances, and the other AZ has four instances, the load is still distributed evenly across the AZs. Best practice is to use the same number of instances in each AZ. You are charged for data transfers between AZs when cross-zone load balancing is enabled.

User authentication—The ALB allows you to offload the authentication process so it can authenticate users as they request access to cloud applications. The ALB can integrate with AWS Cognito, which allows both Web-based and enterprise identity providers to authenticate.

MAKE SURE TO WATCH THE COMPANION VIDEO "UNDERSTANDING ELB FEATURES."

Application Load Balancer (ALB)

The ALB is one of the load balancer choices from the ELB service for application-specific features that work at Layer 7 of the OSI model. However, it's not comparable with third-party "application load balancers" offered by F5, Cisco, and Nginx that are more correctly called application delivery controllers (ADC). The ADC offers many advanced applications services, such as compression, SSL offload, caching, and traffic shaping. Amazon's ALB offers none of these features except for SSL offload. The AWS ALB is designed for the load balancing of containers, instances, and private IP addresses using target groups.

A target group is the destination where the listener sends incoming requests. Targets include instances, containers, and IP addresses. A target can also be registered with multiple targets, as shown in Figure 5-20. Target groups are defined by target type; instance (defined by instance ID), IP (defined by private IP addresses), and Lambda (defined by a specific Lambda function). Targeted IP addresses can include instances using any private IP address from any network interface in a VPC or peered VPC, RDS databases, or on-premise resources that are reachable through a Direct Connect or VPN connection. Instance IDs defined by a target group use their primary private IP address communication.

Auto scaling uses target groups with defined instance IDs. Each EC2 instance or IP addresses can be associated with the same target by using different ports; the ALB uses this feature to route requests to specific micro services posted on the same EC2 instance. Lambda functions can also be targeted and invoked by an incoming load balancer traffic request.

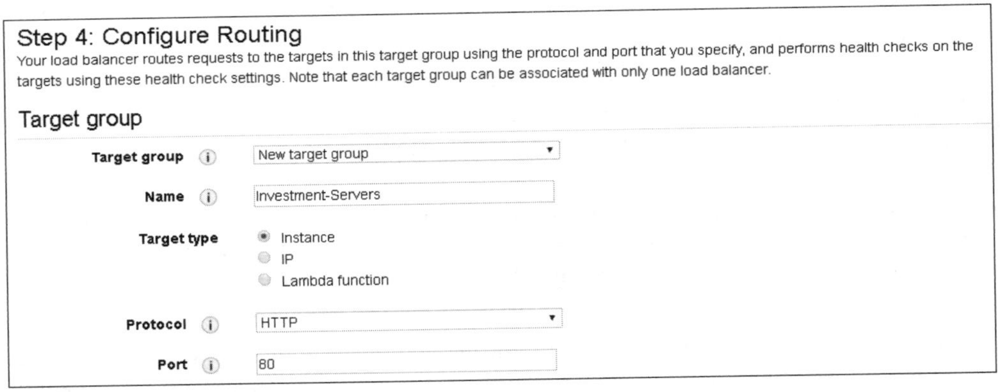

Figure 5-20   Adding a target group to an ALB

Big-Picture Steps: ALB Creation

1. **Choose the load balancer type to install: internal or external.**

   Our first step is to choose what type of load balancer to create. Next, select the scheme: whether the load balancer is accepting public inbound traffic or private inbound traffic. Select the IP address type—IPv4 or IPv6—as shown in Figure 5-21.

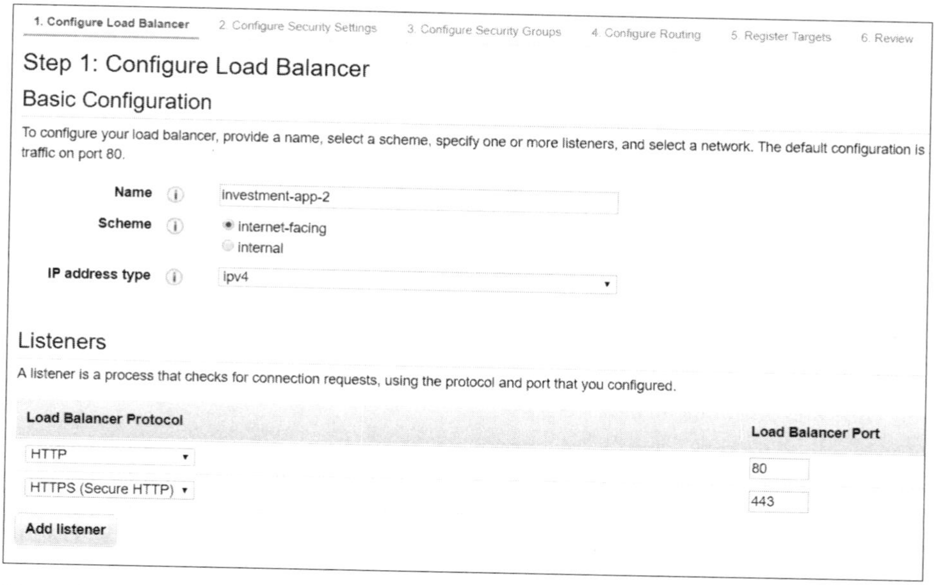

Figure 5-21   Initial configuration of ALB

2. **Configure the VPC, two availability zones, and two subnets.**

We also need to select the VPC and the subnets that the load balancer will be fronting. If it is a public-facing load balancer, it will be hosted in a public subnet. This provides protection for your instances or containers, which can be hosted on a private subnet or subnets and be directly targeted by the load balancer. Subnets from at least two AZs must be selected for availability, as shown in Figure 5-22.

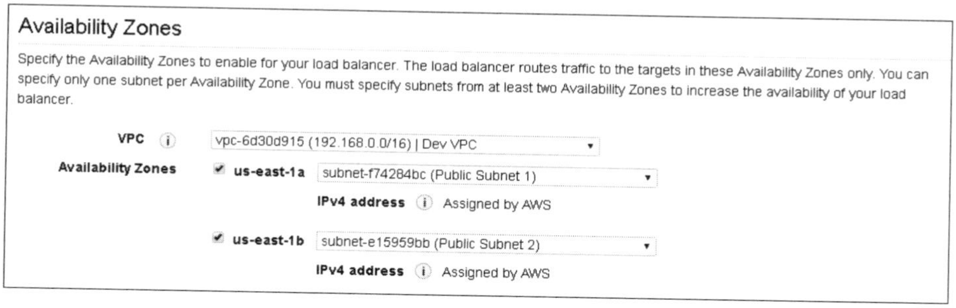

Figure 5-22   AZs and subnets must be chosen

3. **Choose a listener.**

    Load balancers communicate using a process called a *listener*, which continually checks for any incoming requests based on the defined protocol and port that you have configured. Listeners follow rules that determine which target group the incoming connection requests are sent to. The two popular standards are port 80 and port 443; however, you can choose any Transmission Control Protocol (TCP) port you want. The default port is HTTP port 80.

    Each listener monitors all incoming connect requests based on Hypertext Transfer Protocol (HTTP; port 80) and Hypertext Transfer Protocol Secure (HTTPS; port 443) termination between the load balancer and the client. An X.509 certificate must be deployed on either the CLB or the ALB that is using encrypted connections. The AWS Certificate Manager integrates fully with the ELB service, allowing you to easily deploy security certificates on your load balancer.

    Rules can be defined for each listener, defining how user requests are routed to the backend target groups. Additional listeners can be created only after the initial listener has been configured and the load balancer has been launched successfully. Additional listeners can be added, selecting the load balancer after creation and selecting the Listeners tab. You can select existing listeners and view and modify the rules.

    If you're using a listener on port 443, you need to upload your certificate to the load balancer. It's a good idea to first upload your website or domain certificate using the AWS Certificate Manager and then select it while creating the load balancer. You also need to select the security policy that is applied to the front-end connections; uploading a custom security policy is not allowed. Amazon recommends using the latest available policy, which is the most up-to-date security policy listed. The latest security policy is always applied to the back-end connections. Each request accepted by the listener uses two connections:

    - Front-end connection between the client and the load balancer
    - Back-end connection between the load balancer and the associated target

    When either front-end or back-end connections are not idle and are not processing data for 60 seconds, the connections close for obvious security reasons. Depending on the type of connection, you may want to leave the connections open for a longer time period. Connection options can be set at the Web server and on the load balancer by editing the attributes of the load balancer.

4. **Create Rules.**

    Each listener has a default rule. Default rules are simple because they cannot have additional conditions. Therefore, the default rule for HTTP: Port 80 has one action: forward traffic to the defined targets, as shown in Figure 5-23.

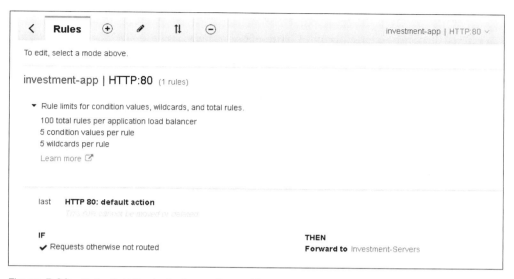

Figure 5-23   Default ALB rule for forwarding traffic

Rule Choices

Rules are precise actions to be carried out by the listener the rules are assigned to. The actions that can be carried out using rules follow:

- **forward**—Send requests to the named target group.

- **redirect**—Redirect the request from one URL to another. Usable components include the protocol (HTTP to HTTP, HTTP to HTTPS, and HTTPS to HTTPS), hostname, port, or path.

- **authenticate-cognito**—AWS Cognito is used to authenticate users, as shown in Figure 5-24. After creating a Cognito user pool, you must create a user pool app client that supports using an AWS ELB authentication session cookie to be authenticated by the load balancer and whitelist to call back URLs for the DNS domain name of the load balancer and the canonical name (CNAME) of your application.

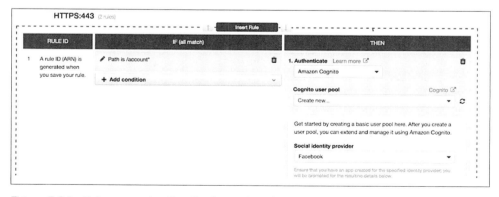

Figure 5-24   Rules can set authentication options for ALB

- **authenticate-oidc**—OpenID Connect authentication.

- **fixed-response**—Send a custom HTTP response to the end user.

> **Note**
>
> Rule conditions can also be defined. Each rule can have one host condition or one path condition. Rule actions are carried out only if the conditions are met.

Host-based routing—This routing option forwards requests to a target group based on the domain name contained in the host header. When the hostname in the host header matches the hostname in the listener rule, the request is routed. Wildcard characters can be used in the first part of the hostname, but not in the name after the period (*name*.com).

For example, requests to a.example.com could be sent to one target group, and requests to b.example.com could be sent to another target group. Rules can be created that combine path and host-based routing allowing you to route requests to a specific path such as */productiondocs*, as shown in Figure 5-25. Up to 75 rules can be applied per ALB.

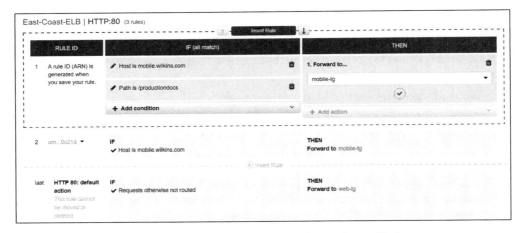

Figure 5-25   Host- and path-based rules can be defined for precise traffic flow

Path-based routing—If the path in the URL matches the path pattern defined in the listeners rule, the request is routed. Instead of just the root domain being able to be used as the path to send requests, endpoints can be defined at the ALB directing the traffic requests, as shown in Figure 5-26.

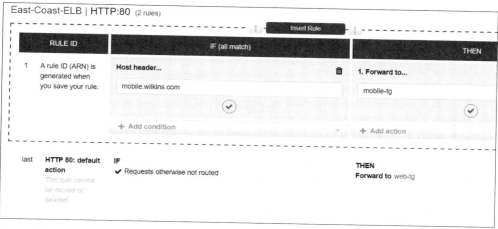

East-Coast-ELB | HTTP:80 (2 rules)

Figure 5-26   Path rules match the request to defined URL rules

Both path- and host-based routing allow you to control the compute environment where the requests are being directed. Certain requests such as API calls may be processed on a compute-optimized instance target group; other requests can be directed to memory-optimized instances in another target group.

MAKE SURE TO WATCH THE COMPANION VIDEO "CREATING LISTENER RULES."

HTTPS Listener Security Settings

There are several security settings that must be defined during the installation of the ALB for the HTTPS listener:

- As previously mentioned in ELB features, a security group must be attached to allow communication to the registered targets. The load balancer communicates with the resources in each target group and carries out health checks on the resources to ensure their availability. The security group must be assigned that allows both inbound and outbound traffic for the listeners and health checks in both directions, from the resources in the target group to the load balancer.

- The ALB uses an X.509 certificate (SSL/TLS), and each certificate is associated with the domain name. As shown in Figure 5-27, you can choose a certificate that has been preloaded to the Certificate Manager. Optionally, if Certificate Manager is not supported in your region, you can use the AWS command-line interface (CLI) to upload your security certificate to IAM.

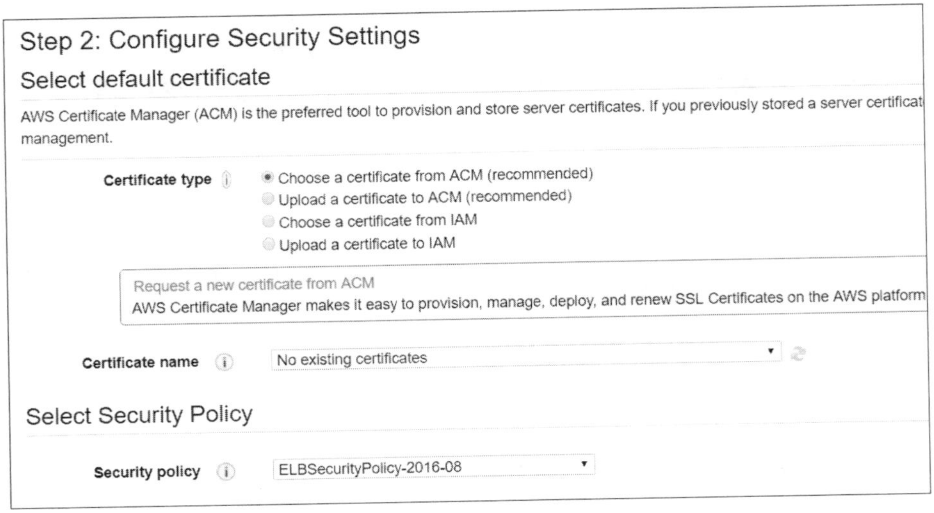

Step 2: Configure Security Settings

Select default certificate

AWS Certificate Manager (ACM) is the preferred tool to provision and store server certificates. If you previously stored a server certificate management.

Certificate type ⓘ
    ● Choose a certificate from ACM (recommended)
    ○ Upload a certificate to ACM (recommended)
    ○ Choose a certificate from IAM
    ○ Upload a certificate to IAM

Request a new certificate from ACM
AWS Certificate Manager makes it easy to provision, manage, deploy, and renew SSL Certificates on the AWS platform

Certificate name ⓘ   No existing certificates ▾ ↻

Select Security Policy

Security policy ⓘ   ELBSecurityPolicy-2016-08 ▾

Figure 5-27   Choose security certificate for ALB

- The security policy for front-end connections for the HTTPS listener can be chosen; AWS recommends that you select the most current policy available, which is always used on the back-end connections. Custom policies cannot be deployed on an ALB.

Note

Certificates uploaded to the ALB from Certificate Manager are automatically renewed by the Certificate Manager service.

Target Group Routing

Now that we have selected our listeners and our certificate and defined our security group, it's time to target the resources that the load balancer will route traffic to. The protocols supported by target groups are HTTP and HTTPS, and optionally any TCP port number from 1 through 65535. Your configuration may use a single listener listening for HTTP traffic on port 80, yet have several target groups with different routing connections defined by the assigned rules to the listener. We have three choices per target group:

- **Instance**—Instances are always defined by the instance ID; traffic is always using the private primary private IP address on the primary network interface.

- **IP**—IP addresses are private IP addresses that can be defined on any network interface.

- **Lambda**—This is a single targeted Lambda function.

Targets (instance or private IP address) are registered in target groups located in an AZ. At least one registered target must be in each target group.

As soon as the target has finished registering and has passed its health checks, the load balancer can start routing user requests to the target. When a target is deregistered, the load balancer waits until any requests that are in process are completed.

Target Group Attributes

Each instance or IP target group's operation can be controlled by several attributes, as shown in Table 5-2.

Table 5-2   **Target Group Attributes Can Be Used for Instance or IP Targets**

Attribute	Details
deregistration_delay_timeout_seconds	How much time before a target (instance or IP) is deregistered; default is 300 seconds.
slow_start.duration_seconds	The time a new target (instance or IP) is sent a gradually increasing number of connection requests; up to 15 minutes. No default setting.
stickiness.enabled	Enabled or disabled.
stickiness.lb_cookie.duration_seconds	Cookie expiration in seconds; default is one day.
stickness.type	Must be set to lb_cookie.

Maintaining User Sessions

If a load balancer is presenting an application that is merely providing generic information, then maintaining a specific user session may not be required. However, for applications where the user is interfacing with an initial server, maintaining the same session between the end user and the back-end server is important. If you are buying something online, you expect your session to begin and end properly without problems.

Because the ALB is between the user and the back-end application server, and SSL offload is being performed by the ALB, the back-end server won't know the IP address protocol and the port used between the front-end connection from the user to the load balancer. The ALB uses specific X-forwarded headers to pass client connection information to the back-end servers for front-end connection using HTTPS and HTTP/2 connections.

- **X-Forwarded-For**—This request header allows forwarding of the client's IP address to the back-end servers in the form *X-forwarded-For: client-ip-address*.

- **X-Forwarded-Proto**—This request header allows back-end servers to identify the HTTP or HTTPS protocol that a client used when connecting to the load balancer in the form *X-forwarded-Proto: originatingProtocol*. The protocol passed to the back-end server allows the application or website to redirect the user request to the desired URL.

- **X-Forwarded-Port**—This request header allows back-end servers to identify the port that the client used to connect to the load balancer.

Sticky Session Support

ELB also supports sticky sessions, which allow the load balancer to bind the user's active session to a specific instance, ensuring that all users' requests are sent to the initial instance the session was started on. With sticky sessions enabled on a load balancer, after a request is routed to a target, a cookie is generated by the load balancer and returned to the client. All requests from the client from this point forward include the cookie; the information contained in the cookie ensures that the request is routed by the load balancer to the same back-end server. The enabling of sticky sessions and the parameters for the stickiness of the cookie are defined by editing the target group attributes, as shown in Figure 5-28.

What happens when the back-end server that the user is connected to fails and is no longer available? The load balancer automatically chooses a new healthy instance and moves the user to the new instance for the remainder of the session, even if the old instance comes back. This does not mean the new instance knows anything about the user; sticky sessions are useful when everything works, but they're not so useful when things break.

If you don't use sticky sessions and choose to replicate the user session information to all other servers in the cluster using session replication, a busy application cluster with lots of user requests might be flooded with too much user information to keep track of.

Rather than using sticky sessions, you could consider using a central storage location for user session information, using a DynamoDB table or a hosted ElastiCache Redis cluster or Memcached nodes. This adds complexity, but for massive user sessions, it may be the best option.

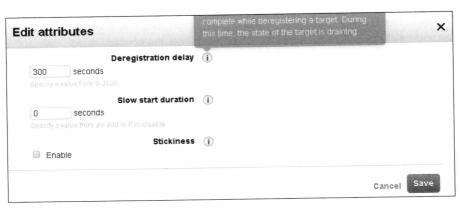

Figure 5-28   Target group attributes

Configuring Health Checks

Health checks can be configured for each target group against the registered targets. There are several settings to understand when creating health checks, as listed in Figure Table 5-3. As discussed earlier in this chapter, health checks ensure your resource is available and ready to accept user requests. Depending on the ongoing results of health checks, a registered target is typically defined as *healthy* or *unhealthy*.

A newly added target to the target group is defined as *initial*; once its health check is successful, the target is defined as *healthy*. When the target is being removed and connection draining is underway, the target is marked as *draining*.

Table 5-3   **Health Check Settings**

Health Check Setting	Details
Health Check Protocol	HTTP or HTTPS can be used.
Health Check Port	The port used for performing health checks on targets. The default is the communications protocol port, 80, or 443
Health Check Path	The destination ping path on the target. Default is /.
Health Check Timeout Seconds	No response from the target in the listed timeout (2–60 seconds) is a failed health check.
Health Check Interval Seconds	The time between each health check (5–300 seconds).
Healthy Threshold Count	Consecutive health checks required from an unhealthy target before the target is considered healthy.
Unhealthy Threshold Account	Consecutive failed health checks resulting in an unhealthy target.
Matcher	Successful HTTP code from a healthy target (200–499).

Terra Firma can use health checks to ensure that resources placed behind load balancers are available as required. EC2 auto scaling can also take advantage of ELB health checks when applications are automatically scaled using auto scale groups. You'll read more about EC2 Auto Scaling in a few pages.

Monitoring Load Balancer Operation

There are several AWS services available for monitoring your ALB or NLB operations, including CloudWatch, and access logs that can be enabled for each load balancer.

CloudWatch—ELB metrics can be used to monitor and ensure your system is performing as you expected. Only when your load balancer is responding to user requests will metrics be reported to CloudWatch for analysis. Table 5-4 lists several metrics that provide operating details based on the sum of the totals.

Table 5-4   **CloudWatch Metrics for ELB**

ELB Metric	Details
ActiveConnectionCount	Concurrent TCP front-end and back-end connections
ConsumedLCUs	Number of load balancer capacity units used
NewConnectionCount	Total number of TCP connections from clients to load balancer to targets
ProcessedBytes	Total number of bytes processed by the load balancer
RequestCount	Number of requests processed with responses from a target
HealthyHostCount	Number of targets that are healthy
UnhealthyHostCount	Number of targets that are unhealthy
RequestCountPerTarget	Average number of requests received by each target in a group

Access logs—You can also choose to enable access logs, which provide detailed information about all requests sent to your load balancer. Once enabled, ELB captures the logging detail and stores it in the desired S3 bucket. Additional security can be provided by enabling server-side encryption on the bucket to encrypt each access log file. Choosing S3-managed encryption keys (SSE-S3) ensures each log file is encrypted with a unique AWS managed key that has multifactor authentication enabled, and automatic key rotation carried out by default.

Log files are published every 5 minutes. Log details include the type of request or connection (HTTP, HTTPS, http2, WebSockets, WebSockets over SSL/TLS) and the timestamp, client port, and target port, request and target processing time, and sent and received bytes. All the details provided by CloudWatch logging can be provided by access logs for a fraction of the cost of CloudWatch metrics.

Network Load Balancer

A Network Load Balancer (NLB) is designed for supporting private resources using the TCP protocol and port number at the fourth layer of the OSI stack. Listeners, target groups, health checks, and most of the features are similar but not exactly the same as an ALB because the NLB is designed for private access. You could use it as an Internet-facing load balancer; however, the NLB doesn't support SSL offload, HTTPS, and cannot be protected by the WAF. In addition, security groups are not available with a NLB—you have to rely on the instance's security groups for controlling access. Container support is also much more advanced using the ALB with path and host-based routing.

One of the primary reasons for NLBs at AWS is the support of VPC Endpoint Services, also called AWS PrivateLink, which use NLBs in front of private application stacks hosted in VPCs. Additional details on AWS PrivateLink can be found in Chapter 3, "AWS Networking Services," and by watching the companion video on NLB setup.

MAKE SURE TO WATCH THE COMPANION VIDEO "CREATING A NETWORK LOAD BALANCER."

Scaling Applications

Terra Firma has a Web application designed and operating on EC2 instances; in fact, it has followed best practices and has the application load spread across multiple AZs on multiple instances. The application works just fine, with adequate speed for 2,000 users. But last week the application was made available to a few additional users, and the application response started to slow down. That's when the developers decided to add some additional instances, and everyone was happy once again.

This manual solution does work, but it's not ideal. Manual analysis of the existing EC2 instances, or waiting for complaints from the application users, is not proactive. The application in question is going to have many more users in the future, so why not just add a few more instances into the mix? Users won't complain. However, there's a new issue now: cost. If more compute instances are running 24/7, the cost of hosting the application has also increased.

Amazon had this exact problem in its early days of running the Amazon.com website. Running excessive compute capacity was expensive. This problem was solved with EC2 Auto Scaling.

EC2 Auto Scaling

At the start of this chapter, we talked about the three AWS services I called the gang of three: CloudWatch, ELB, and EC2 auto scaling. Together, these services make sure that you have enough compute power for your applications that are running in the AWS cloud.

If your applications hosted in your on-premise data centers can't scale, auto scaling may offer a solution. It's likely that you have a private cloud hosted on-premise in your own data centers. Scale in this case is probably constrained by the number of bare-metal servers that you have, perhaps space, and the other available resources such as load balancing. At AWS in a typical Amazon data center, there are typically between 50,000 and 80,000 bare-metal servers. They simply have more resources. AWS uses monitoring, load balancing, and auto scale to run most of its managed services.

At AWS, we can vertically scale instances that are running any application, including database instances; however, vertical scaling is a manual task. Even if you automate the vertical scaling command, there will be downtime because the compute instance will be offline during reconfiguration.

In a nutshell, EC2 Auto Scaling makes sure that the compute power required by your application is always available. EC2 instances are grouped together in what is called an Auto Scaling group (ASG). Once you define the minimum number of instances for each ASG, auto scaling ensures that the minimum defined instance number is always available. You can also define a maximum number of instances in the ASG; auto scaling manages the maximum number as well. Perhaps you want to maintain a desired capacity of compute instances; that's also an available option. Desired capacity was defining the number of EC2 instances that are started when auto scaling is first launched. If you defined a desired capacity of 2 instances, then 2 instances will be maintained by Auto Scale. The desired compute capacity can also be scaled out or in based on CloudWatch alarm triggers, which can order a change in the number of instances plus or minus. If a desired capacity value is entered, the desired capacity is maintained.

You may already have a cluster of servers targeted behind a load balancer. You can think of this initial number of instances as your desired state. Adding auto scale to this design allows you to scale out or scale in your overall compute power based on CloudWatch alarms.

You can also use auto scaling without a load balancer if you want to maintain a desired state of compute power. In this case, minimum and maximum values are not needed.

Finally, you can choose to add a bit of automation into the mix using the other two services we've talked about in this chapter: CloudWatch and ELB.

Besides the EC2 auto scaling benefit of maintaining the right amount of compute capacity, there are other benefits to consider:

- **Cost management**—EC2 auto scaling helps to save money; if your application has just the right amount of capacity—not too much and not too little—then you're not wasting compute power that you're not utilizing. Automating your capacity saves you a lot of money.

- **Fault tolerance**—EC2 auto scaling integrates with AWS load balancing services (ELB) and AZs. Auto scaling makes the load balancer's job easier because the resources available in each AZ can be scaled up and down based on demand.

- **Health checks**—EC2 auto scaling can detect when instances are unhealthy. You may remember that the load-balancing service could also do health checks on targets in target groups. Auto scaling can not only detect unhealthy instances but remove and replace the instance that's unhealthy with a new instance.

EC2 Auto Scaling Components

EC2 auto scaling works with three main components: a launch template, also called a launch configuration; ASGs; and a defined scaling policy.

Launch Configuration

The launch configuration is a template used by the ASG to launch EC2 instances. Creating a launch configuration is like the steps you would take when manually launching an EC2 instance from the management console. The launch configuration is prestaging the EC2 that will be built by the ASG. Each launch configuration matches up against one ASG at a time. The template includes numerous system components, including the instance ID of the AMI, the instance type to build, the key pair for authentication, desired security groups, and a block storage device. Launch configurations have been superseded by the launch template, which has many additional settings that can be used by an ASG when deploying instances.

Launch Templates

A launch template is similar to a launch configuration, with the added feature of versioning. A default launch template can be created as a source template; then other versions of the template can be created and saved. AWS recommends that you use launch templates rather than launch configurations and specify specific tags or additional core information that your company wants to embed in each launch configuration, such as AZs and subnets, as shown in Figure 5-29.

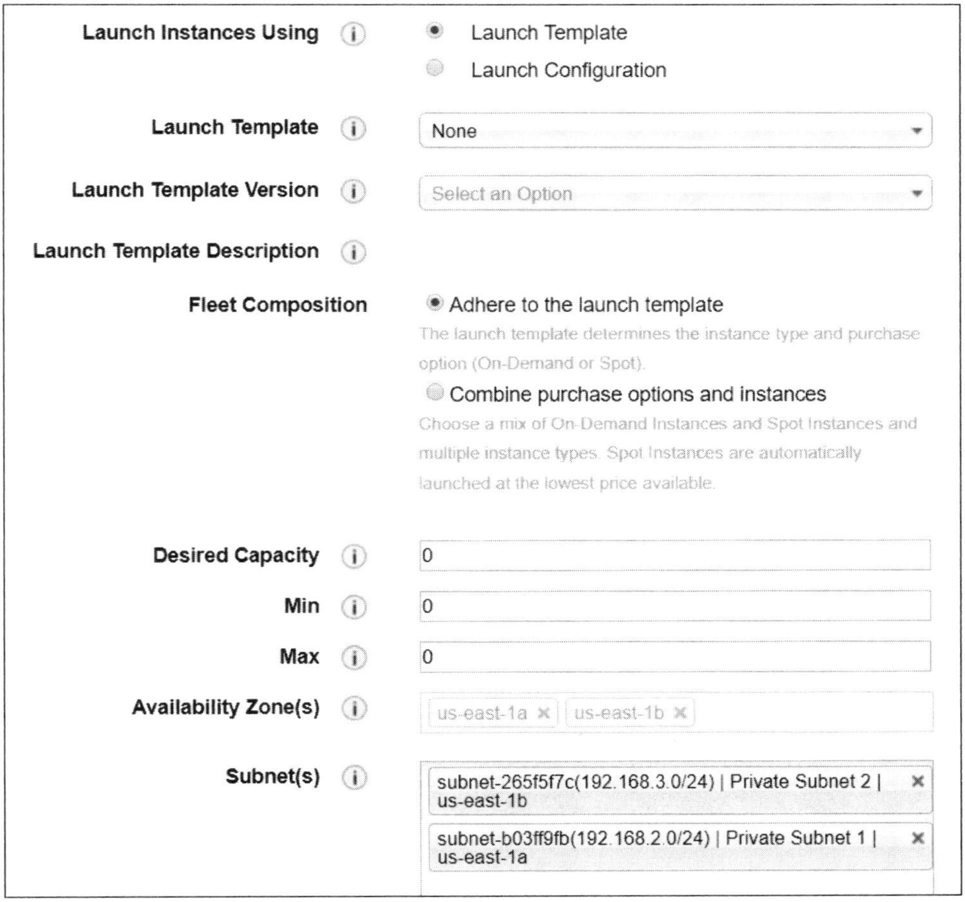

Figure 5-29   Launch configurations

MAKE SURE TO WATCH THE COMPANION VIDEO "CREATING LAUNCH TEMPLATES."

Auto Scaling Groups (ASGs)

An Auto Scaling group (ASG) is built from a collection of EC2 instances that have been generated from the associated launch configuration or launch template. Each ASG launches instances following the parameters of the launch template to meet the defined scaling policy. There is some overlap between some of the settings that can be defined in an ASG and a launch configuration template. Network settings, including AZs, and subnets can also be defined in an ASG, as shown in Figure 5-30.

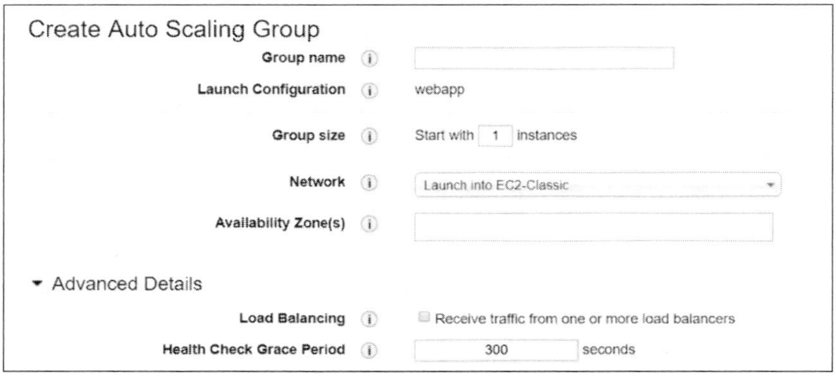

Figure 5-30   Auto Scaling group setting options

Scaling policies can also be attached to ASGs to help dynamically increase or decrease the number of EC2 instances. You can also choose to manually override the defined settings of an ASG and scale the number of instances up or down as necessary.

The instance types that can be added to an ASG include on-demand, spot, or reserved instances across multiple AZs. You can also define the percentage of on-demand and spot instances' capacity for additional cost savings. If you manually select and configure an EC2 instance during the creation of the ASG, AWS creates a launch template based on your manual choices.

ASGs can be associated with an existing load balancer, which then routes traffic to the ASG instances. EC2 auto scaling supports both the Classic, Application, and Network Load Balancers.

ASGs perform health checks on instances added to an ASG; we also know that load balancers can perform health checks on instances in target groups. Auto Scale health checks are checking availability of the instance using the EC2 status check. If instances added to an ASG fail their status checks after boot, they are considered unhealthy, terminated, and re-added to the ASG. Load balancer health checks are a little more complicated when carrying out their health checks, as we have discussed; therefore, ASGs can be configured to also use ELB health checks. This combination of health checks provides the added benefit of performing health based on the status check and on the load balancers' health check tests. If either of the health checks fails, the instances are terminated.

Note

If your ASG is not associated with a load balancer, the ASG health checks are used.

Scaling Options for Auto Scaling Groups

Manual scaling—You can make manual changes to your ASGs at any time by changing the maximum, minimum, or desired state values to start capacity changes.

Maintain current instance levels—Set the desired capacity and health checks to determine the health and automatically replace any instances that are determined to be unhealthy by the auto scaling health check or the load-balancing health check, whichever is selected.

Target tracking—Increase and decrease the ASG based on a metric, as shown in Figure 5-31, to maintain a target value across all instances. You can select several metrics, such as CPUUtilization to support target tracking. Setting CPUUtilization to 60% results in instances being added or removed to maintain the desired CPU utilization. Slightly more instances are typically added than necessary when maintaining the desired CPU utilization because the math behind the scaling calculations plays it safe by rounding up the number of instances to add or remove.

Increase Group Size

Name:	Increase Group Size
Execute policy when:	No alarm selected ▼ ↻ Add new alarm
Take the action:	Add ▼ 0 instances ▼
And then wait:	300 seconds before allowing another scaling activity

Create a scaling policy with steps ⓘ

Figure 5-31   Target tracking variables for increasing group size

Simple scaling policies are also bound to a *cooldown period*; in other words, let's not rush it. Here's an example of where a cooldown period could be useful. Terra Firma has a three-tier application running in test mode on AWS consisting of Web servers, application servers, and the RSA database tier. Separate ASGs are created for the Web tier and for the application tier. Each tier uses CloudWatch alarms to scale out whenever the CPUutilization for each tier exceeds 70 percent. The firing of the alarm instructs the ASG to launch and configure an additional instance.

Each instance uses a User Data script to help install and set up the instance, installing software and updates, before the instance is ready to be placed into service. These additional tasks take time, usually 4–5 minutes. After all, it's the cloud. Sometimes update and build tasks take a little longer than usual.

While the new instance is being readied and an unexpected increase in CPUutilization occurs, the CloudWatch alarm fires once again, ordering the ASG to launch another instance.

Because a cooldown period is in force, after the ASG launches an instance on request, any further scaling requests are ignored until the cooldown period finishes. The default cooldown is 300 seconds, but this can be changed when you create the ASG. The cooldown period is either a cooldown during scaling out or a cooldown period before termination.

> **Note**
>
> Amazon recommends that metrics used for target tracking should be set for a 1-minute frequency to ensure a faster response time. Detailed monitoring must be enabled to utilize 1-minute intervals.

Scale based on a schedule—Scaling can also be defined by time and date values, which instructs auto scaling to scale up or down at a specific time. The start time, minimum, maximum, and desired sizes can be set for recurring actions. The issue with scheduled scaling is that there is still compute waste. It's much better to enable scaling on-demand, and it's not hard to set up.

Scale on demand policy—Demand scaling allows users custom metrics that will determine the scaling out and in of your defined fleet of EC2 instances. Multiple policies can be attached to an ASG that can both control the scaling out and in. Multiple scaling policies can provide scaling control. For example, a scaling policy might react to the CloudWatch metric Network Utilization and scale out when network traffic is greater than (>) a certain percentage. Or a scaling policy could measure the depth of messages in an SQS queue and scale out when the number of messages is over a certain value. Both simple scaling and step scaling support the following parameters for scaling instances:

- **ChangeInCapacity**—Increase or decrease the capacity of the ASG by the defined number of instances.

- **ExactCapacity**—This value defines the capacity of the ASG to the defined number. For example, if the current capacity is four instances and an adjustment to the ASG is three instances, the capacity is set to seven instances.

- **PercentChangeInCapacity**—This changes to the capacity of the ASG by either a positive or a negative percentage value.

- **Step Autoscaling Policy**—Using steps is the most advanced option because it allows you to have multiple policies for scaling out and in. Step scaling allows you to define a lower and upper boundary for the metric being used and to define the amount by which to scale in or scale out the instances, as shown in Figure 5-32, with incremental steps in or out.

    - A first instance is added when CPU utilization is between 40% and 50%.

    - The next step adds two instances when CPU utilization is between 50% and 70%.

    - In the third step, three instances are added when CPU utilization is between 70% and 90%.

    - When CPU utilization is greater than 90%, add a further four instances.

The step policy also defines the warm-up period, which is defining the amount of time required before the instance is running and ready to go. Keep in mind: instances may need to apply updates, finish configuration, and pass health checks. Only after a successful warmer is the next step in the policy applied. The same steps in reverse can be designed to scale back in.

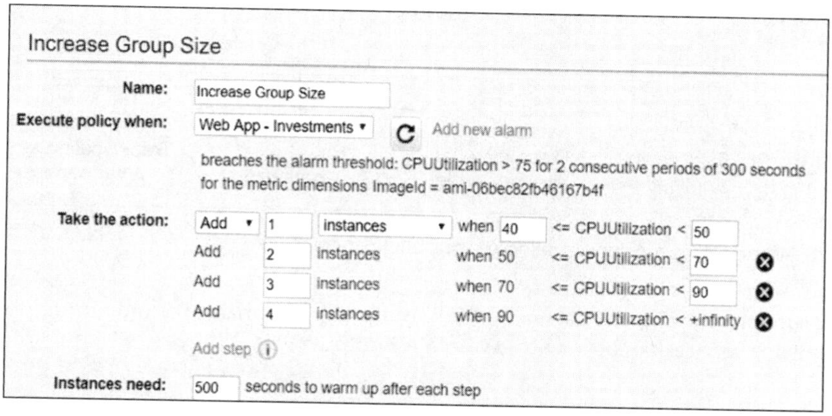

Figure 5-32   Step scaling parameters

MAKE SURE TO WATCH THE COMPANION VIDEO "EC2 AUTO SCALING."

Lifecycle Hooks

Custom actions can be created and carried out on instances that an ASG launches or terminates. The instance is placed into a wait state and held from becoming registered in the ASG or from being terminated for one hour. While being held in the wait state, custom actions can be performed on the instance. Think of the wait state as an opportunity to perform any task you want on the instance before it is added or removed from the ASG. The maximum amount of time an instance can be frozen is up to 48 hours. During the wait time, the following custom actions are allowed:

- Call a Lambda function to perform a specific task.
- Send a message to a defined SNS notification.
- Execute a script as the instance starts and remains in the defined wait state.

You can add a lifecycle hook to an ASG using AWS CLI commands populating the User data location in a launch template, as shown here:

```
aws autoscaling put-lifecycle-hook --lifecycle-hook-name <lifecycle code> --auto-
scaling-group-name <ASG here > --lifecycle-transition autoscaling:EC2_INSTANCE_
LAUNCHING
```

AWS Auto Scaling

You now know about EC2 auto scaling, but there's another scaling option in the console called AWS Auto Scaling. What's the difference? This version is a management tool for scaling across application stacks using the familiar ELB service for load-balanced distribution of EC2 compute instances (see Figure 5-33).

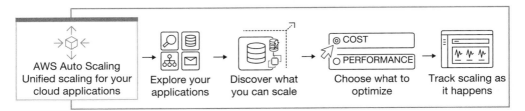

Figure 5-33   AWS Auto Scaling provides scaling of your application stack

AWS Auto Scaling supports the ECS and database solutions that utilize DynamoDB and Aurora. Currently, the following services can be managed with AWS Auto Scaling:

- EC2 ASGs
- EC2 Spot Fleets
- ECS
- DynamoDB throughput table (read-write) capacity
- Aurora replicas for Amazon Aurora

AWS Auto Scaling uses a feature called predictive scaling, which uses machine learning models to analyze the applications, and traffic pattern history to forecast potential changes in the future. Predictive scaling currently only works with EC2 instances. After two weeks of analysis, it begins to forecast future traffic patterns for the next 48 hours of application operation.

In Conclusion

One of the advantages of using public cloud services is that the setup and operations—including monitoring—are heavily automated. Our goal is to get to the same level of automation for applications that are hosted in the cloud. If you can set aside the need to fully understand how AWS load balancing works and focus on the service's stability and availability, then it's possible that using load balancing, auto scaling, and built-in monitoring services provided by AWS can save you a great deal of time and money.

I don't think there's any debate left about the fact of wanting and needing scale for our hosted cloud applications. Using the AWS gang of three essential services (ELB, CW, and AS) means you need to select an application ready to be moved to the cloud and begin testing with the goal of creating a stateless and automatically scalable application. On to the discussion points!

Top 10 Big-Picture Discussion Points: Scale, Availability, and Monitoring Decisions

To have your application work effectively with scale, it must be properly designed to work in a horizontal scaling cluster. This means it can't have any local dependencies; all depended micro-services in services must be hosted externally to the Web server or application server. No data must be stored on the instance—just the operating system, application code, middleware, and other generic components that are installed on every other instance in the cluster. This also means that a lift and shift approach from on-premise to the cloud probably isn't going to work because the odds are close to 100% that there will be dependencies in that application that will have to be stripped out.

It's time to discuss what you have and where you need to go regarding your applications that are moving to the cloud.

1. Do you have golden images for your Web and application servers?

2. Can you replace existing third-party load balancers with ELB services?

3. Are your applications hosted in public subnets?

4. Should you be tracking CloudTrail APIs using CloudWatch log groups and metric filters?

5. Can CloudWatch help monitor your on-premise servers with the installation of the CloudWatch agent?

6. Can launch configurations help you plan your auto scaling deployments?

7. Are billing alarms enabled to manage your developer's project costs?

8. Can Lambda functions be created to help automate solutions with CloudWatch alerts?

9. Will step scaling policies help improve application performance?

10. Will step scaling policies help you save even more money?

6

Cloud Storage

In this chapter, we are going to explore the storage options that are offered by AWS and contrast them with what you may be using on-premise. By the end of this chapter, you will understand the choices available for storing your precious data in the AWS cloud. There are many storage options available at AWS. In fact, most of the storage options could not be replicated on-premise; they're simply too large and durable.

Picking the right storage solution involves some learning and testing on your part and will most certainly involve an element of change, and of trust. And, as we all know, changing something that isn't broke is usually hard to do. In the past, you may have always selected network-attached storage (NAS) or spun up a particular version of relational database without thinking about any other storage possibilities because there weren't any other choices available.

The reality faced today by companies that have not yet moved to the public cloud is that you're probably close to running out of local network storage. If you're not yet at a crisis regarding available storage, you're going to be. Some companies have made the decision that applications that are hosted in the cloud, and the associated storage for the application data, has to be in the cloud due to latency issues. The application is too far away from the local data store. Some companies have decided that certain data records are never going to be moved to the cloud due to compliance issues. Other companies just have a general overall uneasy feeling about losing complete control of where and how their data is stored.

AWS has made great strides in providing storage solutions for companies that want to work in a hybrid mode of operation, where some data will be stored on-premise because of security concerns, rules, and regulations. Amazon has figured out that some customers, such as financial customers, are not allowed to move certain data resources to the cloud. For these types of customers, the hybrid cloud is here to stay. Therefore, create services that allow customers to decide what they want or are allowed to do: store data in the AWS cloud, or access data from their on-premise cloud storage arrays. The reality is, if you connect to AWS with a fast Direct Connect connection of 10 Gbps, the choice of location is yours to make. However, many companies, once they get comfortable with AWS, end up moving their data records to the cloud.

The overall goal of this chapter is to present enough information about the storage option at AWS to allow you to make an informed decision about the available storage options and the data transfer options available at AWS. After all, if you have lots of data and you're running out of space, you probably want to know how to move that data to the AWS cloud or back on-premise.

The topics for this chapter include these:

- **File systems**—For both Windows (FSx) and Linux (elastic file system [EFS])
- **EBS**—Elastic block storage for Elastic Compute Cloud (EC2) instances
- **S3**—The Simple Storage Service and S3 Glacier: unlimited object storage for static assets and archived storage
- **RDS**—Managed relational database service solutions
- **Aurora**—AWS's favorite relational database solution for MySQL and PostgreSQL-compatible databases
- **DynamoDB**—A horizontally scalable transactional database service
- **ElastiCache**—In-memory storage solutions
- **Data transfer options**—How to move data to and from the AWS cloud

> **Note**
>
> Certainly, some crown jewels will not be moving to the cloud. Amazon has thought about this reality and is offering a variety of hybrid storage offerings.

At Terra Firma, the cloud will be used for many different types of data records:

- Database instances for relational databases such as MySQL for storing the human resources department's records
- Developers who want to explore using DynamoDB for newer applications that don't need complicated queries
- Application caching that was held in RAM for databases and for the caching of user sessions
- Archival storage for documentation that needs to be stored somewhere and possibly never read again
- Unlimited cloud storage with automated lifecycle rules to ensure cost-effective storage
- Shared storage for Linux and Windows applications needing access to the same files
- Backups of database and computer instance boot drives and data volumes

Cloud Storage

When you think about what is stored in the cloud, certainly personal records take the prize for the largest amount of storage being used. Corporations and software as a service (SaaS) applications are increasingly using the cloud to store vast quantities of data for everyday tasks like Word and Excel files, machine learning, online gaming results, and anything else you can think of. The reality is that your storage totals in the public cloud will only grow and not shrink. Therefore, the cheap advertised price of storage will get more expensive over time as you hang onto your data records, typically for a long period of time. Out-of-sight data records become expensive to store over time.

Just think of taking a picture with your phone. It's probably synchronized to store that picture with a public cloud storage service. Billions of pictures are uploaded to the cloud daily. And we've all heard about Big Data, which we could summarize as a lot of data that needs to be analyzed for metadata patterns. Some customers have trillions of objects stored in Amazon S3 object storage.

At AWS, there is a wide breadth of storage options—namely, block, object, and file storage—that are similar but not the same as your on-premise storage options shown in Figure 6-1.

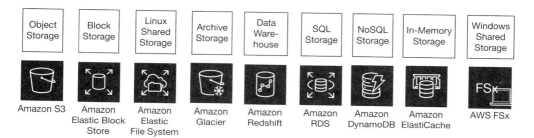

Figure 6-1   AWS-hosted storage options

Amazon EFS—Shared scalable file service accessed through a simple interface for multiple EC2 instances at the same time. Data is stored natively as files in a directory tree that is shared over your selected virtual private cloud (VPC) subnets. EFS data records can be accessed by multiple Linux clients at the same time over AWS's private network using the common protocol NFS 4.x. EFS is as close as we can get to a hosted NAS solution at AWS.

Amazon ElastiCache—In-memory store managed services supporting Memcached and Redis designs.

Object—Object storage at AWS is called Amazon S3. S3 is the Simple Storage Service, and its companion, S3 Glacier, is the archiving component. Each file is defined as an object that is stored in a bucket, and each file is identified by a unique key. The S3 storage array can be thought of as just a great big room—a flat file space where the objects are accessed and managed through simple application programming interface (API) calls, such as GET and PUT requests. The original design for S3 was for accessing content across the Internet. S3 is fast, scalable, durable, and extremely cost-effective cloud storage designed as a static file storage object service. When a file is stored in S3, the entire file is uploaded. When changes to the file are uploaded, the entire file is replaced. S3 is useful for hosting a website's static content, media files, storage for big data analytics, and archiving records in long-term storage vaults in S3 Glacier. Amazon uses S3 storage to store everything: snapshots, logs, reports, and backups. Everything ends up in S3 storage.

Block storage—Block storage at AWS is called elastic block storage (EBS), or ephemeral storage. Amazon EBS storage arrays are built using solid-state drives (SSDs) or hard disk drive (HDDs) to provide persistent block storage at both slower to faster speeds that are only accessible across the private AWS network. Enabling direct public access to the EBS storage is not possible.

Both Windows and Linux use block disk volumes at AWS presenting block data in the file system format understood by each operating system to applications or directly to the end user. Each EBS volume can be attached to only one EC2 instance at a time.

Many EC2 instance families also include local storage volumes, called ephemeral storage (block storage). Because ephemeral storage, also called instance storage, is actually a local SSD hard drive located on the bare-metal server that hosts the EC2 instance, it's incredibly fast, but it has no long-term durability. Local instance block storage is designed to be temporary storage only; it *can* survive an instance reboot but is discarded when an EC2 instance is powered off or fails.

Amazon RDS—Relational database service for a variety of popular database engines including Oracle, SQL Server, MySQL, PostgreSQL, and MariaDB. Behind the scenes, RDS uses EBS volumes when building database instances and stores snapshots in S3 storage.

Amazon FSx for Windows File Server—Fully managed native Microsoft Windows storage with the familiar Windows file shares built with SSD storage on Windows servers. It has full support for the New Technology File System (NTFS) and Server Message Block (SMB) protocols, the Distributed File System (DFS), and integration with existing Active Directory environments.

Amazon FSx for Lustre—Designed for high-speed analysis of high-performance computing (HPC), machine learning, and media processing workflows that store their data in S3. FSx for Lustre provides extreme data processing up to hundreds of Gbps throughput with millions of input/output per second (IOPS) at low latency. FSx for Lustre is integrated with S3 storage, allowing data stored in S3 to be moved to FSx for processing. Then the results are written back to S3.

Which Storage Matches Your Workload?

Before choosing a storage solution at AWS, there's work to be done on your end. Your application, your operating system, your performance, and your data storage needs dictate what storage solution or solutions to consider using. Review the chart shown in Table 6-1 as a starting point for reviewing how you are currently using on-premise storage compared with what you can do in the AWS cloud.

Table 6-1 **Discussion Points for Storage Needs**

Storage Considerations	Details
Operating system	Linux and Windows are the supported operating systems at AWS. Windows can support EBS volumes, S3 storage, and Amazon FSx. Linux can use S3, EBS, and EFS. For obtaining the best performance possible from EFS, your Linux distribution and kernel should be current.
File-sharing protocol	Amazon EFS uses NFSv4; Windows uses SMB, which is compatible with Amazon FSx.
Performance	How fast, predictable, or unpredictable does your storage burst need to be? Each type of application has different requirements. Except for S3, storage solutions at AWS are designed to handle sudden burst requirements.

Storage Considerations	Details
Compliance	You may have external requirements you need to follow (Payment Card Industry (PCI), FedRAMP, or internal rules and regulations. Cloud solutions at AWS have achieved various levels of compliance. The question worth considering is this: Are you in control of your data if all the copies of your data are stored in the cloud?
Capacity	What are your daily, monthly, and yearly requirements? What about in two years? Five years?
Encryption	What needs to be encrypted for compliance? Data records at rest, or data in transit across the network.
Clients	How many clients are going to be accessing the file system at the same time?
Input/output (I/O) requirements	What is the percentage of reading and of writing files? Is it balanced or unbalanced?
Number of files	How many files will you be storing in the cloud daily, weekly, or long term?
Current file design	How many subdirectories deep is your file tree? Is it an efficient design to continue?
File size per directory	What is the smallest file size per directory? What's the largest file size?
Throughput on-premise	What is your average throughput on-premise? Are you expecting higher levels of performance in the cloud? Are there specific IOPS requirements?
Latency	What can your application live with in terms of overall latency?

EBS Block Storage

You probably have a storage area network (SAN) providing block-level storage to multiple clients connected to a virtual SAN storage array. You may also still have a separate SAN network running across fiber channel or iSCSI protocols that present the logical unit numbers (LUNs) as hard disks to each client. AWS also has block storage that can be chunked into virtual volumes called EBS volumes. They have a variety of hard drives you can choose from and a variety of speeds, but there is no fiber channel or iSCSI offerings at the customer level.

EBS is a block storage service that is accessed only across the private AWS network. Each EBS volume is equivalent to what you think of as a virtual hard disk and can be thought of as an independent storage resource; EBS volumes do not have to be attached to an instance to persist.

When you create an EBS volume, the blocks for the volume are spread across multiple storage arrays, providing a high level of redundancy and durability. Once EBS volumes are created, they are stored within the same availability zone (AZ) where your instances reside, as shown in Figure 6-2, and they provide 99.99 availability. Each single EBS volume can be attached or detached to and from any EC2 instance located in the AZ where it is stored; in addition, multiple EBS volumes can be attached to a single instance at a time.

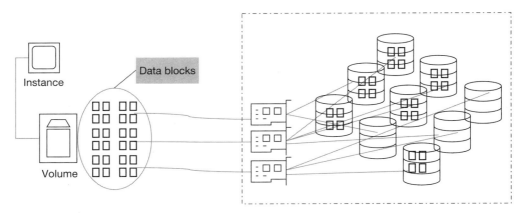

Figure 6-2   EBS data storage architecture

> **Note**
> EBS boot and data volumes should always be separated. Never store data records on the boot drive of an instance.

EBS Volume Types

Several EBS volume types are available depending on your use case. Your decisions for the type of EBS volume chosen will obviously depend on your workload. Different workloads will have different performance needs. For example, different IOPS or throughput needs can be selected for database storage volumes, choosing volumes for boot volumes, or for storage that is not accessed frequently. The general storage requirements for a boot volume will probably not need to be as fast or as large as a data drive for a database instance. In the EBS storage world, there are several choices:

- General-Purpose SSD volumes provide a baseline of 3 IOPS per GB with a minimum speed of 100 IOPS that can burst to 3,000 IOPS.

- Provisioned IOPS SSD volumes have a maximum IOPS from 100 to 64,000 IOPS.

- Throughput Optimized HDD volumes provide good throughput performance for sequential I/O of 40 MBs per TB.

- Cold HHD volumes have a baseline of 12 MB/s per TB.

- Magnetic HDD volumes average 100 IOPS.

Note

For AWS customers, EBS volumes are used to create boot instances and are typically used as data drives for other customer-built application solutions that involve EC2 instances such as RDS, EMR, ElastiCache, or the data warehousing solution Redshift. Other than these examples, EBS should not always be chosen for storage without considering EFS and FSx or S3. These storage options have no capacity limitations and should be strongly considered for data storage for records that are not being stored in a database. AWS managed service storage solutions use EBS drives in the background (S3 storage arrays, DynamoDB and EFS, and FSx). We just don't have direct access to the EBS volumes.

General-Purpose SSD (gp2)

The baseline for a general-purpose SSD is designed with a minimum baseline of 100 to 10,000 IOPS with an average of 3 IOPS per GB. Volumes up to 1 TB can burst up to 3,000 IOPS. Volumes larger than 3,000 GB have a baseline of 10,000 IOPS. Bursting is for a use case where applications have periods of idle time followed by periods of high IOPS. The smallest gp2 drive can burst to 3000 IOPS while maintaining a single-digit millisecond latency with throughput up to 160 MB/s.

All EBS storage volumes that support bursting use a burst token bucket design, as shown in Figure 6-3. During quiet idle times, each gp2 volume accumulates burst tokens at a rate of 3 IOPS per GB per second. When the drive needs additional performance using the acquired burst tokens, it can burst up to 3,000 IOPS per second. As your EBS volumes gets larger, your volume is assigned additional burst credits, allowing the drive to burst for a longer time frame. For example, a 300 GB volume can burst up to 40 minutes, 500 GB volumes can burst for almost an hour, and even larger 900 GB volumes can burst for almost 10 hours.

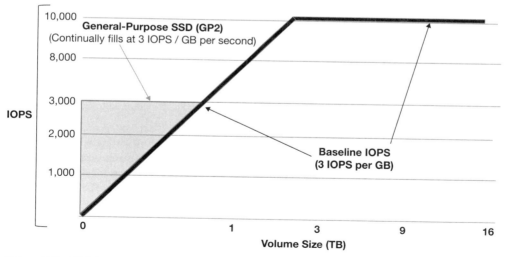

Figure 6-3   EBS burst bucket architecture

For cold storage and throughput-optimized volumes, burst credits are always accumulating based on the size of the drive. A storage-optimized volume accumulates 40 MB/s per TB; a cold storage volume accumulates 12 MB per TB. Proper testing of your applications is required to know if your data transfer requirements are going to be sequential or random in nature.

- For example, if you have a large sequential workload working for three hours on a throughput optimized volume, approximately 5.4 TB of data will be transferred.

- If your workload is random in nature, using the same drive in the same working timeframe of three hours, 87 GB of data will be transferred.

Keep in mind that the maximum data transfer speeds are only going to be achieved with modern instances with the latest versions of Windows or Linux.

Note

To do your workload testing on a Linux system, you could use the utility iostat. For Windows systems, use Perfmon. The results will be displayed in sectors. You will then need to know the number of bytes you're using per sector and multiply the sectors by the number of bytes to come up with the current workload size.

Provisioned IOPS (io1)

EBS volumes, defined as provisioned IOPS, are available from 100 to 64,000 IOPS with throughput up to 320 MB/s. io1 drives are designed for applications and databases that require sustained IOPS. Capacity ranges from 4 GB to 16 TB have a much more consistent single-digit millisecond latency than the general-purpose SSD drives. When you select your IOPS target, AWS hits your target more than 99.9% of the time. For Terra Firma database servers, provisioned IOPS will certainly be a consideration.

Note

You also need to make sure to match your application with its required bandwidth needs regarding storage. If a 2 TB volume is attached to a c4.large instance with a 16 KB workload, the GP2 volume functions close to 6,000 IOPS. Moving to a c4.2xlarge, which has double the dedicated EBS bandwidth, means that your storage bandwidth is increased to 8,000 IOPS.

Ordering storage-optimized EC2 instances provides even higher levels of storage and network throughput than provisioned IOPS EBS drives, as shown in Table 6-2. This additional performance is because storage-optimized instances include local ephemeral storage devices that have much higher random I/O performance and low latency due to the use of directed attached local NVM Express (NVMe) SSD drives utilizing flash storage. In addition, network bandwidth streams are separated from the application bandwidth. For instances hosted by the Nitro hypervisor, the separation of data and network communication channels is enabled by default.

Table 6-2   **Increasing Performance with NVMe SSD Drives**

Bare-Metal Instance Size	100% Random Read IOPS	Write IOPS
i3.large	100,125	35,000
i3.xlarge	206,250	70,000
i3.2xlarge	412,500	180,000
i3.4xlarge	825,000	360,000
i3.8xlarge	1.65 million	720,000
i3.16xlarge	3.3 million	1.4 million

If you need more speed and you want the security of persistent EBS volumes, you can choose to stripe your data volumes together. However, avoid using Redundant Array of Independent Disks (RAID) for redundancy because EBS data volumes are already replicated at the back end. RAID 5 designs using EBS volumes also lose 20% to 30% of usable I/O because of parity checks. However, if your needs are less than what is offered for throughput by storage optimized instances, EBS volume choices should be compared regarding throughput, performance, and cost.

Throughput-optimized volumes—What if overall throughput is more important than high-speed IOPS? Are you looking at small blocks with random I/O, or larger blocks with sequential I/O? For smaller blocks with random I/O requirements, you should first start testing with the general-purpose SSD. However, if you require more than 1,750 MB/s of throughput, you should consider the D2 instance family. Keep in mind that we're back to looking at ephemeral volume stores instead of persistent EBS storage.

Throughput performance—Consider the throughput-provisioned volumes, which are magnetic drives with a baseline throughput of 40 MB/s up to 500 MB/s. They can also burst at 250 MB/s per TB up to 500 MB/s per volume. The maximum capacity for all block volumes is 16 TB, but the smallest throughput volumes start at 500 GB. These are useful to consider for large block, high-throughput sequential workloads like Hadoop and MapReduce.

Magnetic HDD—If cost is your main concern, the other choice offered is defined as a cold magnetic drive. Applications associated with this type of platter don't require a high-performance baseline—just storage and cheap cost. Magnetic drives have a much lower baseline of 12 MB/s per TB up to 192 MB/s, with the ability to burst from 80 MB/s up to 250 MB/s per volume. Magnetic drives are ideal for applications that require some throughput but with lower specifications.

> **Note**
>
> EBS volumes have 5 9s reliability for service availability. For durability, the annual failure rate of EBS volumes is between .1% and .2% compared to 3% for commodity hard drives in the industry. If you have 1,000 EBS volumes, you could potentially expect 1 to 2 of those volumes to fail per year.

Elastic EBS Volumes

EBS volumes are an elastic volume service that allows you to increase or change the current volume size and to increase or decrease the provisioned IOPS in real time, as shown in Figure 6-4. There is no maintenance window required when manually scaling volumes. Elastic volumes can also provide cost savings because you do not have to overprovision your storage volumes by planning for future growth; instead, monitor your volumes with CloudWatch metrics, and make changes when necessary.

Figure 6-4   Increasing volume size with elastic volumes

Attaching an EBS Volume

When an EBS volume is attached to an instance, a couple background processes begin running, depending on the hypervisor being used to host the instance:

- **Instances hosted on the Xen hypervisor**—These are associated with a system component called an I/O domain. When an EBS volume is attached, it is attached to the I/O domain. Another system component, called a *shared memory segment*, is set up at the hypervisor level acting as a queue to handle data access from the instance to the EBS volume.

  - When your instance wants to perform an I/O call, it first submits a system call to the kernel. Assuming it's a read request, a block of data is placed in the hypervisor queue. Next, the I/O domain takes the data from the hypervisor queue and sends it to another storage queue, which delivers the data blocks to the EBS volume.

- **Instances hosted on the Nitro hypervisor**—A PCI interface is now used to directly interface with the EBS volume. EBS volumes are attached directly to the Nitro card, which presents a direct storage interface to the EC2 instance. Storage requests are submitted directly to the PCI interface; the Nitro hypervisor has no part to play in communication with EBS storage volumes. This provides a huge performance impact with minimal latency when compared to instances hosted on the Xen hypervisor.

> MAKE SURE TO WATCH THE COMPANION VIDEO "CREATING EBS VOLUMES."

To access the companion videos, register your book at informit.com/register.

> **Note**
>
> The cost for provisioning any of the available EBS volume types is a per-month storage charge based on the number of used GB prorated down to the second. General-purpose solid-state drive (SSD) volumes are charged at $.10 per GB.
>
> Provisioned IOPS volumes are charged at 12.5 cents per GB plus a $0.65 charge per provisioned IOPS.
>
> Throughput volumes range from $0.25 to $0.45 per GB depending on the volume type selected.
>
> Snapshots can be created from any type of EBS volume, and the storage charge for the snapshots is $.05 per GB per month.

EBS Volume Encryption

Both EBS boot and data volumes can be encrypted; the encryption of each volume is performed using separate encryption keys. Note that both encrypted and unencrypted volumes can be attached to the same EC2 instance at the same time. The encryption of EBS volumes is supported by most instances, including the c4, i2, i3, m3, m4, r3, and r4 families. Encryption is no longer a performance issue for EC2 instances hosted on the Nitro hypervisor because the encryption process has been offloaded to custom chipsets on the host, bare-metal server. However, if you choose to use a third-party software encryption process running on an instance rather than the AWS encryption process, the instance's CPU will have to perform the encryption process at the application level, creating a potential performance issue.

> **Note**
>
> Data encrypted by the EBS encryption process is encrypted before it crosses the network. It also remains encrypted in-flight and at rest and remains encrypted when a snapshot is created of the encrypted volume.

The customer master key used in encryption can be used by all identity and access management (IAM) users of the AWS account once they have been added as key users in the key management service (KMS) console, as shown in Figure 6-5. The customer master key shown in Figure 6-5 protects all the other keys issued for data encryption and decryption of your EBS volumes within your AWS account. All AWS-issued customer master keys are protected by envelope encryption, meaning that AWS is responsible for creating and protecting the "envelope" containing the master keys of all AWS accounts.

After enabling your customer-managed key using the KMS for your AWS account, for additional security, it's a good idea to add another key administrator and to enable key rotation of your customer master key. You can also control the additional users in your account who can use each KMS key for encryption and decryption services. Terra Firma decided to use the KMS provided by AWS, create an additional administrator, and enable key rotation of its customer master key.

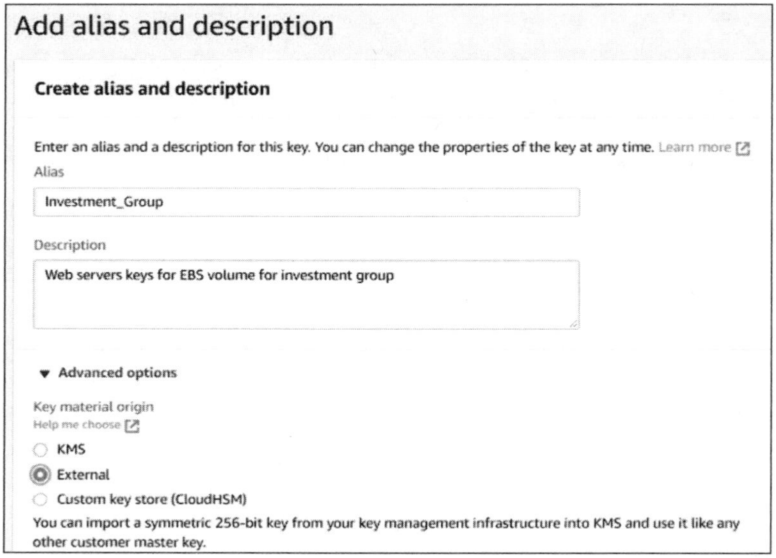

Figure 6-5   Creating a new master key

EBS Snapshots

An EBS snapshot is a point-in-time copy of your EBS volume that is stored in S3 object storage. Because S3 storage is designed for 11 9s durability, your snapshot is safely stored.

The first time a snapshot is taken, every modified block of the EBS volume is part of the master snapshot that is captured and stored in S3. Every additional snapshot from this point forward is defined as an incremental snapshot that records the changes since the last snapshot. Only the blocks that you've written and changed are pushed to the snapshot. When you delete a snapshot, only data that is exclusive to that snapshot copy is deleted.

Note

Deploying a daily snapshot schedule greatly reduces the possibility of data loss. AWS has two options for managing snapshots. First, the Data Lifecycle manager allows you to schedule the creation and deletion of EBS snapshots. Second, AWS Backup allows you even more control of your storage by allowing you to centrally manage EBS, RDS, and Storage Gateway snapshots and EFS and DynamoDB backups.

Taking a snapshot from a Linux instance—After starting a snapshot, the snapshot process continues in the background. If there have not been a large number of blocks changed, the process may be quick. If there have been many changes, the process could take several hours to complete. The first thing that you should do before beginning the snapshot process for a boot volume is to *quiesce* the drive; this means to stop ongoing I/O processes and write all data records currently cached in memory to the volume. You could execute either the *sync* or the *fsfreeze* command directly on the EBS volume to quiet the file system. However, the safest method to stop I/O is to simply unmount the drive. After starting the snapshot process, as shown in Figure 6-6, you receive a snapshot ID, which is your confirmation from AWS that the snapshot parameters are confirmed, and the snapshot is being taken in the background.

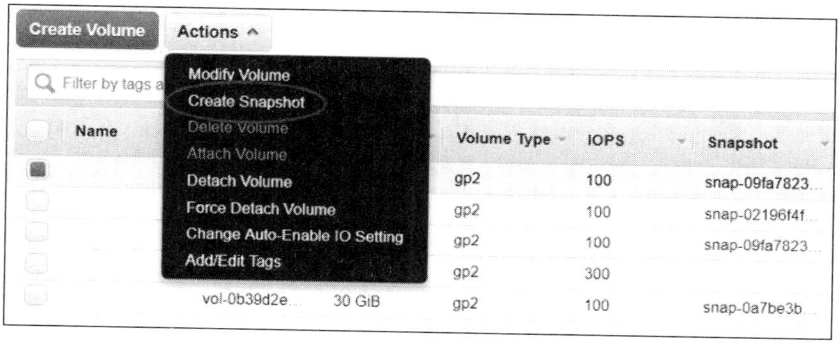

Figure 6-6   Creating a snapshot

Taking a snapshot from a Windows instance—For Windows systems, you can use the *sync* utility to quiesce the file system and then perform the snapshot. Windows also has a built-in operating system service utility called the volume shadow copy service (VSS) that can be used to take application-consistent snapshots. The Simple Service Manager (SSM) now integrates with the Windows VSS, and commands such as *ec2-createVSSSnapshot* can be executed to create snapshots of Windows applications. The latest Windows Server image (AMI) 2017.11.21 and higher includes the SMM VSS snapshot utilities.

What can we do with snapshots?

- **Within a region**—Snapshots can be used to create an EBS volume within any AZ in the region. Remember: VPCs can span all AZs within the region.

- **To another region**—Using the EBS copy utility, snapshots can be copied to another AWS region, which allows you to prestage, or quickly set up a disaster recovery site in another geographical AWS region.

- **For automating snapshots**—You can use the Amazon EC2 Run command and tags to build your own custom snapshot management system that sets parameters for daily or weekly snapshots and snapshot retention.

- **Rebuild instances**—If the snapshot is a boot drive, you can use it to create a new EC2 instance.

- **Rebuild a database**—If the snapshot is a database instance, you can use it to create a new database instance.
- **Create volumes**—Snapshots can be used to create new EBS volumes.

Tagging EBS Volumes and Snapshots

The one process you should make part of your company's mandated workflow is the creation of tags when you create AWS resources. Each tag is a key-value pair, and fifty individual tags can typically be created for each AWS resource. Tags can be used for automation, analysis, reporting, compliance checks, and billing to control the creation of a resource. Custom tags can be used for many reasons, including the following examples:

- **Tags on creation**—Tags can be created for EBS volumes at the time of creation.
- **Cost allocation tags**—These allow you to have visibility into your actual snapshot storage costs. In the billing dashboard, selecting Cost Allocation Tags, as shown in Figure 6-7, is where you select and activate tags that can be used for the billing process. Reports and budgets can then be generated, which allows you to view the costs and the usage, broken down by the assigned tags. Alerts can also be created for resources that have been tagged when costs have exceeded 50% of the budget.
- **Enforced tags**—IAM security policies can enforce the use of specific tags on EBS volumes and control who can create tags.
- **Resource-level permissions**—Neither the *CreateTags* nor the *DeleteTags* functions can be controlled by IAM resource-level permissions that mandate that EBS volumes be encrypted.
- **Managed services**—AWS Config, AWS Inspector, S3 Inventory, Lambda, AWS Budgets, and Cost Explorer are services that require tags for identification purposes.

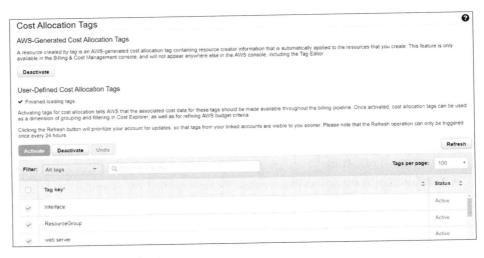

Figure 6-7   Cost allocation tags

EBS Best Practices

There are many best practices for managing your EBS volumes; here are several that apply to every use case:

- Create a schedule using AWS Backup to back up your attached EBS volumes with EBS snapshots.

- Don't store data records on your root EBS boot volumes.

- Use separate EBS volumes for the operating system, and if necessary, for persistent data records.

- Ensure that your EBS data volumes have been set to be deleted after an instance termination; after all, you have a snapshot schedule in place already backing up your data.

- Use ephemeral storage volumes for storing temporary files instead of EBS volumes.

MAKE SURE TO WATCH THE COMPANION VIDEO "CREATING SNAPSHOTS."

S3 Storage

It may still sound enticing that you can sign up to the AWS cloud and provision unlimited storage; however, unlimited storage comes with an unlimited price. The initial price for S3 storage is inexpensive at first, but storage at AWS is assessed a monthly charge, plus potentially a data transfer fee that is applied when you retrieve, replicate, or download files from AWS. It's a great advantage to have unlimited storage, but we need to make sure we are getting the best bang for our buck. Once you have content stored at S3, storage charges continue forever; fortunately, there are tools available to help minimize storage costs as much as possible when using S3.

S3 storage, launched March 14, 2006, was one of the first AWS services offered. It provided unlimited storage in a container called a *bucket* that can be made available publicly across the Internet or privately across Amazon's private network. The default is always private; you must make the decision to make your private S3 bucket public. Whether or not you've signed up and are using the S3 storage service directly at AWS, you're still using S3 storage. Internally, pretty much every data component makes its way to S3 storage, including AMIs, EC2 instance images, database backups, database snapshots, continuous backups from DynamoDB, Redshift, CloudWatch logs, and CloudTrail trails, to provide just a few examples.

Tens of trillions of objects are stored in S3 across many millions of hard drives. There are more than 235 distributed microservices alone that make up the S3 storage service. Objects that are stored in S3 are also subjected to continuous integrity checks through checksums, end-to-end, from the source upload to final bucket destination. Amazon is incredibly serious about ensuring that the S3 storage arrays stay up as much as possible, and if issues occur, solutions execute in the background without anyone noticing.

> **Note**
>
> In a single AWS region, S3 will manage access peaks of up to 60 TB per second per day.

The storage arrays that host S3 storage are the same design as the storage arrays that host EBS, or EFS storage. The difference is how you can access and use the storage; S3 can't be used as a boot drive or to install software. S3 is primarily designed for unlimited storage capacity with decent read performance and the ability to scale up to handle the many customers who store and retrieve objects from S3 buckets. S3 storage also has a number of durability levels that can be chosen, depending on the type of records being stored. Workloads that you might want to consider using S3 for include these:

- **Website static records**—Stored in S3 Standard and moved to S3-1A or back based on usage using intelligent tiering

- **Thumbnail images**—Could be stored in S3-1A reduced redundancy storage because thumbnails could be re-created

- **Surveillance video**—Could first be stored in S3 Standard using lifecycle policies to automatically move to S3 Glacier for long-term storage or deletion

- **Historical records**—Directly stored in encrypted in S3 Glacier for archival storage

- **Backups**—Stored in S3 delivered by snapshots, AWS Backup, or the Storage Gateway service

- **Big Data**—Stored in S3 and analyzed by Elastic MapReduce (EMR) or FSx Lustre

> **Note**
>
> S3 storage was designed for use by developers first using available software development kits (SDKs) for a variety of popular languages, including Java, .NET, and Ruby Version 3. There are several clients also available for using S3 as the back end for storing anything you can think of; however, direct access to S3 is as easy as accessing a cloud storage such as Dropbox or Microsoft OneDrive. You can directly upload content using the S3 Management Console or by using the command-line interface (CLI). AWS Snowball can also be used to migrate massive amounts of data directly into S3.

Buckets, Objects, and Keys

Following are the key concepts and terms you will come across when working with S3:

- **Buckets**—The containers that store S3 objects.

- **Unlimited storage**—Upload as many objects as you want into an S3 bucket. The only limitation is the size of each object, which is 5 TB each. Use the *multipart upload* API for objects larger than 5 MB to 5 TB.

- **Permissions**—Define the levels of public or private access to your buckets and objects.

Each AWS account is controlled by a number of soft limits that apply to every AWS service. For S3 buckets, you can create up to 100 buckets per AWS account, and this initial soft limit number of buckets can be increased upon request. An S3 bucket resides in an AWS region that you select. There is no limit to the objects that can be stored in a single bucket, just the size of each object (5 TB). You also can't create buckets inside of buckets, but you can use delimiters (backslashes) for organization of your objects within each bucket.

Before selecting a particular AWS region for your S3 buckets, you need to consider the factors of compliance, latency, and cost of the S3 service based on its location. As part of the S3 service-level agreement (SLA) with AWS, objects that are stored in a specified AWS region never leave the region unless you decide to transfer them to another region location.

Names for S3 buckets are domain name system (DNS) names that are stored in Route 53, AWS's global DNS service. Bucket names are defined as global and must be globally unique.

Each object in a bucket contains some mandatory parts, including the data portion and the associated metadata portion, which is the name of the object itself. Each object is identified by a unique key and stored in a bucket with an attached version ID. Optionally, you can add some additional custom metadata to each object when it is being stored. Keep in mind that custom metadata is not encrypted. You can see the mapping for each object showing the bucket + key + version of each object in Figure 6-8.

Figure 6-8   S3 object details

When you create an S3 bucket, several configuration options are available, as shown in Table 6-3.

Table 6-3   **S3 Bucket Configuration Options**

S3 Feature	Details
Region	Choose the region for bucket creation
Policy	Select S3 bucket security with bucket policy and access control lists (ACLs)
Website	Configure an S3 bucket to host a static website
Logging	Track access requests to an S3 bucket
Notifications	Receive notifications when S3 bucket events happen (GET, PUT, DELETE)
Versioning	Store multiple versions of the same object within a single S3 bucket
Lifecycle	Create rules for object retention and movement across S3 storage classes
Cross-region replication	Automatically replicate objects to other S3 buckets hosted in other S3 regions within your AWS account
Encryption	Enable encryption; objects are not encrypted by default
Tagging	Add cost allocation tags to help track costs or inventory or to help automate tasks
Request payment	Charge the data transfer costs to the end user
Object lock	Enable write once read many (WORM) policy on objects or buckets
Transfer acceleration	Securely transfer files quickly using CloudFront edge locations for ingress to AWS

S3 Data Consistency

Objects stored in an S3 bucket are replicated many times to at least three other separate physical storage locations within the region where your bucket is located, providing a high level of durability for each stored object. Replicated data records can't be instantly consistent in separate physical stored locations; however, Amazon guarantees read-after-write consistency for PUTs for all new objects stored in your S3 bucket. This isn't difficult to guarantee. Amazon merely reads the location where the object was first stored, thereby guaranteeing a successful first read after write. All objects that are overwritten or deleted follow the rules of eventual consistency; eventually, all copies of each object in all linked storage locations will be the same. With multiple copies of data, replicating updates and deletions takes time to complete.

S3 Storage Classes

S3 storage classes have been designed for different use cases when storing objects in S3 buckets, as shown in Table 6-4.

Table 6-4   **S3 Storage Classes**

Storage Classes	Standard	Intelligent Tiering	Standard-1A	One Zone-1A	Glacier	Glacier Deep Archive
Access Frequency	NA	Moves objects to Standard-1A after 30 days	Infrequent— minimum 30 days	Re-creatable data	Archive data	7 to 10 years
Access speed (Millisecond) ms	ms	ms	ms	ms	Minutes to hours	Hours
Number of AZs	3		3	1	3	3
Cost to retrieve	$0.0210/ GB	$0.0210/GB to $0.0125 /GB	$0.0125/GB	$0.0100/GB	$0.00040/ GB	$0.00099/ GB
Minimum duration (days)	None	30	30	30	90	180
Availability	99.99%	99.9%	99.9%	99.5%	N/A	N/A
Minimum object size	N/A	N/A	128 KB	128 KB	40 KB	40 KB

S3 Standard—This is for data that is regularly accessed by online cloud-hosted applications. It is designed for high performance and durability, offering 11 9s of durability, and 4 9s of availability. Amazon states, "If you store 10,000 objects in S3, on average, you may lose one object every 10 million years." We'll have to take Amazon's word on this.

S3 Intelligent-Tiering—Rules for automatic tiering analyze and move your less accessed objects to lower cost storage classes and back as required. Movement is based on the access of the object and can be defined by the bucket or the object moving from S3 standard to S3 S3-1A, One Zone-1A, or S3 Glacier. Intelligent tiering optimizes your storage costs by monitoring your access patterns at the object level, automating cost savings for your stored objects in S3.

After 30 days of inactivity, your objects are moved from the frequent access tier to the infrequent access tier on an object by object basis. If the infrequent data objects begin to be accessed more frequently, they are moved back to the frequent access tier. The minimum storage duration fee has been removed when using intelligent tiering and replaced with a monitoring fee per object of $2.50 per million objects. Here are several examples where intelligent tiering may save you a great deal of money and management time:

- Move all objects older than 90 days to S3-1A.

- Move all objects after 180 days to S3 Glacier.

- Move all objects over 365 days to S3 Glacier Deep Archive.

S3 Standard-1A—This is designed for less frequently accessed data but offering the same performance of 11 9s durability. The design concept is that you don't need to access your data frequently. Therefore, in use cases where object access is greater than 30 days, this is a cheaper option than S3 Standard.

S3 One Zone-1A—This is designed for less frequently accessed data that could be re-created if necessary, but with less durability than S3 Standard-1A because it is stored in a single AZ instead of across three AZs. The price point is 20% less than S3-1A.

S3 Glacier—This is long-term archival storage. Even though it's designed for archival storage, if you need your archived data back quickly, you can get it back within minutes. You do pay additional fees for the expedited access.

S3 Glacier Deep Archive—The concept with this storage option is to remove the need for on-premise tape libraries. It is the cheapest price for storage at AWS, with a price of 4/10 of $.01 per MB. The assumption is that you don't need this information back, but if you do, retrieval times are within 12 hours.

MAKE SURE TO WATCH THE COMPANION VIDEO "CREATING S3 BUCKETS."

S3 Management

S3 buckets have a variety of powerful controls to help manage your stored data:

S3 Batch Operations—Although you could sit down and build this yourself using the existing CLI commands, customers have told AWS to "build it." This service allows you to manage your data, regardless of the size and scale of your S3 storage. The first step is to gather your objects together that you want to analyze; this is most easily done by using the S3 management service S3 Inventory, as shown in Figure 6-9, or you can provide your own comma-delimited text file of S3 resources. Once your S3 inventory has been gathered, you can choose to automate several numbing manual tasks you probably wouldn't get around to, including copying objects between S3 buckets, replacing existing tags, or changing access controls. You can even run custom Lambda functions to execute your own custom logic.

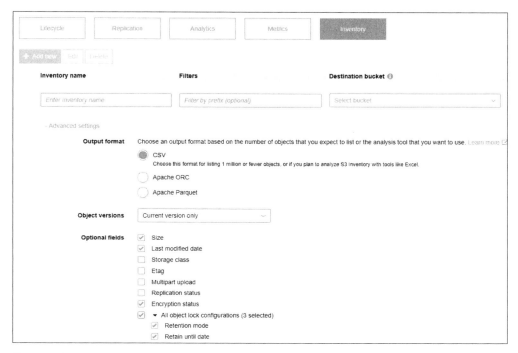

Figure 6-9   Creating S3 inventory

S3 Object Lock—Retention policies can be enforced by defined "Retain until dates" or "Legal hold dates." The storage class of the object does not affect S3 object lock settings; however, you must first turn on versioning at the S3 bucket level before you can use the object lock feature.

When objects are written to an S3 bucket, retention management can also control the retention date of the object. Until the defined retention date is reached, the object itself cannot be deleted or modified. Retention management can be deployed at the object level or S3 bucket level. For example, you could add a three-year or a five-year retention policy at the bucket level; from this point forward, all objects placed in the specific S3 bucket inherit the retention policy. This data protection level has added customers who need to adhere to SEC Rule 17-a 4(f), CFTC Regulation 1.3.1, and FINRA Rule 4511. S3 buckets can also be assigned immutable protection at the bucket level, or for specific object in the bucket; that's (WORM) write once, read many times, as shown in Figure 6-10. There are two modes of protection available for locking S3 objects:

- **Compliance mode**—All deletes are disallowed even for Root AWS accounts.

- **Governance mode**—Allow privileged deletes for WORM-protected buckets or objects.

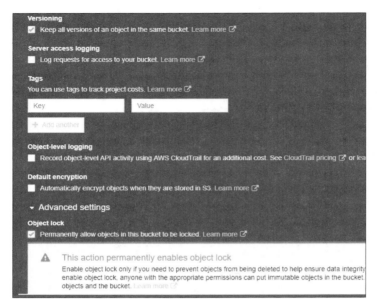

Figure 6-10   Enabling object lock on an S3 bucket

Cross-Region Replication (CRR) —This can be performed from any AWS region to any other region to any S3 storage class and across AWS accounts. The replication process is carried out by enabling CCR at the source bucket for the entire bucket contents or by a prefix or tag, as shown in Figure 6-11. In addition, lifecycle rules can be configured to replicate objects stored in S3 Standard to other S3 storage classes on the destination bucket, or optionally to S3 Glacier. To ensure security, CCR replication is encrypted. The cost for performing CRR is for the copy request, plus an inter-region data transfer charge for the replicated object.

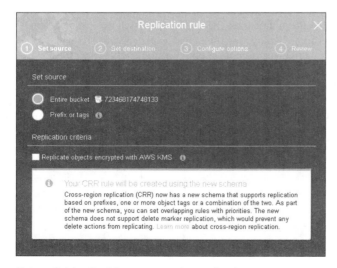

Figure 6-11   Enabling cross-region replication

S3 Inventory—If you want to find details about your current object inventory in S3, you can run an inventory process using S3 Inventory. After you select the source bucket for analysis, S3 Inventory creates a flat CSV file based on your query criteria and stores the inventory listing in a specified destination S3 bucket. The inventory listing encompasses current objects and their associated metadata, including the object's key name, version ID, encryption and replication status, retention date, storage class, object hold status, and object size. The inventory list file can be encrypted using S3-managed or KMS-managed keys.

> **Note**
>
> For S3 buckets, request rate performance rates on the S3 storage array are currently set at 3,500 write transactions per second and 5,500 read transactions per second, per bucket partition. Because of these performance levels, most customers no longer need hashing or randomizing of your key names. Key names are now automatically partitioned, and any buckets that don't achieve the current read/write transaction specifications have additional partitioning added by AWS. Performance levels are analyzed through machine learning analysis that happens in the background, increasing the performance of each S3 bucket as necessary.

S3 Storage Class Analysis—Through machine learning processes, your S3 storage is categorized into groups of less frequently accessed data by carrying out analysis of retrievals against storage. Analysis can be performed by bucket, protects, or object tags.

Object Tags—Up to 10 tags can be added to each S3 object. The following actions can be performed based on the assigned object tags:

- **IAM Policy**—Which users or groups of users can read an object

- **Replication**—Which objects to be replicated to a bucket in another region

- **Lifecycle policies**—Control lifecycle policies

Versioning

Versioning can be enabled on an S3 bucket, protecting your objects from accidental deletion. Versioning should be enabled before any objects are stored in the S3 bucket, guaranteeing all objects will be protected from deletion. After versioning has been enabled:

- Every new PUT of an existing object is created as a new object with a new version ID.

- The newest version is defined as the current version, and the previous versions are retained and not overwritten.

- Requesting just the S3 key name of an object presents you with the current version of the object.

- When a user attempts to delete an object without specifying a version ID, any further access is removed to the object, but the object is retained.

After versioning has been enabled, additional lifecycle management rules for the versioned content, as shown in Figure 6-12, can be created. These define a lifecycle expiration policy that dictates the number of versions that you want to maintain. Lifecycle rules help you manage previous versions of objects by transitioning or expiring specific objects after a certain number of days.

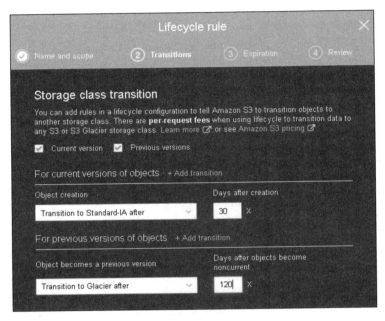

Figure 6-12   Lifecycle rules

> **Note**
> S3 also offers an event notification that alerts you at no additional cost when deletions occur. Versioning with MFA delete can also be enabled on S3 buckets, requiring two forms of authentication to build the leading object.

MAKE SURE TO WATCH THE COMPANION VIDEO "S3 MANAGEMENT FEATURES."

S3 Bucket Security

By default, only the owner who created the S3 bucket has access to its objects. There are several methods for controlling security for an S3 bucket:

ACL—Controls basic access from other AWS accounts for list and write objects and read and write bucket permissions, public access, and access to S3 logging information. ACLs are available because of backward compatibility and are the weakest type of S3 security.

IAM policy—Granting granular access to other AWS users and groups of IAM users is possible by using IAM trust policies in partnership with resource policies.

Bucket policy—Control direct access on the S3 bucket by creating a bucket policy that is assigned directly to the S3 bucket. A bucket policy can control anonymous access (HTTP/HTTPS), encryption settings, and the source IP address range allowing S3 bucket access.

Note

If you require public access to objects in an S3 bucket, it's recommended that you create a separate AWS account specifically used for allowing public S3 object access.

S3 block public access—Buckets always start as private, with no default public access. Once S3 block public access is enabled, the attempted changing of security settings to allow public access to objects in the S3 bucket is denied. Block public access settings can be configured on an individual S3 bucket or all S3 buckets in your AWS account by editing the public access settings for your account using the S3 management console. Choices for S3 block public access include the following:

- **Public**—Everyone has access to list objects, write objects, and read and write permissions.

- **Objects can be public**—The bucket is not public; however, public access can be granted to individual objects by users with permissions.

- **Buckets and objects not public**—No public access is allowed to the bucket or the objects within the bucket.

Note

Amazon Macie is another interesting AWS security service that uses artificial intelligence (AI) and machine learning technology to analyze your S3 objects and classify the S3 data based on discovered file formats, such as personally identifiable information (PII) and critical business documents. After analysis, you can create custom policy definitions and receive alerts when S3 documents are moved or specific business documents are shared.

S3 analytics—This allows you to visualize the access patterns on how your stored S3 object data is being used. Analyze your S3 data by bucket, prefix, object tag, or date of last access, as shown in Figure 6-13.

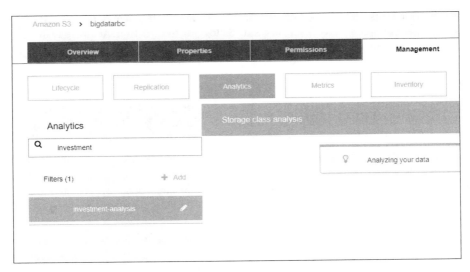

Figure 6-13   Analyze access patterns with S3 analytics

Amazon S3 Glacier Archive Storage

S3 Glacier is an extension of S3 storage that has the lowest cost of any managed storage service at Amazon. The design concept for S3 Glacier is that you don't want to access the content stored in S3 Glacier very often or ever. In fact, the minimum storage time is 90 days; accessing the content sooner results in a penalty.

Glacier encrypts all stored objects automatically and has the same 11 9s durability as S3 storage. Data is stored in vaults and archives, and these can be set up through the S3 management console. Delivering content into S3 Glacier can be carried out using the following methods:

- CLI commands
- S3 lifecycle rules
- Direct use of the REST API
- Use of an SDK
- Direct PUT—Store objects directly into S3 Glacier using the S3 API
- CRR—Replicate objects to S3 Glacier in another region using CRR and a lifecycle rule

To retrieve objects from S3 Glacier, create a retrieval job using the Management console or by using the S3 API. The retrieval job creates a separate copy of your data and then places it in S3 Standard-1A storage, leaving the actual archived data in its original location in S3 Glacier. You can then access your temporary archived data from S3 using an S3 GET request.

Note
You can retrieve up to 10 GB of Glacier data per month for free.

S3 Glacier Vaults and Archives

An S3 Glacier vault is used for storing archives, as shown in Figure 6-14. Each S3 Glacier vault is stored in the AWS region of your choosing, up to 1,000 vaults per AWS region. The term *archive*, when working with S3 Glacier, is defined as an object (file, document, photo, or video) that is stored. You can store an unlimited number of archives within a single S3 Glacier vault.

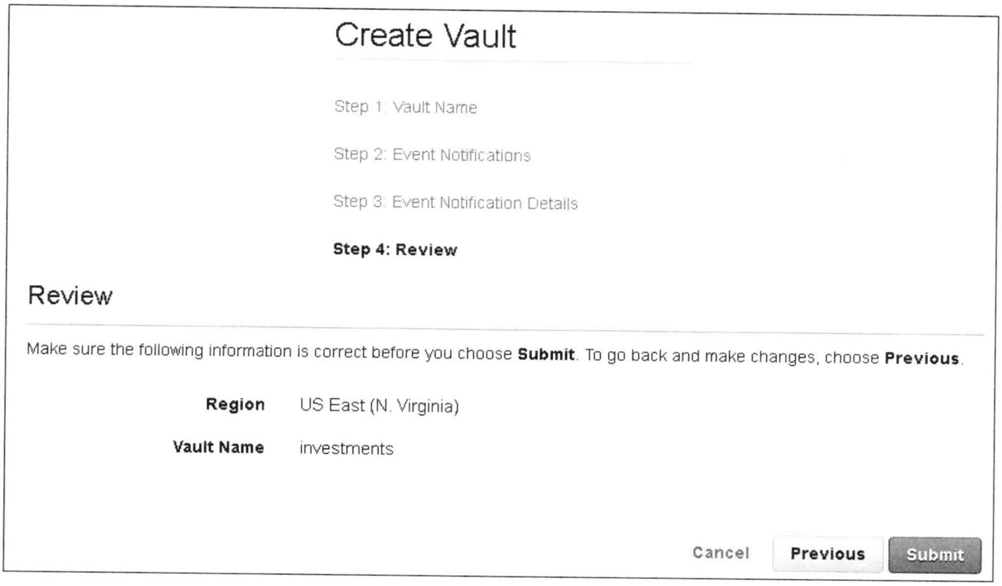

Figure 6-14   Creating S3 Glacier vaults

Shared File Systems at AWS

We've looked at virtual hard drives (EBS) and cloud object storage (S3). There are also several choices at AWS when it comes to storage that can be shared among multiple servers at the same time. Your on-premise storage solutions might include NAS, which is supplied by a dedicated hardware or software appliance serving shared files to multiple clients across the network. Typical file-sharing protocols utilized are the network file system (NFS), SMB, Windows file shares (CIFS), and perhaps even the Apple Filing Protocol (AFP). At AWS, there are shared file system choices for both Windows and Linux clients utilizing most of these popular protocols; here's an initial summary of the shared storage options at AWS.

EFS—The EFS provides a shared file system using NFS 4.1 designed for both cloud-hosted and on-premise Linux workloads. It is designed to scale on-demand up to petabytes in size and can be shared across many thousands of EC2 instances and accessed from on-premise servers through virtual private network (VPN) and Direct Connect connections.

Amazon FSx for Windows File Server—FSx is a fully managed native Windows file server storage fully compatible with Active Directory Domain Services providing Windows ACLs and a native NTFS Windows Explorer experience. FSx provides GB/s of scaling throughput with sub-millisecond latency and also complies with the Payment Card Industry Data Security Standard (PCI-DSS) and HIPAA compliance standards.

Amazon FSx for Lustre—Lustre provides optimized scale-out storage for short-term processing of compute-intensive workloads, such as high-performance computing (HPC) or video processing. Performance can scale to hundreds of gigabytes per second of throughput, with millions of IOPS performing with sub-millisecond latencies. FSx is integrated with S3 storage, allowing you to initially store massive data sets for analysis in S3, copy data into FSx Lustre for analysis, and then store results back in S3 storage. FSx for Lustre is POSIX compliant and supports PCI-DSS and HIPAA workloads.

AWS Shared Storage Use Cases

Corporations have used various storage solutions for serving a variety of data-sharing needs. AWS storage options can be used for the following:

- Home directories: EFS can be used for Linux clients needing shared storage
- FSx can be used for Windows clients needing shared storage
- S3 buckets can be used for shared data for multiple Web servers; EFS can also be used
- Standard line-of-business applications: Either EFS or FSx depending on the type of client and application
- Content management systems: EFS or FSx storage arrays can be used
- Development environments: EFS and S3 buckets can be used for shared development resources
- Backup and disaster recovery: Both S3 and S3 Glacier can be used for backup and long-term storage, including archiving

Elastic File System (EFS)

EFS is a completely managed file system that scales on demand up to petabytes for EC2 Linux instances. EFS removes the need to provision and attach EBS volumes for data storage, and it is a shared storage service allowing you to serve instances hosted on subnets within select VPCs using NFS mount points. The key features of EFS include these:

- **No networking or file layer to manage**—With just a few API calls, your file system is ready right away. You only pay for the storage used and the level of performance. There are no EBS drives to provision, manage, and pay for.

- **Elastic**—The file system automatically grows and shrinks as you add and remove files; you do not have to plan for a final storage size.

- **Scale**—EFS can scale to petabytes of capacity. As EFS grows, performance can scale along with the growth. As the file system grows, the latency remains low, regardless of the number of clients accessing your file system.

- **Performance**—Two performance modes are available: general-purpose and max I/O, which is designed for thousands of instances that need access to the same files at the same time.

EFS Performance Modes

General-Purpose—When you order EFS, the default mode of operation is assigned a throughput performance that supports up to 7,000 operations per second per file system and is recommended as the starting point. Amazon recommends that you monitor your file system using the CloudWatch metric *PercentIOLimit*; if your file system is operating close to 100%, choose Max I/O instead.

Max I/O Performance—This mode of operation can scale to a much higher level of throughput and operations per second and was designed for situations where thousands of EC2 instances are attached to your file system.

EFS Throughput Modes

The default throughput mode for EFS is called a burst model using performance credits. You can also control the exact throughput of your elastic file system by selecting the provisioned through-put mode and entering any level of throughput up to 1 GB per second.

Using the default burst mode; when your EFS file system reads or writes data to the file system but throughput remains below the assigned baseline rate, it earns burst credits. This may sound like the most boring game ever, but these burst credits are being accumulated for future throughput needs. When your file system requires more throughput, the saved burst credits are cashed in, allowing performance throughput above the current baseline.

Throughput is designed to increase as the number of stored files increases. As files are added to your file system, the amount of throughput allowed is increased based on the allotted file size. For example, a 5 TB EFS file system can burst to 500 MB/sec throughput (5 TB X 100 MB/sec per TB); a 10 TB file system can burst to 1,000 MB/sec of throughput. Using the CloudWatch metric *BurstCreditBalance*, you can monitor your positive burst credit balance. After testing, you might decide to move up to provisioned throughput with a few mouse clicks, as shown in Figure 6-15.

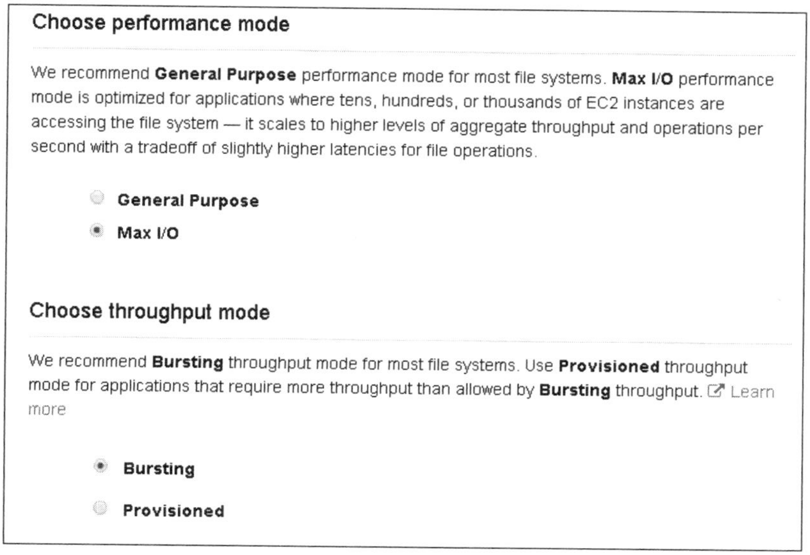

Choose performance mode

We recommend **General Purpose** performance mode for most file systems. **Max I/O** performance mode is optimized for applications where tens, hundreds, or thousands of EC2 instances are accessing the file system — it scales to higher levels of aggregate throughput and operations per second with a tradeoff of slightly higher latencies for file operations.

- ○ **General Purpose**
- ● **Max I/O**

Choose throughput mode

We recommend **Bursting** throughput mode for most file systems. Use **Provisioned** throughput mode for applications that require more throughput than allowed by **Bursting** throughput. ☑ Learn more

- ● **Bursting**
- ○ **Provisioned**

Figure 6-15   Selecting EFS performance

EFS Security

After creating your file system and mount points in your selected VPC, you can use security groups and optionally network ACLs to further control the EC2 instance and subnet access to the EFS mount points. Access to the files and directories themselves is controlled by your application or operating system user and group permissions. All data stored within the EFS is encrypted at rest, and encryption keys are managed by the AWS KMS.

> **Note**
>
> At a minimum, use a Linux kernel version 4.0 and up when using EFS, or you won't be happy with the performance levels.

Storage Performance Compared

The available managed storage options at AWS all have different performance characteristics, as shown in Table 6-5.

- EBS provides the lowest overall latency when compared to EFS or S3 storage. Remember: EBS volumes are accessible from a single server. There is no ability to further scale the performance of a single block volume when it is under load because the amount of maximum throughput is defined at creation of each volume. EC2 instances use EBS volumes as boot volumes or for database drives with mandated higher IOPS requirements.

- EFS is in the middle of latency specs when compared to EBS or S3 object storage. As discussed, EFS has a scalable amount of throughput, resulting in latency levels higher than EBS block storage, but not as high as S3 object storage. EBS also has the advantage of file and record locking, a recognizable tree-storage structure, and the ability to share the contents with multiple clients.

- Before the EFS, customers were forced to create their own do-it-yourself file storage systems with multiple EBS volumes for boot and storage needs attached to each instance. EBS is required as a boot device for each instance and for database instances; the rest of your storage does not have to use EBS volumes.

- EFS has a lower latency than S3 object storage but a higher latency than an EBS volume. However, there are higher levels of throughput available for scaling the EFS throughput to the many gigabytes per second when using the provisioned throughput mode.

- S3 object storage can achieve decent levels of throughput and scalability; however, it has a higher level of latency when compared to EFS or EBS volumes, which makes it inadequate for latency-sensitive applications.

Table 6-5   **Comparing S3, EFS, and EBS Storage**

Feature	Simple Storage Service (S3)	Elastic Block Storage (EFS)	Elastic File System (EFS)
Costs of storage	Scaled cost based on first 50 TB of storage used and the number of requests made (POST, GET) Data transfer per GB out of S3	General-purpose SSD $.0.10 per GB per month Provisioned IOPS SSD $.0.125 per GB per month; $.0.065 per provisioned IOPS per month Throughput-optimized HD $.0.045 per GB per month Cold HD $.0.025 per GB per month	Standard storage $0.030 GB used per month Infrequent access storage $0.045 GB used per month Infrequent Access Requests (per GB transferred) $0.01
Storage size	No limit	Maximum storage size 16 TB	No limit
File size	5 TB	No limit	47.9 TB single file
Data throughput	Supports multipart upload PUT maximum of 5 GB	SSD, SSD IOPS, and throughput optimized	3 GB/sec per client
Performance	Supports up to 3,500 PUT/LIST/DELETES requests per second per partition Supports 5,500 GET requests per second per partition	3 IOPS per GB Provisioned IOPS up to 32,000 Single volumes can be scaled on-demand	Supports up to 7,000 file system operations per second
Data location	Data stays within region or requested AZ	Data stays within the same AZ	Data is stored within the region
Data access options	Public (HTTP, HTTPS) or private network endpoints (Gateway)	Private network from a single instance	Private network from multiple instances
Permissions	ACLs, bucket policies, IAM polices	IAM policies, Operating system security settings (Linux and Windows)	Linux operating system only
File access and updates	Entire file must be replaced	Block-level file changes	POSIX support or file and record locking for access by multiple clients

Feature	Simple Storage Service (S3)	Elastic Block Storage (EFS)	Elastic File System (EFS)
Encryption	SSE—Amazon S3, AWS-KMS, SSE-C	AWS—KMS—Managed customer master key (CMK) with AES 256-bit encryption	AWS—KMS—Managed CMK with AES 256-bit encryption
Durability	11 9s stored in three separate facilities	99.95 multiple copies within the AZ	Highly available design
Access Control	Pre-signed URLs, OAI	Security group, NACL, IAM	Security group, IAM
Availability	4 9s can survive the loss of two facilities	Cannot survive AZ failure	Stored across multiple AZs
Ideal file type	Static files	Boot drives, database instances SQL, NoSQL	Big data analytics, media workflows (media editing, studio production), or home directories

EFS File Sync

EFS File Sync allows you to sync data from an on-premise NFS to EFS. It is available as an installable agent that runs on EC2 instances, or VMware ESXi environments.

EFS File Sync can be used to copy files from EFSs hosted in different AWS regions. It is much faster than standard Linux copy commands, and the upload is designed for encrypted parallel data transfer to AWS.

Compared to EFS sync, using rsync is a much slower choice because rsync is a single-threaded utility. If you use fpsync, your performance will be much better because you are now working with a multithreaded utility.

You do not have to set up a VPN connection or use a more expensive Direct Connect connection when using EFS file sync.

MAKE SURE TO WATCH THE COMPANION VIDEO "CREATING EFS STORAGE."

Amazon FSx for Windows File Server

Although the number of companies running Windows workloads at AWS has dropped compared to Linux workloads, 38% of customers still use Windows Servers. EFS is limited to a Linux client; however, Windows clients now can use FSx for Windows File Server to set up a completely compatible Windows file system, as shown in Figure 6-16. Features include the following:

Windows Shares—FSx is built using Windows file servers and accessed using the SMB protocol 2.0 to 3.11, allowing you to support Windows 7 clients and Windows Server 2008.

File System—Built on SSD drives, FSx file systems can be up to 64 TB with more than 2 Mb per second of throughput. Multi-AZ support for FSx allows you to use Microsoft DFS to replicate between multiple locations supporting up to 300 PB of storage.

Redundancy—Data is stored within an AZ, and incremental snapshots are automatically taken every day. Manual snapshots are supported as well.

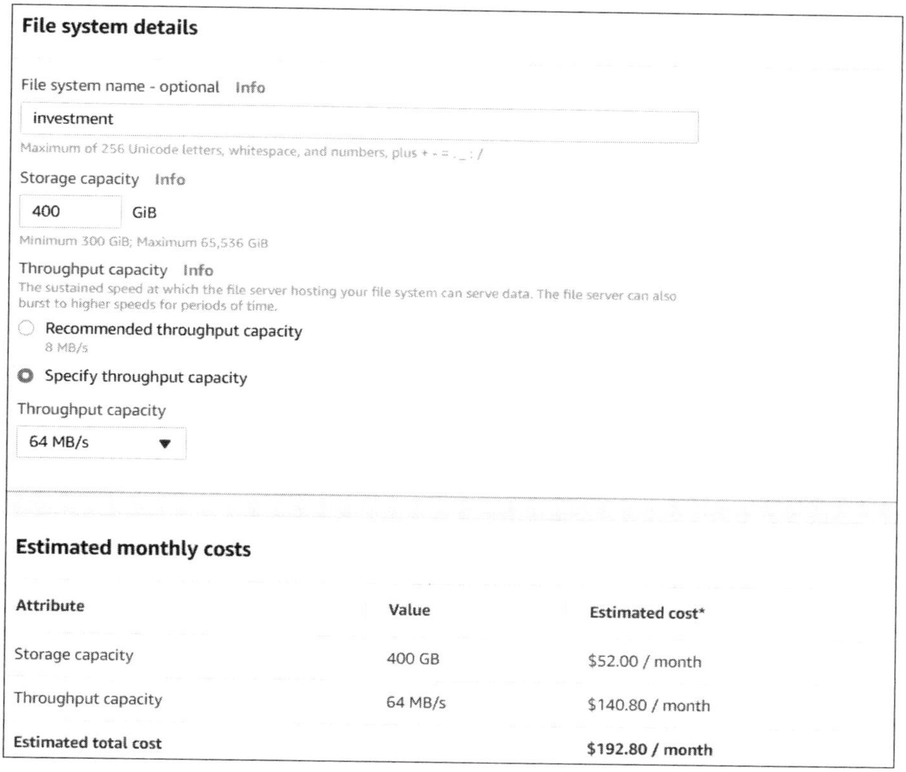

File system details

File system name - optional   Info

investment

Maximum of 256 Unicode letters, whitespace, and numbers, plus + - = . _ : /

Storage capacity   Info

400   GiB

Minimum 300 GiB; Maximum 65,536 GiB

Throughput capacity   Info

The sustained speed at which the file server hosting your file system can serve data. The file server can also burst to higher speeds for periods of time.

○ Recommended throughput capacity
  8 MB/s

◉ Specify throughput capacity

Throughput capacity

64 MB/s   ▼

Estimated monthly costs

Attribute	Value	Estimated cost*
Storage capacity	400 GB	$52.00 / month
Throughput capacity	64 MB/s	$140.80 / month
Estimated total cost		**$192.80 / month**

Figure 6-16   Ordering FSx

MAKE SURE TO WATCH THE COMPANION VIDEO "FSX SETUP FOR WINDOWS."

Relational Database Service (RDS)

Just like networking services at AWS, the odds are 100% that you're using databases. Databases at AWS are hosted by several database services, including RDS, which hosts a variety of popular relational database engines, as shown in Table 6-6. Because AWS completely manages RDS, all you need to do is focus on your data and leave the running, monitoring, backing up, and failover of your database instances to Amazon. If this isn't your style, Amazon has no issue with your building your own EC2 instances and managing every aspect of your database infrastructure.

Table 6-6 **RDS Database Engines**

Database Engine	Data Recovery Support	SSL Support	Replication	Encryption	Real-Time Monitoring	Compliance Support
MariaDB 10.0,1,2,3	InnoDB for version 10.2 and XtraDB version 10.0, and 10.1	yaSSL, Open SSL, or TLS	Point-in-time restore and snapshot restore	AES-256	Yes	HIPAA
MySQL 5.5–8.0	InnoDB	yaSSL, Open SSL, or TLS	Point-in-time restore and snapshot restore	AES-256	Yes for 5.5 or later	HIPAA, PHI, FedRAMP
SQL Server 2008–2017	All versions support data recovery	SSL	SQL Server Mirroring, SQL Always On	AES-256, TDE	Yes	N/A
Oracle 12c, 11g	All versions support data recovery	SSL or NNE	Point-in-time restore and snapshot restore	AES-256, TDE	Yes	N/A
PostgreSQL	All versions support data recovery	SSL	AWS Synchronous Replication	AES-256	Yes	HIPAA, PHI, FedRAMP

Perhaps you don't want to build and maintain the virtual servers for your databases anymore; if this sounds like you, join the club. There are thousands of AWS customers who have decided that they need databases; they just don't want to manage the infrastructure anymore. The essential components that make up the relational database service hosted by RDS and managed by AWS include the complete management of the instances hosting your data, automatic backups, synchronous replication from the master to the standby database instance, and automatic failover and recovery as required.

RDS Database Instances

Under the hood of an RDS deployment is a familiar compute component: the EC2 instance. When you order your RDS database instance, the CPU, memory, storage, and its performance (IOPS) are ordered as a bundle. These initial values can be changed later. RDS supports a variety of standard, memory-optimized, and burstable performance EC2 instances that also support Intel hyperthreading, which allows multiple threads to run concurrently on a single Intel Xeon CPU core. Threads are represented as virtual CPUs (vCPUs). RDS pricing can use on-demand EC2 instances. The odds are that you want to use reserved instance (RI) mean pricing, giving you a price break up to 70%. This makes the most sense because your databases are typically always running.

Storage for your database instances is with EBS volumes, which are automatically striped for you, providing additional performance. Volume types can be either general-purpose SSDs, provisioned IOPS SSDs, or magnetic hard drives. (Magnetic drives show up for backward compatibility because some older customers still use them. For production databases, Amazon does not recommend magnetic drives. Furthermore, the drives are limited to 4 TB.) MySQL, MariaDB, Oracle, and PostgreSQL volumes can be from 20 GB to 32 TB. SQL Server is limited to 16 TB storage volumes. General-purpose SSD storage uses burst credits, allowing sustained burst performance; the length of sustained performance depends on the size of the volume. You can have up to 40 RDS database instances for hosting MySQL, MariaDB, or PostgreSQL; these values are defined by AWS account soft limits and can be increased upon request. For more information on burst credits, review the EBS section found earlier in this chapter.

For typical production databases, the recommendation is to use provisioned IOPS, which range from 1,000 to 40,000 IOPS depending on the database engine being used.

> **Note**
>
> For databases running in production, multi-AZ deployments with provisioned IOPS for the master and standby databases and read replicas should be used.

As mentioned, as your needs change, you can independently scale the size of your database compute and change the size and the IOPS of your storage volumes, as shown in Figure 6-17. While changes are being made to compute resources attached to your database instance, your database is unavailable. If your database services are hosted and maintained by the RDS, you don't have direct access to your database compute instance because Amazon is carrying out the backup, patching, monitoring, and recovery of your database instances for you.

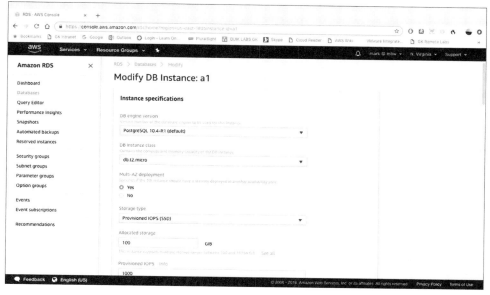

Figure 6-17   Changing database instance parameters

Each database instance runs a specific database engine and version that you choose at installation. RDS supports MySQL, MariaDB, PostgreSQL, Oracle, and Microsoft SQL Server. Just because these database engines are supported by RDS doesn't mean every version of every listed database engine available is supported by RDS. You must carefully check out the database engines supported and decide if RDS matches your needs; you may have to build your required database design from scratch.

If you decide to build your own database instances, you have to provision the right EC2 instance size, attach appropriate EBS volumes and IOPS, and define and maintain your own database instance snapshot backup schedule. You are also responsible for monitoring the database instances and providing all the maintenance, including failover. It's no wonder RDS is popular.

High Availability for RDS

Production databases can and should use multi-AZ deployments, which provide failover support with the master database instance located in one AZ and the standby database instance in the other AZ. The technology used for database failover and the master to the standby depends on the database engine type. Most RDS deployments use Amazon's failover technology. However, SQL Server uses SQL Server mirroring to perform its failovers.

When you order a multi-AZ deployment, it's Amazon's job to provision and maintain the master and standby replicas in different AZs, as shown in Figure 6-18. The primary database instance is synchronously replicated to the standby replica, providing data redundancy. Transaction logs are backed up every 5 minutes. Data replication between the database instances creates increased write and commit latencies because of the synchronous data replication between the master and the standby instances. Your database instances and volumes must be sized to be able to perform synchronous replication quickly and reliably without affecting the overall performance required of your database service.

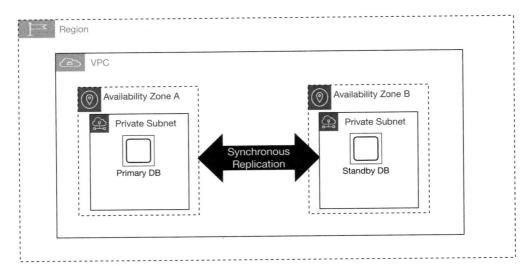

Figure 6-18   RDS multi-AZ design

Note

For most RDS designs except for Aurora, the standby replica is treated as a true standby instance and therefore is not used for additional read requests. Additional read replicas can be automatically created using the RDS service. Place the read replicas in the desired regions to handle any additional read requirements.

When issues occur, as they will, the RDS database failover is an automated process that swings into action when problems occur, such as a failure of the primary database instance, or an AZ failure. Failover can also occur if maintenance is being performed. Perhaps the primary and secondary database instance server types are being changed, or software patching is being performed.

When failure happens during the failover process, RDS automatically switches over to the standby replica, as shown in Figure 6-19. The standby replica now becomes the master database instance. Route 53, the AWS DNS service, modifies the RDS endpoint to point to the new master, the standby replica; this process should happen quickly. Re-establishing the availability of the new standby database instance takes a bit more time; the EC2 instance has to be built, and snapshots have to be applied. After the new standby replica is re-created, to ensure all changes have propagated from the master to the standby database, Amazon replays what is called the redo log from the last database checkpoint, making sure all changes have been applied before the new master database is made available.

This recovery process isn't magic. It's simply an automated recovery process that you want Amazon to carry out on your behalf. Other real-world issues might be happening on the network with Route 53, the DNS service, or Murphy's Law.

Note

Database event subscriptions can be created to notify you via text or email that a failover is underway.

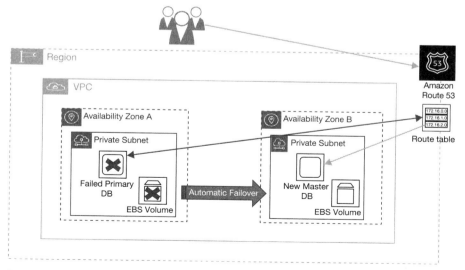

Figure 6-19   RDS failover

Big-Picture RDS Installation Steps

The process for installing a database using RDS is similar for all the supported database engine types except for Aurora. After selecting the database engine, the database instance details are chosen. The initial options that you can define depend on the database engine, as shown in Table 6-7.

Table 6-7   Initial RDS Setup Questions

Database Instance Settings	Details
License model	Bring your own license (BYOL), general-purpose
Database engine version	Select desired version to deploy
Database instance	Standard, memory-optimized, and burstable performance
Multi-AZ deployment	Synchronous AWS replication service; SQL Server uses Native Mirroring or Always On
Storage type	SSD, provisioned IOPS, or HDD volumes
Amount of storage to allocate	1–16 TB (sizing follows EBS limits)
Database instance identifier	Unique identifier if required by database engine
Master username and password	For database authentication

The advanced database instance settings options that can be configured are shown in Table 6-8.

Table 6-8   Advanced RDS Setup Questions

Advanced Database Instance Settings	Details
Database port	Database engine default value
VPC	VPC to host database instance
Database subnet group	Predefined subnet for database instance
Public accessibility	Default is private
Availability zone	Specify AZ
Security group	Control access to database instance
Database name	Unique database name
Database port	Default access port of database engine
Parameter group	Predefine database engine, database instance, and allocated storage
Option group	Additional features per database engine, such as encryption
Copy tags to snapshot	Tags to be added to database snapshots
Encryption	Encryption type dependent on database engine

Advanced Database Instance Settings	Details
Backup retention	Number of days automatic backups of database to be retained
Backup window	Specific time for database backup
Enhanced monitoring	Enables metrics to be gathered in real time
Log exports	Publish select logs to CloudWatch
Auto minor version upgrade	Allow database engine to receive minor database engine version upgrades automatically
Maintenance window	30-minute window to apply database modifications

Monitoring Database Performance

Once your RDS database has been deployed, you should establish a CloudWatch baseline to calculate the ongoing performance of your database under different times of day to establish an acceptable normal level of operation. Using the RDS console, you can select a variety of metrics that allow you to monitor the number of connections to the database instance, read and write operations, and the amount of storage, memory, and CPU being utilized. A sampling of CloudWatch metrics as shown in Table 6-9 allows you to use metrics to create alarms that can alert you when problems and issues occur.

Table 6-9 **CloudWatch RDS Metrics**

CW Metric	Definition	Reporting	Values
IOPS	Input and output operations per second	Average read/write per minute	Tens of thousands per second
Read and write latency	Time it took from request to completion	One-minute interval	Per second
Throughput	Bytes transferred to or from the database volume	One-minute interval	MB/second
Queue depth	I/O requests waiting to be carried out	One-minute interval	From zero to several hundred

Best Practices for RDS

There are numerous best practices to carry out when utilizing an RDS deployment:

- Monitor your infrastructure with CloudWatch alerts to ensure you are notified when you are about to overload your capacity.

- Monitor database performance to define what is acceptable as normal operation. Define baselines for the minimum, maximum, and average values at defined intervals (hourly, half-day, seven days, one week, and two weeks) to create a normal baseline.

- Performance metrics to evaluate include CPU utilization, available memory, amount of free storage space, read-write (IOPS, latency, throughput), network receive and transmit throughput, database connections, high CPU or RAM consumption, and disk space consumption.

- Provisioned IOPS storage must be matched with the desired EC2 instance for the best performance.

- Caching of the DNS name of your database EC2 instance should use a time to live (TTL) of less than 30 seconds to ensure that if failover occurs, the client application connects to the new master server quickly. A longer TTL would cause problems because the failover to the new master would not occur for a longer period.

- For the best performance, each database instance should have enough allocated RAM, so the working set of your database resides in memory.

- Use IAM users and groups to control access to RDS resources.

MAKE SURE TO WATCH THE COMPANION VIDEO "ORDERING RDS."

Aurora

Another SQL type database service hosted by RDS is Aurora, a fully compatible MySQL and PostgreSQL-managed database as a service (DBaaS). If either MySQL or PostgreSQL is currently being used on-premise and is due to be moved to the AWS cloud, Aurora is well worth evaluating. Comparing the performance of Aurora to MySQL on the same hardware, Aurora has up to five times the performance confirmed by SysBench testing due to use of an SSD virtual SAN showing a cluster storage array replicated six times across three AZs. When deploying Aurora, there are three interesting choices, as shown in Figure 6-20.

- **Aurora Provisioned**—This is the standard deployment where the customer defines the instance class and the advanced details of placement, accessibility, encryption, backup, and failover required.

- **Provisioned with Aurora parallel query enabled**—A single query can be distributed across all the available CPUs in the storage layer, greatly speeding up analytical queries. More than 200 SQL functions, equijoins, and projections can run in parallel format. This feature is only currently available for the MySQL 5.6 compatible version of Aurora that is running on the r3 or r4 family of EC2 instances.

- **Serviceless**—This deployment option is an on-demand deployment of Aurora that works with the MySQL-compatible addition of Aurora. When your application is up and running, a serviceless Aurora database cluster is deployed that scales based on the defined minimum and maximum performance requirements of the application. When your application enters a period of light or minimal activity, the Aurora database is scaled in to the minimum allocated size but remains online and continues to service application requests scaling back out as required.

Rather than defining the database instance class size, for the serviceless option of Aurora, you set the minimum and maximum capacity required. Behind the scenes, the database endpoint points to a fleet of resources that are automatically scaled based on your minimum and maximum requirements. For example, your serviceless database cluster can scale up if the CPU utilization of the application rises above 60% or the connections to the application are more than 80%. The cluster can then scale down if the application CPU load is below 25% utilization and less than 30% of the connections were utilized. Consider a retail environment with multiple branch locations using a centralized point-of-sale. As more customers enter the store and begin purchasing, the system can scale accordingly up and down.

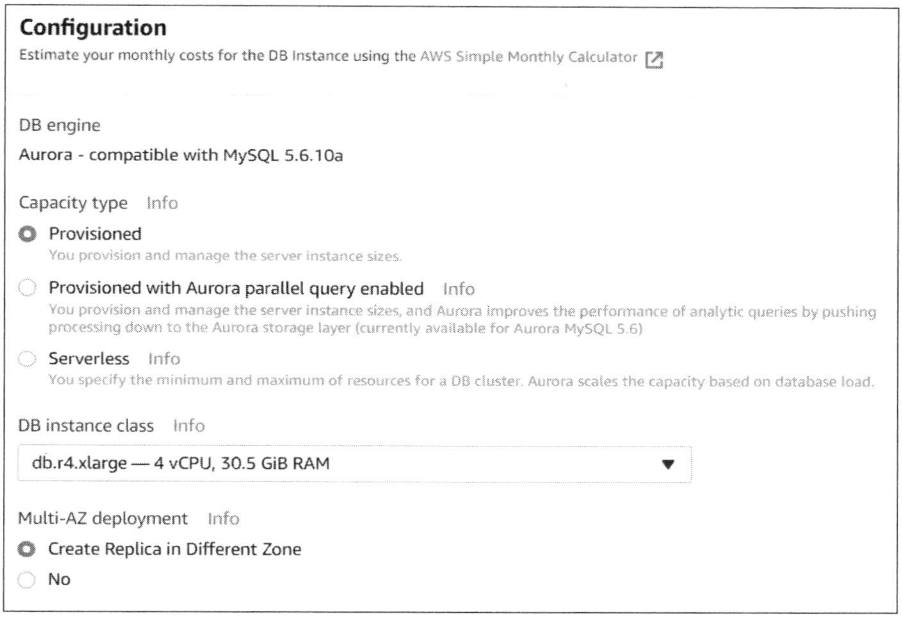

Configuration
Estimate your monthly costs for the DB Instance using the AWS Simple Monthly Calculator 🗗

DB engine
Aurora - compatible with MySQL 5.6.10a

Capacity type   Info
◉ Provisioned
   You provision and manage the server instance sizes.

○ Provisioned with Aurora parallel query enabled   Info
   You provision and manage the server instance sizes, and Aurora improves the performance of analytic queries by pushing processing down to the Aurora storage layer (currently available for Aurora MySQL 5.6)

○ Serverless   Info
   You specify the minimum and maximum of resources for a DB cluster. Aurora scales the capacity based on database load.

DB instance class   Info

db.r4.xlarge — 4 vCPU, 30.5 GiB RAM ▼

Multi-AZ deployment   Info
◉ Create Replica in Different Zone
○ No

Figure 6-20   Aurora deployment options

Aurora Storage

When comparing Aurora to SQL databases supported by RDS, there is no need to provision storage in advance for future growth. The internal design of the Aurora storage engine allows for the automatic scaling of its distributed storage architecture from a starting point of 10 GB, up to 64 TB in 10 GB chunks that are stored across multiple SSD drives across multiple AZs, as shown in Figure 6-21. Aurora replicates six copies of its data records across three AZs, providing enhanced durability and 99.99% availability.

The quorum across the three AZs is all six data nodes; the write set is four nodes, and the read set is the two remaining nodes spread across three AZs. Data is stored in a shared cluster storage volume of Aurora data stored on multiple SSD drives. The shared storage volume spans the multiple AZs. The result is that each AZ has a copy of the database cluster data.

Aurora performance enhancements are due to the design of the storage plane, which is an SSD-backed virtualized storage array. Aurora has at a minimum a primary database instance, and it can have up to 15 additional Aurora replicas. Beyond the storage durability, the data transaction logs are being backed up continuously to S3 storage.

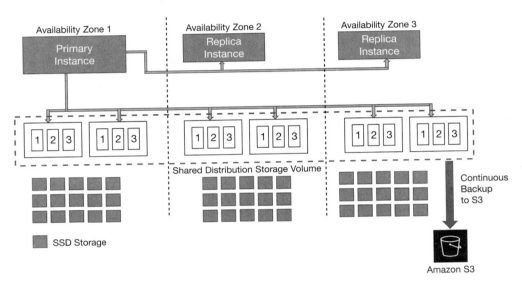

Figure 6-21   Aurora data storage architecture

Aurora has been designed by locating the underlying SSD storage nodes that make up Aurora's shared storage volume into what Amazon calls a cell spread across the three AZs helping to limit the size of the blast radius when failures occur.

Aurora's cluster design has the primary and replica database instances connecting to the same storage plane. The primary database instance carries out the write operations to the cluster volumes in each AZ and offloads the read operations to the replica database instances, as shown in Figure 6-22. This design is different from standard RDS MySQL or PostgreSQL deployments, where standby database instances do not perform read requests.

If the primary database instance becomes unavailable, there is automatic failover to an Aurora Replica. The failover priority for the available Aurora Replicas can also be defined.

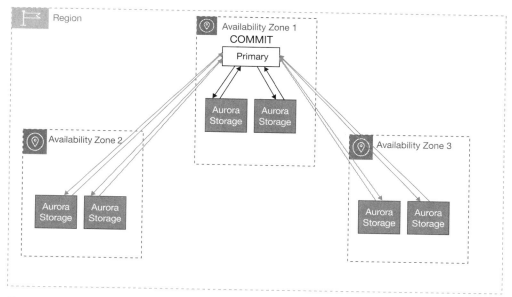

Figure 6-22   Aurora cluster design

When failover occurs, the speed of the failover process is in seconds. Assuming there are additional Aurora replicas in the same or different AZs, which there will be for a production deployment, the canonical name record (CNAME) is changed to point to the Aurora Replica that has been promoted to be the new primary database.

With Aurora, you can lose access to two copies of data without affecting the writing process, and you can lose up to three copies without affecting the ability to read your data. In the background, Aurora is constantly checking and rechecking the data blocks and discs, performing repairs automatically using data from the volumes in the cluster. In addition, Aurora Replicas can be created in different AWS regions. The first Aurora Replica created in a different region acts as the primary Aurora Replica in the new region. You can also add Aurora Replicas in different AWS regions that share the same storage plane.

> **Note**
>
> In the near future, Aurora will be able to operate in a multimaster design where multiple read/ write master database instances can be deployed across multiple AZs, improving Aurora's high-availability design. If one of the master database instances were to fail, other instances in the cluster could take over immediately, maintaining both read and write availability for the cluster.

Communicating with Aurora

Communication with the Aurora cluster is performed with specific endpoints, as shown in Figure 6-23.

The cluster endpoint to the Aurora database cluster is a single URL containing a host address and a port address to simplify connectivity to the primary database instance for all writes, including inserts, updates, deletes, and changes. When failovers occur, the cluster endpoint automatically points to the new primary database instance.

The reader endpoint connects to one of the available Aurora replicas for the database cluster; if there are multiple Aurora replicas, the endpoint uses load balancing to support the read requests. If your Aurora deployment is small, containing a single primary instance, the reader endpoint services read requests from the primary database instance.

The instance endpoint points to the current primary database instance of the database cluster.

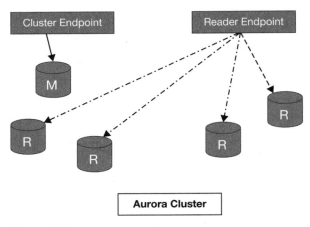

Figure 6-23   Aurora endpoints

> **Note**
> Dow Jones used the AWS data migration service to migrate its legacy environment to Aurora. It uses a 1 TB Aurora cluster that can handle 200 transactions per second. Alfresco used Aurora to scale to more than a billion documents with throughput of 3 million transactions per hour.

MAKE SURE TO WATCH THE COMPANION VIDEO "CREATING AURORA DATABASES."

DynamoDB

Another popular database offered by AWS is DynamoDB. Amazon had internally developed DynamoDB in 2006 and initially started using it to host the familiar shopping cart in the online Amazon store. DynamoDB was publicly launched as a NoSQL database service in 2012 designed for Internet performance at scale for applications hosted at AWS. These days, the Amazon store is completely backed by DynamoDB.

> **Note**
>
> For older applications that are joined at the hip with an SQL database, there may be no reason to change. After all, AWS has use cases for customers using SQL with millions of customers. For newer applications with no legacy concerns or requirements, a nonrelational database such as DynamoDB might be something to consider.

DynamoDB has been designed as a nonrelational database that doesn't follow the same rules as the standard SQL database (see Table 6-10).

Table 6-10   **SQL vs DynamoDB Compared**

Features	SQL Server	DynamoDB
Database type	Relational database management system (RDBMS)	Nonrelational
Structure	Tables with rows and columns	Collection of JavaScript Object Notation (JSON) documents, key-value, graph, or column
Schema	Predefined	Dynamic
Scale	Vertical	Horizontal
Language	SQL structured	JavaScript
Performance	Good for online analytical processing (OLAP)	Built for online transaction processing (OLTP) at scale
Optimization	Optimized for storage	Optimized for read/write
Query type	Real-time ad hoc queries	Simple

When you initially order DynamoDB, all you can view is the table, sort, and query definitions in addition to optional performance controls. There is no access to the underlying infrastructure. DynamoDB tables can be global in scope, synchronized across multiple AWS regions. There are no limits to the table size you can create, and you also define the read/write performance of each DynamoDB table. The tables contain small pieces of data, but potentially many hundreds of thousands of pieces of data, including website clicks, online gaming, advertising, inventory updates, tweets, voting, and user session state. DynamoDB tables also can horizontally scale; any of the listed examples may require an increase in performance at a moment's notice.

With an SQL database, there is a defined set of data rules, called the *schema*, which could be one or more interlinked tables, columns, data types, views, procedures, relationships, and primary keys, to name a few of the components (refer to Table 6-10). With SQL, the database rules have been defined *before* any data is entered into the rows and columns of the relational databases table following Structured Query Language (SQL).

In comparison, DynamoDB stores its data in tables but doesn't follow the same rules as a relational database. First, its data is stored in several JSON formats: graph-based, key-value, document, and column. There's more to DynamoDB than just a simple table, but first let's think about databases and why we store data there. Databases keep our precious data safe, secure, and reliable. Relational databases have stored and secured our data reliably for years. And some relational databases at AWS can now automatically scale their compute performance and data storage; for example, Aurora Serviceless can now scale on-demand, and all versions of Aurora scale data records automatically. At AWS, some of the operational lines between SQL and DynamoDB are starting to be blurred.

> **Note**
>
> When Amazon looked at how its data operations on its internal Oracle databases were being carried out internally at AWS, it found the following facts. They made Amazon realize that DynamoDB could completely replace its Oracle databases, a task that it completed in 2019.
>
> - 70% of the queries were single SQL query against the primary key of a single table with a single row of information being delivered.
> - 20% of the queries were queries against multiple rows of a single table.
> - 10% of the queries were complex relational queries.

Database Design 101

DynamoDB has been built for OLTP at scale and stores its data in the format in which the application is going to use it. As a result, there's no need for complex queries across multiple tables as an SQL database. DynamoDB design uses a single table for the application (see Figure 6-24). An SQL database query can also be plenty fast when it's performing a search within a specific table.

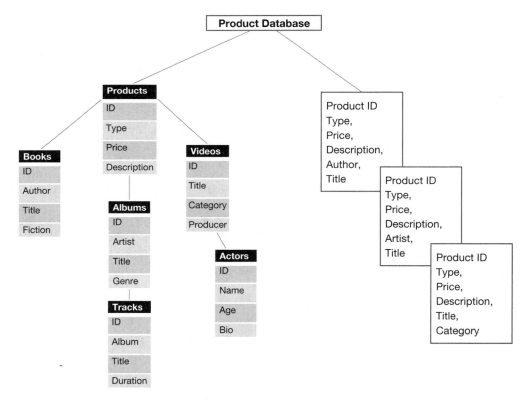

Figure 6-24   Comparing SQL (left) and DynamoDB queries (right)

When you query your data, you want specific results, such as items per order or orders for each customer, regardless of the database type. Taking the SQL example of a product catalog for a company, as shown again by Figure 6-24, on the left side under Products, you could have links to books, albums, and videos. These categories could be broken down into further details such as tracks and actors. There would be relationships defined as one-to-one between product and books, one-to-many between albums and tracks, and many-to-many between videos and actors.

For the SQL database in this example, it would be a complex SQL query to summarize a list of all your products. You would require three distinct queries: one for books, one for products, and one for videos. There would also be several joins and mapping tables that would be used to produce the list.

As a result, the CPU of the database instance could be under a fair amount of load to carry out a complex query task. And because the query request data is stored in multiple tables, it must be assembled before it can be viewed. With DynamoDB, on the right side the same data is stored in a collection of JSON documents.

If you want the total number of products, your DynamoDB query for the database example shown in Figure 6-25 on the right side can be very simple. For example, it might be **Select*from Products where type = book**. The DynamoDB query process is much simpler. The DynamoDB query gets the data from the single table; it does not have to construct the view of the data from multiple tables.

```
$ aws dynamodb query
\ --table-name Orders
\ --key-condition-expression
"Username = :username"
\ --expression-attribute-values '{
":username": { "S": "markw" } }'
\ $LOCAL
```

DynamoDB query

```
SELECT customer.cust_name, salesperson.name,
salesperson.city
FROM salesperson, customer
WHERE salesperson.city = customer.city;
```

SQL query

Figure 6-25   Comparing SQL and DynamoDB queries

Note that the structure of the DynamoDB—the schema, if you will—is contained within each document. There is no mandatory schema that defines the fields, of all the records, in a DynamoDB database. DynamoDB makes simple queries, which are less taxing on the application.

DynamoDB Tables

In a DynamoDB table, data is stored as groups of attributes, also known as *items*. This concept is similar to the rows and columns found in other relational databases.

Each item stored in a DynamoDB database can be stored and retrieved using a primary key that uniquely identifies each item in the table.

When you construct a table in DynamoDB, you must define a primary key. In Figure 6-26, the primary key is defined as the station_id. A hash value is computed for the primary key, and the data in the table is partitioned into multiple partitions, each linked to the primary key hash for the table; in this case, it's station_id. You can also choose to have a secondary index, such as LastName.

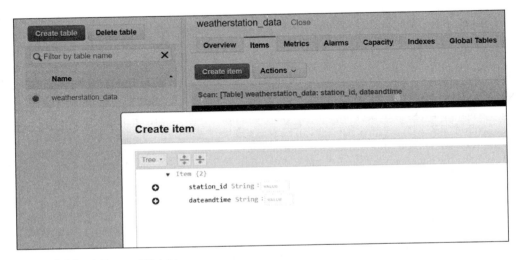

Figure 6-26　A DynamoDB table

Provisioning Table Capacity

DynamoDB performance is defined in what is called *capacity unit sizes*:

- **A single read capacity unit** means a strongly consistent read per second, or two eventually consistent reads per second for items up to 4 KB in size.

- **A single write capacity unit** means a strongly consistent write per second for items up to 1 KB in size.

Your design requires some level of read and write capacity units shown in Figure 6-27. The design might require only a defined amount of read and write performance because your tables could initially be small. The default provision capacity is 5 read and 5 write capacity units. However, over time, your design needs may change, and you may have to, or wish to, scale your table performance to a much higher level. With DynamoDB, you can make changes to your read and write capacity units applied to your table by switching from the default provisioned read/write capacity to on-demand and quickly adjusting the amount of scale that your application and therefore your DynamoDB table requires.

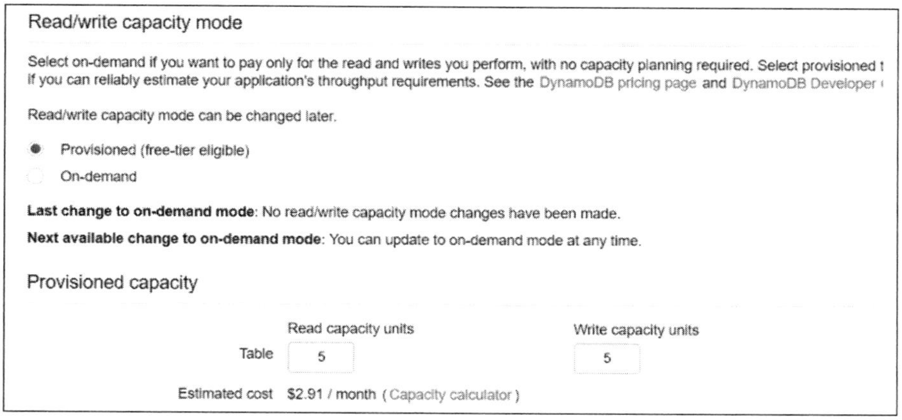

Read/write capacity mode

Select on-demand if you want to pay only for the read and writes you perform, with no capacity planning required. Select provisioned t
If you can reliably estimate your application's throughput requirements. See the DynamoDB pricing page and DynamoDB Developer (

Read/write capacity mode can be changed later.

● Provisioned (free-tier eligible)
○ On-demand

Last change to on-demand mode: No read/write capacity mode changes have been made.

Next available change to on-demand mode: You can update to on-demand mode at any time.

Provisioned capacity

	Read capacity units	Write capacity units
Table	5	5

Estimated cost $2.91 / month (Capacity calculator)

Figure 6-27   Adjusting table capacity

With DynamoDB, both the read capacity units (RCUs) and the write capacity units (WCUs) can be defined for the table; that is, how many reads and writes do you need per second for your table? A single read allows you to read up to 4 KB of data; if your object is under 4 KB, then a single read allows you to gather all the information. A 20 KB object would need 5 RCUs to perform the full read of the object. The same math applies to the writes.

If you provision 300 RCUs for your table, DynamoDB splits up the reads across the three storage partitions. RCUs work on a system using the available tokens for the required read performance. Each token bucket has what is called a *fill rate* that matches the defined RCUs. For our example, the token bucket is refilled at the RCU rate of 100 tokens per second, ensuring the table has enough tokens for the requested performance. Tokens are emptied from the token bucket at the rate of one token per read request. The number of tokens that are deducted from the bucket depends on the number of read requests and the size of the item read. The larger the item, the more tokens that are required to read the entire item.

When a read request is performed, if there are no tokens left in the token bucket, the read request is throttled. To get around this problem, the token bucket also has a burst token added to your bucket, which is calculated based on the rate of the number of provisioned RCUs multiplied by 300. This equals 5 minutes of additional performance at your defined RCU baseline; for spikes in read and write traffic to your table, you will have up to five minutes of performance credits available to handle the increased load. In addition, anytime your DynamoDB table is not being read or written to, burst tokens are being added to your token bucket up to a maximum of 30,000 tokens.

If you need to exceed read and write capacity throughput units higher than the maximum of 40,000, you can contact Amazon directly to request the desired unit increase.

Adaptive Capacity

To solve the problem of your table being throttled when it runs out of burst credits, DynamoDB has introduced a feature called *adaptive capacity* that increases the fill rate to the token bucket based on several parameters: the traffic to your table, your provisioned RCU capacity, the throttling rate, and the current multiplier. Adaptive capacity also provides additional burst tokens, so you have a longer period for bursting and don't run out of tokens as quickly as you would without adaptive capacity being enabled. There are still limits to how many burst credits you will get, which is why DynamoDB introduced a feature called Auto Scaling.

Auto Scaling, as shown in Figure 6-28 allows you to set a lower and upper limit of performance capacity and a desired level of utilization. CloudWatch metrics for monitoring table performance are published to CloudWatch, the monitoring engine at AWS, and alarms are defined to alert Auto Scaling when additional or less performance capacity is required for table reads and writes.

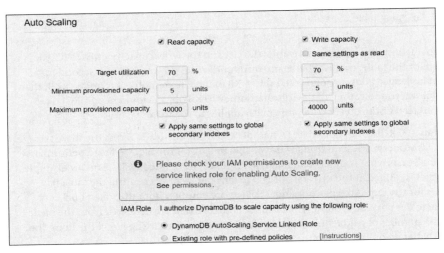

Figure 6-28   DynamoDB Auto Scaling settings

Let's look at the case for a gaming company that uses DynamoDB as its database for millions of gamers. The information pieces that are being stored—such as game scores—are small, but potentially millions of scores need to be stored at scale. Data is stored in DynamoDB by first issuing a PUT request that is sent to a request router, which checks with the authentication services to see if the requested task is allowed. Assuming everything checks out with security, the request is sent to the DynamoDB storage services, which determine where to first write the items to disk and then replicate to the other storage nodes. DynamoDB employs hundreds of thousands of request routers and storage nodes following a cell-based architecture design to limit when failures occur by storing request routers and storage nodes in multiple partitions and AZs throughout the AWS region, as shown in Figure 6-29.

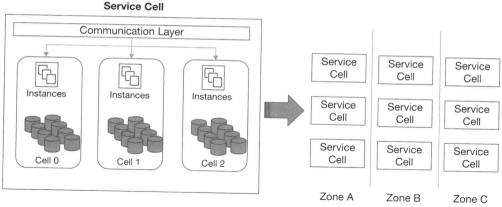

Figure 6-29   DynamoDB cell-based design

Data Consistency

Because data is written into the three partition locations across each AZ, data is not initially consistent in all storage partitions; however, after some time, all data locations across all AZs will be consistent. With DynamoDB, you have a choice of how consistent you want your data to be: Eventually Consistent or Strongly Consistent.

- If you choose Strongly Consistent, a strongly consistent read produces a result from the storage nodes that performed a successful write of the information being requested.

- If you choose Eventual Consistency, the leader node makes a random decision as to which of the storage nodes that are hosting the partition to read from.

The odds are that you will get a consistent read even when eventual consistency has been chosen because two storage partitions out of the three will always have up-to-date data. Typically, the single storage node that is not consistent with the other two nodes is only milliseconds away from being up to date. One of the associated storage nodes will be assigned as the leader node: the initial node that performs the first data write.

Once two of the associated storage nodes have acknowledged a successful write process, the leader storage node communicates with the request router that the write process is successful, which passes that information back to the application and end user.

Each PUT request talks to the leader node first. Then the data is distributed across the AZs, as shown in Figure 6-30. The leader node is always up to date, as is one of the other storage nodes, because there must be an acknowledgment that the PUT is successful into storage locations for a write process to be successful.

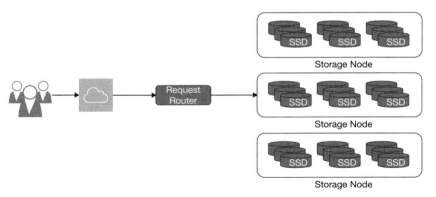

Figure 6-30   DynamoDB storage node design

Paxos is the defined technical method to get the multiple storage systems to agree on a particular leader for the peer storage nodes. The leader storage node is always up to date. The leader and the peer storage nodes are also joined with a heartbeat that fires every 1.5 seconds with the associated storage peers. If the peer storage nodes fall out of sync with the leader storage node, an election is performed, and one of the peer storage nodes becomes the new leader node.

The request routers are stateless devices; it does not matter which request router you communicate with that in turn talks to the leader node of the associated storage partition.

As your DynamoDB database scales, the internal design ensures predictable performance through a process called *burst capacity*. When partitions start to get overloaded, the partition is automatically split and resharded into multiple partitions, which spreads the current read and write capacity units across the available partitions to be able to better serve the required reads and writes of the DynamoDB table.

ACID and DynamoDB

Relational databases promise and deliver great reliability in the exact content of the data being stored. Relational database transactions achieve extremely high levels of storage consistency due to design principles like ACID, which states that your database transactions have a high level of validity due to the properties of atomicity, consistency, isolation, and durability. The ACID standard is followed by relational databases such as Oracle, MySQL, PostgreSQL, and SQL Server; transactions follow the ACID principles as a single process with four conditional variables.

- **Atomicity**—Each database transaction completes successfully, or it's not accepted.

- **Consistency**—Database transactions are successfully written to disk and validated.

- **Isolation**—Database transactions are isolated and secure during processing.

- **Durability**—Database transactions are committed to persistent storage and logged.

Amazon also supports ACID with DynamoDB across one or more tables hosted within a single AWS region. Two internal DynamoDB operations handle these transactions:

- **TransactWriteItems**—This is a batch write operation with multiple PUT, UPDATE, and DELETE item operations that check for specific conditions that must be satisfied before updates are approved.

- **TransactGetItems**—This is a batch read operation with one or more GET item operations. If the GET item request collides with an active write transaction of the same item type, the read transactions are canceled.

With replicated DynamoDB data, the records must also be exact on the primary and the standby database instances. The process of data replication takes time; it *can* be fast, but the process of verification does take additional time.

Global Tables

Standard DynamoDB tables are hosted within an AWS region. A global DynamoDB table is multiple DynamoDB tables replicated across multiple AWS regions, as shown in Figure 6-31, synchronized with the same data records. Because the partitions are stored in multiple AWS regions, IAM roles ensure the proper level of security is enforced when writing records to the global DynamoDB table. Data is transferred from one AWS region to the other using a synchronized replication engine in the source and destination AWS region.

The local replication engine compiles all the PUTS, UPDATES, and DELETES to the DynamoDB table and then replicates the local changes across the private AWS network to the associated DynamoDB table in the destination AWS region. Global tables are multimaster by design, so updates performed in one region are repeated and updated in the other AWS region. Both the outbound and the inbound replication engines need to determine what updates are local and need to be shipped to the other region and what updates are replicated. The replicated updates need to be compared using version numbers and millisecond timestamps to ensure data consistency across the DynamoDB global table. Replicated data from global tables works with a last-write conflict resolution; if the timestamps are the same, the local AWS region where the change was initiated wins.

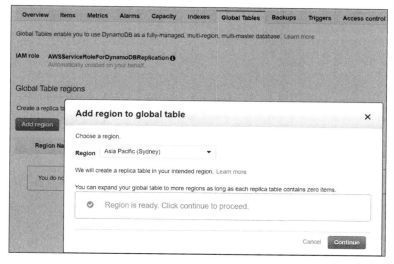

Figure 6-31   DynamoDB global tables

DynamoDB Accelerator (DAX)

DynamoDB response times can be increased to eventually consistent data levels with microsecond latency by adding an in-memory cache to the design. E-commerce online sales, applications with read-intensive needs, and applications performing in-depth analysis over a long-term time frame are some of the use cases that can take advantage of DAX. Your DAX cluster, once provisioned, will be hosted in the VPC of your choice. Applications can use the DAX cluster after the DAX client is installed on the EC2 instances hosting the associated application.

DAX can be designed to be highly available, with multiple nodes hosted across multiple AZs within the AWS region, and can scale out up to 10 replicas. Read operations that DAX will respond to include *GetItem, BatchGetItem, Query*, and *Scan* API calls. Write operations are first written to the table and then to the DAX cluster. Write operations include *BatchWriteItem, UpdateItem, DeleteItem,* and *PutItem* API calls.

Backup and Restore

There are two options for backup at DynamoDB: point-in-time recovery and on-demand backups.

Point-in-time recovery backup—This allows you to restore your DynamoDB table for up to 35 days. This is a fixed value of retention and cannot be changed. A point-in-time restore point can be chosen up to 5 minutes before the current time. Once point-in-time recovery has been enabled for DynamoDB, continuous backups are performed to S3.

On-demand backup—This allows you to create full backups of DynamoDB tables for long-term storage. The on-demand backup is created asynchronously, applying all changes that happen to a snapshot stored in S3. Each on-demand backup backs up the entire DynamoDB table data each time.

A restored table, regardless of the backup type, includes local and global secondary indexes, encryption settings, and the provisioned read and write capacity of the source table at the time of restore. Only after the table has been restored can you manually re-create any auto scaling policies, assigned IAM policies, tags, and TTL settings that were previously applied.

> MAKE SURE TO WATCH THE COMPANION VIDEO "CREATING DYNAMODB TABLES."

ElastiCache

To improve performance of existing applications and supported databases, ElastiCache in memory Redis or Memcached caches can be deployed. The two platforms supported by ElastiCache are Redis, up to version 5.0, and Memcached version 1.5 rev. 10. A memory cache is designed for short-term storage of information, unlike DynamoDB or RDS, where the data is persistently stored. ElastiCache is designed to improve application performance by reducing the reads and writes to persistent storage and direct the traffic to an in-memory cache. Common uses include deploying ElastiCache as a read-only database replica or storage queue or as an in-memory read-write NoSQL database.

One of the best examples of using an in-memory cache is for storing session state for a user session; the user session information needs to be stored, but not for the long term, as shown in Figure 6-32. Rather than storing the user session information on the Web instance that the user is connecting to, the user information is instead stored in an in-memory cache; if the Web instance fails, when the user is routed to another Web instance, the user session information is still being held in the separate memory cache and remains available for the duration of the user session. ElastiCache for Redis would be a good choice for storing user state information. Redis use cases include session cache storage, queues, and full webpage cache. Memcached use cases include application caching for database performance, real-time analytics, media streaming, session state, and message queues. ElastiCache features include the following:

- **Fast performance**—Sub-millisecond response time
- **Management**—AWS management of all hardware and software setup and monitoring
- **Scalable**—Read scaling with replicas, write in-memory scaling
- **Reliable**—Multi-AZ and design with automatic failover
- **Compliant**—HIPAA, PCI, and FedRAMP support with encryption at rest and in transit

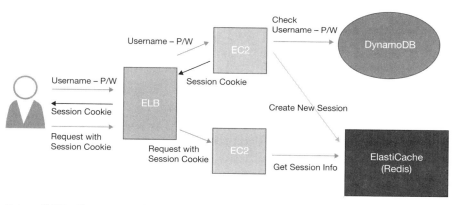

Figure 6-32   User state information stored in ElastiCache

AWS Data Transfer Options

Regardless of the location of your data, there is an ever-increasing number of tools and services to move your data from on-premise locations—even remote locations off-grid into the AWS cloud.

You need to answer several questions before you can choose the proper solution for data transfer into AWS:

What kind of data do you need to transfer from on-premise to AWS?

Data	AWS Transfer Option
Virtual server images	Server migration tools, Export-Import service
Virtual hard disks	Server migration tools, Export-Import service
Database	Database migration tools
Bulk storage files	AWS transfer for SSH File Transfer Protocol (SFTP), AWS Storage Gateway

Where will the data be used at AWS?

Daily use at AWS	AWS DataSync, Direct Connect
Archived use	Glacier
Stored forever	Glacier
On-premise	Direct Connect

How much data needs to be transferred?

Gigabytes	AWS Transfer for SFTP
Terabytes	AWS Snowball, or Snowball Edge
Exabytes	AWS Snowmobile

What are solutions for offline data transfer and hybrid?

Private network connection to AWS	AWS Direct Connect
Edge location transfer	S3 transfer acceleration
Internet transfer	AWS DataSync, AWS Transfer for SFTP
Offline data transfer	Snowball, Snowball Edge, Snowmobile
Hybrid storage	AWS Storage Gateway

AWS Direct Connect—This allows you to create a private connection from your on-premise data center using a fiber-optic connection to AWS. On the Amazon side, the Direct Connect connection connects to a Direct Connect router. A Direct Connect connection can also be partitioned into up to 50 private virtual interfaces to serve public and private resources at AWS across the Direct Connect connection. In addition, you can use a Direct Connect gateway connection to connect your Direct Connect connection to VPCs within your AWS account that are in the same or a different region, as shown in Figure 6-33.

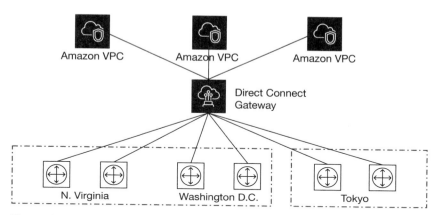

Figure 6-33   Direct Connect Gateway architecture

AWS DataSync—This is a managed data transfer service that helps you automate the movement of large amounts of data from on-premise locations to either S3 buckets or EFS storage. Communication can be over the Internet or across a Direct Connect connection. Both one-time and continuous data transfer are supported using the NFS protocol and parallel processing for fast data transfers. The data sync agent is installed by downloading and deploying the OVA template on a virtual machine that is hosted on your VMware ESXi network. Next, create a data transfer task from your data source (NAS or file system) to the AWS destination—either Amazon EFS or S3 bucket—and then start the transfer. Data integrity verification is continually checked during the transfer process, and data transfers are encrypted using Transport Layer Security (TLS). AWS DataSync also supports both PCI and HIPAA data transfers.

The Snow Family

Meet the Snow family, the new official name of the Snowball and Snowmobile device family: Snowball devices or Snowmobile trucks on demand. Yes, real transport trucks.

AWS Snowball—Petabyte data transfer is possible with multiple Snowball devices; each device can hold up to 80 TB of data. After creating a job request, as shown in Figure 6-34, a Snowball device is shipped to you via UPS. Once you receive your device, hook it up to your local network using its RJ-45 connection. You have to install the client software and enter predefined security information before you can start the data transfer. Once your data transfer has finished, call UPS and ship the Snowball device back to AWS; AWS deposits your data into an S3 bucket. You can also reverse this process and transfer data from AWS back to your on-premise network. All data that is transferred to a Snowball device is encrypted with 256 bit-encryption keys that can be defined using the AWS KMS.

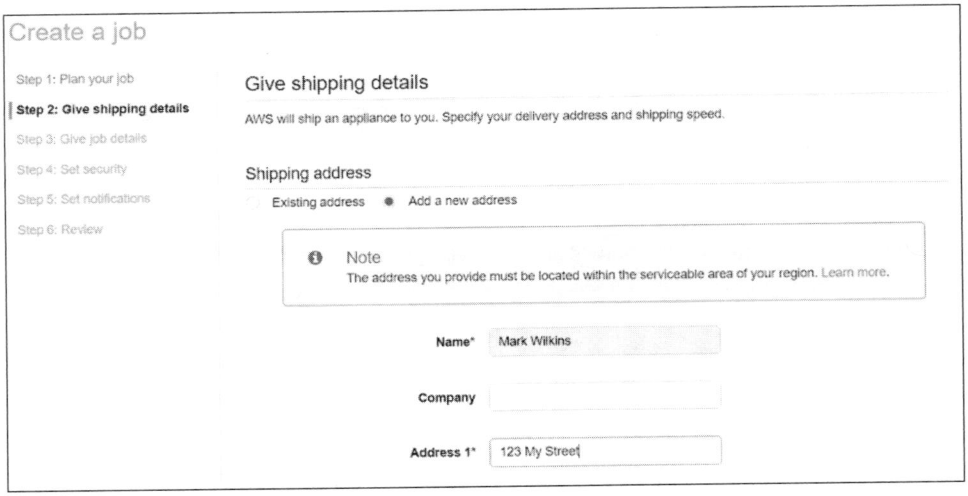

Figure 6-34   Creating a Snowball job

AWS Snowball Edge—Up to 100 TB of capacity and two levels of built-in compute power can be selected with the Snowball Edge device. The two available options are either Storage Optimized or Compute Optimized. The Compute Optimized Snowball device is designed for data processing and storage for remote sites or locations that are not connected to the grid. Perhaps while your data is being transferred to the Snowball device, it could use some additional processing or analysis before being stored. The Snowball Edge device supports the installation of a local EC2 instance, which can carry out the local processing duties; the instance can be built from your instance AMIs.

AWS Snowmobile—Up to hundreds of petabytes of data can be moved with a specialized truck called a Snowmobile. After ordering, AWS employees show up with a 45-foot truck and attach it to your data center. After the truck is filled with data, it is carefully driven back to AWS and uploaded into an S3 bucket of your choice. The truck has a logo "faster than cloud" for easy identification. Okay, that's not true, but your data does have an escort vehicle for additional safety.

AWS transfer for SFTP—A fully managed transfer service for transferring files into and out of an S3 bucket using the secure SFTP. Simply point your existing SFTP software to the SFTP endpoint at AWS, set up user authentication, select your S3 bucket, and after assigning IAM access roles, you are ready to start transferring data.

AWS Storage Gateway Family

Storage Gateway allows you to integrate your on-premise network to AWS so that your applications and utilities can utilize S3, S3 Glacier, and EFS storage seamlessly. You can use the storage gateway to back up and archive documents, migration services, and tiered storage.

Protocols supported include NFS, SMB, and iSCSI. The actual gateway device can be a hardware device such as a Dell EMC PowerEdge server with a preloaded storage gateway or a virtual machine image that can be downloaded and installed in your VMware or Hyper-V environment. There are three configuration choices available for deploying a storage gateway.

- **File Gateway**—Interfaces directly into S3 storage, which allows you to store and retrieve files using either the NFS or SMB protocol file shares, as shown in Figure 6-35.

- **Volume Gateway**—Provides S3 cloud storage that can be mounted locally as iSCSI devices for on-premise applications. Data can be stored in S3 buckets with a copy of frequently accessed data cached locally. Alternatively, all data can first be stored locally and then asynchronously backed up to S3.

- **Tape Gateway**—Virtual tape drive that supports a variety of third-party backup applications, such as Veritas or Commvault. It allows you to store and archive data in S3 bucket storage as virtual tapes.

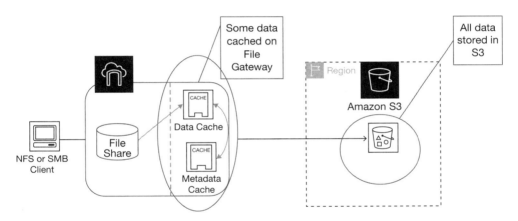

Figure 6-35   Storage Gateway: File Gateway architecture

MAKE SURE TO WATCH THE COMPANION VIDEO "DATA TRANSFER OPTIONS AT AWS."

In Conclusion

Whew. There are a few storage options to consider in the AWS cloud! Storage services are different from compute or networking services at AWS because storage is holding the one component we can't afford to lose: our precious data.

Amazon certainly gives us enough choice when it comes to storage in the cloud, and it seems to realize that you're probably going to operate in a hybrid mode of operation for the time being.

Of course, I could be completely wrong. You may be planning to move absolutely everything to the cloud. However, you probably want some of your documents under absolute control, which means there may be the possibility of storing certain records on-premise. Only after careful testing of each chosen storage solution will you know whether you have a winner.

Look at the big-picture discussion points below, and start planning your migration to AWS storage. Review some of the charts and figures in this chapter to help you make some initial decisions as to which storage solution is best for your needs.

Top 10 Big-Picture Discussion Points: Storage Options and Considerations

Before deciding on a storage platform, you must decide what you are trying to accomplish.

1. What is your storage use case that you are trying to solve?
2. What is your database currently being used for?
3. Can your existing database be migrated to AWS?
4. What compliance rules and regulations do you have to follow?
5. What is the structure of the data that needs to be moved to AWS? Can it live in S3 or S3 Glacier storage?
6. How often will you need to read or write to your storage?
7. Do both Linux and Windows workloads need shared data access? Can EFS or FSx offer a solution?
8. What are your current data processing speeds? Are they adequate? Can AWS match or exceed your current data speeds?
9. What backup/restore/recovery solution do you need?
10. Can replicated database storage solve any of your issues?

Security Services

Any company that has moved some or a portion of its on-premise IT services to the cloud is worried about security breaches happening to its hosted stuff—and more specifically, how and when these security breaches occur, and how to prevent them from happening again. After all, security breaches happen regularly. Regardless of where you live, security issues are a reoccurring news item. Although many of the breaches that were publicized in the past 5 years were related to on-premise point-of-sale systems having security issues, by 2018, many of the data breaches focused on compromised payment systems that affected both debit cards and credit cards of millions of customers, and of course, we are some of those customers.

It's only natural to think that the same security issues and concerns could happen and possibly be more widespread when you are operating in the AWS cloud. The latest security bulletins published by AWS at https://aws.amazon.com/security/security-bulletins/ show that there were various Xen security advisories that Amazon needed to keep on top of on behalf of all AWS customers. There are other security bulletins that potentially can affect your compute operations at AWS if you are using specific versions of Docker, Kubernetes, and several other AWS services. Amazon's job of patching its infrastructure, managed services, and many other integral system components never ends.

Amazon is responsible for maintaining security for the infrastructure being used; that's the job security of the cloud. Our job is maintaining our stuff—what's hosted and stored in the cloud.

Certainly, the job of securing our resources hosted in the AWS cloud never ends, whether it's patching Web and application servers or the operating systems or properly configuring AWS services. For example, in 2014, security vulnerabilities with the Bash shell were discovered. These security issues weren't new; they just weren't discovered until 2014.

Operating in the AWS cloud, customers require absolute security. Fortunately, the toolbox of AWS services in the cloud-hosted operating system includes a decent global security service called identity and access management (IAM). Like the moniker says, the management of access to AWS resources to users that we know or identify with is the job of the IAM service.

At the end of this chapter, hopefully you will feel comfortable with the concept of how to secure your AWS resources; create security policy for users, groups, servers, and AWS managed services; and have a better understanding of the additional security and auditing tools available at AWS for your use in maintaining a decent level of security.

The topics for this chapter include the following:

- IAM
- Authorization and authentication
- IAM users and groups
- The concept of temporary authorization with IAM roles
- Creating security policy
- Policy options
- AWS Organizations
- AWS RAM (Resource Access Manager)
- AWS Secrets
- AWS Inspector
- GuardDuty

Terra Firma is interested in maintaining security for its hosted applications and the administrators who work with its AWS accounts and services. The company also wants to control access for users who will be using a federated logon process—that is, single sign-on (SSO). Terra Firma also must work with third-party consultants who need access to AWS resources. The internal auditing team wants to know what tools are available to help maintain and manage Terra Firma's overall AWS security and existing compliance levels. Upper management also has specific questions and concerns about the following items:

- Creating users and groups for administrative duties at AWS
- Defining an appropriate password policy
- Setting limits on what administrators can do
- Managing the company's multiple AWS accounts centrally
- Using AWS security services to monitor existing AWS resources
- Analyzing EC2 instances for proper security levels
- Protecting credentials for Web and application servers

In a nutshell, deploying and maintaining security at AWS revolves around a framework of security policies and integrated management services. Security policies define what users, groups, servers, and services can and can't do. There are also different types of users at AWS. There are administrator types, and then there are AWS users who may not be aware that they actually have anything to do with AWS. For an example of the latter, a mobile user using mobile applications on her phone very possibly has no idea that the back end to an important application is hosted at AWS. Let's start off with IAM.

Identity and Access Management

IAM was introduced to AWS accounts on September 1, 2010. The simplest definition of IAM is that it can provide controlled access to resources hosted in each AWS account to IAM users, groups of users, and the AWS applications and services, as shown in Figure 7-1. *Can* is used here because you must deploy IAM security policies to select IAM users and groups before IAM has power to control anything.

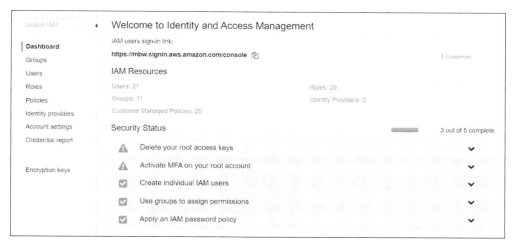

Figure 7-1   The IAM console

> **Note**
>
> IAM checks and confirms that the API calls requested by an authenticated user are allowed to be carried out.

IAM lives its electronic life as a paranoid security service, and we *want* it to be paranoid. IAM's default mind-set is no access to anything. Explicit deny is the initial mind-set of IAM. Maintaining and enforcing security is the number-one duty that Amazon can't mess up and we don't want to mess up either. Even though it's our responsibility to secure our own applications and data and access to AWS services, AWS also is responsible for providing us the toolset to do so. After all, it's Amazon's cloud.

> **Note**
>
> Creating your first IAM user account, you must add all the required permissions; there are no default permissions assigned to a new IAM user account.

IAM allows us to control access to our resources hosted at AWS from users, groups of users, computer instances, and AWS management services. Access to our AWS resources could be from end users using a mobile device, administrators who need to perform administrative tasks, or developers who may need to share AWS resources among themselves, possibly from different AWS accounts. Amazon services that need access to resources in your account to do their job, such as AWS Config and GuardDuty, also rely on IAM policies assigned to a role that defines a level of access for a temporary period of time. Before we dive under the hood of IAM, here are some of its main features:

- **Full integration with AWS's services**—Every AWS service can be controlled to some degree using IAM security. One of your jobs as an AWS account administrator is to review the current and ever-expanding documentation on each AWS service you want to deploy to keep up with the breadth of support IAM provides. The features of IAM continually change and increase in power every couple of months.

- **Bundled in the price**—You are not charged anything for setting up and using IAM; however, you are charged for accessing AWS resources as an IAM user. As previously mentioned, with IAM, you get to control the access to AWS resources. IAM potentially saves you money by controlling what users can and can't do. For example, you can restrict which EC2 instances developers are allowed to spin up; therefore, properly deployed IAM policies provide the required security and save you money.

- **Controlled access to your AWS account resources in all regions**—Each IAM user can be assigned security policies that control the access to AWS resources in any AWS account in any AWS region. Therefore, you can mandate which AWS regions accessed within an AWS account IAM users *can't* access.

- **Granular permission control**—Completely control access to any AWS resource or resources at a granular level. Be as detailed and concise as you have to be. For example, if you want to define that an IAM user can describe a load balancer's attributes and that's it, you can do so.

- **Define the level of access an AWS service has to resources hosted in your AWS account**—AWS Config monitors your AWS account for acceptable levels of compliance based on Config rules that you define. When you sign up for an AWS management service, such as AWS Config, it is granted access only to your AWS account resources through a mandated IAM security policy assigned to the requesting AWS management service, as shown in Figure 7-2.

- **Multifactor authentication (MFA)**—Using a variety of multifactor devices—both hardware and software—you can implement an additional level of authentication security to any IAM user or to the root user of the AWS account. In simple terms, MFA provides an additional security code—from a software or hardware device that is linked to your AWS account—that must be entered and verified before authentication to AWS is successful.

- **Identity Federation/SSO access to AWS services**—Allows externally authenticated users temporary access to AWS services. This might involve externally authenticating from your corporate network or from a third-party identity provider such as Google or Facebook.

```
AWS Config role*

Grant AWS Config read-only access to your AWS resources so that it can record configuration information, and grant it permission to send this information to
Amazon S3 and Amazon SNS.

   ●   Create AWS Config service-linked role
   ○   Choose a role from your account
```

Figure 7-2   AWS management services require IAM security roles to be assigned before operation is approved

IAM is a global AWS service protecting AWS resources that are located around the world in the 20 AWS regions. To control access, the IAM security service operates outside of the AWS regions; if you don't get access through IAM, you are denied access. The IAM service has a single global endpoint located at https://sts.amazonaws.com. All API requests must also use Hypertext Transfer Protocol Secure (HTTPS) due to the security nature of all IAM requests.

> **Note**
>
> Because it's a global service, security changes and additions to the IAM service take time to replicate worldwide.

IAM Policy Defined

Each IAM policy is ultimately a set of rules that, under the right conditions, define the actions of the AWS entity that the IAM policy is attached to and can perform on specific AWS resources. The first sentence is full of terms used by IAM that need additional explanation. Plus, there are additional related terms used that we need to understand to make sense of IAM.

> **Note**
>
> Who is allowed to do what is the job of IAM.

Entities—There are two entities that IAM authenticates: a user account, which is assigned permanent credentials; and a role, which does not have credentials (no password or access keys). Instead, temporary authentication credentials and a session token are assigned only after verification that the identity can assume the role.

Identity—This means the AWS identification of the entity—the IAM user, group, or role. Each identity is where an IAM security policy is attached.

Roles—A role provides temporary access to AWS resources, but only after the role is linked to an IAM user account.

Users—Only local IAM users and externally authenticated users can authenticate to AWS. An example of an externally authenticated user could be a corporate user who first authenticates to the corporate Active Directory network. Then, after AWS verifies the user's credentials, temporary credentials are assigned using an IAM role, allowing the external authenticated user access to AWS resources as required. Other external user examples supported by AWS are Google and Facebook.

Groups—A group of IAM users who share the IAM policies assigned to the group, but only after each member of the group has successfully first authenticated to AWS.

Policy objects—Each AWS service is broken down into many granular policy objects that can be crafted into a security policy.

Statement—Policy statements define who can do what to the listed AWS resource.

Principal—The principal is a user, or role, or a software application hosted on an Elastic Compute Cloud (EC2) instance or managed AWS service that the policy is attached to for performing the listed task or tasks on the defined AWS service. When policies are attached to resources or to AWS users from other AWS accounts, the principals needing access are defined in the policy by using their Amazon resource number (ARN). If the principal is a defined role for an application carrying out a task on an AWS resource, the principal will be the AWS service that the application needs access to. The defined tasks can be broadly defined as creating, reading, writing, modifying, or deleting AWS resources. If the IAM Management console is used to create IAM policy for a user or role, the IAM Management console carries out the task of linking a trust policy to the specified user or role automatically.

Resources—These are always defined as AWS resources.

Condition—The conditions that need to be present for this policy to work. Does a specific principal, IP address, date, or even tag need to be present for this policy to be approved? Conditions are optional.

IAM Authentication

Before you can make a request to carry out a task on an AWS resource, you should be authenticated as an IAM user or as an externally authenticated user with a IAM role. You could also use the root user account of your AWS account to carry out any task; however, using the root user for daily AWS administration is not recommended. We will discuss the root user and its role in a few pages. The other IAM option—authenticating as an external user—means the user has first authenticated to a third-party security system, such as Active Directory or Facebook. Externally authenticated users use IAM roles, which provide a set of access keys and temporary credentials that can be used for a defined period of access time. The default is set for one hour of allowed access before the temporary credentials are discarded.

An IAM user wanting to use the AWS Management console to perform administration can do so after signing in with a recognized IAM username and password and having the required IAM policies assigned to his user or group account. If multifactor authentication has also been enabled on an IAM account that is authenticating, a numerical code has to be entered before authentication is successful.

Authentication requests can also be carried out when running commands or scripts from the AWS command-line interface (CLI) or from software development kit (SDK) calls; however, a pair of access keys also has to be provided for these types of requests to be successful. Other than

AWS Management console logons, a valid access key and secret access key assigned to the IAM user account making the request must be provided and validated before authentication succeeds. Logon to the AWS Management console logon requires only a username and a password; additional access keys are not required.

When an IAM user account is created, the option is available to create additional access keys. The first access key is the *ID key*, which is an uppercase alphabetic string of characters starting with AKIAXXXXXXXXXXXX, as shown in Figure 7-3. The second access key is called the *secret access key*, which is a base64 string, 40 characters in length. Temporary access keys are issued from the AWS service that issues temporary keys and tokens: the security token service (STS). Temporary access keys issued from STS start with an alphanumeric string such as ASIAXXXXXX.

Figure 7-3   IAM user account access keys

> **Note**
>
> IAM is protecting AWS resources at the infrastructure and service level. Therefore, IAM users and groups are administrators at some level because there is some administrative task that the user or groups of users need to carry out at AWS. IAM does not provide credentials to log on to a client service, locally to a Windows or Linux server, or to a database server. IAM users can only utilize AWS services.

Before creating an IAM user, you must understand the different types of access available and what IAM does and doesn't do.

- If you need to log on locally to a Linux or Windows operating system instance, note that IAM does not control operating system logons.

- If you need to log on locally to a database server, note that IAM does not control database logons.

- If you're using SSO, you very well could be using a federated identity using Active Directory or a supported SAML 2.0 product. IAM supports this type of external authentication using IAM roles, which are attached to the externally authenticated user after verification of their identity using STS.

- If you're developing mobile applications that run on AWS, the authentication of end users into the applications is not what a full IAM user account is for. Because mobile applications are running typically on phones, AWS supports authenticating from a mobile application using one of the popular public identity providers such as Facebook, Google, Login with Amazon, or any other provider that supports OpenID Connect. Signing in successfully using one of the well-known external identity providers (IdPS) generates an authentication token that can be presented to AWS's secure token service. Verification of the external authentication token by STS results in temporary security credentials being provided for access to the desired AWS resources. Again, the access is provided by the linking of an IAM role to the externally authenticated user. You can also use AWS Cognito, which helps you manage the multiple identity providers in one place and allows you to add user sign-in and access control to your applications for authenticated mobile.

- If you need to log on as an administrator or developer and work with AWS services, this type of authentication and access control is what a full IAM user account is designed for.

Requesting Access to AWS Resources

Only after AWS has successfully authenticated you are you authorized to make a request to access AWS resources. When the principal (IAM user or role) requests permission to perform an action, the request is sent to either IAM for the IAM user or to IAM and then STS for the issuing of temporary credentials if the IAM user has an assigned role attached to her user account. Several IAM components work together when a request is made for access to AWS resources:

- **The Principal**—Defines what IAM user or IAM user with an assigned role has sent the request.

- **Operation**—The operation is always an API call being executed. The request is for an API operation from the Management console through a script, a CLI manual command, or an application defined using one of the AWS SDKs utilizing RESTful calls across HTTP with JavaScript Object Notation (JSON) as the data exchange format.

- **Action**—This lists the specific action the principal wants to perform. Actions might be for information (List or Get requests) or to make changes (creating, deleting, or modifying).

- **Resource**—Every created AWS resource has a unique ARN for identification purposes, as shown in Figure 7-4.

- **Environmental data**—Lists where the request is originating from, such as from a specific IP address range; additional required security information; and the time of day.

- **Resource data**—Provides additional details about the resource being accessed, such as a specific Simple Storage Service (S3) bucket, a DynamoDB table, or a specific tag on the AWS resource being accessed.

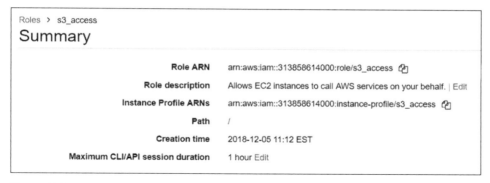

Figure 7-4   Every AWS resource has a resource number (ARN)

> **Note**
> Authorized requests are only allowed to authenticated users.

The Authorization Process

IAM reviews each request against the associated policies of the principal that was requesting authorization and determines whether the request will be allowed or denied, as shown in Figure 7-5. Note that the principal may also be a member of one or more IAM groups, which may increase the number of assigned policies needed to be evaluated before authorization is approved. The mind-set of IAM is this: when in doubt, deny. The evaluation logic of IAM policies follows three strict rules:

- By default, all requests are implicitly denied.

- An explicit allow can override the default deny.

- An explicit deny overrides any allows forever.

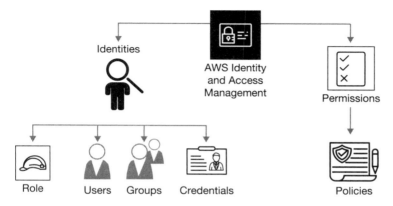

Figure 7-5   The IAM authorization request

When a principal makes a request to AWS, the IAM service checks whether the principal is authenticated, signed in, authorized, and has the necessary permissions assigned.

> **Note**
>
> You have probably lived this type of authorization process as a teenager. "Hey, Dad. Can I go to the movies?" "Nope. All requests are denied." So, you wait until Mom gets home. "Hey, Mom. Can I go to the movies?" "I think so, but let me see whether you cleaned your room. Nope. You can't go to the movie because you didn't clean your room." Mom was sneaky because she threw in a condition; that's what IAM policies can use for additional leverage.

Behind the scenes, the IAM security system takes all the provided information, checks out the policies assigned to the user or group of users, and either approves or denies the request. It takes but a single denied action for the request to be denied. As I've mentioned, IAM functions with a high level of paranoia, starting off by implicitly denying everything by default. Your request will only be authorized if every part of the request is allowed, as shown in Figure 7-6:

- The evaluation logic follows some exact rules that can't be bent for anyone, not even Jeff Bezos.

- All requests are implicitly denied by default for IAM users.

- A default deny can only be overruled and allowed by an explicit permission allow.

- Each permission allow can also be controlled by a defined permission boundary.

- An explicit deny in any policy overrides any allows.

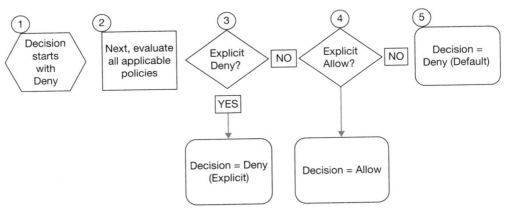

Figure 7-6   Policy evaluation logic

Actions

Assuming your request has been authorized, IAM approves the actions or operations requested to the AWS resources in your AWS account, or optionally, to resources in another AWS account. Actions are the tasks you can perform on an AWS resource, such as creating, editing, and deleting the resource. There can be a number of choices when looking at the available actions for each resource; for example, the user resource has more than 40 different actions that can be allowed or denied, including create user, delete user, get user, or update user, as shown in Figure 7-7. Once specific actions have been approved, only these actions listed in the policy can be performed on the defined resource.

Each AWS resource will have several or many actions that can be carried out; the initial access level choices are typically List, Read (typically Get or List), and Write (typically Create, Put, Delete, Update) or other options. The type of AWS resource determines the action choices available. A handy resource has been created by cloudonaut.io referencing all IAM actions for all AWS services. You can find this online resource at https://iam.cloudonaut.io/.

Figure 7-7   Actions approved by IAM

IAM Users

AWS didn't always have an integrated security system, but as mentioned earlier, it got serious about cloud security starting back in 2010 when it wanted to attract government and corporate clients. Without having a security framework such as IAM in place, AWS never would have been audited successfully against a compliance standard and therefore would not have been accepted by major corporations and government institutions.

It may help to think of our AWS account as a complete hosted cloud operating system with comparable security features similar to the Red Hat Enterprise Linux operating system or Microsoft Active Directory Domain Services. At AWS, our cloud operating system and all its features and tools are available the moment we log in to an AWS account.

Usually when we think of the word *account*, it relates to a user account, or a group account in the context of an operating system. At AWS, the "account" that you initially signed up for was probably designed for a company, but instead it is used by individuals for their company. And larger companies typically have many accounts—perhaps one or more per developer. Within each AWS account, all available AWS resources can be deployed; the end result is that your company will probably have, or does have, multiple AWS accounts, and it's potentially a mess. We will talk about some of the options available for managing multiple AWS accounts for easier management of account and user security later in this chapter, when we discuss AWS Organizations, and Resource Access Manager (AWS RAM). For now, within a single AWS account, IAM user identities come in four flavors:

1. The common first scenario is the user (think administrator-type) who needs access to the AWS Management console.

2. The second flavor is the administrator or developer who needs additional access to the AWS APIs, whether the APIs are fired using the Management console, at the AWS CLI prompt, or through development of applications using AWS SDKs, such as JavaScript or .NET.

3. The third is a corporate user who is first authenticated at work, perhaps through Active Directory. This user requires access to a hosted AWS resource. Through the process of external identity federation, temporary AWS credentials and access are provided to the requested AWS resource.

4. The fourth type of user is the mobile user who has no idea that the mobile application is even accessing AWS back-end resources.

Terra Firma certainly needs to consider the number of administrators and developer user accounts that need to be created, and the number of AWS accounts that need to be managed.

The Root User

Every AWS account has a root user; that's the very first user, and the owner of your AWS account. The root user credentials are the email address and password that you entered when you created your AWS account; perhaps you're still using that account.

If you want to, although it's not recommended, you can continue to log on using the root account in your AWS account; however, the reason this is a bad idea is because the root user from your AWS account is not controlled by IAM. Ever. Think of the root account as your backdoor account that carries out a few specific tasks that primarily deal with the AWS account; however, the root user is not meant for daily administration duties. The root account was used the first time you logged into your AWS account; after all, there weren't any other accounts available. If the root account is the only available user account that you have, your next job should be creating IAM users and groups to safeguard access to your AWS account resources.

Here's a quick way to see if you're using the root account. What are your security credentials to log into your AWS account? If your answer is "an email address" as shown in Figure 7-8, well, congratulations. You are accessing your AWS account as the root user; you cannot be controlled, and you cannot be locked down. Now think about how many people could potentially be using that same account logon; one of those people could potentially delete everything in your AWS account. If that happens, there's no way to stop it because there are no controls on the root account.

Figure 7-8   The root user logon

Why would Amazon start with a user account with unlimited power? It's not like Amazon didn't warn us. There certainly have been a few notifications from AWS alerting you to create additional users to protect your AWS account. However, the first account in any operating system must have the most power, just like an Active Directory domain controller enterprise administrator or the root user for the Linux operating system. Like any other networking operating system, the root credentials need to be protected.

The root account doesn't have many tasks that must be carried out as the AWS account root user; however, there are some, including these:

- Modifying the root user account details, including changing the password
- Closing an AWS account forever
- Changing your AWS support plan from free to Developer, Small business, or Enterprise
- Enabling billing for the account or changing your payment options or billing information
- Creating a CloudFront key pair
- Enabling MFA on an S3 bucket in your AWS account
- Requesting permission to perform a penetration test
- Restore IAM user permissions that have been revoked

Terra Firma needs to do some detailed inventory about how many AWS accounts it currently has and how many root accounts are being used.

> **Note**
>
> After you sign in for the first time using the root user for your account, best practice is to create an IAM user for yourself, add the required administrative privileges to your new IAM user, and stop using the root account unless it is necessary to do so.

The IAM User

An IAM user is either a person or an AWS service that uses specific IAM user account authentication components (username/password combination, or a validated access key and secret key pair) before being able to interact with AWS resources. Every IAM user can access AWS resources using the Management console with a username/password, or optionally has been provided programmatic access using an associated access key ID and secret access key, or both types of access: Management console access *and* programmatic access. When you are running a script or command from an AWS CLI prompt, the script or command does not execute unless an IAM user's account access ID and secret access key are provided. The access keys need to be validated before the execution of any CLI command or script.

> **Note**
>
> Remember, an IAM user is not a typical user account; instead, an IAM user is a user within an AWS account.

There are two quick ways to identify an IAM user:

- The most common way is using the name of the user account that is listed in the IAM Management console when the user account was created. The common username will also show up in each IAM group listings of associated IAM users.

- Every entity that is created at AWS also has a unique resource name: the ARN. The ARN can uniquely identify an IAM user across all AWS user accounts; for example, creating an IAM policy and needing to specify a user as a principal would follow the format of *arn:aws:iam::account ID:user/mark*.

Creating an IAM User

Creating a user, regardless of the procedure used, is carried out by calling the AWS API. The easiest way to start creating IAM users is to use the IAM service in the AWS Management console and click Add User, as shown in Figure 7-9.

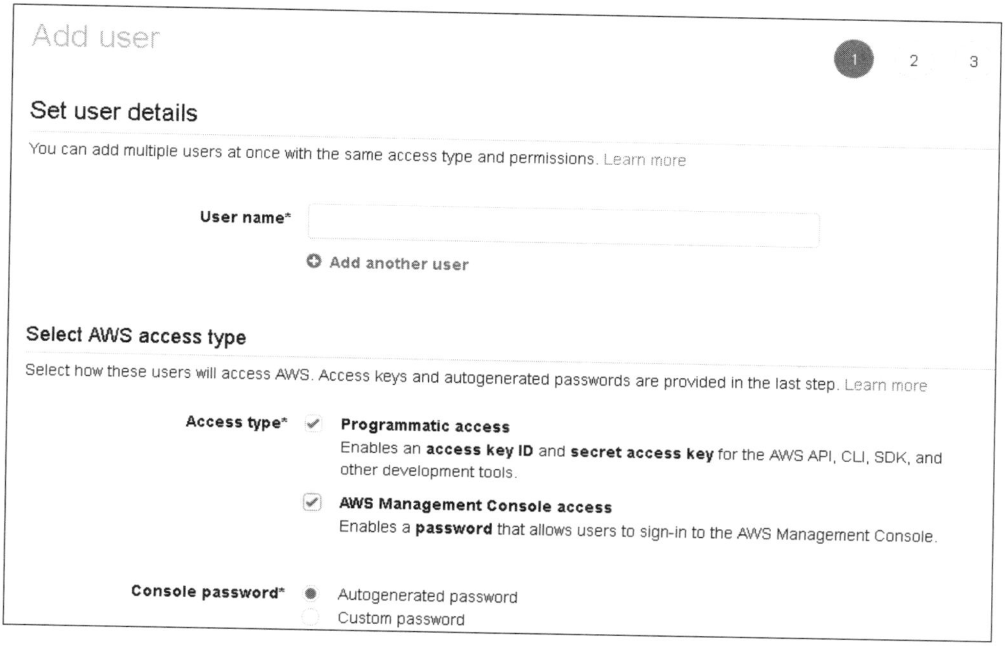

Figure 7-9   Creating an IAM user

The first decision you must make is the type of access you want to allow your new IAM user to have: Management console, programmatic access, or both types of access.

- **Management console**—Access to the console requires a username and password. If console access is all that is required, access keys (an access key ID and secret access key) are not required.

- **Programmatic access**—This involves working from a command prompt using the AWS CLI, by using the Tools for Windows PowerShell, or through an application/API call.

> **Note**
>
> If you're taking over an existing AWS environment, you may find that IAM users have access keys assigned to their accounts, but they don't actually need the assigned access keys, as they're not carrying out programmatic tasks. If this is the case, the access keys should be deleted. In the future, if you decide the users need access keys, you can add new ones. The root account access keys should also be removed for safekeeping; this certainly is a best practice to follow.

IAM User Access Keys

You can use access keys as credentials when they're linked to an IAM user or to the AWS account root user. As we have discussed, access keys are required when using the AWS CLI, as shown in Figure 7-10, running scripts, running PowerShell scripts, or calling the AWS API directly or through an application. Each user account can have two access keys: the access key ID that can be viewed through the console, and a secret access key that is not viewable after creation. Think of the integration of the two access keys like the combination of a username/password for logging into the Management console; the access keys must also be used when requesting authentication.

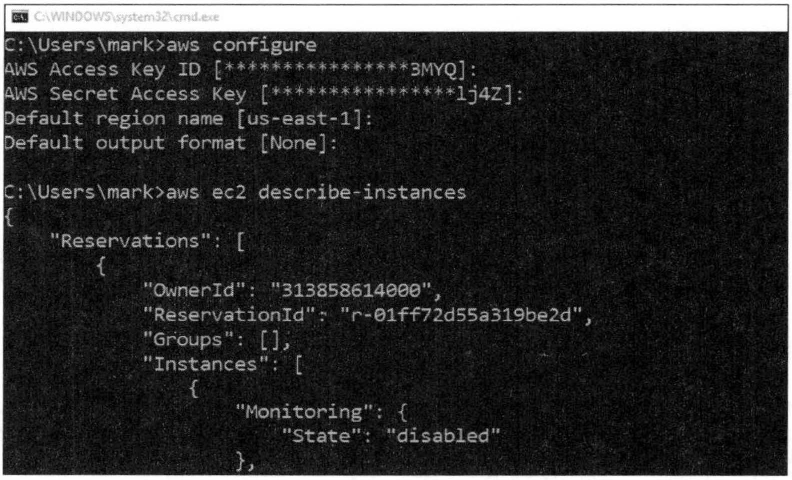

Figure 7-10   Access keys to be used at the AWS CLI prompt

Once an IAM user account has been created successfully, you are prompted to save the access keys (access key ID and secret access key). The option to save a copy of the secret access key is a one-shot deal; if you don't download a copy of the secret access key at the completion of the user account creation process, you cannot view the secret access key again. Of course, you can always request a new set of access keys for an already created IAM user (access ID and secret access key) again.

Creating a new IAM user without adding additional permissions or groups creates an extremely limited IAM user. There are no security policies assigned by default; a new IAM user can't even change her own password. You can add a number of pre-created IAM policies, group accounts, and security options to a new IAM account, as shown in Figure 7-11:

- Existing IAM policies—Policy options created by AWS or by you
- Copying permissions from existing IAM users to the user being created
- Adding the user to an IAM group or multiple groups with attached IAM policies
- Adding a permissions boundary—A permission boundary defines the maximum amount of permission that can be assigned to an IAM user.

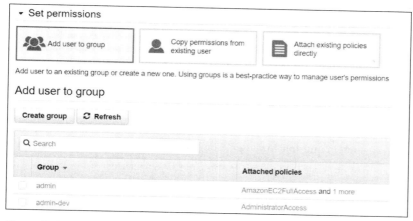

Figure 7-11   IAM user account creation options

During creation of an IAM user account using the Management console, Amazon gives you plenty of options to add permissions to the user account you're creating. If you don't follow Amazon's suggestions, as mentioned, you are creating a user with no permissions. The best practice is to add your new user to an existing IAM group, which has the defined necessary permissions that match the IAM user accounts tasks. Even if you are creating an IAM user for a specific AWS task that only this user will carry out, you may want to think about adding this person to an IAM group if there's the possibility of multiple IAM users carrying out the same task. Or you may want to create a single IAM user for a single specified AWS task. That's perfectly okay; just make sure that this use case is well documented; obviously, it's easier to manage by groups.

MAKE SURE TO WATCH THE COMPANION VIDEO "CREATING IAM USERS AND GROUPS."

To access the companion videos, register your book at informit.com/register.

Note

What an IAM user can and can't do at AWS is defined by either an explicit allow permission to carry out a task against an AWS resource or by an explicit deny permission, which denies the user from being able to carry out the requested task. Note that an explicit deny in any policy assigned to an IAM user account overrides any other allows.

IAM Groups

An IAM group is a collection of IAM users. IAM users in an IAM group have their own authentication credentials and possible membership in additional IAM groups. Each IAM group that IAM users are members of is assigned the permissions assigned to the IAM groups they belong to only after they have successfully authenticated to AWS. IAM groups are to be used to delegate security policies for a specific group of IAM users. As mentioned previously, IAM groups make assigning permissions for IAM users much easier than having to modify multiple individual IAM user accounts. The characteristics of IAM groups follow:

- Each IAM group can contain multiple IAM users from the same AWS account.

- IAM users can belong to multiple IAM groups in the same AWS account.

- IAM groups can't be nested; IAM groups can only contain IAM users, but not additional IAM groups.

- There are no default IAM groups that include All Users like Microsoft Windows.

- There are initial soft limits as to the number of IAM groups you can have in your AWS account, and a limit to how many IAM groups an IAM user can be in. You can be a member of 10 IAM groups, and the maximum number of IAM users in an IAM group is 5,000.

Terra Firma needs to consider what group strategy to use for developers, administrators, and auditors. It next needs to create the IAM groups and associate the desired IAM policies before creating IAM users.

Signing In as an IAM User

After IAM users have been created, to make it easier for your IAM users to sign into the Management console, you can create a custom URL that contains your AWS account ID, as shown in Figure 7-12.

Figure 7-12   A custom URL for IAM users can be created

IAM Account Details

Each IAM user account displayed in the IAM console shows some useful information about each IAM account listing the IAM groups that the IAM user belongs to, the age of the access keys assigned to the IAM user account, the age of the current password, the last activity of the IAM account, and whether MFA has been enabled. Clicking the gear icon in the IAM user account console provides several additional account options that can be displayed, including listing the ARN of the account, the access key ID, the access key last used, and any assigned certificates, as shown in Figure 7-13.

Figure 7-13   IAM user account options

IAM User Account Summary

The summary of each IAM user account provides a wealth of useful information, as shown in Figure 7-14, including the following options:

- **Permissions attached directly**—A listing of applied policies and the policy type
- **IAM groups attached**—Attached policies due to group membership
- **Tags**—Key/value pairs (up to 50) that can be added for additional information
- **Security credentials**
  - Manage console password: enable or disable console access and manage password
  - Assigned MFA device: manage MFA virtual or hardware device

- Signing certificates
- Access keys
- **Access Advisor**—The service permissions that have been granted to the IAM user and when the AWS services were last accessed within the calendar year

Figure 7-14   User account summary information

MAKE SURE TO WATCH THE COMPANION VIDEO "CREATING IAM USERS AND GROUPS."

Creating a Password Policy

Password policies can be defined per AWS account for all IAM user accounts by selecting Account settings in the IAM console. The password options are the familiar options such as password complexity, password expiration and reuse, and whether IAM users can change their own password, as shown in Figure 7-15.

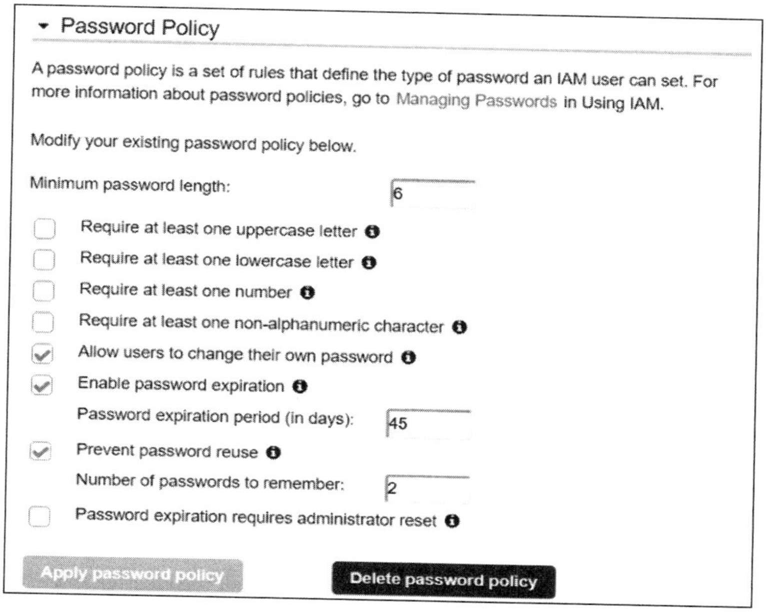

Figure 7-15 Password policy options

Terra Firma needs to review what its corporate policy currently is for passwords and consider whether more stringent rules need to be followed for working in the AWS cloud. If rules need to be tightened around password policy, perhaps the rules for the current on-premise password policy and the password policy defined in the AWS cloud need to be analyzed and possibly unified.

MAKE SURE TO WATCH THE COMPANION VIDEO "DEFINING A PASSWORD POLICY."

Rotating Access Keys

Once an IAM user account has been created with assigned access keys, the access keys are not changed unless they are manually rotated or you use an automated process such as a script or a custom Lambda function. The best practice is to rotate a user's access keys, preferably at the same time the IAM user password is changed to maintain a higher level of security and avoid issues that can arise from stolen access keys. Access keys can be viewed in the properties of the IAM user account on the Security credentials tab. Each IAM user account can have two active access keys. When a request is received to create a new access key, an associated secret access key is created along with the new access key ID, as shown in Figure 7-16.

Figure 7-16   Changing an IAM user's access key manually

Obviously, the IAM administrator who is given the ability to create and rotate access keys must be a trusted individual. Permissions to rotate access keys can be accomplished by assigning the policy shown in Figure 7-17 to the trusted IAM administrator account that will be carrying out the task of key rotation. Note that the actions of Get, Create, List, Update, and Delete are required to rotate access keys successfully.

```
{
  "Version": "2012-10-17",
  "Statement": [
  {
  "Sid": "ManageAccessKeysForUser",
  "Effect": "Allow",
  "Action": [
  "iam:DeleteAccessKey",
  "iam:GetAccessKeyLastUsed",
  "iam:UpdateAccessKey",
  "iam:GetUser",
  "iam:CreateAccessKey",
  "iam:ListAccessKeys"
  ],
  "Resource": "arn:aws:iam::*:user/${aws:username}"
  },
  {
  "Sid": "ListUsersInConsole",
  "Effect": "Allow",
  "Action": "iam:ListUsers",
  "Resource": "*"
  }
  ]
}
```

Figure 7-17   Policy settings for rotating access keys

> **Note**
>
> Rotating access keys without a great deal of thought can be disastrous. After all, if scripts and applications depend on a specific set of access keys, the applications and scripts have to be changed and updated as well. Don't forget this part of the equation.

Using Multifactor Authentication (MFA)

Every AWS user account—both the root account and the IAM user account—supports the addition of MFA, which forces each user during the authentication process to AWS to provide an additional security code, in addition to the user's username and password credentials to access AWS resources. There are several options available at AWS for deploying MFA:

- **Virtual MFA device**—A software app such as Google Authenticator or Gemalto MP-1 software tokens that typically is installed on the user's phone can generate a 6-digit code that can be entered during authentication.

- **U2F security key**—A USB device that generates a security code when tapped. These devices are part of the fast identity online (FIDO) alliance and are supported by many industry leaders, including Microsoft, Google, AWS, VMware, Intel, and others.

- **Hardware MFA device**—A hardware device such as a Gemalto SafeNet security appliance that generates the MFA security code. Gemalto devices can provide end-to-end management of the entire encryption process.

> MAKE SURE TO WATCH THE COMPANION VIDEO "ENABLING MFA PROTECTION."

IAM Policy Types

The IAM policies that we create or assign to control access to AWS resources and products have certain features and powers that depend on the associated AWS service and the IAM actions available. The choices for controlling AWS services with IAM policies are forever increasing in choices; features for most AWS services are added frequently. Make sure to check the exact documentation of each AWS service for the up-to-date choices. Let's look at the policy types that can be attached to IAM identities (users, groups, or roles).

Identity-Based Policies

Identity-based policies are categorized as permission policies; each policy contains permissions controlled by actions that can be attached to IAM users, groups, or as a role defining what actions the user, group, or role can carry out. The listed permissions are either allowing or denying access and, optionally, which additional conditions must be met before access is allowed to the listed AWS service or services defined in each policy.

There are three identity-based policy types:

- A managed policy created by AWS
- A job function policy created by AWS
- A custom policy that you create

Managed policies—These are read-only stand-alone identity-based policies that you can select and attach to a single IAM user or multiple users, IAM groups, or roles created within an AWS account, as shown in Figure 7-18. AWS creates and manages managed policies internally. These policies look similar in scope to the available security options you would find when you're setting up users and groups for Microsoft Active Directory Domain Services. Here are some definitions to understand when working with managed policies:

- Managed policies can be attached and detached from any identity (user, group, role).
- Managed policies can be customized after being imported and saved as a custom policy.
- Managed policies cannot be deleted. When we detach a managed policy, we remove it from the selected identity, user, group, or role; however, a managed policy is still available in the library of managed AWS policies for reuse.
- Custom policies can be attached, detached, and deleted.
- Each managed policy can be applied to multiple users, groups, and roles.

Policy name ▾	Type	Attachments ▾	Used as
▸ 📦 ViewOnlyAccess	Job function	0	*None*
▸ 📦 TranslateReadOnly	AWS managed	0	*None*
▸ 📦 TranslateFullAccess	AWS managed	0	*None*
▸ 📦 TagPoliciesService...	AWS managed	0	*None*
▸ 📦 TagGovernancePolicy	AWS managed	0	*None*
▸ 📦 SystemAdministrator	Job function	0	*None*
▸ 📦 SupportUser	Job function	0	*None*
▸ StatesExecutionPoli...	Customer managed	1	Permissions policy

Figure 7-18   Managed policy choices

Job function policies—These are specialized managed policies based on a generic job description, as shown in Figure 7-19, that are also created and maintained by AWS. Job function policy choices include Administrator, Billing, Database Administrator, Security Auditor, System Administrator, and more. Job function policies might seem like an excellent idea. However, you need to be careful when assigning job function policies because you may be inadvertently assigning more permissions than you expected or need. For example, the System Administrator policy allows the creation and maintenance of resources across a wide swath of AWS services, including CloudTrail, CloudWatch, CodeCommit, CodeDeploy, Config, Directory Service, EC2, IAM, Lambda, relational database service (RDS), Route 53, Trusted Advisor, virtual private cloud (VPC), and more. Job function policies can be useful as a starting policy template that's imported as a custom policy and then making modifications to suit your needs.

Policy name ▼	Type
ViewOnlyAccess	Job function
SystemAdministrator	Job function
SupportUser	Job function
SecurityAudit	Job function
PowerUserAccess	Job function
NetworkAdministrator	Job function
DataScientist	Job function
DatabaseAdministra...	Job function
Billing	Job function
AdministratorAccess	Job function

Figure 7-19   Job functions

Custom policies—Each managed policy can be selected as a starting point, modified for your use, and then saved as a custom policy in your AWS account. You can also elect to start with a blank page when creating a custom policy document and create the entire policy from scratch. Each custom policy created by you is defined as a customer-managed policy; you've either authored the policy from scratch or started by importing a managed service policy and then making and saving changes to the original security policy document under a new policy name. Once you've created a custom policy, it's your responsibility to manage and maintain each policy document.

Resource-Based Policies

As we know, identity-based policies are attached to an IAM user, group, or role, defining what each identity is allowed or not allowed to do. Resource-based policies are a little different in functionality because they are attached directly to the AWS resource. Resource policies are supported by several AWS resources; the most common examples are S3 buckets, but there are other AWS services that support resource-based policies, including S3 Glacier vaults, simple notification service (SNS), AWS Simple Queue Service (SQS), AWS ElastiSearch records, and AWS Lambda functions. Because resource policies are attached directly to the AWS resource, each policy needs to define the access rules for the AWS resource regardless of the user or group that accesses the resource. Resource-based policies are also sometimes called in-line policies due to the direct attaching of the policy to the resource; if the resource is deleted, the security policy is unattached and discarded. Resource-based policies are always a custom action; there are no examples of managed resource-based policies that AWS creates. Within a single AWS account, an IAM user can be assigned a managed IAM policy and a resource-based policy for the same AWS resource, as shown in Figure 7-20. Mark has an identity-based policy that allows him to list and read an S3 bucket A. The resource—in this case, the S3 bucket—has an attached resource-based policy that identifies that Mark can list and write on S3 bucket A. On S3 bucket C, a resource policy is attached that has denied access to Mark. Note that Julian also has a combination of identity- and resource-based policies, but Jan has no managed policies assigned. She does, however, have access to S3 bucket C because she is specifically listed in the resource policy using her IAM user ARN.

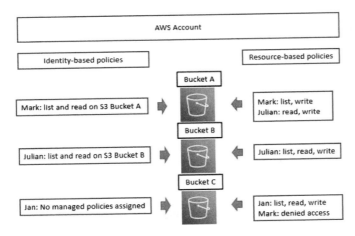

Figure 7-20   Identity and resource-based policies working together

In-Line Policies

Another method of attaching policies is through the process of what is called in-line or embedded. Policies attached in-line help you maintain a strict one-to-one relationship between the attached policy and the entity the policy is attached to. When the entity is deleted, so are the attached policies. In comparison, using a managed policy allows you to reapply the policy to multiple entities, and all updates to a managed policy apply automatically to all entities that have the managed policy assigned. Each in-line policy must be managed individually; therefore, an in-line policy should be a custom policy that has been designed for your custom needs. For example, let's say a specific user with high security clearance within your company has been assigned the task of managing AWS CloudHSM, a security service that uses single-tenant hardware security modules (HSMs) for storing your company's symmetric and asymmetric keys. You've decided to manage the security for this service by using in-line policies to ensure that only this person can carry out the specific task. Perhaps you have two security administrators to be safe, and you use in-line policies to ensure that the policies are only assigned to these two individuals. Once their IAM user accounts are deleted, the in-line policies, because they have been embedded with the user accounts, are removed as well.

IAM Policy Creation

The format of an IAM policy is crafted in JSON format and linked to your AWS account. We can create and view the existing IAM policies using the IAM Management console or by using the AWS CLI. Assuming you are just starting with AWS, it's probably best to start with the IAM Management console view where the users, groups, policies, and rules can be viewed easily.

Each policy can define just one permission or multiple permissions. Multiple policies can also be attached to a user, group, or role. When creating custom policies, keep them as simple as possible to start; don't mix resource types in a single policy just because you can. Separate policies by resource type for easier deployment and troubleshooting. Policies can be created in several methods:

- Policies can be created and added to by importing policy settings in JSON format into your account using standard copy and paste techniques.

- Policies can be created using the visual editor found in the IAM console and shown in Figure 7-21.

- Policies can be created using the JSON editor found in the IAM console and shown in Figure 7-21.

- Policies can be created by using a third-party IAM tool that has been installed and properly configured, like the process that initially sets up the AWI CLI software. After authenticating to AWS using a recognized IAM user with valid access keys, you can create your users, groups, and roles with any third-party tool, such as OneLogon or Ping Identity, instead of using the IAM Management console.

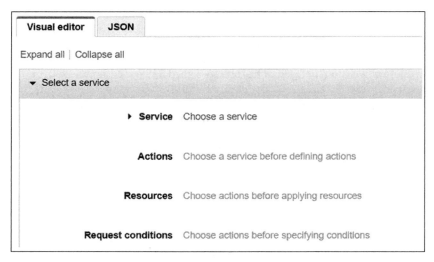

Figure 7-21   The Visual Editor and JSON tabs

Policy Elements

Each policy contains mandatory and optional elements that need to be understood.

Version—This element is the version of the policy language, as shown in Figure 7-22, that the policy is using. The date/time version number is added automatically when you are manually creating a policy document in the Management console. It is best practice to add the latest version to your custom policies if they are created outside the IAM Management console to ensure that any new IAM features you are using in your policy are supported by the version number. If no version number is listed, the oldest version number is used, which can cause problems. For example, if you were using tags for determining access or permission boundaries in a custom policy with no listed version number, these newer features would not work without the latest version number present.

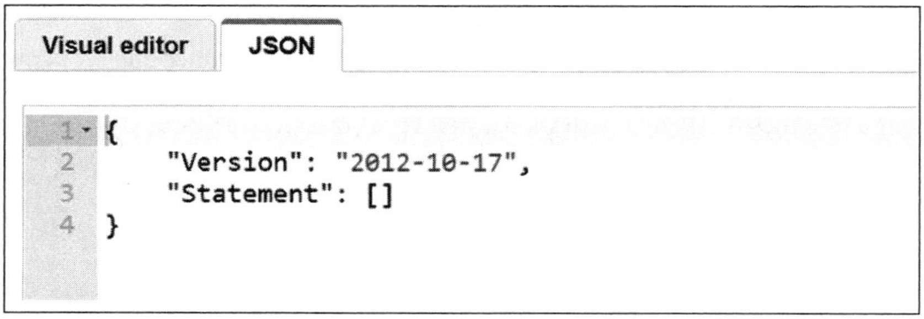

```
Visual editor    JSON

1 ▾ {
2       "Version": "2012-10-17",
3       "Statement": []
4 }
```

Figure 7-22   Version information

Statement—(Mandatory) Each policy has at least a single statement; multiple statements in a policy are allowed. It might be cleaner or simpler to limit each statement to a single policy when beginning to craft custom policies.

Sid—(Optional) This element is a unique ID statement for additional identification purposes.

Effect—(Mandatory) The effect of any listed action is Allow or Deny.

Action—(Mandatory) Each action lists the type of access that is allowed or denied.

Principal—(Optional) The account, user, role, or federated user the policy allows or denies access to a resource.

Resource—(Mandatory) The AWS resource that the actions in the statement apply to.

Condition—(Optional) This element defines the absolute circumstances that must be met before the policy is applied.

MAKE SURE TO WATCH THE COMPANION VIDEO "CREATING IAM POLICIES."

Reading a Simple JSON Policy

There are syntax and grammar rules to follow when creating IAM policies. One missing brace (that's a curly bracket {), or missed comma or colon can cause lots of pain when creating or troubleshooting IAM policy. First, the rules:

1. Text values—that is, string values—are always encased in double quotes.

2. String values are followed with a colon.

3. The data parts in a policy are defined as name-value pairs.

4. The name and the value are separated with a colon. Example: "Effect": "Allow"

5. When data in a policy has multiple name-value pairs, each name-value pair is separated using commas.

6. Curly brackets, also called *braces*, contain objects.

7. Each object can hold multiple name-value pairs.

8. If square brackets are used, there are multiple name-value pairs, separated by commas.

```
1. {
2.   "Version": "2012-10-17",
3.   "Statement": {
4.     "Effect": "Allow",
5.     "Action": "s3:ListBucket",
6.     "Resource": "arn:aws:s3:::graphic_bucket"
7.   }
8. }
```

9. Each policy starts with a curly left bracket that defines the start of the policy statement block. Once the policy statement block finishes, a curly right bracket denotes the finish.

10. The current version of IAM policies is next; both "Version" and the version number are in quotation marks because the values within the quotes are string values. Treat the version line in an IAM policy as a mandatory policy element. The version number is a name-value pair; therefore, the name and the value are separated by a colon. Because there are multiple name-value pairs in this policy, there is a comma at the end of lines that have name-values: lines 2, 4, and 5.

11. The first statement in the policy is defined as a "Statement" in quotes followed by a colon (:) and another inner left curly bracket ({) that denotes the start of the statement block—namely, Effect—Action—Resource.

12. The "Effect" in quotation marks followed by a colon (:) is "Allow," also in quotation marks: a name-value pair with a comma at the end. The effect is either Allow or Deny.

13. The "Action" in this policy is to allow the listing of an S3 bucket: a name-value pair with a comma at the end.

14. The "Resource" being controlled by this policy is the S3 bucket: graphic_bucket. The resource references the ARN—the unique Amazon name that is assigned to each resource at creation. Resource lines in policies don't have commas because a resource is a name-resource listing, not a name-value pair.

15. The right curly bracket indicates that the statement block is complete.

16. The final right curly bracket indicates that the policy statement block is complete.

Policy Actions

When creating custom policies, you may have to provide more actions than you first thought for the user to be able to carry out the task. Take, for example, creating a policy for a user whom you want to be able to create, change, or remove her own IAM user account password. The actions that need to be listed in the policy have to include the following:

- **CreateLoginProfile**—The user needs the ability to create a login profile.

- **DeleteLoginProfile**—The user must be able to delete her login profile if she wants to make changes.

- **GetLoginProfile**—The user has to be able to access the login profile.

- **UpdateLoginProfile**—After making changes, the user has to be able to update her login information.

If you want an IAM user to be able to perform administration tasks for a group of IAM users, the actions required would include creation, deletion, listing users and groups, removing policies, and renaming or changing information. To be able to make changes to an AWS resource, you must be able to modify and delete. The policy listed in Figure 7-23 provides the details for this policy.

```
{
"Version": "2012-10-17",
"Statement": [
{
"Sid": "AllowUsersToPerformUserActions",
"Effect": "Allow",
"Action": [
"iam:ListPolicies",
"iam:GetPolicy",
"iam:UpdateUser",
"iam:AttachUserPolicy",
"iam:ListEntitiesForPolicy",
"iam:DeleteUserPolicy",
"iam:DeleteUser",
"iam:ListUserPolicies",
"iam:CreateUser",
"iam:RemoveUserFromGroup",
"iam:AddUserToGroup",
"iam:GetUserPolicy",
"iam:ListGroupsForUser",
"iam:PutUserPolicy",
"iam:ListAttachedUserPolicies",
"iam:ListUsers",
"iam:GetUser",
"iam:DetachUserPolicy"
],
"Resource": "*"
},
{
"Sid": "AllowUsersToSeeStatsOnIAMConsoleDashboard",
"Effect": "Allow",
"Action": [
"iam:GetAccount*",
"iam:ListAccount*"
],
"Resource": "*"
}
]
}
```

Figure 7-23   IAM policy for performing administrative tasks

Additional Policy Control Options

You can add a variety of additional control options to a security policy. These optional policy options give you great power in how you manage security options for users and groups. Terra Firma wants to use permission boundaries to control the maximum tasks that junior administrators can carry out at AWS—in particular, AWS accounts.

Permission boundaries—You can apply a permission boundary policy for both the IAM user and the role. A managed policy can define the maximum permissions that an identity-based policy can grant to a particular IAM user or role. Adding an additional permission boundary provides another level of control. The user or role can only carry out the actions that are allowed by *both* the assigned identity-based policy and the permission boundary policy. Therefore, the permission settings defined in a management policy can be controlled by a permission boundary policy that establishes the maximum permissions the management policy is allowed to use.

The first step is to create a policy that defines the permission boundary for the user or role. Let's suppose you want your administrator Mark to be able to fully manage S3 buckets and EC2 instances, and that's all. The next step is to create the policy shown in Figure 7-24 that defines the permissions boundary for Mark—namely, that he can fully administrate S3 buckets and EC2 instances.

```
{
"Version": "2012-10-17",
"Statement": [
{
"Effect": "Allow",
"Action": [
"s3:*",
"ec2:*"
],
"Resource": "*"
}
]
}
```

Figure 7-24   Mark's permission boundary

Once this permission boundary has been added to Mark's IAM account, as shown in Figure 7-25, the only two AWS services that Mark will have full administrative control over are the two listed AWS services S3 and EC2 instances. In the future, if a policy is added to Mark's account that allows him to work with AWS CloudTrail and create alerts and alarms, when Mark goes to carry out any of these actions using CloudTrail, he would be denied because the permission boundary does not define that Mark can use CloudTrail. Remember: the permission boundary policy settings must match up with the additional policy settings that are applied to Mark's IAM user account.

The permission boundary shown in Figure 7-24 could be much more stringent; instead of listing full control, the permission boundary could spell out a specific listing of tasks that Mark could carry out for both S3 and EC2 instances.

Figure 7-25   Adding a permission boundary to a user account

Organizations SCPs—AWS has a management service, called AWS Organizations and discussed at the end of this chapter, that allows you to manage security settings across multiple AWS accounts. One of the features of AWS Organizations is an option called service control policy (SCP) that acts like a permission boundary at the organizational level for AWS accounts included in an AWS Organization that define the maximum permissions allowed. The types of permission policies that can be mandated by an SCP are a little more flexible because they support both identity-based policies and resource-based policies for IAM users and roles and the root user in any AWS accounts that the SCP is applied against. The organizational service control policies act just like permission boundaries. They don't grant permissions; instead, they limit the permissions that can be granted to IAM users, the root user, and roles. Both the SCP and the controlled policy must have matching permissions in the SCP and the identity-based or resource-based policy for the desired permissions to be allowed, as shown in Figure 7-26. With AWS Organizations, AWS provides centralized services and procedures to help you avoid making security mistakes. One last time: permissions are allowed only if the IAM user or role policy and the SCP policy list the identical permissions in both policies.

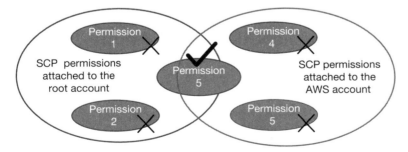

Figure 7-26   Effective permissions using a service control policy

Access control lists (ACLs)—ACLs are present for defining simple permission controls on S3 buckets for cross-account permission access only. They cannot be used to grant permissions to entities in the same AWS account. ACLs are only present because of backward compatibility; it's a much better idea to use roles to control cross-account access.

Session policies—Session policies are another version of a permission boundary to help limit what permissions can be assigned to federated users using roles, or IAM users and groups with assigned roles, as shown in Figure 7-27. Developers can create session policies when they are creating a temporary session using a role with a custom application. When session policies are deployed, the effective permissions for the session are either the ones that are granted by the resource-based policy settings or the identity-based policy settings that match the session policy permission settings.

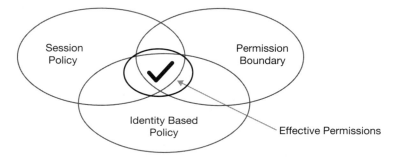

Figure 7-27   Session policies

MAKE SURE TO WATCH THE COMPANION VIDEO "CREATING PERMISSION BOUNDARIES."

Reviewing the Policy Permissions Applied

Trying to figure out the assigned access levels, the available resources, and any additional conditions that have been allowed or denied within each policy can be tough to troubleshoot. Thankfully, AWS provides these details in *policy summary tables*, as shown in Figure 7-28, making it easier to troubleshoot or analyze what an IAM user, group, or role combined with a select IAM policy can do. Policy summaries can be found on both IAM users and roles for all attached policies. You can view policy summaries by first selecting the individual policy, and from its summary page clicking Policy Summary. Information is displayed for the different types of policies: both custom and AWS-managed policies and the newer AWS-managed job function policies.

The information is contained in three tables:

- **Policy summary (Services)**—Information is grouped into explicit deny, allow, and uncategorized services when IAM can't figure out the service name due to a typo or its being a custom third-party service. Recognized services are listed based on whether the policy allows or explicitly denies the use of the service.

- **Service summary (Actions)**—Information displayed includes a list of the actions and permissions (list, read, write) that have been defined in the policy for a particular service.

- **Action summary (Resources)**—Information includes a list of resources and the conditions that control each action. Details include the resources, the region where the resources have been defined, and what IAM accounts the actions are associated with.

Figure 7-28   Policy summary tables

IAM Policy Versions

After you've created an IAM policy, you may want to make additions, deletions, or both. Regardless of whether the policy is a customer-managed policy that you have created or an AWS managed policy that Amazon has made changes to, any changes to the newer policy don't overwrite the older version of the policy as a new version of the policy is created.

Amazon stores up to five versions of a managed policy. To define the default version of a customer-managed policy to be used, after selecting the policy, select the Policy Versions tab, and from the displayed versions, select the version of the policy that you want to define as the default version to be used. From this point forward, the selected version of the policy becomes the default version, as shown in Figure 7-29. If you want to roll back changes later, you can change the current version of the policy to another older version of the policy.

| Policy ARN | arn:aws:iam::aws:policy/service-role/AmazonEC2RoleforSSM |
| Description | Default policy for Amazon EC2 Role for Simple Systems Manager service role. |

Permissions   Policy usage   **Policy versions**   Access Advisor

Each time you update a policy, you create a new version. You can have up to 5 versions. Learn more

Version	Creation time
▶ Version 7 (Default)	2018-10-24 15:37 EST
▶ Version 6	2018-08-15 10:24 EST
▶ Version 5	2017-09-22 17:04 EST
▶ Version 4	2017-08-10 16:49 EST

Figure 7-29   Viewing versions of IAM policies

Using Conditional Elements

The conditional elements of a JSON policy allow you to provide optional parameters that must be met before the policy is approved. Conditional elements are typically global, as shown in the examples in Table 7-1. Terra Firma is looking to use the aws:SourceIP to control the range of IP addresses from which their administrators can log on to AWS.

Table 7-1   **Conditional Elements**

Conditional Elements: Global	Details
aws:CurrentTime	Check for date/time conditions
aws:SecureTransport	The request must use the secure sockets layer (SSL)
aws:UserAgent	Use to allow certain client applications to make requests
aws:MultiFactorAuthPresent	Use the BoolIfExists operator to deny requests that do not include MFA
Bool	Value must be true
StringEquals	The request must contain a specific value
Conditional Elements: Service Specific	**Details**
aws:PrincipalOrgID	Must be a member of a specific AWS Organization
aws:PrincipalTag/tag-key	Check for specific tags
aws:RequestTag/tag-key	Check for a tag and a specific value
aws:PrincipalType	Check for a specific user or role
aws:SourceVpce	Restrict access to a specific endpoint
aws:RequestedRegion	Control the regions that API calls can be made to
aws:SourceIp	IPv4 or IPv6 address, or range of addresses
aws:userid	Check the user's ID

Using Tags with IAM Identities

Most AWS resources allow you to define a number of tags for the resource you are creating or using. You can add custom attributes using tags to both the IAM user and the role. For example, you can define the key **location** and the tag value **Toronto**. Note that you can tag IAM users or roles, but not IAM groups or IAM policies.

Once you have tagged your IAM users and roles, you can use the tags to control these IAM users and roles and their access to AWS resources. Tags are added as a conditional element of each policy mandating what tags need to be attached before the permission request is allowed. The following logic can be controlled by conditional tags:

- **Resources**—Tags can be used for IAM users and roles to determine whether access is allowed or denied to the requested resource based on the attached tags.

- **Requests**—Text can be used to control the tags that can be added, changed, or removed from an IAM user or role.

- **Principles**—Tags with boolean logic can be used to control what the IAM user is allowed to do.

In the example shown in Figure 7-30, administrators can only delete users who have the tempuser=canterminate tag and a Principal tag attached to useradmin = true.

```
{
  "Version": "2012-10-17",
  "Statement": [{
  "Effect": "Allow",
  "Action": "iam:DeleteUser",
  "Resource": "*",
  "Condition": {"StringLike": {"iam:ResourceTag/tempuser": "canterminate"}}
  }]
}


{
  "Version": "2012-10-17",
  "Statement": [
  {
  "Effect": "Allow",
  "Action": "iam:*",
  "Resource": "*",
  "Condition": {"StringEquals": {"aws:PrincipalTag/useradmin": "true"}}
  }
  ]
}
```

Figure 7-30   Using tags to control deletions

IAM Roles

Roles are used to provide temporary access to AWS resources. An IAM role is a security policy defining a set of permissions, without an assigned identity. Only after a role is assigned to an AWS identity (user or group) is the policy attached to the role able to be assumed by the principal. There is also an additional policy required when roles are used, called a *trust policy*. The trust policy is assigned to the identity who can assume the role as shown in Figure 7-31. A role does not have credentials (no password or access keys); temporary authentication credentials and a session token are only assigned to an IAM user or federated user after verification that the identity can assume the role. If a role is set up using the IAM console, the trust policy document is created and applied automatically. If the role is assigned to a user in the same AWS account, no trust policy is required, as the user is already known. If the role is assigned to an IAM user residing in another AWS account, a trust policy must be assigned to the IAM user to gain access. If the AWS CLI is used instead of the Management console, both the trust policy and the permissions policy must be created.

```
{
   "Version":"2012-10-17",
   "Statement": {
   "Effect":"Allow",
   "Principal": {"AWS: "arn:iam::123456789:root" },
   "Action":"sts:AssumeRole",
   }
}
```

Figure 7-31   A trust policy must include an STS assume action statement

When to Use Roles

AWS services that need to perform actions in your AWS account on your behalf—These roles, called *service-linked roles*, make it easier to assign the required permissions that allow the service to carry out its job. AWS Config, AWS Inspector, CloudWatch logs, and the elastic file system (EFS) are examples of AWS services that require a role with the required permissions attached so the service can carry out its prescribed job. With temporary credentials, the service-linked role is granted access to carry out requested tasks as required, rather than allowing access all the time.

AWS service roles for EC2 instances hosting applications that need access to AWS resources— This is one of the best examples of roles being used to control access to AWS resources by a hosted application. For the application to function properly, it needs valid AWS credentials to make its API requests to AWS resources. You could (but this a bad idea!) store a set of IAM users' credentials on the local hard disk of the application or Web server and allow the application to use these credentials.

Or (and this is a really good idea, and the recommended best practice) you could create an IAM role that provides temporary credentials for the application hosted on the EC2 instance. Because you are using a role, you don't have to worry about managing credentials; Amazon handles that. When the IAM role is used, temporary credentials are supplied that the application can use to make calls to the required AWS resources. Each instance can have a single role assigned; all applications hosted on the instance can use the role. However, the single role can be assigned to multiple instances, and changes made to the role are propagated to all instances that are using that role. The addition of a role to an instance is carried out by creating an *instance profile* that is attached to the instance either during creation, as shown in Figure 7-32, or after creation.

Each role assigned to an EC2 instance contains a permissions policy that lists the permissions to be used, plus a trust policy that allows the EC2 instance to be able to assume the assigned role and retrieve the temporary credentials. This allows access for a defined period of time; one hour is the default. The temporary credentials are stored in the memory of the running instance and are part of the instances metadata store under *iam/security-credentials/role-name*.

Using temporary security credentials for the EC2 instance provides an additional advantage; the security credentials are automatically rotated just before their temporary session expires, ensuring that a valid set of credentials is always at hand for the application. Terra Firma uses roles to control Web and application server access to S3 buckets.

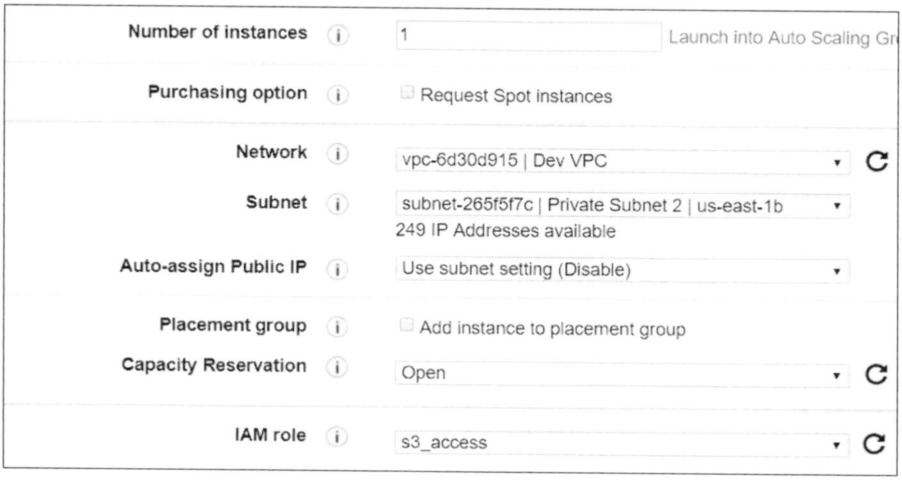

Figure 7-32   Adding an IAM role during instance installation

Mobile applications—For mobile applications that require authentication, Amazon has a service called Cognito, discussed previously in this chapter. Cognito is designed for scalable and secure mobile authentication for hundreds or thousands of users, as shown in Figure 7-33. Your choices for authentication can also be through social media providers such as Google and Facebook, or even Logon Amazon. In addition, there is support for enterprise federation using Microsoft Active Directory and SAML 2.0, and newer protocols such as Oauth 2.0 and OpenID Connect. Cognito also supports creating user pools of email addresses or phone numbers that can be linked to the desired application along with the type of authentication needed: through the user pool, or by federating through a third-party identity provider. The beauty of using Cognito is that it manages multiple identity providers—both identity federation and Web-based federation options that mobile applications use for authentication and access to AWS resources.

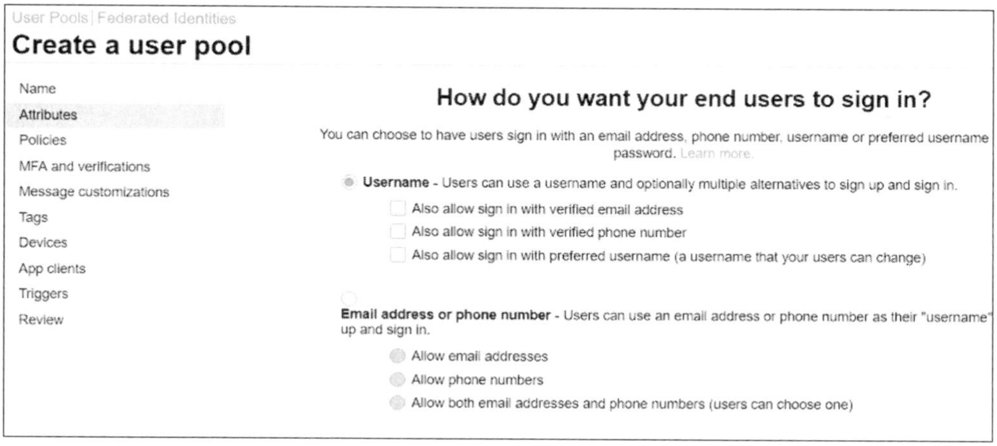

Figure 7-33   Cognito is designed for mobile application authentication

Cross-Account Access to AWS Resources

Perhaps you want to allow access to resources in your AWS account from users in other AWS accounts. Rather than creating an IAM user account within your AWS account for this type of access, you can instead provide temporary access by using an IAM role. This feature is called *cross-account access*. Let's assume a developer's group account in another AWS account needs access to the S3 bucket **corpdocs** in the production AWS account.

1. Create an IAM policy called **access-s3** in the production account controlling access to the S3 resource. The policy created is merely a custom policy allowing access to the specific S3 resource, as shown in Figure 7-34.

```
{
"Version": "2012-10-17",
"Statement": [
{
"Effect": "Allow",
"Action": "s3:ListAllMyBuckets",
"Resource": "*"
},
{
"Effect": "Allow",
"Action": [
"s3:ListBucket",
"s3:GetBucketLocation"
],
"Resource": "arn:aws:s3:::corpdocs"
},
{
"Effect": "Allow",
"Action": [
"s3:GetObject",
"s3:PutObject",
"s3:DeleteObject"
],
"Resource": "arn:aws:s3:::corpdocs/*"
}
]
}
```

Figure 7-34   Security policy for corpdocs bucket access

2. Create an IAM role called **get-access**, which is assigned to the developers IAM group that is linked to the policy **access-s3**. Now the policy has been linked to a specific role in the production account.

3. Get the ARN of the **get-access** role. We need this information to be able to populate the custom IAM policy that allows the developers IAM group to successfully switch accounts and access the **get-access** role.

4. Grant access to the role to the developers IAM group by creating an in-line custom policy allowing members of the group to access the **get-access** role, as shown in Figure 7-35.

```
{
"Version": "2012-10-17",
"Statement": {
"Effect": "Allow",
"Action": "sts:AssumeRole",
"Resource": "arn:aws:iam:::PRODUCTION-AWS-ACCT-ID:role/get-access"
}
}
```

Figure 7-35   Custom policy allowing developers to assume the get-access role

5. Any member of the developers group can now switch roles using the Management console by clicking the Switch Role menu below the username listing, as shown in Figure 7-36.

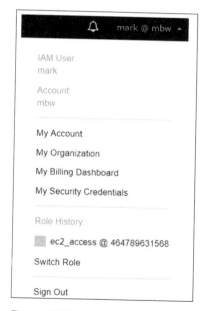

Figure 7-36   Using the Switch Role option for cross-account access

The AWS Security Token Service (STS)

Running in the background at AWS is a global AWS service that provides temporary credentials upon request for IAM users or roles. STS uses a default global endpoint located in the US East, North Virginia region at https://sts.amazon.com; you can also choose to make STS API calls to other AWS regions if faster responses are needed. Temporary security credentials are just as defined; they're temporary rather than permanent when compared to access credentials linked to an IAM user. Temporary credentials are provided only on request. The advantages of using the security token service to provide temporary credentials at AWS follow:

- There's no need to rotate security credentials; STS performs credential rotation when temporary credentials are renewed.

- Applications use temporary credentials when they're hosted on EC2 instances with assigned roles, removing the need for IM User account credentials and passwords.

- The STS manages and secures temporary credentials.

- Access to AWS resources can be defined without requiring a full IAM user account.

Here are a few valid scenarios for using temporary credentials and the STS:

- **Federation**—SSO federation with SAML 2.0, Web-based federation (Amazon, Google, Facebook), or by using OpenID Connect. The action in the policy will be AssumeRoleWithSAML or AssumeRoleWithWebIdentity. For both of these actions, STS is called. After verification, STS returns temporary credentials (access key, secret access key, and security token) that are valid for one hour by default. Editing the maximum CLI/API session duration as shown in Figure 7-37 allows you to control the exact length of validity for the assigned security credentials from 1 to 36 hours, or by defining a custom length of time.

- **Roles for cross-account access**—IAM user identities in one AWS account use IAM roles to assume access to AWS resources in other AWS accounts using defined roles and policies allowing authentication using STS. The action in the policy is AssumeRole.

- **Roles for controlling access to AWS services**—Only AWS RoboMaker, AWS QuickSight, AWS Amplify, and AWS Rekognition can't use temporary credentials. The action in the policy is AssumeRole.

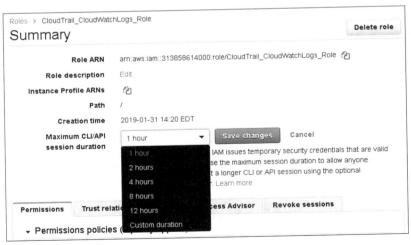

Figure 7-37   Changing the temporary credentials' validity timeframe

Identity Federation

If your users already authenticate to a corporate network such as Active Directory, you don't have to start over by creating separate IAM users. Instead, your user corporate identities can be *federated*, or stored in AWS. If your corporate network is compatible with SAML 2.0 (Security Association Markup Language), it can be configured to provide an SSO process to gain access to the AWS Management console. There are many options available for SSO in the industry, including Cognito, STS, Web Identity, SAML 2.0, and Open ID Connect. The choices available are due to the changes in authentication over the past 20 years. Most companies have Active Directory Domain Services (AD DS), which has supported the security association markup language (SAML) for many years. SAML is a protocol that needs to be supported by the cloud providers in order to support most major corporations' ability to authenticate using SSO to the cloud.

Ever since Steve Jobs popularized the mobile phone, mobile applications have come to the forefront, requiring a different type of authentication. No longer were we just linking a corporate computer/user account to an application hosted in the cloud. We also needed to link our phones running the application to the cloud provider. The first so-called identity provider to gain market share was OpenID, which is best described as an authorized nation protocol. OpenID typically allowed you to gain access to a website without providing a full set of credentials, instead using an identity provider such as Google or Facebook to vouch for or authorize your identity.

The next popular method for authorization was the OAuth protocol, which used access tokens and was used with many hosted service providers. Neither Open ID nor OAuth is as secure as SAML 2.0, which uses a set of *claims* for identification.

Amazon provides several services to handle the different levels of federation used in the industry today. Cognito allows you to manage the variety of authentication providers in the industry, including Facebook, Google, Twitter, OpenID, SAML, and even custom authentication providers that can be created from scratch. The odds are that you will use several of these methods for controlling authentication and access to applications hosted in AWS. Active Directory networks with Active Directory Federated Services installed can take advantage of the AWS Directory Services to build a trust relationship between your corporate Active Directory network and an AWS account.

1. Register your identity provider used at work, such as Active Directory with AWS. You must create and provide a metadata XML file, as shown in Figure 7-38, that lists your identity provider and authentication keys used by AWS to validate the authentication requests from your organization.

Figure 7-38   Adding a metadata xml file

2. Create IAM roles that provide access to the AWS resources. For the trust policy of the role, list your identity provider as the principal. This ensures that users from your organization will be allowed to access AWS resources.

3. Define what users or groups to map to the IAM roles, as shown in Figure 7-39, that provide access to the required AWS resources.

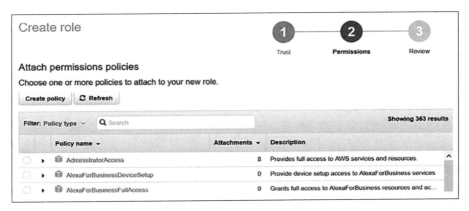

Figure 7-39   Select policies for IAM role

> **Note**
>
> Setting up SSO and creating identity and user pools using AWS Cognito is a procedure that is outside the scope of this book. The good news is that the deployment of AWS Cognito and Identity Federation is well documented at https://docs.aws.amazon.com.

IAM Best Practices

There are several best practices you should follow when dealing with IAM.

- **Managing the root account**—Don't forget the password for an AWS root account by creating such a complicated password you can't remember it. And don't write it down! When you need access to the root account, reset the password. In addition, always enable MFA on a root account. Make sure your access keys for the root account have been deleted. You can check whether you have active access keys for your root account by logging on as the root user, opening the IAM console, and checking the graphics, as shown in Figure 7-40. The goal should be shiny green check boxes for all options.

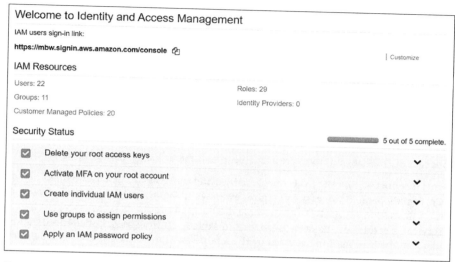

Figure 7-40   A properly set up root account

- **Create individual IAM users and groups for administration**—Even single users that you create should first be placed in an IAM group. At some point, each single user's duties need to be assumed by someone else due to holidays or illness. It's much easier to add a new IAM user to an existing IAM group.

- **Permissions**—Grant least privileges when assigning IAM permissions, and take the time to get proficient at deploying management policies and, if necessary, creating custom IAM policies for specific administrative access. Remember: most IAM accounts are administrator accounts if they have a fully fledged IAM user account. The goal should be to use IAM roles wherever possible because roles use temporary credentials that STS assigns and manages.

- **Groups**—Don't manage by IAM users; instead, manage with delegating access using IAM groups.

- **Conditions**—Consider restricting access with additional conditions. Consider adding a mandatory IP address range for administrators who need to perform administration; force authentication from a specific location.

- **Use CloudTrail logs**—By default, CloudTrail tracks all API calls to every AWS account and stores them for 90 days. You can extend the length of storage to permanent storage by creating a trail that saves all logs of all API calls from all AWS regions to a defined S3 bucket.

- **Passwords**—Make sure to create a strong password policy that aligns with your corporate policies.

- **Rotate security credentials**—Consider rotating the security credentials on a timeline that matches the password change for each account. Even better, redesign your IAM security to use roles for administrative tasks to ensure temporary credentials are used and managed by STS/AWS.

- **MFA**—Enable MFA for IAM users, including the root user of your AWS account. At the very least, use a software-based security code generator such as Google Authenticator or Authy.

- **Use IAM roles for application servers**—Use IAM roles to share temporary access to AWS resources for applications hosted on EC2 instances. Let AWS manage the credentials rather than us humans.

IAM Security Tools

Various security utilities and tools are available to make your job of managing IAM security easier.

Credential report—From the IAM console or by using the AWS CLI, you can request and download a comma-separated values (CSV) report, as shown in Figure 7-41, listing the current status of IAM users in an AWS account. Details include the status of the access keys (usage, last used, last used service), key rotation, passwords (enabled/disabled, last time used, last changed), and MFA information. The information provided by the report is within the last four-hour timeframe.

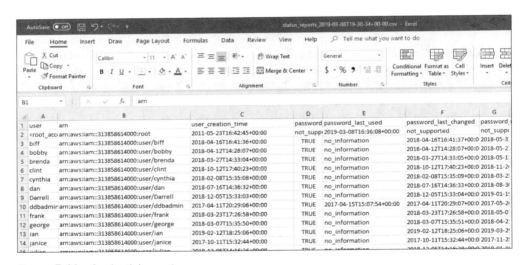

Figure 7-41 Credential report

Access Advisor—Reports can be generated to display the last time an IAM user or role accessed an AWS service. This is called *service last accessed data* in official AWS jargon. Reports can be viewed for each IAM entity by first selecting the IAM user, group, or role; selecting the Access Advisor tab; and then viewing the contents of the Access Advisor tab, as shown in Figure 7-42.

User—The last time an authenticated user tried to access the listed AWS service.

Group—The last time an authenticated group member attempted to access a listed AWS service.

Role—The last time a role was used by an authenticated user.

Policy—The last time an authenticated user or role attempted to access a particular service using a particular policy.

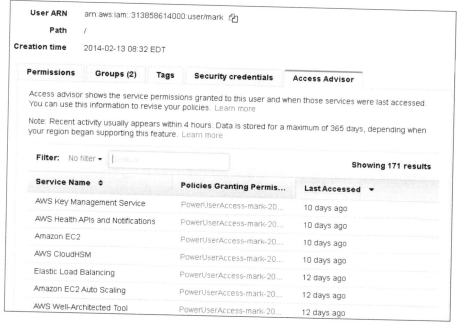

Figure 7-42   Access Advisor details

Policy Simulator—After you've created your first policy, you might get lucky and have it work right off the bat. If you are using the pre-created managed policies provided by AWS, they will work. Creating a custom policy, however, might cause additional levels of stress when it doesn't work as expected. Fortunately, Amazon has a simulator called the IAM Policy Simulator that you can used to test your policies, as shown in Figure 7-43. The simulator evaluates your policy using the same policy evaluation engine that would be used if real IAM policy requests were being carried out.

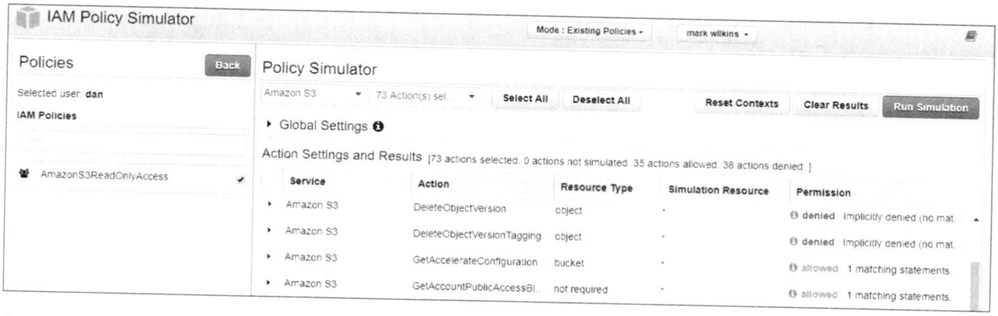

Figure 7-43   IAM Policy Simulator

With the Policy Simulator, you can test IAM policies that are attached to users, groups, or roles within an AWS account. You can select one or all security policies that are attached, and you can test all actions for what is being allowed or denied by the selected IAM policies. You can even add in conditions such as the IP address that the request must come from. Both identity-based and resource policies can be tested with the Policy Simulator. To use the Policy Simulator to test policies attached to IAM users, groups, or roles, it stands to reason that you need the appropriate permissions to be able to retrieve IAM policy. For example, to be able to simulate policies for IAM users and groups, the following actions must be included in your IAM policy:

- iam:GetGroupPolicy and iam:ListGroupsPolicy

- iam:GetPolicy and iam:ListPolicy

- iam:GetPolicyVersion and iam:ListPolicyVersion

- iam:GetUser and iam:ListUser

- iam:ListAtachedUserPolicies and iam:ListGroupsForUser

- iam:GetUserPolicy

MAKE SURE TO WATCH THE COMPANION VIDEO "EXPLORING AWS SECURITY TOOLS."

AWS CloudTrail—All API authentication requests involving IAM users' roles and the STS are logged to CloudTrail logs. You can search the event history held in CloudTrail for information on both successful and unsuccessful authentication requests. Logon failures using the STS actions **AssumeRoleWithSAML** and **AssumeRoleWithWebIdentity** are logged along with any additional identity provider details. In addition, the API requests made to other AWS services are logged with details about which user made the request, as shown in Table 7-2.

Table 7-2   **API Requests Used for Requesting Authentication**

User Type	IAM API	STS API	User Identity
AWS account root user	GetSessionToken		Root identity
IAM user	GetSessionToken		IAM user
IAM user		GetFederationToken	IAM user
IAM user		AssumeRole	Role identity

From the CloudWatch console, you can use a dashboard view of all API calls to your AWS account. Clicking View Event allows you to view the details of each call. In Figure 7-44, a successful console login by IAM user Mark is displayed, including the AWS account ID, username, time, source, and region.

```
{
  "eventVersion": "1.05",
  "userIdentity": {
  "type": "IAMUser",
  "principalId": "AIDAIEAFEX5JDWNZUTPOM",
  "arn": "arn:aws:iam::313858614000:user/mark",
  "accountId": "313858614000",
  "userName": "mark"
  },
  "eventTime": "2019-01-15T14:32:27Z",
  "eventSource": "signin.amazonaws.com",
  "eventName": "ConsoleLogin",
  "awsRegion": "us-east-1",
  "sourceIPAddress": "100.43.117.254",
  "userAgent": "Mozilla/5.0 (Macintosh; Intel Mac OS X 10_14_1) AppleWebKit/537.36
  (KHTML, like Gecko) Chrome/71.0.3578.98 Safari/537.36",
  "requestParameters": null,
  "responseElements": {
  "ConsoleLogin": "Success"
  },
  "additionalEventData": {
  "LoginTo": "https://console.aws.amazon.com/console/home?region=us-east-1&state=has
  hArgs%23&isauthcode=true",
  "MobileVersion": "No",
  "MFAUsed": "No"
  },
  "eventID": "4f85d8b9-7513-410f-a250-3b07d02d81a3",
  "eventType": "AwsConsoleSignIn",
  "recipientAccountId": "313858614000"
}
```

Figure 7-44   Detailed CloudWatch event

MAKE SURE TO WATCH THE COMPANION VIDEO "EXPLORING CLOUDTRAIL EVENTS."

Creating a CloudWatch Trail Event

To store CloudTrail events longer than the default 90-day timeframe, you can create a *trail* that then stores all CloudTrail event information in an S3 bucket, or a CloudWatch log. Trails, by default, capture information from all AWS regions. You can choose to record all management read/write events or just read-only or write-only events to your trail, as shown in Figure 7-45.

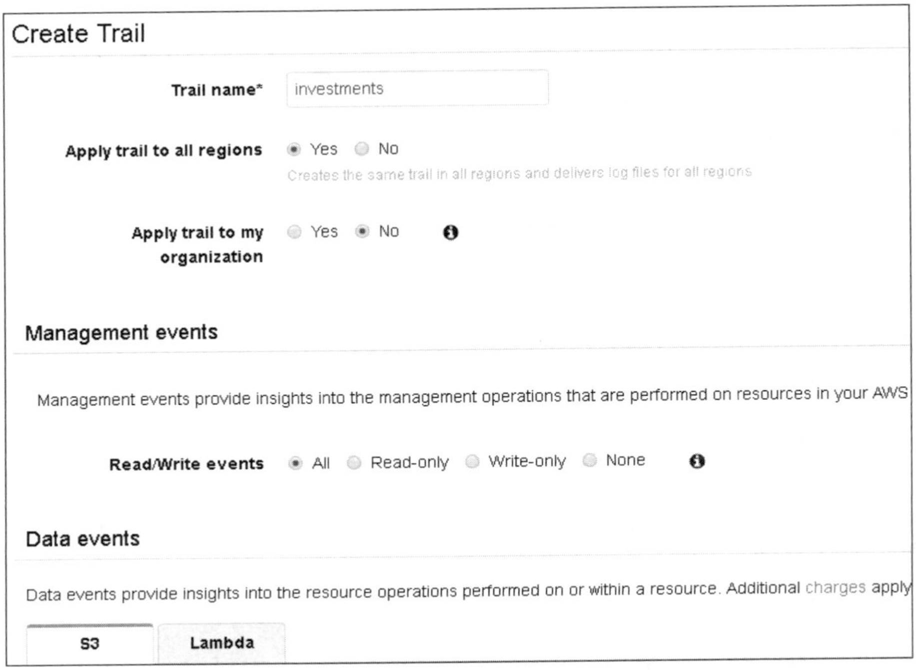

Figure 7-45   Creating a CloudTrail trail

Once data has been logged in a trail, you can analyze it using three methods.

- **S3 bucket**—If your CloudTrail is stored in an S3 bucket, then API activity for the S3 bucket can trigger activities. For example, the PutObject API can generate an event to send notification to an SNS topic or an SQS queue or trigger a Lambda function.

- **Lambda function**—You can also choose to invoke one or many Lambda functions directly on your trail data.

- **CloudWatch logs**—Storing authentication data in CloudWatch logs allows you to define an event rule that can be triggered if an AWS API call is received from IAM. The rule that is defined for the CloudWatch event watches for a specific pattern, such as an AWS API call from IAM, as shown in Figure 7-46. It can alert you when a data pattern is matched.

Figure 7-46   Creating a CloudTrail trail

Other AWS Security Services

Amazon has a variety of services to help you with the management of securing users and AWS resources. Depending on the size of your company or how much time you have available to manage AWS security, one or more of these management services might be just what you are looking for to manage your compliance and overall security settings.

AWS Organizations

Centralized policy-based management for multiple AWS accounts is the goal of AWS Organizations. If you're lucky enough to not yet have AWS accounts, look at AWS Organizations as a great starting point for working your AWS accounts, especially if you know you're going to have several AWS accounts to manage.

The first step to carry out with AWS Organizations is to create your initial organization with a specific AWS account; this account will henceforth be known as the master account, as shown in Figure 7-47. The master account sits at the root of your AWS Organization tree. Note that the master account is also defined as the payer account, which means it's responsible for all the charges carried out by all the AWS accounts that are nested within AWS Organizations.

The feature of consolidated billing is also included in AWS Organizations. Using AWS Organizations, at the root, you can create new AWS accounts or add existing AWS accounts. All additional AWS accounts added to AWS Organizations are defined as member accounts. After grouping your AWS accounts, you can then apply security control policies to them. The policies that can be applied to AWS Organizations are SCPs; these are permission boundaries that help define the effective permissions of applied IAM policies. If the SCP policy and the IAM policy allow the same AWS service actions in both policy documents—that is, the settings match—then the actions are allowed.

Within AWS Organizations, the AWS accounts can be organized into groupings called *organizational units* (OUs), as shown in Figure 7-47. These OUs are not the same as Microsoft Active Directory OUs, but they have some of the same organizational concepts. OUs can be nested so that you can create a tree-like hierarchy that meets your business needs. Nested OUs inherit SCP policy from the parent OU and specific policy controls that can be applied directly to any OU. SCP policies can be defined for the entire AWS Organization, for specific OUs, or for specific AWS accounts. Terra Firma wants to explore the creation of a master account using AWS Organizations. This allows Terra Firma to plan properly for future AWS growth and central control.

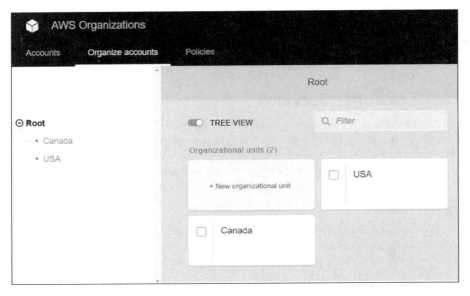

Figure 7-47   AWS Organizations and OUs

Resource Access Manager (AWS RAM)

We know we can control access to AWS resources with IAM users, groups, and roles by assigning the appropriate security policy. However, you may have many AWS accounts, and the prospect of managing resource access hosted in separate AWS accounts may not be possible. Amazon knows that corporations have hundreds if not thousands of AWS accounts and resources, and they need and want to manage these resources centrally. A fairly new service called the Resource Access Manager allows you to centrally manage AWS accounts, IAM policies, and AWS resources.

AWS RAM allows you to share your AWS resources hosted within a single AWS account with other AWS accounts. If you are using AWS Organizations, you can also use AWS RAM to share your AWS resources between the AWS accounts within your organization.

Perhaps you have application servers or even database servers that would be handy to share centrally between different AWS accounts instead of having to create duplicate resources. Ultimately, any EC2 resource hosted on a subnet within the VPC can be shared. Therefore, you can create a central VPC and share the subnets within the VPC with other AWS accounts that belong to the same organization hosted by AWS Organizations.

As the owner of the VPC, you're responsible for the creation and management of all standard VPC resources, including subnets, route tables, VPC endpoints, PrivateLink endpoints, Internet gateways, virtual private gateways, network address translation (NAT) gateways, and transit gateways.

- Once the subnet is shared with you, as shown in Figure 7-48, you can use any resources hosted by the subnet, including EC2 instances, RDS databases, and even Redshift clusters.

- Once a subnet has been shared, you can use the shared subnet to create, modify, and delete your own resources.

- You can share resources within any AWS region that supports resource sharing using AWS RAM.

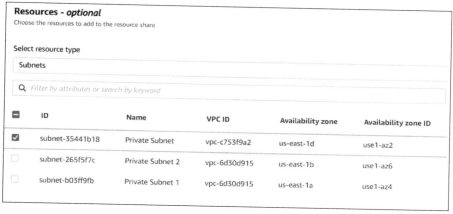

Figure 7-48   Sharing subnets with AWS RAM

The first task to consider is to decide the level of sharing you want to carry out. Which resources that you own would you like to share?

Next, decide which principals you would like to share the resource with. Resource principals can be AWS accounts, OUs, or an entire organization from AWS Organizations.

If your AWS account is part of an organization within AWS Organizations, and sharing within your organization is enabled, any principal in your organization will automatically be granted access to any shared resources. If you are not using AWS Organizations, you will receive an invitation to join the resource share, and after accepting the invitation, you will have access to the shared resource.

After a resource has been shared with an AWS Organization, any new accounts that are added to the organization immediately have access to the shared resources. Even though a resource has been shared with you, you can't turn around and share the resource with somebody else because you're not the owner of the resource. Resource sharing is the responsibility of the resource owner.

Once an owner has shared a resource with your AWS account, you can begin to use the resource. What you can do with the resource depends on the type of resource that's being shared and the IAM security policies and service control policies that have been applied.

Resources can be shared by default with any AWS account; if you want to, you can restrict resource sharing to an organization within your AWS Organizations, specific AWS accounts, or OUs within the AWS Organization.

MAKE SURE TO WATCH THE COMPANION VIDEO "SETTING UP AWS ORGANIZATIONS AND RAM."

Secrets Manager

Secrets Manager allows you to secure and manage secrets for your RDS databases, as shown in Figure 7-49. This includes MySQL, PostgreSQL, and Amazon Aurora, and secrets for Oracle databases hosted on EC2 instances, and OAuth refresh tokens that are used when accessing AWS resources on third-party services and on-premise resources. The rotation of database credentials is automatically configured when secrets are stored in Secrets Manager. Secrets are encrypted at rest using encryption keys stored in the AWS Key Management service. You can specify customer master keys (CMKs) used to encrypt secrets or choose to use the default KMS encryption keys provided for your AWS account.

Developers can replace any hard-coded secrets used in their applications with secrets retrieved from Secrets Manager using the secrets manager APIs. Access to secrets is controlled by the IAM policy that defines the access permissions of both users and applications when retrieving secrets.

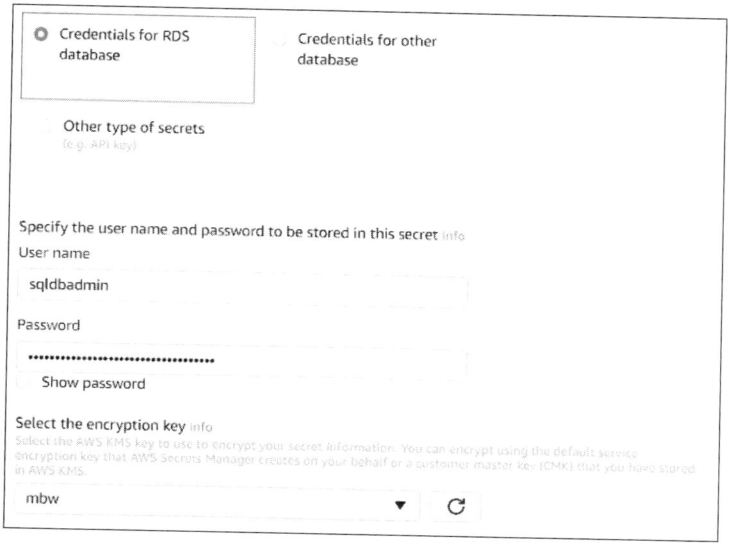

Figure 7-49   Storing RDS credentials as a secret

GuardDuty

GuardDuty is a built-in threat detection service hosted at AWS that you can subscribe to, allowing the continual monitoring and protection of your AWS accounts and services, as shown in Figure 7-50. GuardDuty works within these categories monitoring these security issues:

- **Reconnaissance**—Unusual API activity, failed logons, suspicious network traffic

- **EC2 instance compromise**—Analysis of network protocols, inbound and outbound communication, temporary theft of EC2 credentials

- **Account compromise**—Attempts to disable CloudWatch, suspicious API calls, or infrastructure deployment anomalies

Figure 7-50   GuardDuty settings

GuardDuty relies on machine learning and continual analysis from other integrated AWS security services, including CloudTrail events, VPC flow logs, and DNS logs. GuardDuty performs analysis in near-real-time and does not retain log information it has finished its after its analysis Of course, you can still use the individual AWS services and create and manage your own alerts, but perhaps you don't have the time or skill set necessary to protect your AWS resources adequately.

AWS Inspector

AWS Inspector performs security checks and assessments against the operating systems and applications hosted on Linux and EC2 instances by using an optional inspector agent that is installed in the operating system associated with the EC2 instance. After you define the assessment target for AWS Inspector, which is a group of tagged EC2 instances, AWS Inspector evaluates the state of each instance using several rule packages.

There are two types of rules: network accessibility tests that don't require the inspector agent to be installed, and host assessment rules that do require the inspector agent to be installed, as shown in Figure 7-51. Assessments check for security issues on each EC2 instance. The choices for rule packages comply within industry standards and include the Common Vulnerabilities and Exposures (CVE) checks, the Center for Internet Security (CIS) checks, Operating System configuration benchmarks, and other security best practices.

AWS Inspector rules are assigned severity levels of medium and high based on levels of confidentiality, integrity, and availability of the defined assessment target. AWS Inspector also integrates with Amazon SNS, which sends notifications when failures occur. Remember that SNS notifications can in turn call a Lambda function, which can carry out any AWS task you would like, as Lambda can use all AWS APIs. Terra Firma is exploring the use of AWS Inspector to make sure that there are no missed security holes on its Web and application server EC2 instances.

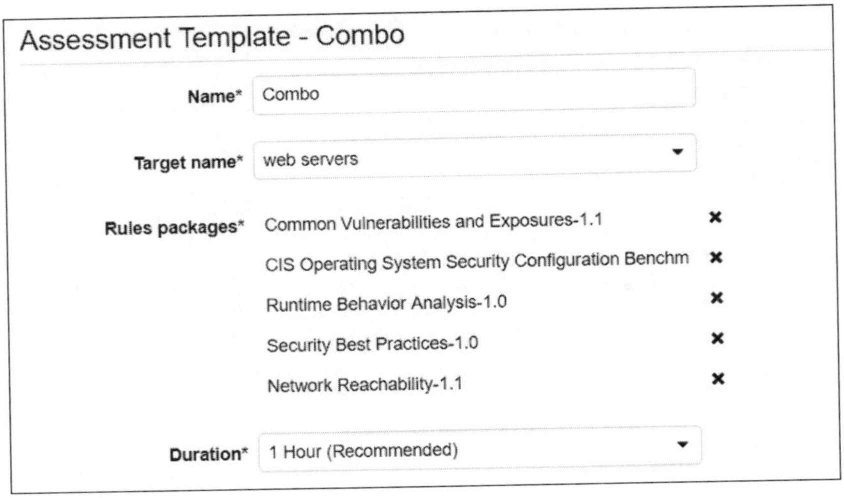

Figure 7-51   AWS Inspector options

In Conclusion

Kudos for hanging in what could be a difficult chapter to grasp with just one read. There are a lot of moving parts and a lot of documentation to wade through. In fact, there are well over 3,000 pages of AWS documents dealing just with IAM. If you're like I am, the first time I am exposed to a new security system, it takes a while to absorb all the details.

Amazon certainly does things in its way, and we mostly looked at dealing with security using the AWS Management console. You can use the AWS CLI tools as well, but you need to look at security settings graphically to get a grasp on the scope of what you want to do. Once the concepts in this chapter make sense, perhaps it's time to try crafting some IAM policies if you're up for it. Look at the companion videos that are an extension of this book. After you watch the videos, if you feel you need some customized policies, remember to test them with the Policy Simulator.

It's probably best to create an AWS account to use as a sandbox or two to play with IAM policies so you can test them before you move them into production. After all, it's easy to cut-and-paste policies from one account to another.

Top 10 Big-Picture Security Discussion Points

Deploying and managing security for your company resources that are hosted in the AWS cloud is the job that never ends. Here are a few more discussion points to consider. Gather everybody into a conference room with a couple of whiteboards, and start discussing and planning. The more you plan, the safer you'll be, and the more you prototype ideas, the more you'll learn.

1. Are you using the root account daily? Why?

2. Do your IAM users currently use MFA? Why not?

3. Do you have your IAM users and groups defined?

4. Are applications hosted on EC2 instances using IAM roles to access AWS services?

5. Does the sharing of VPCs and subnets with AWS RAM simplify your deployments at AWS?

6. Can IAM roles replace current IAM user identities for accessing AWS resources?

7. What permission boundaries should be enforced? At what level? Per user, or per organization?

8. Can AWS Organizations help you manage multiple AWS accounts?

9. Will GuardDuty help you manage the overall protection and compliance of your AWS resources that are hosted in your AWS accounts?

10. Would AWS Inspector help you to further protect your hosted applications on EC2 instances?

8

Automating AWS Infrastructure

There have been many systems put in place over the years to help successfully manage and deploy complicated software applications on complicated hardware stacks. We are living through the next iteration of potential promise in the IT world, and that's the public cloud. Move your applications to the cloud, and you can also "be all in" and think everything is great. It is certainly great for the public cloud providers like AWS. Hundreds of thousands of customers are experimenting and using AWS cloud services, and many companies have been using their services for years.

This book has focused on explaining how the AWS services work and how the services are integrated. Looking at the AWS cloud as a complete entity—an operating system hosted on the Internet—the one characteristic of AWS that stands above all others is the level of integrated automation utilized to deploy, manage, and recover our AWS services. There is not a single AWS service offered that is not heavily automated for deployment and in its overall operation; when you order a virtual private network (VPN), it's created and available in seconds. Order an Elastic Compute Cloud (EC2) instance, either through the Management console or by using the AWS command-line interface (CLI) tools, and it's created and available in minutes. Automated processes provide the just-in-time response we demand when we order cloud services.

Automating with AWS

It wasn't that long ago when you ordered a virtual machine from a cloud provider and waited several days until an email arrived telling you that your service was ready to go.

AWS services are being changed, enhanced, and updated 24/7, with features and changes appearing similarly every day. AWS as a whole is deployed and maintained using a combination of developer agility and automated processes matching the agile definition of *being able to move quickly and easily* with a partnership of developers, system operations, project managers, network engineers, and security professionals working together from the initial design stages, through the development process, to production and continual updates.

AWS wasn't always this automated and regimented; in the early days, Amazon was a burgeoning online e-commerce bookseller. The increasing popularity of the Amazon store introduced problems with being able to scale its online resources to match its customers' needs. Over time, rules were defined at Amazon for all developers mandating that each underlying service that supported the Amazon store must be accessible through a core set of shared application programming interfaces (APIs) that were shared with all developers, and that each service was built and maintained on a common core of compute and storage resources.

These days it may seem that Jeff Bezos, the founder, chairman, CEO, and president of Amazon, and Andy Jassy, the CEO of Amazon Web Services, knew exactly what they were doing, but they say they really had no idea that they were building a scalable cloud-hosted operating system utilizing a combination of custom software and custom hardware components. But that's what they have built. Today, the AWS cloud allows any company or developer to build, host, and run applications on AWS's infrastructure platform using the many custom tools developed internally at AWS to help run the Amazon.com store effectively.

Amazon built and continues to build its hosting environment using mandated internal processes, which I define as a mixture of Information Technology Infrastructure Library (ITIL), SCRUM (a framework for managing product development working together as a development team), Agile (a software development cycle for teams of developers working with the overall tenets of planning, designing, developing, testing, and evaluating as a team with open communications), and currently DevOps (a continuation of the agile framework with full collaboration among the development and operations teams. You may not agree with these definitions as written, and that's okay; there are many different definitions of these terms. The reality is that the work at AWS is being done together in an effective manner; the result is hundreds of changes being made to the AWS hardware and software environment every month. In addition, all AWS services are being monitored, scaled, rebuilt, and logged through completely automated processes. Amazon doesn't use manual processes to do anything, and your long-term goal should be that your company doesn't either.

This book is not going to turn into a Bible of how to operate with a DevOps or Agile mind-set because there are already many excellent books on these topics.

However, as your experience with AWS grows, you're going to want to start using automation to help run and manage your day-to-day operations running AWS and to help you solve problems when they occur. There are numerous services available that don't cost anything additional to use other than the time it takes to become competent in using them. This might sound too good to be true, but most of Amazon's automation services are indeed free to use; what you are charged for are the AWS compute and storage resources that each service uses. AWS charges for compute, storage, and data transfer.

Automation services will always manage your resources more effectively than you can manually. At AWS, the automation of infrastructure is typically called *infrastructure as code*; hopefully this definition makes sense; when we create resources using the AWS Management console, in the background AWS uses automated processes running scripts to finish the creation and management of resources.

Regardless of how you define your own deployment or development process, there are a number of powerful tools in the AWS toolbox that can help you automate your procedures. This chapter is primarily focused on automating AWS's infrastructure rather than exploring the software development in detail, but we will do some exploration of the available software development tools at

AWS. If you're a developer who's been told that your applications are now going to be developed in the AWS cloud, you first need to know the infrastructure components available at AWS and how they work together. Then you must understand the tools that can be used for automation of AWS infrastructure and what tools are also available for coding. We are going to look at some of the software deployment tools AWS offers, such as Elastic Beanstalk, and additional management tools that will help you deploy applications using processes called continuous integration (CI) and continuous deployment (CD). The topics for this chapter include these:

- Automating deployment options at AWS

- CloudFormation stack-based architecture deployments

- Service Catalog to help secure CloudFormation templates

- Exploring the 12-Factor App guidelines for building and deploying cloud-hosted software applications

- Elastic Beanstalk for deploying applications and infrastructure together

- Continuous integration and deployment with CodeDeploy, CodeBuild, and CodePipeline

- Serviceless computing with Lambda functions

- The API Gateway

Terra Firma wants to do the following:

- Learn how to automate the creation of its AWS infrastructure

- Move toward a DevOps mind-set utilizing its programmers to manage AWS system operations through automation processes

- Deploy a self-serve portal of its AWS infrastructure stacks allowing developers to build test environments quickly and properly the first time

- Create a hosted application using serviceless computing components for conference registrations

- Explore using an AWS hosted code repository rather than Git

From Manual to Automated Infrastructure with CloudFormation

In this book, we've looked at deploying a variety of AWS resources, such as EC2 instances, elastic block storage (EBS) and Simple Storage Service (S3) storage, virtual private cloud (VPC) networks, elastic load balancers (ELB), and EC2 auto scaling groups. For those beginning to learn AWS, we've focused on using the Management console as the starting point, which is a great place to commence deploying and managing AWS services such as EC2 instances.

Yet, the second and third time you deploy an EC2 instance using the Management console, you will probably not perform the steps the same as the first time. Even if you do manage to complete a manual task with the same steps, by the tenth installation, you will have made changes or will have decided to make additional changes because your needs have changed, or there was a better option available. The point is, a manual process rarely stays the same over time. Even the simplest manual process can be automated at AWS.

Peering under the hood at any management service running at AWS, you'll find the process command-set driven by JavaScript Object Notation (JSON) scripts. At the GUI level, using the Management console, we fill in the blanks; once we click Create, JSON scripts are executed in the background carrying out our requests.

CloudFormation is the AWS-hosted orchestration engine that works with JSON templates to deploy AWS resources, as shown in Figure 8-1. AWS uses CloudFormation extensively, and so can you. More than 300,000 AWS customers use CloudFormation to manage deployment of just about everything, including all infrastructure stack deployments. Each CloudFormation template declares the desired infrastructure stack to be created, and the CF engine automatically deploys and links the resources. Additional control variables can be added to each CF template to manage and control the precise order of the installation of resources.

Of course, there are third-party solutions, such as Chef, Puppet, and Ansible, that perform automated deployments of compute infrastructure. CloudFormation is not going to replace these third-party products but can be a useful tool for building automated solutions for your AWS infrastructure if you don't use one of these third-party orchestration tools. AWS has a managed service called OpsWorks in three flavors that might be useful to your deployments at AWS if your company currently uses one the following Chef or Puppet versions:

- **OpsWorks Stacks**—Manage applications and services that are hosted at AWS and on-premise running Chef recipes, bask, or PowerShell scripts.

- **OpsWorks for Chef Automate**—Build a fully managed Chef Automate server that supports the latest versions of Chef server and Chef Automate, any community-based tools or cookbooks, and native Chef tools.

- **OpsWorks for Puppet Enterprise**—A fully managed Puppet Enterprise environment that patches, updates, and backs up your existing Puppet environment and allows you to manage and administrate both Linux and Windows server nodes hosted on EC2 instances and on-premise.

Figure 8-1   The CloudFormation console

JSON's extensive use at AWS follows the same concept as Microsoft Azure and its extensive use of PowerShell; at AWS, JSON scripts are used internally for many tasks and processes: creating security policy with IAM and working with CloudFormation are the two most common examples that you will come across.

If you use Windows EC2 instances at AWS, you can also use PowerShell scripting. Both Microsoft and AWS heavily rely on automation tools. Let's compare the manual deployment process at AWS against the automated process starting with CloudFormation.

Time spent—Over time, running manual processes at AWS becomes a big waste of time for the human carrying out the process. In the past, maintaining manual processes such as building computer systems and stacks would have been your job security; these days it's just not a prudent way to deploy production resources. For one thing, there's just too many steps in a manual process to consider. Every CloudFormation deployment does take time, but much less time than a manual process because each step in a CloudFormation script is essential. There are no wasted steps, and all steps are in the proper order. Over time, executing an automated process to build EC2 instances will save you hours if not weeks of time; the CF process runs in the background, allowing you to do something else. CloudFormation can also perform updates and deletions to existing AWS resources.

Security issues—Humans make mistakes, and manual changes can end up being huge security mistakes due to the lack of oversight. CloudFormation templates can be secured and controlled for usage by specific IAM users and groups. Templates also carry the same steps every time they are executed, which helps solve any fat-finger mistakes we humans make. Service Catalog, another AWS service, integrates with CloudFormation, mandating which users or accounts can use CloudFormation templates to build infrastructure stacks.

Documentation—It's difficult to document manual processes if they constantly change, and who has the time to create documentation anyway? CloudFormation templates are readable, and once you get used to the format, they are actually self-documenting. Again, there are no wasted steps in a CloudFormation script; what is described is exactly what is deployed; if there are mistakes found in a CloudFormation script during deployment, all changes that have been carried out are reversed.

Repeatability—If you're lucky, you can repeat your manual steps the same way every time. However, you're just wasting valuable time in the long run. With a CloudFormation script, you can deploy and redeploy the listed AWS resources in multiple environments, such as separate development, staging, and production environments. Every time a CloudFormation template is executed, it is repeating the same steps.

Cost savings—CloudFormation automation carries out stack deployments and updates much faster than manual processes ever could. In addition, CloudFormation automation can be locked down using a companion service called AWS Systems Manager, discussed later in this chapter. ensuring only specific IAM users and groups can access and execute specific CF deployment tasks.

CloudFormation Components

CloudFormation works with templates, stacks, and change sets. A *CloudFormation template* is an AWS resource blueprint that can create a complete application stack, or a single stack component such as a VPC network complete with multiple subnets, Internet gateways, and NAT services all automatically deployed and configured. A template type called a change set can be created to help you visualize how proposed changes will affect AWS resources that were deployed by a current CloudFormation template.

CloudFormation Templates

Each CloudFormation template is a text file that follows either JSON or YAML formatting standards; CloudFormation responds to files saved with JSON, YAML, or txt extensions. Each template can deploy, or update a multiple AWS resource, or a single resource such as a VPC or an EC2 instance JSON format as shown in Figure 8-2; to compare Figure 8-3 displays the same information but in YAML format. It's really a matter of personal preference as to which format you use. When creating CloudFormation templates, you might find YAML easier to read, which could be helpful in the long term. YAML seems more self-documenting because it's easier to read.

```
{
  "AWSTemplateFormatVersion" : "2010-09-09",
  "Description" : "EC2 instance",
  "Resources" : {
  "EC2Instance" : {
  "Type" : "AWS::EC2::Instance",
  "Properties" : {
  "ImageId" : "ami-0ff8a91497e77f667",
  "InstanceType" : "t1.micro"
  }
  }
  }
}
```

Figure 8-2   CloudFormation template in JSON format

```
AWSTemplateFormatVersion: '2010-09-09'
Description: EC2 instance
Resources:
EC2Instance:
Type: AWS::EC2::Instance
Properties:
ImageId: ami-0ff8a91497e77f667
```

Figure 8-3   CloudFormation template in YAML format

CloudFormation templates can utilize multiple sections, as shown in Figure 8-4; however, the only mandated section that must be present is *Resources*. Like any template or script, the better the internal documentation, the better the understanding can be for the individual who needs to understand the script but wasn't its author. It is highly recommended to use the *Metadata* section for comments to ensure the understanding of the script while it is being written, and much later when somebody is trying to remember just what this script is supposed to do.

```
"AWSTemplateFormatVersion": "version date",
"AWSTemplateFormatVersion" : "2010-09-09"
<TemplateFormatVersion: Defines the current CF template version>

 "Description": "Here are additional details about this template and what it does",
<Description: Describes the template; must always follow the version section>

"Metadata": {
  "Metadata" : {
  "Instances" : {"Description" : "Details about the instances"},
  "Databases" : {"Description" : "Details about the databases"}
 }
},
<Metadata: Additional information about the resources being deployed by the
template>

  "Parameters" : {
  "InstanceTypeParameter" : {
    "Type" : "String",
    "Default" : "t2.medium",
    "AllowedValues" : ["t2.medium", "m5.large", "m5.xlarge"],
    "Description" : "Enter t2.medium, m5.large, or m5.xlarge. Default is
t2.medium."
  }
}
<Parameters: Defines the AWS resource values allowed to be selected and used by
your template>

"Mappings" : {
  "RegionMap" : {
    "us-east-1"      : { "HVM64" : "ami-0bb8a91508f77f868"},
    "us-west-1"      : { "HVM64" : "ami-0cdb828fd58c52239"},
    "eu-west-1"      : { "HVM64" : "ami-078bb4163c506cd88"},
    "ap-southeast-1" : { "HVM64" : "ami-09999b978cc4dfc10"},
    "ap-northeast-1" : { "HVM64" : "ami-06fd42961ce9f0d75"}
  }
}
<Mappings: Defines conditional parameters defined by a "key"; in this example, the
AWS region and a set of AMI values to be used>

 "Conditions": {
 "CreateTestResources": {"Fn::Equals" : [{"Ref" : "EnvType"}, "test"]}
 },
<Conditions: Defines dependencies between resources, such as the order when
resources are created, or where resources are created. For example, "test" deploys
the stack in the test environment>
```

(Continued)

```
"Resources" : {"Resources" : {
  "TestEC2Instance" : {
    "Type" : "AWS::EC2::Instance",
    "Properties" : {
      "ImageId" : "ami-0ef8b91705f77f867"
      {
    }
  }
}<Defines the stack resources and its properties>

<Resources: Defines the resources to use the stack, such as the EC2 instance and
AMI>

"Outputs" : {
  "InstanceID" : {
    "Description": "The Deployed EC2 Instance",
    "Value" : { "Ref" : "Test EC2Instance" }
  }
{
<Defines the stack outputs displayed in the CloudFormation console after a
successful deployment>
```

Figure 8-4　Valid sections in CloudFormation template

MAKE SURE TO WATCH THE COMPANION VIDEO "ANALYZING A CLOUD FORMATION TEMPLATE."

To access the companion videos, register your book at informit.com/register.

Stacks

AWS has many sample CloudFormation templates that you can download from the online CloudFormation documentation, as shown in Figure 8-5, and are available to deploy in many AWS regions. A CloudFormation stack can be as simple as a single VPC or as complex as a complete three-tier application stack complete with the required network infrastructure and associated services. CloudFormation can be useful in deploying infrastructure at AWS, including the following areas:

- **Network**—Define a baseline template for developers to ensure that their VPC network setup matches company policy.

- **Front-end infrastructure**—Deploy Internet gateways, associated route table entries, or load balancers into existing AWS network infrastructure.

- **Back-end infrastructure**—Create complete mastery in standby database infrastructure, including subnet groups and associated security groups.

- **Two-tier application**—Using a two-tier CloudFormation script allows you to rebuild a complete application stack with required network and infrastructure components when failures or disaster occur, or launch the application stack in another AWS region.

- **Windows Server Active Directory**—Deploy Active Directory on Windows Server 2008 R2 instances in a VPC.

- **Demo applications**—Define an application stack for demonstrations, allowing the sales team or end users to quickly create the entire environment.

- **AWS managed services**—CloudFormation template that can be used to automate the setup of any AWS managed services; for example, AWS Config or Inspector could be enabled and set up using a CloudFormation template.

> **Note**
>
> There are many standardized CloudFormation templates available from AWS at https://aws. amazon.com/quickstart/ that have been built by AWS solution architects and trusted partners to help you deploy complete solutions on AWS. These templates are called AWS Quick Starts and are designed following the current AWS best practices for security and high availability.

AWS Documentation » AWS CloudFormation » User Guide » Sample Templates » EU (London) Region » **Sample Solutions**

Sample Solutions

Sample solutions templates show you how to create an end-to-end solution with common applications. The applications in these samples are not supported or maintained by AWS and are only for demonstrating the capabilities of AWS CloudFormation templates.

Template Name	Description	View	View in Designer	Launch
SharePoint® Foundation 2010	Deploys SharePoint® Foundation 2010 running on Microsoft Windows Server® 2008 R2.	View	View in Designer	Launch Stack ●
Microsoft Windows Server Active Directory	Creates a single server installation of Active Directory running on Microsoft Windows Server® 2008 R2.	View	View in Designer	Launch Stack ●

Figure 8-5   AWS has many sample solutions complete with CloudFormation templates

Creating an EC2 Instance with EIP

If you're like I am, you will want to see examples that work when looking at using a programming or scripting utility. I highly recommend looking at the AWS Quick Starts website https://aws. amazon.com/quickstart/ to see how powerful CloudFormation can be. Here's a simple example that creates an EC2 instance using a CloudFormation template, as shown in Figure 8-6. The template parameters are easily readable from top to bottom. Under *Properties*, the EC2 instance ID, subnet ID, and EC2 instance type must all be already present in the AWS region where the template is executed; otherwise, deployment will fail. If there are issues in the CloudFormation script during deployment, CloudFormation rolls back and removes any infrastructure that the template created. The *Ref* statement is used in this template to attach the elastic IP (EIP) to the defined EC2 instance that was deployed and referenced under the listed resources in *EC2 Machine*.

```
AWSTemplateFormatVersion: 2010-09-09
Description: EC2 Instance Template
"Resources": {
 "EC2Machine": {
 "Type": "AWS::EC2::Instance",
 "Properties": {
  "ImageId": "i-0ff407a7042afb0f0",
  "NetworkInterfaces": [{
  "DeviceIndex": "0",
  "DeleteOnTermination": "true",
  "SubnetId": "subnet-7c6dd651"
  }],
  "InstanceType": "t2.small"
  }
 }
},
"EIP": {
 "Type": "AWS::EC2::EIP",
 "Properties": {
 "Domain": "VPC"
 }
 },
"VpcIPAssoc": {
 "Type": "AWS::EC2::EIPAssociation",
 "Properties": {
 "InstanceId": {
 "Ref": "EC2Machine"
 },
 "AllocationId": {
 "Fn::GetAtt": ["EIP",
  "AllocationId"]
 }
 }
}
```

Figure 8-6   CloudFormation templates for creating an EC2 instance

MAKE SURE TO WATCH THE COMPANION VIDEO "CREATING EC2 INSTANCES WITH CLOUDFORMATION."

Updating with Change Sets

When a deployed CloudFormation resource stack needs to be updated, change sets allow you to preview how your existing AWS resources will be modified, as shown in Figure 8-7. Selecting an original CloudFormation template to edit, the desired set of changes to be made are inputted; CloudFormation then analyzes your requested changes against the existing CloudFormation stack, producing a change set that you can then review and approve the changes for or cancel.

Multiple change sets can be created for various comparison purposes. Once a change set is created, reviewed, and approved, CloudFormation updates your current resource stack.

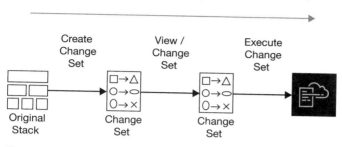

Figure 8-7   Using change sets with CloudFormation

MAKE SURE TO WATCH THE COMPANION VIDEO "CREATING CHANGE SETS WITH CLOUDFORMATION."

Working with CloudFormation Stack Sets

Stack sets allow you to create a single CloudFormation template to deploy, update, or delete AWS infrastructure across multiple AWS regions and AWS accounts. When a CloudFormation template will be deploying infrastructure across multiple accounts, as shown in Figure 8-8, and AWS regions, you must ensure that the AWS resources that the template references are available in each AWS account or region; for example, EC2 instances, EBS volumes, and key pairs are always created in a specific region. These region-specific resources must be copied to each AWS region, where the CloudFormation template is executed. Global resources such as IAM roles and S3 buckets that are being created by the CloudFormation template should also be reviewed to make sure there are no naming conflicts during creation, as global resources must be unique across all AWS regions.

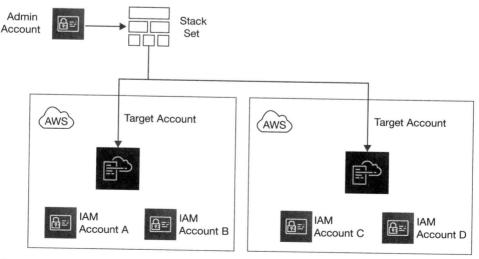

Figure 8-8   Stack sets with two AWS target accounts

Once a stack set is updated, all instances of the stack that were created are updated as well. For example, if you had 10 AWS accounts across 3 AWS regions, 30 stack instances would be updated when the master stack set is executed. If a stack set is deleted, all corresponding stack sets will also be deleted.

A stack set is first created in a single AWS account. Before additional stack instances can be created from the master stack set, trust relationships using IAM roles must be created between the initial AWS administrator account and the desired target accounts.

For testing purposes, one example available in the AWS CloudFormation console is a sample stack set that allows you to enable AWS Config across selected AWS regions or accounts. Just a reminder: AWS Config allows you to control AWS account compliance by defining rules that monitor specific AWS resources to ensure the desired level of compliance has been followed.

AWS Service Catalog

Using a CloudFormation template provides great power for creating, modifying, and updating AWS infrastructure. Creating AWS infrastructure always costs money; therefore, perhaps you would like to control who gets to deploy specific CloudFormation templates. Using Service Catalog allows you to manage the distribution of CloudFormation templates as a product list to an AWS account ID, an AWS Organizations account, or an Organizational Unit contained within an AWS organization. Service Catalog is composed of portfolios, as shown in Figure 8-9, which are a collection of one or more products.

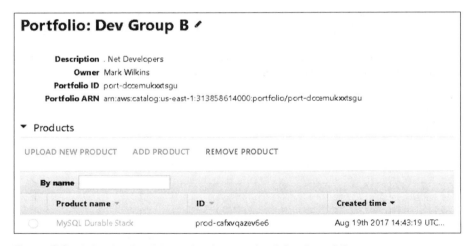

Figure 8-9   A Service Catalog product is part of a defined portfolio

When an approved product is selected, Service Catalog delivers the Confirmation template to CloudFormation, which then executes the template creating the product. Third-party products hosted in the AWS Marketplace are also supported by Service Catalog, as Software appliances are bundled with a CloudFormation template.

Each IAM user in an AWS account can be granted access to a Server Catalog portfolio of multiple approved products. Because products are built using common Confirmation templates, any AWS infrastructure components, including EC2 instances and databases hosted privately in a VPC, can be deployed. In addition, VPC endpoints using AWS PrivateLink allow access to the AWS Service Catalog service.

When you're creating Service Catalog products, constraints using IAM roles can be used to limit the level of administrative access to the resources contained in the stack being deployed by the product itself. Service actions can also be assigned for rebooting, starting, or stopping deployed EC2 instances, as shown in Figure 8-10.

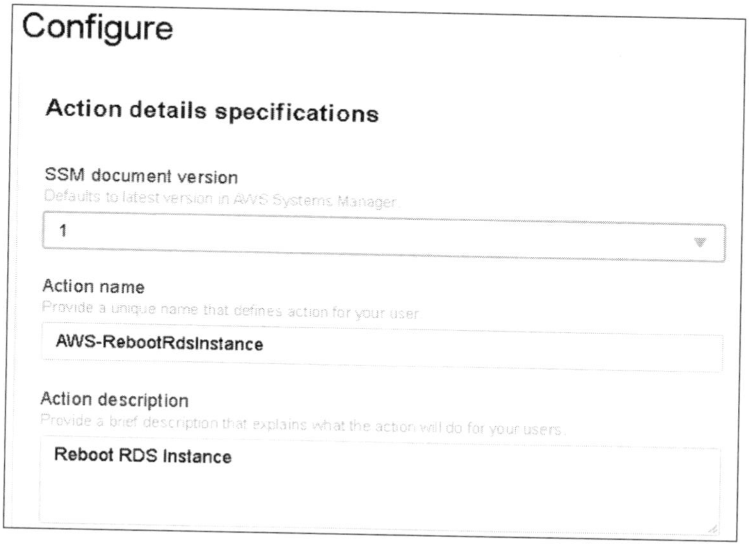

Figure 8-10   Server action constraints controlled by Service Catalog

In addition, rules can be added that control any parameter values that the end user enters; for example, you could mandate that specific subnets must be used for a stack deployment. Rules can also be defined, which allow you to control which AWS account and region the product can launch.

Each deployed product can also be listed by version number, allowing end users to select products by the latest version so they could update currently deployed products that are running an older version. Terra Firma will use CloudFormation and Service Catalog in combination to create a self-serve portal for developers.

MAKE SURE TO WATCH THE COMPANION VIDEO "CREATING PRODUCTS WITH SERVICE CATALOG."

The 12-Factor Methodology

For developers getting ready to create their first application in the cloud, there are several rules generally accepted by developers for successfully creating applications that run exclusively in the public cloud. These rules are called the 12-factor app rules.

> **Note**
> The original website for the 12-factor app rules is https://12factor.net/.

Several years ago, Heroku cofounder Adam Wiggins released a suggested blueprint for creating native software as a service (SaaS) applications hosted in the public cloud. Heroku is a managed platform as a service (PaaS) provider that Salesforce owns. Incidentally, Heroku is hosted at AWS. The software engineers at Heroku were attempting to provide guidance for applications that were going to be created in the public cloud based on their real-world experience.

These guidelines can be viewed as a set of best practices to consider utilizing. Of course, depending on your deployment methods, you may quibble with some of the rules, and that's okay. The point is, these are handy rules to consider and discuss before deploying applications in the cloud. Your applications that are hosted in the cloud also need infrastructure; as a result, these rules for proper application deployment in the cloud don't stand alone; cloud infrastructure is also a necessary part of the 12 rules. Let's look at these 12 rules from an infrastructure point of view and identify the AWS services that can help with the goal of each defined rule.

Rule 1. Codebase—One Codebase That Is Tracked with Version Control Allows Many Deploys

In development circles, this rule is non-negotiable; it must be followed. Creating an application usually involves three separate environments: development, testing, and production, as shown in Figure 8-11. The same code base should be used in each environment, whether it's the developer's laptop, a set of testing server EC2 instances, or the production EC2 instances. If you think about it, operating systems, off-the-shelf software, dynamic-link libraries (DLLs), development environments, and application code are all controlled by versions. And each version of application code needs to be stored separately and securely in a safe location.

All developers likely use a code repository such as GitHub to store their code. As your codebase undergoes revisions, each revision needs to be tracked; after all, a single codebase might be responsible for thousands of deployments. Documenting and controlling the separate versions of the codebase just makes sense. Amazon also has a code repository, called CodeCommit, that might be more useful than Git for applications hosted at AWS. We will cover CodeCommit in the next section.

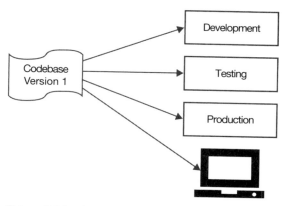

Figure 8-11   One codebase regardless of location

At the infrastructure level at Amazon, we also have dependencies. The AWS components to keep track of include these:

- **AMIs**—Images for Web, application, database, and appliance instances. Each AMI should be version controlled.

- **EBS volumes**—Boot volumes and data volumes should be tagged by version number.

- **EBS snapshots**—Snapshots used to create boot volumes will be part of an AMI.

- **Containers**—Each container image is referenced by its version number.

AWS CodeCommit

CodeCommit is a hosted AWS version control service with no storage size limits, as shown in Figure 8-12. It allows AWS customers to privately store their source and binary code that are automatically encrypted at rest and at transit at AWS. CodeCommit allows Terra Firma to store its code versions at AWS rather than at Git and not worry about running out of storage space. CodeCommit is also HIPAA eligible and supports Payment Card Industry Data Security Standard (PCI DSS) and ISO 27001 standards.

Figure 8-12   A CodeCommit repository

CodeCommit supports common Git commands and, as mentioned, there are no limits on file size, type, and repository size. CodeCommit is designed for collaborative software development environments. When developers make multiple file changes, CodeCommit manages the changes across multiple files. You may remember that S3 buckets also support file versioning, but S3 versioning is really meant for recovery of older versions of files. It's not designed for collaborative software development environments; as a result, S3 buckets are better suited for files that are not source code.

Rule 2. Dependencies—Explicitly Declare and Isolate Dependencies

Any application that you have written or will write depends on some specific components, whether it's a database, a specific operating system version, a required utility, or a software agent that needs to be present. Document these dependencies so you know the components and the version of each component required by the application. Applications that are being deployed should never rely on the assumed existence of required system components; instead, each dependency needs to be declared and managed by a dependency manager to ensure that only the defined dependencies will be installed with the codebase. A dependency manager uses a configuration file to determine what dependency to get, what version of the dependency, and what repository to get it from. If there is a specific version of system tools that the codebase always requires, perhaps the system tools could be added into the operating system that the codebase will be installed on. However, over time software versions for every component will change. An example of a dependency manager could be Composer, which is used with PHP projects, or Maven, which can be used with Java projects. The other benefit of using a dependency manager is that the versions of your dependencies will be the same versions used in the dev, test, and production environments.

If there is duplication with the operating system versions, the operating system and its feature set can also be controlled by AMI versions, and CodeCommit can be used to host the different versions of the application code. CloudFormation also includes a number of helper scripts that can allow you to automatically install and configure applications, packages, and operating system services that execute on EC2 Linux and Windows instances.

- **cfn-init**—Can install packages, create files, and start operating system services

- **cfn-signal**—Can be used with a wait condition to synchronize installation timings only when the required resources are installed and available

- **cdn-get-metadata**—Can be used to retrieve metadata from the EC2 instance's memory

Rule 3. Config—Store Config in the Environment

Your codebase should be the same in the development, testing, and production environments. However, your database instances or your S3 buckets will have different paths, or URLs, used in testing or development. Obviously, a local database shouldn't be stored on a compute instance operating as a Web or an application server. Other configuration components, such as API keys, plus database credentials for access and authentication, should never be hard-coded. We can use AWS Secrets for storing database credentials and secrets, and we can use identity and access management (IAM) roles for accessing data resources at AWS, including S3 buckets, DynamoDB tables, and RDS databases. API Gateway can also be used to store your APIs. You'll learn more about the API Gateway at the end of this chapter.

Development frameworks define environment variables through configuration files. Separating your application components from the application code allows you to reuse your backing services in different environments using environment variables to point to the desired resource from the dev, test, or production environment.

Amazon has a few services that can help centrally store application configurations:

- AWS Secrets allows you to store application secrets such as database credentials, API keys, and Oauth tokens.

- AWS Certificate Manager allows you to create and manage any public secure sockets layer/transport layer security (SSL/TLS) certificates used for any hosted AWS websites or applications. ACM also supports creating a private certificate authority and issuing X.509 certificates for identification of IAM users, EC2 instances, and AWS services.

- AWS Key Management Services can be used to create and manage encryption keys.

- AWS Systems Manager Parameter Store stores configuration data and secrets for EC2 instances, including passwords, database strings, and license codes.

Rule 4. Backing Services—Treat Backing Services as Attached Resources

All infrastructure services at AWS can be defined as backing services; AWS services can be accessed by Hypertext Transfer Protocol Secure (HTTPS) private endpoints. Backing services hosted at AWS are connected over the AWS private network and include databases (relational database service [RDS], DynamoDB), shared storage (S3 buckets, elastic file system [EFS]), Simple Mail Transfer Protocol (SMTP) services, queues (Simple Queue Service [SQS]), caching systems (such as ElastiCache, which manages Memcached or Redis in-memory queues or databases), and monitoring services (CloudWatch, Config, and CloudTrail). Under certain conditions, backing services should be completely swappable; for example, a MySQL database hosted on-premise should be able to be swapped with a hosted copy of the database at AWS without changing application code; the only variable that needs to change is the resource handle in the config file that points to the database location.

> **Note**
>
> All backing services provided by AWS services have associated metrics that can be monitored using CloudWatch alarms and alerts.

Rule 5. Build, Release, Run—Separate, Build and Run Stages

If you are creating applications that will have updates, whether on a defined schedule or at unpredictable times, you will want to have defined stages where testing can be carried out on the application state before it is approved and moved to production. Amazon has several such platform as a service (PaaS) services that work with multiple stages. Elastic Beanstalk allows you to upload and deploy your application code combined with a config file that builds the AWS environment and deploys your application, as shown in Figure 8-13.

Figure 8-13   Elastic Beanstalk dashboard showing running application and configuration

The Elastic Beanstalk build stage takes your application code from the defined repo storage location, which could be an S3 bucket or CodeCommit, and compiles it into executable code that is combined with the current config file and automatically deployed at AWS. Elastic Beanstalk also supports Blue/Green deployments, where application and infrastructure updates can be seamlessly deployed into production environments using multiple stages.

You can also use the Elastic Beanstalk CLI to push your application code commits to AWS CodeCommit. When you run the CLI command **EB create** or **EB deploy** to create or update an EBS environment, the selected application version is pulled from the defined CodeCommit repository, uploading the application and required environment to Elastic Beanstalk. Other AWS services that work with deployment stages include these:

- CodePipeline provides a continuous delivery service for automating deployment of your applications using multiple staging environments.

- CodeDeploy helps automate application deployments to EC2 instances hosted at AWS or on-premise; details are later in this chapter.

- CodeBuild compiles your source code and runs tests on prebuilt environments, producing executives that are ready to deploy without your having to build the test server environment.

Rule 6. Process—Execute the App as One or More Stateless Processes

Stateless processes provide fault tolerance for the instance running your applications by separating the important data records being worked on by the application and storing them in a centralized storage location such as an SQS message queue. An example of a stateless design using an SQS queue could be a design in which an SQS message queue, as shown in Figure 8-14, is deployed as part of the workflow to add a corporate watermark to all training videos uploaded to an associated S3 bucket. A number of EC2 instances are subscribed to the SQS queue; every time a video is uploaded to the S3 bucket, a message is sent to the SQS queue. The EC2 servers that have subscribed to the SQS queue poll for any updates to the queue; when an update message is received by a subscribed server, the server carries out the work of adding a watermark to the video and then stores the video in another S3 bucket.

Figure 8-14   SQS queues provide stateless memory-resident storage for applications

Others stateless options available at AWS include these:

- AWS Simple Notification Services is a hosted messaging service that allows applications to deliver push-based notifications to subscribers such as SQS queues or Lambda.

- Amazon MQ is a hosted managed message broker service specifically designed for Apache Active MQ, an open-source message broker service similar to SQS queue functionality.

- AWS Simple Email Service is a hosted email-sending service that includes an SMTP interface allowing you to integrate the email service into your application for communicating with an end user.

Each of these AWS services is stateless, carrying out its task as requested and blissfully unaware of its purpose. Its only job is to maintain and when necessary make available the redundantly stored data records. Let's see how stateless services can solve an ongoing problem. At Terra Firma, new employees need to create a profile on their first day of work. The profile application runs on a local server and involves entering pertinent information that each new hire needs to enter. Each screen of information is stored within the application running on the local server until the profile creation has completed. This local application is known to fail without warning, causing problems and wasting time. Moving the profile application to the AWS cloud, a proper redesign with hosted stateless components provides redundancy and availability by hosting the application on multiple EC2 instances behind a load balancer. Stateless components such as an SQS queue can retain the user information in a redundant stateless data store. If one of the application servers crashes during the profile creation process, another server takes over, and the process completes successfully.

Data that needs to persist for an undefined period of time should always be stored in a redundant stateful storage service such as a DynamoDB database table, an S3 bucket, an SQS queue, or a shared file store such as the EFS. Once the user profile creation is complete, the application can store the relevant records in a DynamoDB database table and can communicate with the end user using the Simple Email Service.

Rule 7. Port Binding—Export Services via Port Binding

Instead of your using a local Web server installed on the local host and accessible only from a local port, services should be accessible by binding to an external port where the service is located and accessible using an external URL. Therefore, for this example, all Web requests are carried out by binding to an external port where the Web service is hosted and accessed from. The service port that the application needs to connect to is defined by the development environment's configuration file, defined in Rule 3: Config—Store Config in the Environment. Backing services can be used multiple times by different applications and the different dev, test, and production environments.

Rule 8. Concurrency—Scale Out via the Process Model

If your application can't scale horizontally, it's not designed for cloud operation. As we have discussed, many AWS services are designed to automatically scale horizontally:

- **EC2 instances**—Instances can be scaled with EC2 auto scaling and CloudWatch metric alarms.

- **Load balancers**—The ELB load balancer infrastructure horizontally scales to handle demand.

- **S3 storage**—The S3 storage array infrastructure horizontally scales in the background to handle reads.

- **DynamoDB**—DynamoDB horizontally scales tables within the AWS region. Tables can also be designed as global tables, which can scale across multiple AWS regions.

- **AWS Managed Services**—All infrastructure-supporting AWS management services scale horizontally based on demand.

Rule 9. Disposability—Maximize Robustness with Fast Startup and Graceful Shutdown

Except for our stateful and short-term stateless storage of data records in ElastiCache in-memory queues, SQS message, or SNS notification queues, everything else in our application stack should be disposable. After all, our application configuration and bindings, source code, and backing services are being hosted by AWS managed services, each with its own levels of redundancy and durability. Data is stored in a persistent packing storage location such as S3 buckets, RDS, or DynamoDB databases, and possibly, EFS or FSx shared storage. Processes should shut down gracefully or automatically fail over when issues occur:

- A Web application hosted on an EC2 instance can be ordered to stop listening through auto scale or load balancer health checks.

- Load balancer failures are redirected using Route 53 alias records to another load balancer, which is assigned the appropriate elastic IP address (EIP).

- The RDS relational database master instance automatically fails over to the standby database instance. The master database instance is automatically rebuilt.

- DynamoDB tables are replicated a minimum of six times across three availability zones (AZs) throughout each AWS region.

- Spot EC2 instances can automatically hibernate when resources are taken back.

- Compute failures in stateless environments return the current job to the SQS work queue.

- Tagged resources can be monitored by CloudWatch alerts using Lambda functions to shut down resources.

Rule 10. Dev/Prod Parity—Keep Development, Staging, and Production as Similar as Possible

"Similar in nature" does not relate to the number of instances or the size of database instances and supporting infrastructure. Your development environment must be exact in the codebase being used but can be dissimilar in the number of instances or database servers being utilized. Other than the infrastructure components, everything else in the codebase must remain the same. CloudFormation can be used to automatically build each environment using a single template file with conditions that define what infrastructure resources to build for each dev, test, and production environment.

Rule 11. Logs—Treat Logs as Event Streams

In the dev, staging, and production environments, each running process log stream must be stored externally. At AWS, logging is designed as event streams. CloudWatch logs or S3 buckets can be created to store EC2 instances' operating system and application logs. CloudTrail logs, which track all API calls to the AWS account, can also be streamed to CloudWatch logs for further analysis. Third-party monitoring solutions support AWS and can interface with S3 bucket storage. All logs and reports generated at AWS by EC2 instances or AWS managed services eventually end up in an S3 bucket.

Rule 12. Admin Processes—Run Admin/Management Tasks as One-Off Processes

Administrative processes should be executed in the same method regardless of the environment in which the admin task is executed. For example, an application might require a manual process to be carried out; the steps to carry out the manual process must remain the same, whether they are executed in the development, testing, or production environment.

Take what you can from the 12-factor steps. The goal is to think about your applications and infrastructure and over time to implement as many of these steps as possible. This might be an incredibly hard task to do for applications that are simply moved to the cloud. Newer applications that are completely developed in the cloud should attempt to follow these steps as closely as possible.

Elastic Beanstalk

A common situation that a developer faces today when moving to the AWS cloud is this: Develop a Web app, or migrate an existing Web app with little time and budget into the AWS cloud while adhering to the company's compliance standards. The Web application needs to be reliable, able to scale, and easy to update. Perhaps for these situations, Elastic Beanstalk can be of some help.

Elastic Beanstalk has been around since 2011 and was launched as a PaaS offering from AWS to help developers be able to easily deploy Web applications in the AWS cloud hosted on AWS Linux and Windows EC2 instances. As briefly mentioned earlier in this chapter, Elastic Beanstalk auto-mates both the application deployment, as shown in Figure 8-15, and the required infrastructure components, including single and multiple EC2 instances behind an elastic load balancer hosted in an auto scaling group. Monitoring of your Elastic Beanstalk environment is carried out with CloudWatch metrics for monitoring the health of your application. Elastic Beanstalk also integrates with AWS X-Ray, which can help you monitor and debug the internals of your hosted application.

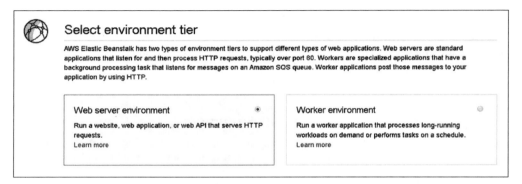

Figure 8-15   Elastic Beanstalk creates the infrastructure and installs the application

Elastic Beanstalk supports a number of development platforms, including Java (Apache HTTP or Tomcat) for PHP, Node.js (Nginx or Apache HTTP), Python (Apache HTTP), Ruby (Passenger), .NET (IIS), and Go. Elastic Beanstalk allows you to deploy different runtime environments across multiple technology stacks that can all be running AWS at the same time; the technology stacks can be EC2 instances or Docker containers.

Developers can use Elastic Beanstalk to quickly deploy and test applications on a predefined infra-structure stack. If the application checks out, that's great. If not, the infrastructure can be quickly discarded at little cost.

Make no mistake, Elastic Beanstalk is not a development environment like Visual Studio. Your application must be written and ready to go before Elastic Beanstalk is useful. After your appli-cation has been written, debugged, and approved from your Visual Studio (or Eclipse develop-ment environment combined with the associated AWS Toolkit), upload your code. Then create and upload your configuration file that details the infrastructure that needs to be built. Elastic Beanstalk finishes off the complete deployment process for the infrastructure and the application. The original goal of Elastic Beanstalk was to remove the timeframe for hardware procurement for applications, which in some cases could take weeks or months.

Elastic Beanstalk also fits into the mind-set of corporations that are working with a DevOps mentality, where the developer is charged with assuming some of the operational duties. Elastic Beanstalk can help developers automate the tasks and procedures previously carried out by administrators and operations folks when your application was hosted in your on-premise data center. Elastic Beanstalk carries out the following tasks for you automatically:

- Provisions and configures EC2 instances, containers, and security groups using a CloudFormation template.

- Configures your RDS database server environment.

- Stores the application server's source code, associated logs, and artifacts in an S3 bucket.

- Enables CloudWatch alarms that monitor the load of your application, triggering auto scaling of your infrastructure out and in as necessary.

- Routes access from the hosted application to a custom domain name.

Elastic Beanstalk is free of charge to use; you are only charged for the resources used for the deployment and hosting of your application. The AWS resources that you use are provisioned within your AWS account, and you have full control of these resources, unlike other PaaS solutions where the provider controls access to the infrastructure resources. At any time, you can go into the Elastic Beanstalk configuration of your application and make changes, as shown in Figure 8-16. Although Beanstalk functions like a PaaS service, you still have access to tune and change the infrastructure resources, as desired.

Figure 8-16   Modify capacity of Elastic Beanstalk application infrastructure

Applications supported by Elastic Beanstalk include simple HTTPS Web applications, or applications with workers' nodes that could be subscribed to SQS queues to carry out more complex, longer running processes.

After your application has been deployed by Elastic Beanstalk, AWS can automatically update the selected application platform environment by enabling managed platform updates, which can be deployed during a defined maintenance window. Updates are minor platform version updates and security patching but are not major platform updates to the Web services being used. Major updates must be initiated manually.

Database support includes any EC2 instance that can be installed on an EC2 instance, RDS database options, or DynamoDB. The database can be provisioned by Elastic Beanstalk during launch or be exposed to the application using environmental variables. You can also choose to deploy your instances hosting your applications in multiple AZs and control your application HTTPS security and authentication by deploying an Application Load Balancer.

> MAKE SURE TO WATCH THE COMPANION VIDEO "DEPLOYING ELASTIC BEANSTALK."

Updating Elastic Beanstalk Applications

New versions of your application can be deployed to your Elastic Beanstalk environment in several ways, depending on the complexity of your application. During updates, Elastic Beanstalk archives the old application version in an S3 bucket. The methods available for updating Elastic Beanstalk applications include these:

- **All at once**—The new application version is deployed to all EC2 instances simultaneously. With this choice, your application will be unavailable while the deployment process is underway. If you want to keep your older version of your application functioning until the new version is deployed, choose the Immutable or Blue/Green update method.

- **Rolling**—The application is deployed in batches to a select number of EC2 instances defined in each batch configuration, as shown in Figure 8-17. As the batches of EC2 instances are being updated, they are detached from the load balancer queue. Once the update is finished, and after passing load-balancing health checks, the batch is added back into the load-balancing queue once again. The first updated batch of EC2 instances must be healthy before the next batch of EC2 instances is updated.

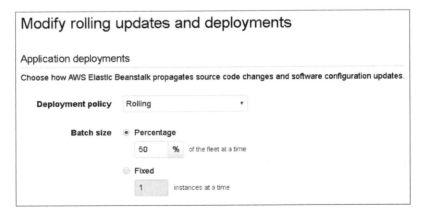

Figure 8-17   Apply rolling updates to Elastic Beanstalk application

- **Immutable**—The application update is only installed on new EC2 instances contained in a second auto scaling group launched in your environment. Only after the new environment passes health checks will the old application version be removed. The new application servers are made available all at once. Because new EC2 instances and auto scaling groups are being deployed, the immutable update process takes longer.

- **Blue/Green**—The new version of the application is deployed to a separate environment. After the new environment is healthy, the CNAMEs of the two environments are swapped, redirecting traffic immediately to the new application version. In this scenario, if a production database is to be used to maintain connectivity with the database, the database must be installed separately from the Elastic Beanstalk deployment. Externally installed databases remain operational and are not removed when the new Elastic Beanstalk application version is installed and swapped.

> MAKE SURE TO WATCH THE COMPANION VIDEO "UPDATING ELASTIC BEANSTALK WITH A BLUE/GREEN DEPLOYMENT."

CodePipeline

Perhaps your application changes are faster than every couple of months. Perhaps you need continuous delivery. AWS CodePipeline provides a delivery service for environments that want build, test, and deploy software on a continuous basis.

The CodePipeline works with a defined workflow that mandates what testing must happen to updates at each stage of development before it is approved as production code. CodePipeline creates a workflow composed of stages. Creating your first pipeline, AWS CodePipeline stores the software contents that will be controlled by the workflow managed by the pipeline into a CodeCommit repository or an S3 bucket, as shown in Figure 8-18. CloudWatch events monitor and alert when any additions occur to the CodePipeline-defined software stages, starting the analysis of the software update as it begins to travel through the CodePipeline and its defined stages.

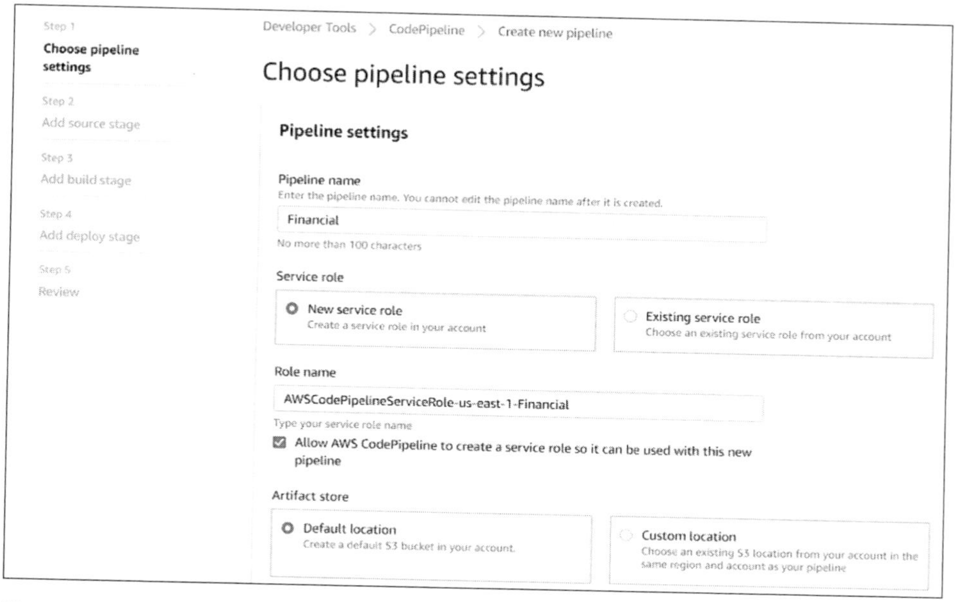

Figure 8-18   Initial setup of CodePipeline

Each stage in the CodePipeline workflow is linked to a test runtime environment, where your code is tested. Each stage can have multiple defined actions that must be carried out before testing is complete. Actions are carried out in a defined order of operation. The first stage in the pipeline is defined as the source stage. The defined location of the code to the pipeline is shown in Figure 8-19. Pipeline processing begins when a change is made to the code in the source location. Optionally, you can manually start the workflow processing cycle.

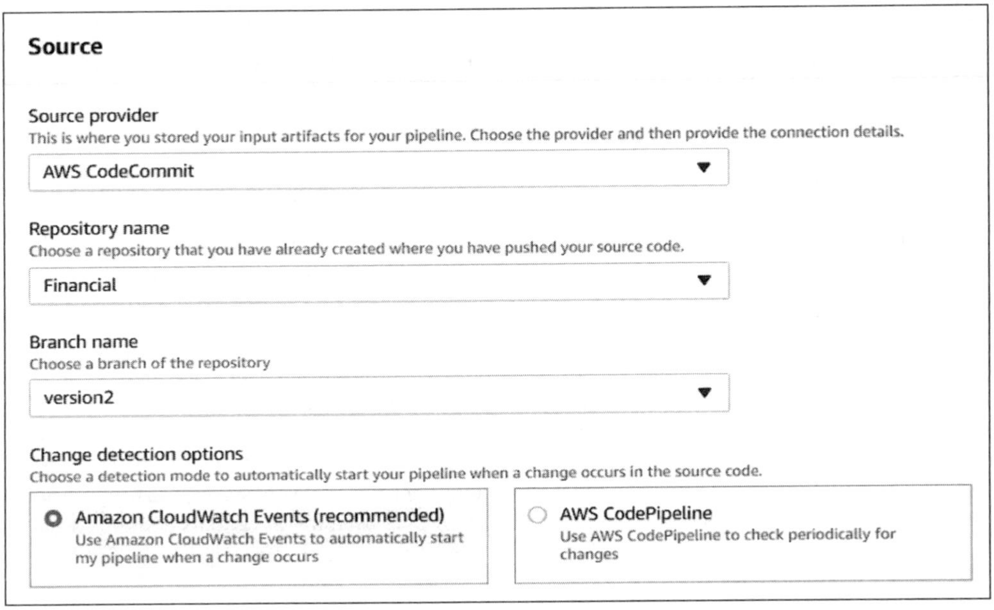

Figure 8-19   Adding the source stage to the CodePipeline workflow

After a stage has completed testing of the source code, all revisions and testing notes or changes created by the testing process are delivered to the next stage in the pipeline. All changes that have been carried out by the actions in each stage and associated testing notes are stored in the associated S3 bucket.

Only one source code revision can run through each stage in the CodePipeline workflow at a time. Approval actions are required before the testing process moves to the next stage. Any failures that occur by any action at any stage in the workflow cause the software being tested not to move to the next action in the stage it is currently in or to the next stage in the pipeline until the failed actions are retried. Once testing is complete and approved, your workflow enters the next deployment stage, as shown in Figure 8-20. Companion services at AWS that support the AWS CodePipeline include CloudFormation, CodeDeploy, Elastic Beanstalk, Service Catalog, and ECS.

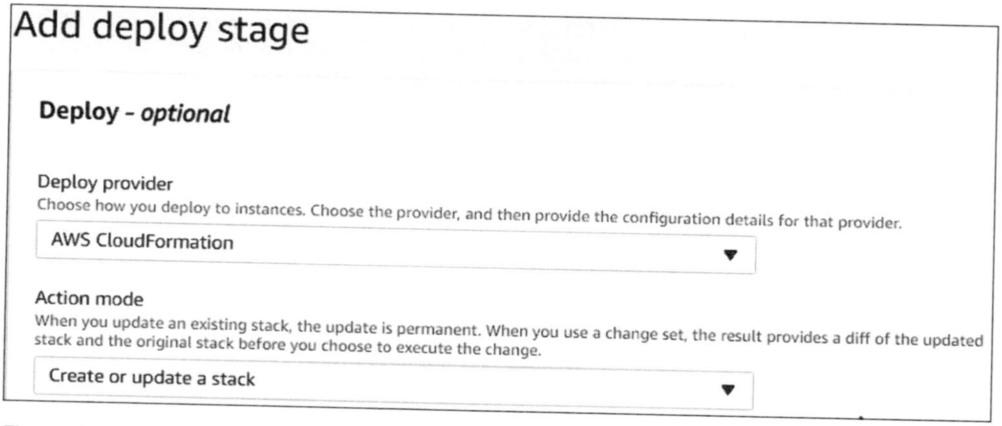

Figure 8-20   Deployment stage options for CodePipeline

AWS CodeDeploy

AWS CodeDeploy allows you to coordinate your application deployments and updates across test and production environments on a variety of server options, including containers, EC2 instances, on-premise servers running Ubuntu 14.04 LTS, RHEL 7.x, Windows Server 2008 R2 and later, and serverless deployment using Lambda functions. Instead of manually spinning up EC2 instances, loading your custom code, and testing it manually, CodeDeploy can carry out your application deployment and updates.

The type of application files that can be managed by CodeDeploy include application code, configuration files, executables, and deployment scripts. CodeDeploy can interface with storage locations such as S3 buckets or integrate with a repository like CodeCommit, Git, and CodePipeline. Updates to applications hosted on compute instances, containers, and serviceless environments are performed with Blue/Green updates, like Elastic Beanstalk, but with much more granular control:

- **Instances**—Traffic is shifted from an original set of instances to a replacement set of instances.
- **Containers**—Traffic is shifted from an ECS task set to a replacement task set.
- **Lambda function**—Traffic is shifted from an existing function to a newer version of the Lambda function based on a defined percentage of network traffic flow.

CodeDeploy to EC2 Instances: Big-Picture Steps

1. Tag EC2 instances for CodeDeploy.
2. Create a service role for CodeDeploy to access your EC2 instances.
3. Install the CodeDeploy agent using user data, or bundle the agent into the current AMI.

4. Create an AppSpec file that defines the source file location for your application version to be tested and the scripts that need to be run during each stage of the deployment/testing process. For example, script bundles and their location can be defined to be carried out on the EC2 instance before and after installation, after the application has successfully started, and during final validation checks.

5. Upload the AppSpec file and application content to be deployed to the S3 bucket.

6. Describe your deployment scheme to CodeDeploy, and create a deployment group describing your EC2 instance configuration, as shown in Figure 8-21.

7. The CodeDeploy agent installed on the EC2 instance begins polling CodeDeploy for instructions on when to start the deployment/test process.

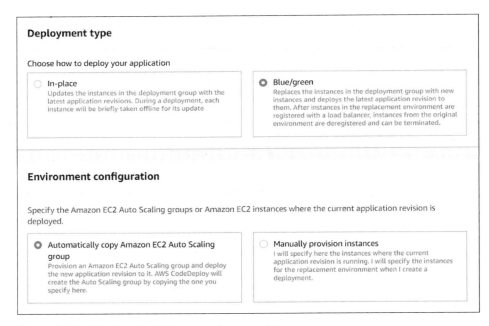

Figure 8-21   Plan how CodeDeploy performs updates

Serviceless Computing with Lambda

Serviceless computing is one of the fancy buzzwords being bandied about today in the cloud, but it's been around for quite a while. The first concept to understand with serviceless computing is that there are still good old EC2 instances in the background running the requested code functions. We haven't reached the point yet of artificial intelligence being able to dispense with servers. However, the code being run on the EC2 instance managed by AWS is being defined per function; and each function is being executed in a firecracker VM after being triggered by an event. At AWS, serviceless computing means Lambda. With Lambda, you are charged for every function that runs based on the RAM/CPU and processing time the function consumes. With a serviceless environment, there are no EC2 instances that you need to manage, and you're not paying for idle processing time. Therefore, the coding hosted by Lambda is focused on the single function based on the logic that is required at the time. Serviceless computing is how you will get the best bang for your buck at AWS; after all, you're not paying for EC2 instances, EBS volumes, Auto Scaling, ELB load balancers, or CloudWatch monitoring; Amazon takes care of all those functions for you. At AWS, we have been able to use serviceless computing with a variety of AWS management services that have been integrated with Lambda:

- **S3 bucket**—A file is uploaded to a bucket, which triggers a Lambda function. The Lambda function, in turn, converts the file into three different resolutions and stores the file in three different S3 buckets.

> MAKE SURE TO WATCH THE COMPANION VIDEO "S3 BUCKETS AND ALERTS USING LAMBDA."

- **DynamoDB table**—An entry is made to a DynamoDB table, which triggers a Lambda function that could perform a custom calculation and deposit the result into another field in the table.

- **CloudWatch alerts**—Define a condition for an AWS service such as IAM; for example, fire off a Lambda function, which alerts you whenever the root account is used in an AWS account.

> MAKE SURE TO WATCH THE COMPANION VIDEO "CLOUDWATCH ALERTS AND LAMBDA."

- **AWS Config**—Create rules that analyze whether resources created in an AWS account follow a company's compliance guidelines. The rules are checked using Lambda functions; if the result is an AWS resource that doesn't meet the defined compliance levels, a Lambda function is executed to remove the out-of-bounds resource.

Lambda allows you to upload and run code from many languages, including Java, Go, PowerShell node.js, C#, and Python. Code can be packaged as zip files and uploaded to an S3 bucket; uploads must be less than 50 MB. Lambda is the engine behind many mobile applications. The application functions run on Amazon servers, therefore, you don't have to maintain servers anymore, just your code. How would you call a Lambda function from a mobile app? You'd use the API Gateway.

> MAKE SURE TO WATCH THE COMPANION VIDEO "CREATING LAMBDA FUNCTIONS."

API Gateway

The API Gateway allows customers to publish APIs they have crafted to a central, hosted location at AWS. But what's an API? The stock definition of an API is application programming interface, which in English means that an API could be considered a defined path to a back-end service, or function. To a user's app hosted on a phone running a mobile application, the API or APIs for the application could be hosted back at AWS. The API is part of the source code or the entire source code for an application, but its location is at AWS. Let's expand the definition of API a bit more:

- The **A** in *application* could be a custom function, the entire app, or somewhere in between.

- The **P** is related to the type of *programming* language or platform that created the API.

- The **I** stands for *interface*, and the API Gateway interfaces with HTTP/REST APIs or WebSocket APIs. Both API types can direct HTTP requests to AWS on the private AWS network; the APIs, however, are only exposed publicly with HTTPS endpoints.

APIs are commonly made available by third-party companies for use on other mobile and Web applications. One of the most popular APIs you have used is the API for Google Maps. When you book a hotel room using a mobile application, the application will probably be using the Google API to call Google Maps with a location request and receive a response back. Most websites and social media sites have several third-party APIs that are part of the overall application from the end user's point of view.

> **Note**
>
> For an older example, think of an EXE file, which is matched up with a library of DLLs. The library file contains any number of functions that, if called by the EXE file, would be fired carrying out a job. If the EXE was a word processor, the associated DLL could contain the code for calling the spell check routine or review.

Think of the API Gateway as a doorway into any service of AWS that you need to integrate with your mobile or Web application. You can also think of the API Gateway as the front door that, once authenticated, allows entry to the AWS back door where the selected AWS service resides that you need to communicate with. Remember, the API Gateway is another one of the AWS managed services hosted by a massive server farm running a custom software program that accepts the hundreds of thousands of requests to the stored APIs. Both HTTP/REST APIs and WebSocket APIs are accessed from exposed HTTPS endpoints, as shown in Figure 8-22.

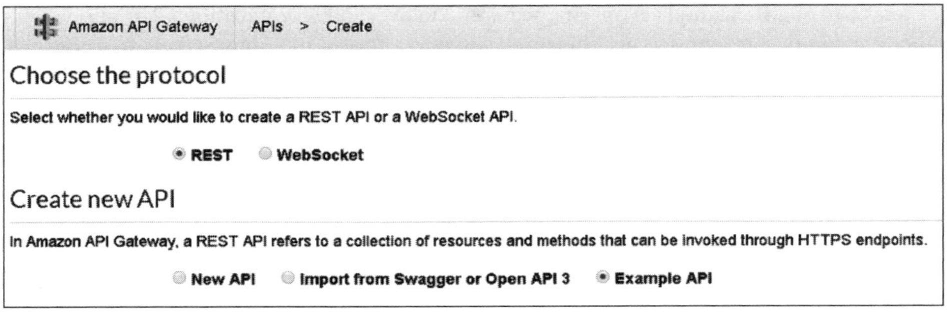

Figure 8-22   Choose the API protocol to create

> **Note**
> API Gateway can call Lambda functions hosted in your AWS account or HTTP endpoints hosted on Elastic Beanstalk or EC2 instances.

If you're programming applications that will be hosted at AWS, you should consider hosting your applications' APIs using API Gateway. API Gateway has the following features:

- **Security**—API Gateway supports IAM and AWS Cognito for authorizing API access.

- **Traffic throttling**—API responses to incoming requests can be cached and take the load off the back-end service, as cached responses to an API with the same query can be answered from the cache. The number of requests an API can receive can also be defined; metering plans for an API's allowed level of traffic can also be defined.

- **Multiple version support**—Multiple API versions can be hosted at the same time by the API Gateway.

- **Metering**—Using metering allows you to throttle and control desired access levels to your hosted API.

- **Access**—When an API is called, API Gateway checks whether an authorized process can carry out the task that the API needs done. Choices are either a Lambda authorizer or a Cognito user pool; API Gateway then calls the selected Authorizer, as shown in Figure 8-23, passing the incoming authorization token for verification. Remember: a Cognito user pool can be configured to allow a mobile application to authenticate an end user request in a variety of methods, including single sign-on (SSO), use of Oauth, or their email address to access the back-end application components.

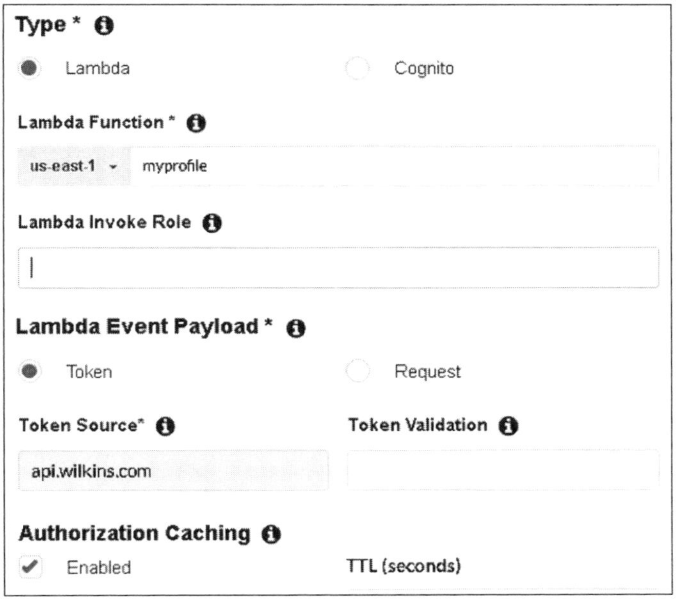

Figure 8-23   Selecting authorizer for API Gateway

> **Note**
>
> API Gateway can create client-side SSL certificates to verify that all requests made to your back-end resources were sent by API Gateway using the associated public key of the certificate. Private APIs can be created for use only with select VPCs across private VPC endpoints.

Building a Serverless Web App

Terra Firma wants to use Lambda to create an event website to sell tickets to its next corporate function. The Web-based interface will be simple and allow users to register for the corporate function after they have registered as attendees.

Create a Static Website

The first step is to create a website that can be hosted in an S3 bucket, as shown in Figure 8-24. The website is going to be hosted in an S3 bucket; therefore, it can be a simple static website with no dynamic assets. After configuring the S3 bucket for website hosting, all the HTML, cascading style sheets (CSS), images, and Web server files are uploaded and stored. A URL is provided using a registered domain owned by Terra Firma via email to each corporate user who wants to sign up for the conference. To host a website, the S3 bucket must also have public read access, and the DNS records must be updated on Route 53 by adding alias records that point to the website.

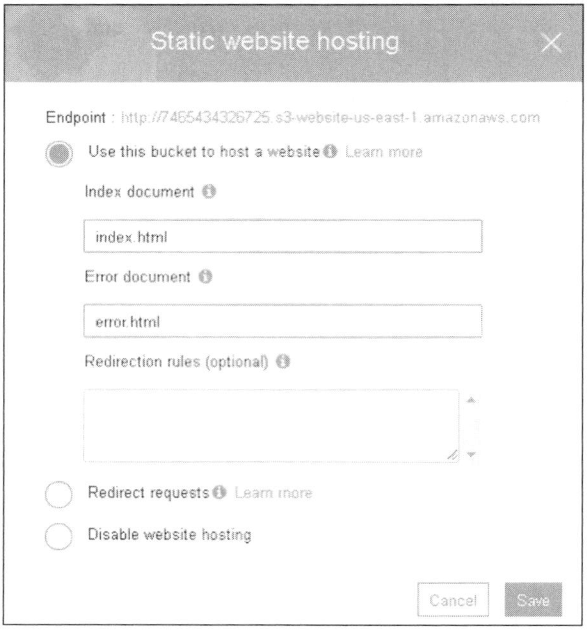

Figure 8-24   Using an S3 bucket for static website hosting

User Authentication

A Cognito user pool needs to be created for the users who will be registering for the conference (see Figure 8-25). The corporate users will use their corporate email addresses to register themselves as new users on the website. After they register on the conference website, Cognito has been configured to send them a standard confirmation email that includes a verification code they will use to confirm their identity.

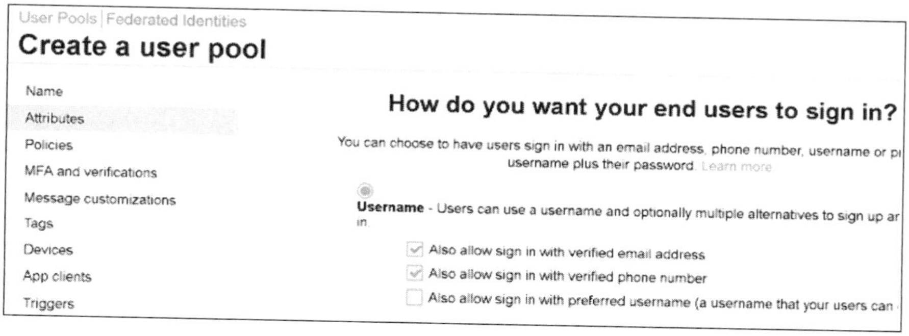

Figure 8-25   Create authentication pool using Cognito

After the users have signed in successfully to the website, a JavaScript function communicates with AWS Cognito authenticating them using the Secure Remote Password protocol and returning a Web token that will be used to identify users as they request access to the conference.

Serverless Back-End Components

The Lambda function, which registers users to the conference and sends them an attendance code, runs at AWS. When each user registers for the conference, the request is first stored in a DynamoDB table and then returns the registration code to the end user (see Figure 8-26).

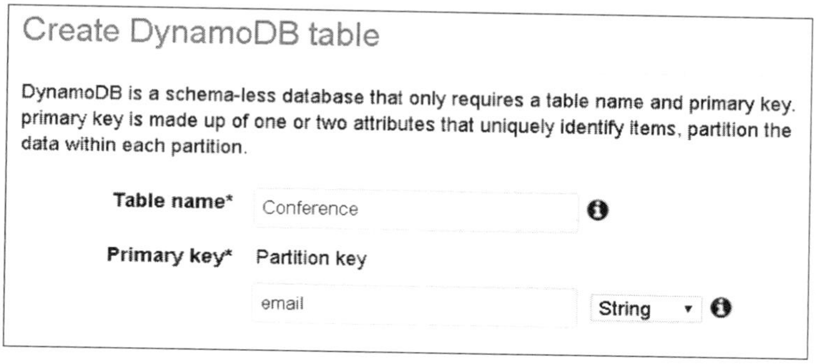

Figure 8-26   Creating DynamoDB table

Set Up the API Gateway

The registration request invokes the Lambda function, which is securely called from the user's browser carrying out the registration as a RESTful API call to the Amazon API Gateway (see Figure 8-27). This background process allows registered users to register to the conference. Remember: the registered users have already been approved through registration and verification by being a member of the Cognito user pool.

The users, unbeknownst to them, are utilizing JavaScript in the background to register for the conference using the publicly exposed API hosted by the API Gateway and carrying out a stateful RESTful request. Representational State Transfer (REST) is a key authentication component of the AWS cloud, and the API Gateway and RESTful APIs are the most common AWS API format. REST uses HTTP verbs to describe the type of each request:

- GET (request a record)
- PUT (update a record)
- POST (create a record)
- DELETE (delete a record)

When users type a URL into their browser, they are carrying out a GET request. Submitting a request for the conference is a POST request.

RESTful communication is defined as stateless; therefore, all the information needed to process a RESTful request is self-contained within the actual request; the server doesn't need additional information to be able to process the request.

The beauty of this design is that you don't need any of your own servers at the back end; you just need Lambda hosting your functions that are called based on the logic of the application and what application request is carried out by the user.

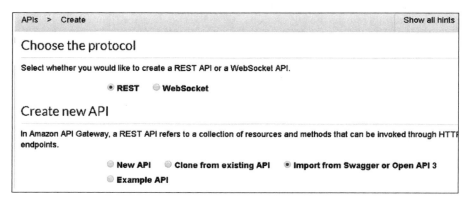

Figure 8-27   Registering the RESTful API with the API Gateway

> MAKE SURE TO WATCH THE COMPANION VIDEO "USING THE API GATEWAY."

In Conclusion

We've looked at several possibilities with automating infrastructure. Automation is the best long-term goal for your application/infrastructure deployments and redeployments at AWS. Automation could be as simple as using a User Data script to build your instances. Certainly, if you are looking at hosting applications that you have written, spend some time with Elastic Beanstalk.

The setup and configuration of Elastic Beanstalk includes most of the infrastructure components that we've looked at in one service: VPCs, instances, AMIs, load balancers, and auto scaling. We also spent some time with CloudFormation, which is a powerful deployment, update, and deletion engine with a somewhat steep learning curve. Despite that, CloudFormation is worthwhile because of what it will save you in time and process. Hopefully as a developer or administrator, you now have a good idea of what AWS has to offer as far as pieces to support, test, and update your code.

Be sure to look at the companion videos bundled with this book to explore these powerful tools in more detail.

This is the last top 10 list of things to consider for your company when moving toward automation at AWS. If you've spent time with the 80 discussion points presented in this book, you've probably come to some positive and useful conclusions that will be great first steps when moving forward with your AWS deployment.

Top 10 Big-Picture Discussion Points: Moving Toward Stateless Design

1. Can CloudFormation templates help you redeploy infrastructure stacks?

2. How useful are CloudFormation templates before deploying VPC network infrastructure?

3. Does using Service Catalog help you lock down infrastructure deployments?

4. Does moving your code hosted at Git to CodeCommit save you money?

5. Who wants to lead the discussion on the 12-factor rules?

6. Can some of your websites be changed to hosted S3 static websites?

7. Do Elastic Beanstalk Blue/Green deployments help you move toward a DevOps mind-set?

8. Which AWS Quick Start can help you in testing AWS services?

9. Which Lambda functions can you create to assist you with automated responses using CloudWatch alerts or S3 bucket uploads?

10. Does the API Gateway help you create mobile apps more effectively?

Index